D1241631

IMPRISONMENT
IN MEDIEVAL ENGLAND

IMPRISONMENT IN MEDIEVAL ENGLAND

RALPH B. PUGH

Professor of English History
University of London

CAMBRIDGE
AT THE UNIVERSITY PRESS
1968

Published by the Syndics of the Cambridge University Press
Bentley House, 200 Euston Road, London, N.W. 1
American Branch: 32 East 57th Street, New York, N.Y. 10022

© Cambridge University Press 1968

Library of Congress Catalogue Card Number: 68–12061

Standard Book Number: 521 06005 2

Printed in Great Britain
at the University Printing House, Cambridge
(Brooke Crutchley, University Printer)

CONTENTS

v

PLATES

vii

PREFACE

For the purpose of this book 'England' has been stretched to cover those parts of Wales and Ireland that were settled by the English. 'Medieval' means the period from the Anglo-Saxon conquest until the summons of the Reformation parliament. The terminus is arbitrary. It is none the less convenient, for it was that parliament which passed the Benefit of Clergy and Gaols Acts (1532) and the Jurisdiction in Liberties Act (1536), all of which, in their several ways, set in motion changes in prison economy.

Special thanks are due to the Committee of Management of the Institute of Historical Research of the University of London, who on two occasions granted me periods of study leave so that I might make progress with this book. One of these periods was spent at the Institute for Advanced Study, Princeton, New Jersey, of which I had the privilege of being made a member for the academic year 1963–4. I very gladly record my warm gratitude to the Trustees of that body as well. Many friends and colleagues have given me most generous help and encouragement while the book was being written. Among them I must single out Miss Joan Gibbs, Mr William Kellaway, Mr R. E. Latham, Mr C. A. F. Meekings, Professor Leon Radzinowicz, and Professor Francis Wormald.

R. B. P.

Hampstead, 1 February 1968

ABBREVIATIONS

Abbrev. Plac.   *Placitorum in domo capitulari Westmonasteriensi asser-*
vatorum abbreviatio...(Record Commission)

Ann. Mon.   *Annales Monastici* (Rolls Series)

Anonimalle Chron.   *The Anonimalle Chronicle 1333 to 1381*, ed.
V. H. Galbraith (Manchester, 1927)

Arch. Ael.   *Archæologia Aeliana* (Proceedings of the Society of
Antiquaries of Newcastle upon Tyne)

Arch. Cant.   *Archaeologia Cantiana* (Proceedings of the Kent Archaeological Society)

Arch. Rev.   *Archaeological Review*

Assoc. Archit. Soc. Rep. & Pap.   *Associated Architectural Societies'
Reports and Papers*

Beds. Coroners' R.   *Bedfordshire Coroners' Rolls* (Bedfordshire Historical Record Society, XLI)

Bk. of Fees   *Liber Feodorum. The Book of Fees commonly called*
Testa de Nevill...

Borough Cust.   *Borough Customs*, ed. Mary Bateson. 2 vols. (Selden
Society, XVIII, XXI)

Bracton   *Bracton de Legibus et Consuetudinibus Angliae*, ed. G. E.
Woodbine. 4 vols. (New Haven, Conn. 1942)

Bristol Chart.   *Bristol Charters*, 1155–1373 (Bristol Record Society, I)

Britton   *Britton*, ed. F. M. Nichols. 2 vols. (Oxford, 1865)

Cal. Chart. R.   *Calendar of...Charter Rolls*...

Cal. Close R.   *Calendar of...Close Rolls*...

Cal. Fine R.   *Calendar of...Fine Rolls*...

Cal. Inq. Misc.   *Calendar of Inquisitions Miscellaneous (Chancery)*...

Cal. Inq. p.m.   *Calendar of Inquisitions* post mortem *and other
Analogous Documents*...

Cal. Lr. Bks.   *Calendar of Letter Books...of the City of London*

Cal. Lib. R.   *Calendar of...Liberate Rolls*...

Cal. of City Coroners' R.   *Calendar of Coroners' Rolls of the City of
London*, ed. R. R. Sharpe

Cal. of Mayor's Ct. R. London   *Calendar of Early Mayor's Court
Rolls...of the City of London*

Cal. Pat. R.   *Calendar of...Patent Rolls*...

Cal. Plea & Mem. R.   *Calendar of Plea and Memoranda Rolls*...
of the City of London

Abbreviations

Cart. Mon. de Rameseia   *Cartularium Monasterii de Rameseia* (Rolls Series)

Cat. Anc. D.   *A Descriptive Catalogue of Ancient Deeds*...

Chron. Abbat. Rameseiensis   *Chronicon Abbatiae Rameseiensis* (Rolls Series)

Chron. Monast. S. Albani   *Chronica Monasterii S. Albani* (Rolls Series)

Chron. Murimuth Contin.   *Adae Murimuth Continuatio Chronicarum* (Rolls Series)

Chrons. Edw. I and II   *Chronicles of the Reigns of Edward I and Edward II* (Rolls Series)

Chrons. of London   *Chronicles of London*, ed. C. L. Kingsford (Oxford, 1905)

Chron. Petroburgense   *Chronicon Petroburgense* (Camden Society original series, XLVII)

Close R.   *Close Rolls of the Reign of Henry III*...

Coventry Leet Bk.   *The Coventry Leet Book*, Vol. I (E.E.T.S. CXXXIV, CXXXV), Vol. II (ibid. CXXXVIII, CXLVI)

Crown Pleas of the Wilts. Eyre   *Crown Pleas of the Wiltshire Eyre, 1249* (Wiltshire Archaeological and Natural History Society, Records Branch, xvi)

Cur. Reg. R.   *Curia Regis Rolls*...

D. &. C   Muniments of a dean and chapter followed by the name of the chapter

D.K. Rep.   *Annual Reports of the Deputy Keeper of the Public Records*. The figure preceding *D.K.* indicates the ordinal number of the report.

Earliest Lincs. Ass. R.   *The Earliest Lincolnshire Assize Rolls, A.D. 1202–1209* (Lincoln Record Society, XXII)

E.E.T.S.   Early English Text Society

E.H.R.   *English Historical Review*

Eyre of Kent   *Year Books of Edward II, The Eyre of Kent*... *A.D. 1313–1314*, I (Selden Society, XXIV), II (ibid. XXVII)

Feud. Aids   *Inquisitions and Assessments relating to Feudal Aids; with other Analogous Documents*...

Fleta   *Fleta*, II, *Prologue, Bk I, Bk II* (Selden Society, LXXII)

Flor. Hist.   *Flores Historiarum* (Rolls Series)

Glanvill   *Tractatus de Legibus et Consuetudinibus Regni Angliae qui Glanvilla vocatur*, ed. D. G. H. Hall (London, 1965)

Gt. Chron. of Lond.   *The Great Chronicle of London*, ed. A. H. Thomas and Isobel D. Thornley (London, 1938)

Abbreviations

Hist. MSS. Com.   Historical Manuscripts Commission's *Reports* followed by the title of the collection reported upon and the volume number if the collection is reported upon in a series of volumes, e.g. *Hatfield* XI

Hust. Wills   Calendar of Wills proved...in the Court of Husting, *London.* 2 vols.

Jorn.   Journals of the Court of Common Council of the City of London, City of London Records Office

Kent Arch. Soc. Rec. Brch.   Kent Archaeological Society, Records Branch

King's Works   The history of the King's Works, ed. H. M. Colvin. 3 vols.

Leis Wl.   Leis Willelme

L. & P.   Letters and Papers, Foreign and Domestic, of the Reign of *Henry VIII* . . .

London Top. Rec.   London Topographical Record

Maitland, *Glos. Pl.*   Pleas of the Crown for the County of Gloucester... *1221,* ed. F. W. Maitland (London, 1884)

Mem. de Parl.   Memoranda de Parliamento. Records of the Parliament holden...in... A.D. 1305 (Rolls Series)

Memorials of Lond. and Lond. Life   Memorials of London and London Life...A.D. 1276–1419, ed. H. T. Riley (London, 1868)

Mirror   The Mirror of Justices (Selden Society, VII)

Mod.   Modern Reports; or Select Cases adjudged in the Courts of *King's Bench,* etc. The figure preceding indicates the volume, that succeeding the page number.

Mun. Acad. Oxon.   Munimenta Academica, *or Documents illustrative of Academical Life and Studies at Oxford* (Rolls Series)

Mun. Gild.   Munimenta Gildhallae Londiniensis (Rolls Series)

Norf. Ant. Misc.   Norfolk Antiquarian Miscellany

Northumb. Ass. R.   Three Early Assize Rolls for...Northumberland . . . (Surtees Society, LXXXVIII)

O.S.   Original Series

Pat. R.   Patent Rolls of the Reign of Henry III . . .

Peerage   Complete Peerage, ed. Vicary Gibbs and others

Pevsner, followed by a county name   The Buildings of England series, ed. Nikolaus Pevsner

Placita Corone   Placita Corone (Selden Society supplementary series, IV)

Plac. de Quo Warr.   Placita de Quo Warranto...(Record Commission)

P.N. Warws. (Eng. Place-Name Soc.) *The Place-Names of Warwickshire* (English Place-Name Society)

P.R.O.   Public Record Office

Proc. before J.P.s *Proceedings before the Justices of the Peace in the fourteenth and fifteenth centuries,* ed. Bertha H. Putnam (London, 1938)

P.R.S.   Pipe Roll Society

Rec. Com.   Record Commission

Recs. of Norwich *The Records of the City of Norwich,* ed. for the Corporation by W. Hudson and J. C. Tingey. 2 vols. (Norwich, etc. 1906–10)

Recs. of Nottingham *Records of the Borough of Nottingham,* published by the Corporation, i (1155–1399), ii (1399–1485), iii (1485–1547)

Rep.   Repertories of the Court of Aldermen of the City of London, City of London Records Office

Registr. Priorat. Wigorn. *Registrum...prioratus Beatae Mariae Wigorniensis* (Camden Society, original series, XCI)

Registrum... episcopi...   The episcopal register of a (named) bishop of a (named) see

Rot. Cart. *Rotuli Chartarum...*(Record Commission)

Rot. de Ob. et Fin. *Rotuli de oblatis et finibus...tempore regis Johannis* (Record Commission)

Rot. Hund. *Rotuli Hundredorum...*(Record Commission)

Rot. Litt. Claus. *Rotuli Litterarum Clausarum...*(Record Commission)

Rot. Litt. Pat. *Rotuli Litterarum Patentium...*(Record Commission)

Rot. Parl. *Rotuli Parliamentorum*

R.S.   Rolls Series

Sel. Bills in Eyre *Select Bills in Eyre, A.D. 1292–1333* (Selden Society, XXX)

Sel. Cases before King's Council *Select Cases before the King's Council, 1243–1482* (Selden Society, XXXV)

Sel. Cases in Exchq. of Pleas *Select Cases in the Exchequer of Pleas* (Selden Society, XLVIII)

Sel. Cases in K.B. *Select Cases in the Court of King's Bench...* I (Selden Society, LV), II (ibid. LVII), III (ibid. LVIII), IV (ibid. LXXIV), V (ibid. LXXVI), VI (ibid. LXXXII)

Sel. Cases of Procedure without Writ *Select Cases of Procedure without Writ* (Selden Society, LX)

Abbreviations

Sel. Pleas of Forest   *Select Pleas of the Forest* (Selden Society, XIII)

Sel. Cases in Star Chamber   *Select Cases before the King's Council in the Star Chamber* . . . [I] (Selden Society, XVI), II (ibid. XXV)

Sess. of Peace in Lincs.   *Records of Some Sessions of the Peace in Lincolnshire, 1360–1375* (Lincoln Record Society, XXX); *1381–1396*, I (Lincoln Record Society, XLIX)

Som. Rec. Soc.   Somerset Record Society

Stat. Realm   *Statutes of the Realm* (Record Commission)

Stubbs, *Charters*   *Select Charters and Other Illustrations of English Constitutional History*, ed. W. Stubbs. The 9th ed. (Oxford, 1921) has been used unless otherwise stated.

Suss. Arch. Coll.   *Sussex Archaeological Collections*

Test. Ebor.   *Testamenta Eboracensia*, i (Surtees Society, IV), ii (ibid. XXX), iii (ibid. XLV), iv (ibid. LIII), v (ibid. LXXIX), vi (ibid. CVI)

Testam. Vetusta   *Testamenta Vetusta*, ed. N. H. Nicholas. 2 vols. (1826)

Toronto Law Jnl   *University of Toronto Law Journal*

Trans. Bristol and Glos. Arch. Soc.   *Transactions of the Bristol and Gloucestershire Archaeological Society*

Trans. R. Hist. Soc.   *Transactions of the Royal Historical Society*

V.C.H.   *Victoria History of the Counties of England*

Will. Salt Arch. Soc.   William Salt Archaeological Society (from 1937 the Staffordshire Record Society)

W.S.L.   William Salt Library, Stafford

Yr. Bk. (R.S.)   The Rolls Series set of *Year Books*

Yr. Bk. (S.S.)   The Selden Society set of *Year Books*

Yr. Bk. (Vulg.)   The Vulgate edition of 1678–9, ed. Sawbridge, Rawlins, and Roycroft

CLASSES OF DOCUMENTS IN
THE PUBLIC RECORD OFFICE USED

CHANCERY:

C 3	Proceedings, Series II
C 47	Miscellanea
C 53	Charter Rolls
C 66	Patent Rolls
C 135	Inquisitions post mortem, Series I, Edward III
C 143	Inquisitions ad quod damnum
C 144	Criminal Inquisitions
C 146	Deeds, Series C

DUCHY OF LANCASTER:

D.L. 37	Chancery Rolls

EXCHEQUER, KING'S REMEMBRANCER:

E 101	Various Accounts
E 143	Extents and Inquisitions

EXCHEQUER, LORD TREASURER'S REMEMBRANCER:

E 364	Rolls of Foreign Accounts
E 372	Pipe Rolls

JUSTICES ITINERANT:

J.I. 1	Assize Rolls, Eyre Rolls, etc.
J.I. 3	Gaol Delivery Rolls

SPECIAL COLLECTIONS:

S.C. 2	Court Rolls
S.C. 6	Ministers' and Receivers' Accounts

I

THE EARLIER USES OF
IMPRISONMENT

IMPRISONMENT in England has no connected history before
the end of the twelfth century. Its origins, however, are an-
tique and certainly stretch back before the days of Alfred.
Once private jurisdictions begin to emerge, and this was perhaps
in the eighth century,[1] some kind of 'prison' may be presumed to
exist. The private franchise-holder, enjoying *infangthief* and *outfangthief*, can hardly do without a place in which to keep delinquents before their trial or punishment. What he needs the king
needs also, and in his version of St Augustine's *Soliloquies* Alfred
presumes that all kings will have a prison.[2] But 'prison' is a
comprehensive term. Often it may not have had to be endured
for long, and in form it may have been as simple as the stocks.[3]
For custodial purposes at least, 'the stocks' is probably our earliest
'prison'.[4]

In Alfred's time the word 'prison' (*carcerr*) first makes its
appearance in a code of laws (*c.* 890). If a man fails in what he

[1] F. Liebermann (ed.), *Die Gesetze der Angelsachsen* (Weimar, 1885), I,
422.
[2] D. Whitelock (ed.), *English historical documents* (London, 1955), I, 845;
H. L. Hargrove, *King Alfred's Old English version of St Augustine's soliloquies*
(Yale Studies in English, XXII, New York, 1904), 46.
[3] Alfred interdicted the unjust use of stocks: Alf. 35 s.2. The word used is
hengen, which later occurs in Cnut's laws for the form of custody provided for
offenders awaiting the ordeal: II Cn. 35. All citations of Anglo–Saxon laws are
from *Laws of the earliest English kings* (Cambridge, 1922), ed. by F. L. Attenborough, and *Laws of the kings of England from Edmund to Henry I* (Cambridge,
1925), ed. by Agnes J. Robertson.
[4] Imprisonment may be analysed according to the object which it is designed
to serve: to hold the prisoner until he can be tried, to punish him after he has
been convicted, or to make life so unpleasant for him that he yields to his captor's
will. In the first case it will be custodial, in the second punitive, and in the third
coercive. The three types tend to merge and in the middle ages were never clearly
kept apart. For a recent analysis see Sir Frank Newsam, *The Home Office* (London,
1954), 144.

has pledged himself to perform he is to be imprisoned, the laws say, in a royal manor for forty days and while there is to submit himself to punishments of the bishop's devising. Should he escape before the forty days are up, he is to be recaptured.[1] Here, surprisingly enough, on its very first documentary appearance, imprisonment is punitive. The laws of Edward and Guthrum (*c.* 925), the legal system which the contestants agreed to observe upon the close of the Danish wars, provide for imprisonment of a delinquent who cannot find surety for the compensation which his delinquency has earned.[2] Here imprisonment seems also to be punitive, but it is a reserve power to be used if a milder punishment cannot be applied. The laws of Athelstan (?925 × ?939) enjoin the imprisonment of certain types of thief. Such a thief is to remain in custody for forty days and is then to be released on the payment of compensation and with a pledge of future good behaviour. Should he steal again, his pledge is forfeit and he must return to prison.[3] Theft is a slight offence and 'prison' is a sufficient punishment for it. Only a very little later, however, men proved guilty of the far graver offences of mortal witchcraft or sorcery, of arson, and of taking the law into their own hands are also awarded 'prison'. Their term is to be 120 days and they are only to be released when compensation has been paid and pledges given for the future.[4] Thus imprisonment continues to have a penal aim. Later pre-Conquest codes do not significantly mention imprisonment and it would be rash to imagine that 'prison', with whatever motive imposed, had anything like its later importance. From a punitive standpoint mutilation, death, outlawry, and, above all, compensation in cash were, in a general way, the proper punishments for what are now called crimes though milder ones were advocated.[5] Imprisonment is always costly to the captor, and in a primitive society there is a strong temptation to enforce a line of conduct on a defaulter by pledges or payments rather than by detaining his body.

---

[1] Alf. 1 s.2, 3, 6.
[2] E. & G. 3.
[3] II As. 1, 1 s.3, 1 s.4, 7.
[4] II As. 6, 6 s.1, s.2.
[5] E.g. II Cn. 2, 2*a*, 2*a* s.1; Leis Wl. 40 (not found in all texts).

On the other hand, there is no doubt that the Normans found a number of prisons in the England that they invaded, particularly upon royal manors in the south, and, in effect, they added to their number. This they did by building many castles in which both king and barons shut up their powerful adversaries[1] and during the Anarchy very many of the common people also.[2]

After the Anarchy the first aspect of imprisonment to become conspicuous is the custodial, that is, the temporary detention of men suspected of serious crimes until they can be tried. Custodial imprisonment does not, however, then originate, for it is deeply rooted in pre-Conquest times. It is a concomitant of the sheriff's authority. By the early eleventh century, if not before, the responsibility for bringing suspects to trial had come to rest upon the sheriffs,[3] and even though that responsibility was eventually shared with the lords of some liberties, the sheriffs remained the chief agents in discharging it. Attachment followed by release on bail was the method that was at first adopted by those officers in securing the arraignment of offenders and it never fell out of use or even grew uncommon. It seems reasonably clear, however, that, as time went on, actual confinement progressively supplemented attachment and bail as the surer means of attaining the needful aim. To trace its development the eye must never leave the sheriff's checker. *Ubi vicecomes ibi gaola.*

The development was slow and unsensational. Until the time of Bracton there is little contemporary literature that defines custodial imprisonment or sets out the way in which it is to be managed. Glanvill refers to it only in a passage in which he shows how those charged with crimes that would by later definition have amounted to treason are to be treated. For those suspect traitors, he says, who are accused merely by common report, there is a choice between attachment by pledges and imprisonment; those who are accused by an ascertainable individual are to be imprisoned only

[1] E.g. Robert of Bellême was long imprisoned in 1112: C. Plummer (ed.), *Two of the Saxon chronicles parallel* (Oxford, 1892–9), I, 243.
[2] Peterborough Chronicle s.a. 1137 in Stubbs, *Charters*, 138.
[3] W. A. Morris, *The medieval English sheriff to 1327* (Manchester, 1927), 28.

1-2

if they cannot find pledges.[1] Imprisonment is thus accepted as a possibility, but, even in so grave a matter as treason, its employment is by no means insisted upon. But though there may be but little doctrine, there is, even in Glanvill's time, substantial evidence that there were both prisons and prisoners, and, since the sheriffs are concerned with both, the conclusion to be drawn is that the prisoners were held upon suspicion or custodially. Thus in 1155–6 the sheriffs of London and Middlesex claim allowance for repairing the Fleet.[2] They also claim the expenses of approvers[3] and in 1157–8 the sheriff of Hampshire pays the wages of the king's gaolers at Winchester.[4] During the next seven years the sheriffs throughout England continue to keep prisoners in their custody. Some of these, indeed, are prisoners of war or hostages.[5] Others, however, are expressly described as approvers[6] or as 'thieves' (*latrones*). The sheriffs support, conduct,[7] or fetter such prisoners.[8] One sheriff incurs expense upon a gaol *ad custodiam latronum*[9] and others build or maintain gaols without any such limitation.[10]

These somewhat sporadic arrangements were made systematic by instructions issued in 1166. These instructions, which have hitherto been accepted as part of the Assize of Clarendon, enjoined all sheriffs to ensure that in counties where no gaols existed gaols should now be built.[11] In these buildings there should be confined

[1] *Glanvill*, 171–2; cf. p. 2.   [2] *Pipe R.* 1155–8 (Rec. Com.), 4.
[3] Ibid.   [4] Ibid. 172.
[5] E.g. ibid. 1161 (P.R.S. IV), 39; 1163 (P.R.S. VI), 4, 6; 1165 (P.R.S. VIII), 31. Some of these men were Welshmen captured in the war against Owain Gwynnedd.
[6] E.g. ibid. 1163, 71–2.
[7] E.g. ibid. 1159 (P.R.S. I), 9; 1164 (P.R.S. VII), 34.
[8] Ibid. 1164, 4.
[9] Ibid. 1159, 38.   [10] See p. 58.
[11] Stubbs, *Charters*, 171. The received text of the 'Assize of Clarendon' has recently been closely scrutinized by H. G. Richardson and G. O. Sayles, *The governance of medieval England from the Conquest to Magna Carta* (Edinburgh, 1963), 438–44. The authors conclude that the document printed by Stubbs is a private compilation and describe it as a 'pseudo-assize'. Naturally, however, it is not disputed that legislation was promulgated at Clarendon in or about 1166 or that directions about gaol-building were issued in that year. As has been said (*Law Quarterly Review*, LXXX, 119), 'the correction is textual rather than substantial'.

4

those presumptive evil-doers who had been arrested by those officers who were accustomed to make arrests or by the sheriffs' own servants. From this time forth the detention of untried suspects in gaols is a common occurrence. Such detention lasted until the prisoner was bailed or judgement was passed on him by a court. Even if bailed he was naturally not quit of the menace of confinement until his trial had ended. So much is implicit in the records, and it is in the end confirmed by the explicit declarations of Bracton.[1] It is not necessary to describe at this point how the system worked.[2] No more need, indeed, be said than that by the mid-thirteenth century custodial imprisonment had, in certain circumstances, come to be not merely permissible but obligatory.

What was true of treason and felony was true also of forest offences. Although Bracton does not talk about it, it was a fact that forest offenders, both clerks and laymen, were by Bracton's time being committed to custodial imprisonment, even for mere trespasses of vert.[3] Thence, like suspect felons, they were often bailed.[4] Over all this the sheriffs, the keepers of the king's castles, and the lords of liberties with the power of imprisonment alike kept watch. Nor need it be supposed that minor offenders, despite the lack of evidence, necessarily escaped such confinement any more than they did in later times.

If custodial imprisonment existed long before it was defined or regulated, so did coercive imprisonment. This form of imprisonment first makes its appearance as a means of securing the payment into the Exchequer of debts due to the crown. When the *Dialogus* came to be written, in Henry II's later years, it was being widely practised, and that treatise describes it, even if somewhat ambiguously. Defaulting crown debtors, we are there told, other than knights, whose debts were put in summons, were to be placed in the custody of the marshal, and each night, while the court was in session, the marshal could imprison them in honourable

---

[1] *Bracton*, II, 345–6, 349–50. The earlier part of the first of these citations is confined to showing how coroners are to behave where a charge *de pace et plagis* has been laid.   [2] For bail see p. 204.

[3] *Sel. Pleas of Forest*, pp. xxxiii–xxxiv, xxxix, lxvi, lxxxvii, lxxxviii.

[4] Ibid. xl.

conditions. Defaulters who were still undischarged after the court had risen were to remain in the lowy of the town in which the court was sitting and might not quit it overnight unless so authorized by the Barons.[1] What was to happen to them in the end if their debts remained persistently in charge is not made clear. A tenant-in-chief, in debt to the crown, who had pledged himself to discharge a debt by a particular day and had failed to do so, was apparently to remain on call, but not in prison, during the session of the court. This was also to be the destiny of a knightly debtor whose debt had been put in summons. If either type of debtor remained in debt after the court had risen, he was to be kept in honourable custody until the king or the president of the court had decided what to do with him. He was, however, to be treated in this honourable fashion only if he was acting as a principal. If he was merely a 'steward', that is to say a bailiff, to use the later term,[2] he might, even though of knightly rank, be imprisoned after the court had risen and he might even be fettered.[3] The general purport of these regulations seems to be that some form of light imprisonment could be applied to all crown debtors at some stage before the discharge of their debts, and that more rigorous imprisonment could be applied to debtors' bailiffs, if their debts became long overdue.

The class distinctions which these regulations draw are not particularly relevant to the narrative at this point.[4] The distinction between the bailiffs and their principals is more so. In the twelfth century it was probably inexpedient to alienate the sympathies of sheriffs and chief officers of boroughs too grossly. Potential sheriffs were in short supply and the crown was largely dependent upon them for securing the surrender of the county issues. Boroughs were favoured by the crown, and their farms were a valuable source of revenue. The agents, however, of the sheriffs and the boroughs had no direct relations with the crown, and the crown did not mind particularly about forfeiting their good

[1] C. Johnson (ed.), *Dialogus de Scaccario* (London, 1950), 21.
[2] T. F. T. Plucknett, *The medieval bailiff* (London, 1954), esp. 5–6, 14.
[3] Johnson, *Dialogus de Scaccario*, 116–17.   [4] See p. 351.

opinion. Prison might well serve as an inducement to such agents to be prompt and honest in their payments, and little was risked by threatening it.

For the period between 1244 and 1322 there have been collected numerous committals of sheriffs, mayors, and other accountants both to the marshal and to prison, the 'prison' always being either the Fleet or the Tower.[1] In 1253 the earl marshal complained about direct committals to the Fleet, alleging that the true custom was to put such defaulters in his own charge or in that of his deputy. The crown promised[2] redress but it is not clear that the promise was kept. By *Fleta*'s time the practice was to commit a sheriff or 'burgess' who was unable to clear his account within a day to the marshal's keeping for the night, and to leave him there in honourable confinement. If he could not discharge himself on the ensuing day, he was to go to the Fleet.[3] An instance of such successive custodies can actually be found in 1309.[4] It seems, however, that the more usual practice was for the marshal to take oath from the accountant that, until he had cleared himself, he would remain in London, or at least that he would sleep there[5] nightly—a mild form of 'gating' barely amounting to imprisonment. From such oaths the Barons of the Exchequer might release the accountant, giving him a day for settlement, and allowing him meanwhile to go home, *ut priso*, on parole.[6] If he failed to keep his day, he could be arrested and imprisoned,[7] and so he might also be if he escaped from the marshal's hands.[8]

Whether a defaulter was entrusted to the marshal or was sent straight to prison may originally have depended on the scale of his debt, the presumed extent of his credit, or the assessment of his character. It might also depend on the condition of the marshalsea. There were periods when the marshal's office was

[1] T. Madox, *The history and antiquities of the Exchequer* (London, 1769 ed.), II, 234, 238, 240.
[2] *Close R.* 1253–4, 196.   [3] *Fleta*, II, p. 133.
[4] Madox, *History of the Exchequer*, II, 241.
[5] Ibid. 241–2; *Fleta*, II, p. 133.
[6] Madox, *History of the Exchequer*, II, 242.
[7] Ibid. 238.   [8] Ibid. 242.

taken in hand[1] and, when this was so, no marshal would have been available to superintend these pernoctations. At such times prison was the only destination possible. Imprisonment of crown debtors in the Fleet was still the practice in the mid-fourteenth century.[2] Gradually, however, the king's marshal established a true prison of his own,[3] and after he had done so, in the 1360s, there can have been little to distinguish 'prison' from 'the custody of the marshal'.

Even in the earliest times coercive imprisonment might be applied to secure quite different ends from those described above. An important instance of its use was to compel the submission of a contumacious excommunicate. If a man was excommunicated and did not seek absolution within forty days after excommunication, a writ *de capiendo excommunicatum* was sent to the sheriff for his arrest. The writ, often called from its opening words a *significavit*, does not expressly enjoin imprisonment, but its counterpart, which reverses the arrest after submission to spiritual authority has been secured, orders release *a prisona nostra*.[4] The procedure was one that was regularly followed and was applied to both clerks and laymen.[5]

With the Statute of Merton (1236), the first statute worthy of the name, yet another form of coercive imprisonment is introduced. Under its sixth clause any layman who abducts or detains an heir under 14 years of age and gives him away in marriage to the detriment of the heir's lord is to be held in prison until he shall have satisfied the lord for the marriage and the crown for the trespass.[6] Thus was the offence of 'ravishing' (or kidnapping) a ward placed upon a statutory footing and given its historic

---

[1] See pp. 158–9.   [2] *Cal. Close R.* 1349–54, 164, 307, 463.
[3] See p. 120.
[4] F. Pollock and F. W. Maitland, *The history of English law before the time of Edward I* (2nd ed. Cambridge, 1898), I, 478; *Bracton*, IV, 327–8.
[5] E.g. *Close R.* 1247–51, 104–5, though the suit there referred to had been wrongly brought in court Christian. For early fourteenth-century examples see *Cal. Close R.* 1302–7, 11 (a layman) and 356 (clerks). The subject is examined in F. D. Logan, *Excommunication and the secular arm in medieval England* (Toronto, 1968) The author's help is gratefully acknowledged.
[6] 20 Hen. III, c. 6: *Stat. Realm*, I. 3.

penalty.[1] The offence and its punishment were not perhaps created by the statute, for in 1227 a man was imprisoned for abducting a female ward from a convent.[2] It is not, however, clear that marriage was intended, nor whether the imprisonment was penal or coercive.

The rolls of the central and itinerant courts for the first three quarters of the thirteenth century record many instances of men being 'taken' (*capiatur*) or 'taken into custody' (*custodiatur*) by judgement of the court. On the face of it these judgements amount to the infliction of prison sentences by summary process. While the circumstances varied a good deal, a high proportion of the offences which earned such sentences can be broadly classified as attempts by fraudulent, frivolous, or ignorant persons to put the machinery of justice out of gear. There is not much legal doctrine that will help us to understand these sentences and no legislation whatsoever. We have to piece the story together from the records and draw our own conclusions.

One way in which a man might incur such a sentence was by his failure, either by non-appearance or by withdrawal, to prosecute an appeal. Glanvill tells us that an appellant who sues out an appeal in a case which affects the crown and then fails to make an appearance must be imprisoned until he is willing to proceed.[3] Several cases ranging from 1201 to 1243 testify that this was not mere dogma.[4] Nor did the requirement soon become obsolete, for it is recorded in the custumals of Romney (1352) and of Lydd (1476).[5] At Lydd the reluctant appellant could choose between two courses: he might spend a year and a day in prison or he might pay a fine to the king and damages to the appellee. In Bracton's time an appellant offering trial by battle and withdrawing on the field was sent to prison, though recommended to mercy.[6]

---

[1] See p. 30.

[2] F. W. Maitland (ed.), *Bracton's note book* (London, 1887), II, no. 256.

[3] *Glanvill*, 21.

[4] E.g. *Cur. Reg. R.* I. 411; IX. 211; Maitland, *Glos. Pl.* pp. 31, 69–70; *Earliest Lincs. Ass. R.* 152; *Miscellanea* II (Surtees Soc. CXXVII), 42. All these are cases of withdrawal. For cases of non-appearance see *Cur. Reg. R.* XI, pp. 72, 239.

[5] *Borough Cust.* I, 86–7.   [6] *Bracton*, II, 401.

The appellant was not necessarily in better case if he prosecuted his appeal and failed in it, whether that failure was due to defeat in combat[1] or to the findings of a jury.[2] In such circumstances also he could be imprisoned. At first sight such a failure will not strike the modern reader as an offence at all but rather as the unfortunate consequence of an unsuccessful suit or lack of bodily skill. But it may be argued that to a contemporary any appeal that failed, whether through lack of application or lack of evidence, was tainted with some kind of falsehood. The appellant had made statements about the appellee which he could not or would not substantiate. Moreover, he might have been responsible for the custodial imprisonment of the appellee before the trial took place and it was not unfair that he should himself suffer the same fate or compensate his adversary in cash. Such a motive for the imprisonment seems to underlie the words of the custumal of Lydd.

The supposition that it was the reprobation of falsehood that brought imprisonment upon the unsuccessful or unwilling appellant is confirmed by much evidence which couples other forms of falsehood and imprisonment together. Glanvill says that jurors who forswore themselves in the grand assize must not only lose their chattels but also be imprisoned.[3] That that punishment was actually inflicted has not indeed been proved and it must in any case have grown increasingly rare as the grand assize itself declined in popularity. But other types of jury could certainly earn imprisonment if they acted in a way deemed to be wrongful. Thus prison was the fate of a Lincolnshire jury (1222) whose verdict was 'attainted',[4] of jurors (1220, 1224) who gave false verdicts in assizes of novel disseisin,[5] and of jurors who testified without knowledge of the facts.[6]

Individuals no less than jurors could be imprisoned for false testimony, particularly appellants who 'counted' falsely.[7] Sometimes the form of the offence is unspecified (1224), which suggests

---

[1] *Bracton*, II, 401; *Placita Corone*, 14.
[2] *Somerset Pleas* [I] (Som. Rec. Soc. XI), 309–10.
[3] *Glanvill*, 35–6.
[4] *Cur. Reg. R.* X. 291.
[5] Ibid. IX. 265; XI, p. 527.
[6] Ibid. XII, p. 443.
[7] *Placita Corone*, 2.

that it was a well-recognized one.[1] There are, however, many instances where the details of the offence are exposed. Thus a man might be imprisoned for falsely stating that he had been wounded in an assault (1225)[2] or that his house had been burgled (1225);[3] for declaring that certain men were villeins, when in fact they were free men (1226);[4] for making untrue statements in court about the contents of a deed (1228).[5] Again 'A' appeals 'B' of assault after he has already appealed 'C' of the same offence in another court (1224);[6] 'A' complains that 'B' has wrongly impleaded him, when in fact it is he who has wrongly impleaded 'B' (1225);[7] 'A' complains that he has been disseised of his tenement by 'B' when he has in fact himself already conveyed that tenement to 'B' (1226);[8] 'A' says that his next-of-kin, 'B', died heirless and that he was consequently entitled to 'B''s land, when in fact he knew that 'B''s widow was pregnant by her deceased husband (1226);[9] 'A' asserts that 'B' had proceeded against him in court Christian against the king's prohibition, when in fact, by 'A''s own admission, 'B' had desisted upon the receipt of the prohibition and the judge had stayed all further proceedings (1231);[10] 'A' denies that a rent is due when the rolls testify to the contrary (1231).[11] In all these cases 'A' is sent to prison.

Other forms of deception were similarly punished. Imprisonment was the fate of a man who produced false charters in court (1224–6),[12] of a man who persuaded a woman to impersonate his wife (1212),[13] and of a married couple who passed off as their own son the infant of another (1211).[14]

Imprisonment was also used to punish or to coerce those who strove to upset judicial decisions already taken or to impede the course of justice. A man who brought an assize of mort d'ancestor for a third time when the assize had already gone against him

---

[1] *Cur. Reg. R.* XI, p. 338.
[2] Ibid. XII, p. 87.
[3] Ibid. pp. 130–1.
[4] *Northumb. Ass. R.* 46–7.
[5] *Bracton's note book*, II, no. 286.
[6] *Cur. Reg. R.* XI, p. 441.
[7] Ibid. XII, p. 311.
[8] Ibid. pp. 342–3.
[9] Ibid. p. 503.
[10] Ibid. XIV, pp. 226–7.
[11] *Bracton's note book*, II, no. 583.
[12] *Cur. Reg. R.* XI, p. 562; XII, p. 359; *Bracton's note book*, III, no. 1105.
[13] *Cur. Reg. R.* VI. 269–70.
[14] Ibid. 169.

twice (1203)[1] was thus remanded, as was a woman who brought a plea in a county court after she had lost her suit at the eyre (1225).[2] In 1231 two men were similarly treated, the one for breaking a final concord and the other for suing for some land by writ of right when he had already lost in another court any interest in it that he might ever have possessed.[3] These may not seem to us to be very grave offences. To contemporaries, however, they probably amounted to contempt of court. It was no doubt because he was deemed to be acting contemptuously that a man was imprisoned in 1223 for retaining some land after it had been decided that he must release it.[4] Of an equally presumptive contemptuousness was the practice of bringing actions in courts Christian against the crown's prohibition (1220, 1223, 1226);[5] that practice was punished in like manner. Irregularities in essoining could also result in imprisonment. Glanvill says that where the overlordship of a tenement is in dispute, each party may summon the several reputed overlords to court. The demandant's lord may essoin thrice but if he then fails to appear his essoiners should go to prison.[6] In 1203 a technically unfit essoiner was treated in the same way.[7] On two occasions essoiners were sent to gaol for declaring that their essoinees were in one place when on investigation they were found to be in another.[8] A man who in 1212 took bribes from recognitors in return for a guarantee that they need not appear *coram rege* found himself in the Fleet.[9]

Such imprisonments are not confined, as the instances cited imply, to the earlier years of the thirteenth century. They are to be found in its last quarter also. Thus, at the Somerset eyre of 1280, three suitors, one of whom was the abbot of Gloucester and another the countess of Aumale, were sentenced to prison

---

[1] *Cur. Reg. R.* II. 146.   [2] Ibid. XII, pp. 94–5.
[3] *Bracton's note book*, II, nos. 496, 498.   [4] *Cur. Reg. R.* XI, p. 136.
[5] Ibid. IX. 107; XI, p. 171; XII, p. 383. In 1201 (ibid. II. 28) another man proceeded in such a court against the prohibition and was gaoled. But he seems to have earned his punishment for other reasons; see next paragraph.
[6] *Glanvill*, 41–2.   [7] E.g. *Cur. Reg. R.* II. 250 n.
[8] Ibid. VIII. 27; X. 312.   [9] Ibid. VI. 289.

for withdrawing pleas of attaint.[1] Another was gaoled for failing in such a plea.[2] A man who falsely claimed (1275) that there were errors in the record of an inquiry made before the justices of the Jews was similarly treated.[3] So was a man who falsely claimed to be an Exchequer messenger (1301).[4] So were the mayor of Exeter, when he sought to defeat the ends of justice by withholding information (1280),[5] and a sheriff's clerk (1296–8) who gave 'false and feigned answers'.[6] *Britton* collectively described such offenders as these as men who had tortiously disturbed the judgement of a royal court, so that it could not be executed, and declared expressly that the proper punishment was imprisonment and fine.[7]

It was mentioned above that one cause of imprisonment was misinforming a court about the substance of a deed.[8] As the ownership or legitimate occupation of land tended to depend more and more upon written testimony, the dangers of forgery and of the falsification of evidences no doubt increased, and imprisonment, which seems to have been the due consequence of committing such forgery, increased with them. In 1292 it was declared to be the law that imprisonment was the proper punishment, in certain circumstances, for denying a deed found on investigation to be genuine.[9] In a somewhat obscure passage *Fleta* states that a man who appended a false seal to a document which had been warranted or was found in possession of such a document might in some circumstances be imprisoned for life.[10]

Nearly all the foregoing offences bear the taint of moral obloquy. There are others, however, from which to the observer of today that taint seems absent. They are those that are concerned with failures to meet the technical requirements of the law. Thus a husband may be imprisoned for failing to produce his wife (1221)

[1] *Somerset Pleas*, IV (Som. Rec. Soc. XLIV), 34–5, 112–13, 271 2.
[2] Ibid. 123–4.
[3] *Sel. Cases in Exchq. of Pleas*, p. 70.
[4] Ibid. p. 213.
[5] Ibid. pp. 105–6.
[6] Madox, *History of the Exchequer*, II, 244.
[7] *Britton*, I, 82.
[8] See p. 11.
[9] *Yr. Bk. 20 & 21 Edw. I* (R.S.), 110.
[10] *Fleta*, II, p. 58.

or a brother his brother (1221).[1] A sheriff's serjeant is put in custody for summoning, *per stulticiam*, men who were not knights, in circumstances where only knights would serve the purpose.[2] At a forest eyre a verderer is imprisoned for saying something in court that did not square with the assertions in his roll,[3] a fault that might have been occasioned by pure forgetfulness. A man was similarly treated in 1229 when found guilty of deforcement: a writ was served upon him to appear before the justices, but he refused to give gage and pledge for so doing.[4] A man who twenty-eight years before had appeared in court to wage his law but could not produce his pledge[5] was also imprisoned; he was perhaps guilty of an involuntary deforcement. It was perhaps of suchlike cases that Bracton was thinking when he said that a man who failed to answer a summons for a minor trespass might be imprisoned.[6] Yet one other instance may be cited of the use of imprisonment to punish those who without any necessarily evil intention interfered with the course of justice. Bracton tells us,[7] and his words are repeated by *Fleta*,[8] that if a bystander at trial by battle interrupted the proceedings by his movements or his words he might be sent to prison and punished in other ways as well at the crown's discretion.

In the vast majority of instances the sentences imposed for the type of fraudulent or vexatious offence described above were *prima facie* of indefinite duration. It is, however, hardly to be supposed that they were often allowed to run for any great length of time. Fines often brought them to a close. Thus the abbot of Gloucester, when judgement had been delivered upon him in 1280, made a fine 'afterwards', and so did the mayor of Exeter. The implication is that they, and all others in like case, were thereupon enlarged. The frequency with which the rolls record such fines led Maitland to believe that imprisonment in these circumstances was fictitious and served merely as sanction for the payment.[9]

---

[1] Maitland, *Glos. Pl.* pp. 43, 58.   [2] *Cur. Reg. R.* XII, pp. 43–4.
[3] *Sel. Pleas of Forest*, p. lxi.   [4] *Bracton's note book*, II, no. 351.
[5] *Cur. Reg. R.* II. 28.   [6] *Bracton*, II, 359.
[7] Ibid. p. 400.   [8] *Fleta*, II, p. 84.
[9] Pollock and Maitland, *History of English law*, II, 517.

No doubt this was sometimes the case. The man already mentioned[1] who was ordered to prison for failing in his appeal was discovered to be poor; he was at once pardoned, apparently before he reached gaol. If the imprisonment had had any other aim than the exaction of a fine, there would not seem to have been any justification for the pardon. But while such cases could no doubt be multiplied it is most doubtful whether the view that all imprisonment in cases of this sort was fictitious can possibly be sustained.

The termination of imprisonment by fine or 'ransom' is, of course, a very old practice. Well before we have any sequence of judicial records we see the payments entered on the Pipe Rolls.[2] It is not, indeed, usually known for what reasons those who paid the 'ransoms' were in prison, but that those persons were actually in prison and were released on payment seems hard to question. Surely it must have been the same with those who were adjudged to prison for their fraudulent or contemptuous doings. Even if, for the sake of argument, the mild word *capiatur* does not imply inclosure in a prison, the stronger word *custodiatur*, which is used with equal frequency, must surely do so. Moreover, the record is not always so laconic. It is sometimes quite specific. Thus in 1220 jurors who made false oath are committed to a named prison, the Fleet, and so are two people who, about the same time, prosecuted in court Christian against the king's prohibition.[3] Not less specific, to say the least of it, is the judgement delivered in 1220 upon two men who withdrew an appeal: *commitantur gaole* reads the record.[4] Four years later a man *qui detentus fuit in gaola* because he had been convicted of false testimony paid an amercement.[5] In the interval, in 1221, occurs the case of the man mentioned above who was ordered into

[1] See p. 10 n. 2.

[2] See for instance the payments for delivery from prison entered on the Pipe Rolls of 1207 (P.R.S. n.s. XXII) and 1209 (P.R.S. n.s. XXIV) (index s.v. *prisona*). It must, however, remain in doubt in each case whether the payment was a fine to enable the prisoner to go free or a payment for bail.

[3] *Cur. Reg. R.* IX. 171, 265.

[4] Ibid. 211.   [5] Ibid. XI, p. 338.

custody for his inability to produce his wife in court. Against the
relevant entry in the roll occurs the word *custodiatur*. This, however, has been struck through, and replaced by a note that the
man made fine.[1] If imprisonment had been merely a fictional
sanction, why should the record have been altered? Moreover, if
imprisonment was always fictitious, why should some actions of
the type described above result in nothing but a fine?[2] The conclusion, therefore, seems to be that these imprisonments were
genuine. Those who deceived the courts, those who sought to
flout the machinery of justice or of government, had behaved
outrageously and not only ought to be but sometimes were imprisoned. The fact that their imprisonment can be liquidated by
a fine does not make it any the less real while it lasts.

Given that it was real, a further question calls for an answer.
Was it penal or coercive or a mixture of the two? The imprisonment of reluctant appellants and breakers of final concords,
mentioned by Glanvill, is evidently coercive;[3] immediately the
appellant decides to prosecute or the fine-breaker to find surety to
perform his covenant, he leaves prison. In all other circumstances
the imprisonment is, in form, penal. The imprisonment of for-
sworn grand assize jurors is so also in fact, for a penal term is
limited. Where the conditions in which the imprisonment will
lapse cannot be predicted, the imprisonment cannot in logic be
coercive. Of course, if it was the case that the crown was more
concerned to secure a payment than to inflict punishment, then
the imprisonment was in fact more coercive than penal. That case,
however, has not been proved.

The hesitation to believe in the genuineness of such imprisonment has been encouraged by a tendency to underestimate the
antiquity of penal imprisonment. For the prevalence of this tendency a passage in Bracton may perhaps be in part responsible.
In words that are often quoted Bracton declared that a prison
ought to be kept for confinement and not for punishment.[4] This

[1] Maitland, *Glos. Pl.* p. 58.
[2] E.g. *Introd. to Cur. Reg. R.* (Selden Soc. LX), 465, 469.
[3] *Glanvill*, 97–8.   [4] *Bracton*, II, 299. Cf. ibid. p. 345.

is Roman doctrine[1] and it died hard. It is repeated in the next century in the *Tractatus de Carceribus* of Bartolus,[2] which while admitting that a prison is necessarily horrible will not allow that it may be so horrible that it becomes a penalty or punishment in itself. But there is not only Roman tradition embedded in such phrases, there is also humanitarianism. Bracton's statement, at all events, when read in its context, is not an abstract pronouncement. It forms part of a passage, of completely practical import, in which the abuse of fetters in custodial imprisonment is reprobated. Other passages make it perfectly clear that Bracton was familiar with penal imprisonment. He admits its existence, for example, in his analysis of the various types of crime and their appropriate punishment. One type of punishment is *corporis coercio*, and this is defined as *imprisonamentum vel ad tempus vel perpetuum*.[3] Even if that passage be dismissed as not much better than rhetoric, there are at least two others that confirm the argument. When writing of lighter charges brought civilly, Bracton says that there are some which result merely in a financial penalty and others which result in such a penalty accompanied by *carceris inclusio*, and that the two are distinguished from one another by the gravity of the offence.[4] Secondly, in a passage in which he is, by implication, distinguishing between repleviable and irrepleviable offences, he says that if a man against whom a charge, albeit a light one, has been preferred, admits much wickedness, he is not to be replevied, but is to undergo *carceris penam et inclusionem*.[5] Thus *carcer*, even custodial *carcer*, is regarded not merely as detention but as *pena*.

The actuality of penal imprisonment in the thirteenth century might have been more readily accepted if it had been sooner realized that such imprisonment was an inherent part of ecclesiastical discipline. Throughout the middle ages the church imprisoned both the secular and the regular clergy. In the early

---

[1] Pollock and Maitland, *History of English law*, II, 516; T. F. T. Plucknett, *Edward I and criminal law* (Cambridge, 1960), 96.

[2] A. T. Sheedy, *Bartolus on social conditions in the fourteenth century* (New York, 1942), 98.   [3] *Bracton*, II, 298.

[4] Ibid. 437–8.   [5] Ibid. 349–50.

thirteenth century it also imposed it on laymen as well. The statutes of Salisbury diocese (1217 × 1219) authorized the imprisonment of those who renounced the religious habit without permission and obdurately refused to return to the cloister.[1] The Council of the Province of Canterbury held at Oxford in 1222 thus punished two lay blasphemers who were sent to a bishop's prison to live out their lives on bread and water.[2] Penitential literature had early recognized that forced confinement could furnish opportunities for reflection upon past misdeeds and a change of heart,[3] and this seems, at least sometimes, to have been the motive for imprisoning monks and nuns.[4] The same philosophy may have underlain the penal imprisonments of pre-Conquest times. While ecclesiastical influence in such matters, so far as laymen were concerned, probably lessened from the beginning of the twelfth century, it is not unreasonable to suppose that a strong tradition survived that 'prison' was a good and proper punishment.

The exceptional importance that was attached in the thirteenth century to the preservation of lawful seisin makes it needful to examine separately the part which imprisonment played in its protection. The Statute of Merton imposed imprisonment on redisseisors, who, if guilty, were to be taken and held until delivered either by 'ransom' or by other means.[5] We have plenty of evidence that, in accordance with the statute, sentence was inflicted.[6] In ejecting the sitting tenant from land adjudged to him, the redisseisor was acting somewhat similarly to those offenders whom we have already met who sought to overturn a final concord or convoked to the county court an issue already settled in eyre. He was, as Bracton expressly states,[7] upsetting a judgement already delivered. Accordingly his offence is one that can logically

---

[1] F. M. Powicke and C. R. Cheney (eds.), *Councils and synods with other documents relating to the English church, A.D. 1205–1313* (Oxford, 1964), II (1), 93, 191.

[2] This incident is recorded by many chroniclers, e.g. the Waverley and Dunstable annalists and Thomas Wykes: *Ann. Mon.* II. 296; III. 76; IV. 63.

[3] Plucknett, *Edward I*, 96.

[4] See p. 382.

[5] *Close R.* 1234–7, 338.

[6] See p. 211.

[7] *Bracton*, III, 202.

be classed with theirs, though, unlike theirs, its punishment is statutory.

Simple disseisin could also lead to imprisonment. The first actual case comes from the record of the Somerset eyre of 1254, which Bracton attended in person. At this eyre the abbot of Athelney was charged with disseising a woman. It was found that not he but the woman's husband was partially guilty of a disseisin and the husband was taken into custody.[1] Other pleas of novel disseisin heard at that eyre had no such outcome. The case, however, was not completely exceptional. A collection of primitive law reports, contemporary with this eyre, defines four sets of circumstances in which imprisonment was possible. If the disseisin was perpetrated by night, if it was effected by force of arms, if it was openly admitted, or if it involved the removal of growing crops—in all these circumstances imprisonment might be inflicted.[2] The man whose wife was involved in the action against the abbot of Athelney had admitted his fault and therefore was covered by a third of these definitions. At the Somerset eyre of 1280 five unsuccessful parties in such pleas were so committed,[3] and four years later a man lay in Oxford gaol for a like conviction.[4] Whether these men fell within any of the categories mentioned above is not revealed in the records. Unlawful disseisin, as has been pointed out,[5] was highly tortious and therefore, from the beginning, had drawn down upon itself punishment in the form of amercement.[6] That it should, later on, have led to imprisonment

[1] *Somerset Pleas*, [i], 426–7.
[2] 'Quatuor modis jacet in gaola in nova disseysina, scilicet, noctanter faciendo disseysinam, item vi et armis, item cognoscendo disseysinam, item per segetes virides asportandas': *Casus Placitorum* (Selden Soc. LXIX), p. lxxxiii. The editor assigns the date 1252–6 to this passage: ibid. p. xxvi.
[3] *Somerset Pleas*, IV, 273–4, 296, 300–1, 339–40, 366.
[4] *Cal. Close R.* 1279–88, 257.
[5] *Introd. to Cur. Reg. R.* (Selden Soc. LX), 156.
[6] Ibid. Mercy is commonly encountered in *Earliest Lincs. Ass. R.*; in *Northumberland Pleas from Cur. Reg. & Ass. R. 1198–1272* (Newcastle Recs. Cttee. Pubs. II), and in that part of the Durham 'assize rolls' (*Miscellanea* II (Surtees Soc.)) which concerns civil pleas affecting Sadberge wapentake, 1235–6. The only instance in these volumes where a reference to imprisonment has been noticed is in the *marginale* to a Lincolnshire plea of 1206: *Earliest Lincs. Ass. R.* 235.

is perhaps to be attributed to some increase in its use by dis-
honest and vexatious suitors and the crown's desire to prevent it
from becoming a fictitious form of action like the common fine.
To use it in that way might have overstrained the resources of
judicial machinery or might, from another standpoint, have legitimately been held to be contemptuous. Disseisin *vi et armis*,
moreover, was tantamount to a breach of the peace and therefore
could be assimilated to those new actions of trespass that were
coming into vogue at the time. Bracton made it plain that those
who coupled disseisin with robbery—and robbery involved *vis
et arma*—incurred a triple penalty. This was mercy for the disseisin, ransom for the robbery, and prison *pro pace*.[1]

Presumably imprisonment remained a possible consequence of
such disseisins as long as the assize of novel disseisin lasted. At all
events it finds a place in the fifteenth-century custumal of Dover,
where the disseisor who uses force is required to go to prison
until he makes fine with the crown. A somewhat similar provision in the custumal of Hereford (1486) imposes imprisonment
for forcible ejection. It is to endure until the ejector is, as a
warning to others, publicly released at a town meeting or in full
court.[2]

Another clear example of the infliction of penal imprisonment
in early times is furnished by the forest law. For those who trespassed in the forest that punishment was statutory. By Henry II's
charter of the forest the man who chased wild beasts by night
whether within the forest or without with the object of capturing
them was to be imprisoned for a year and also to pay a fine and
'ransom' to the crown.[3] There is no significant evidence of the
way in which this provision operated. It was presumably replaced
by Henry III's charter of 1217. This expressly prohibited the
pains of life and limb for venison trespasses and substituted a
heavy 'ransom' for those who could afford to pay. Those who
were too poor to make such recompense were to be imprisoned
for a year and a day. Upon the completion of that term they

[1] *Bracton*, III, 76.   [2] *Borough Cust.* I, 240–2.
[3] Stubbs, *Charters*, 188.

might leave prison if they could find pledges for their future conduct. If they could not they were to abjure.[1]

Upon the eventual appearance of the accused at the forest eyre he was, if convicted, sent to prison. In many instances, however, his imprisonment was commuted to a fine. As the convicted person would have had to redeem himself in any case, both he and the crown may well have seen advantages in arranging for a final payment upon conviction. In assessing fines the justices took into account the time that a man had spent in prison before bailment. Owing to the comparative infrequency of forest eyres it was quite possible for a suspect trespasser to spend more time under custodial imprisonment before trial than the maximum amount of penal imprisonment permitted by the charter of the forest.[2] In one instance, in 1247, two men were released from prison, apparently without a formal pardon and before trial. The king, it was said, not only did not wish to condemn men to death for such offences but also did not wish to inflict bodily torments upon them (*ultra qualitatem delicti sui corporaliter cruciari*).[3] This is not the only indication that Henry III was humane to his prisoners.

Closely akin to trespassing in royal forests was trespassing or, as we should now say, poaching in the parks and fishponds of common persons. The baronage is said to have tried to secure the inclusion in the Statute of Merton of a clause inflicting imprisonment upon such poachers.[4] They failed then, but ten years later prevailed. Thereafter, under a statute whose text does not survive,[5] convicted deer-stealers in parks were to be imprisoned for a year and a day and only to be released atfer paying a stiff 'ransom' and giving surety. The new law is not known to have been much used, but it had important future consequences.[6]

---

[1] Ibid. 346 7.
[2] *Sel. Pleas of Forest*, p. lxiv. Cases are known of a custodial imprisonment lasting 2 years (1253) and 2½ years: ibid. pp. lxvi n., xcii.
[3] *Close R.* 1247–51, 17.
[4] *Sel. Pleas of Forest*, p. cxix, quoting *Stat. Realm*, I.
[5] Ibid. quoting Matthew Paris, *Chronica Majora* (R.S.), VI. 117.
[6] See p. 32.

Before we cross the threshold of Edward I's reign and enter an age in which imprisonments are multiplied by statute, it is necessary to collect together a few instances of imprisonment that do not fit readily into any of the preceding categories. Some of these were imposed in the interests of good government. Thus in 1222 orders were issued out of Chancery to the municipal officers of Canterbury, Norwich, and Oxford to imprison until further order anyone who refused to provide Jews with the necessities of life.[1] In 1254 a man was imprisoned, but subsequently released, because he would not allow certain weirs, presumably in the Thames, to be measured.[2] Sheriffs, gaolers, and other officers who allowed prisoners to escape might in certain circumstances be similarly treated.[3] Sheriffs, says *Britton*, who hold suspects in prison when they ought to have brought them to a gaol delivery are to be both fined and imprisoned, and they and their subordinates who procure approvers to appeal the innocent or hinder them from appealing the guilty are to be imprisoned.[4]

Akin to such offences as these were those committed by crown debtors who were not merely in arrear with their payments but had actually tried to defraud the crown. They also were imprisoned, and we may imagine that this was done rather to punish than to coerce them. Thus in 1236 a debtor paid a mark to an accountant but collected no acquittance from him. The accountant withheld the money from the crown and denied that he had received it. He was handed over to the marshal *tamquam priso*.[5] Next year an accountant swore that he had paid over all that he had received towards a scutage but in fact withheld 6 marks. His fraud was discovered and he was surrendered to the marshal.[6] In the same year an accountant who kept back £13 of a scutage was imprisoned in the Fleet to await the king's pleasure.[7] In 1260 a former sheriff of Yorkshire failed to show in his account that he had received a fine for a venison trespass. He likewise was imprisoned.[8] Irregularities of this kind must have been extremely

---

[1] *Rot. Litt. Claus.* I. 567.
[2] *Close R.* 1253–4, 88.
[3] See pp. 234–5.
[4] *Britton*, I, 87, 89.
[5] *Sel. Cases in Exchq. of Pleas*, pp. 4, 5.
[6] Ibid. pp. 8, 9.
[7] Ibid. p. 15.
[8] Ibid. pp. 44–5.

common and probably were in most cases quickly settled by judicial or administrative action. One form that they took, however, was serious enough to find a place of its own in the Statutes of the Exchequer (1275). It is there explained that crown accountants habitually made false claims when craving allowances for public works that had been undertaken. Those who were convicted of such falsehoods were not only to pay over what was due; they were also to be imprisoned and to be 'punished' at the king's pleasure. The same punishment was to fall on him who concealed charges for which he should have craved allowance—an unexpected requirement which suggests that the man was thought to be acting contemptuously rather than fraudulently.[1]

Little has been said about the length of the sentence which those condemned to penal imprisonment had to endure. Grand assize jurors who forswore themselves remained in custody for at least a year;[2] bystanders who interrupted a trial by battle, for a year and a day.[3] According to one source, those who craved fraudulent allowances at the Exchequer might earn a sentence of a year and forty days.[4] As we have seen, the charters of the forest never sanctioned a longer term than a year and a day.[5] At the other end of the scale there was life-long imprisonment. It was the conventional fate of unpurged clerks.[6] According to *Fleta*, it could in certain circumstances be the fate of two other, presumably rare, classes of offender: inlawed outlaws, who, on being appealed anew on the termination of their outlawries, refused to put themselves upon a jury but demanded battle,[7] and some fraudulent fabricators of seals.[8] By the standards with which we are today familiar these sentences are either very long or very short and do not seem to be in any way related to the gravity of the offence.

Every county gaol and major prison was apt to have its complement of men who had surrendered after exigent or outlawry[9] and of prisoners on remand. Some of the latter were men who had

---

[1] *Stat. Realm*, I. 198. For the date see *Law Quarterly Review*, L, 220 n.
[2] *Glanvill*, 36.   [3] *Bracton*, II, 400.
[4] *Stat. Realm*, I. 198 and n.   [5] See p. 20.   [6] See p. 48.
[7] *Fleta*, II, p. 76.   [8] Ibid. p. 58.   [9] See p. 202.

slain others in self-defence,[1] by accident (1295),[2] or in fits of
lunacy (1445).[3] They awaited the king's pleasure and were often,
if not always, pardoned[4] or bailed.[5] Others were pregnant women,
who could not be put to death (1305)[6] and perhaps, at one time,
could not even be tried (1253)[7] before parturition. By 1350 it
had become the practice, though perhaps not the invariable practice, to pardon them.[8] Clerks convict not claimed by the ordinary
(1397) might also be remanded.[9] There might also be men who
refused to put themselves upon a jury.

The conventional defence in an appeal was for the appellee to
deny the charges and offer battle.[10] If the appellee refused both
battle and a jury, or if the battle could not be waged and the
appellee refused a jury, it was not easy for the justices to know
what to do with him, since after 1219 the ordeal was in effect no
longer available as a means of testing guilt. The justices, no doubt
relying upon the wide discretion which the crown had bestowed
upon them in 1219,[11] acted, when confronted with such a situation,
in different ways. Sometimes they treated the man as guilty and
hanged him;[12] sometimes they allowed him to abjure;[13] but most
commonly they remanded him in custody.[14] The first course perhaps received some encouragement from Bracton, who considered

[1] *Placita Corone*, 19–20. For an actual example (1289) see *Cal. Inq. Misc.*
I, p. 616.

[2] *Cal. Inq. Misc.* I, pp. 642–3.   [3] *Cal. Pat. R.* 1441–6, 389.

[4] *Placita Corone*, 20. For examples of such pardons see *Cal. Pat. R.* 1292–1301,
4, 5, 40, 409, 483, 534; 1361–4, 13, 164, 302, 306, 331, 353, 405, 411, 414, 461,
465, 519.

[5] E.g. *Cal. Close R.* 1288–96, 222, 226–7, 233.

[6] *Abbrev. Plac.* 253.

[7] *Close R.* 1251–3, 501. This is the case of a woman who was condemned to
suffer the death penalty immediately after the birth of her child. The crown stated
that the justices had made a mistake in delivering such a judgement, and ordered
a stay of execution until the facts should be better known.

[8] For examples of pardons see *Cal. Pat. R.* 1350–4, 10; 1381–5, 243; 1391–6,
485; 1408–13, 267.

[9] Ibid. 1396–9, 110–11.   [10] E.g. Maitland, *Glos. Pl.* p. 79.

[11] *Pat. R.* 1216–25, 186.

[12] E.g. Maitland, *Glos. Pl.* p. xxxix; *Bracton's note book*, III, no. 1724.

[13] Maitland, *Glos. Pl.* p. 79.

[14] E.g. *Cur. Reg. R.* XI, p. 460; Maitland, *Glos. Pl.* pp. 43, 51, 103; *Bracton's
note book*, II, no. 136.

the appellee to be quasi-convict in consequence of his refusal.[1] By the 1270s the third course seems to have been accepted as the correct one. It only put off the evil day, however, for the man lay in prison untried and uncertain of his fate. In order to avoid such long and aimless sojourns the justices seem to have decided to make prison very painful so as to force the prisoner to accept a jury.

The 'strong and hard' prison, which had probably long been used as a threat, was in 1275 made the statutory consequence of refusing a jury where a man was of notorious ill fame.[2] This need have meant no more than that the man should be shut up in the worst quarter of the prison.[3] From such beginnings it developed into the regimen (*dieta*) or discipline, which *Fleta* and *Britton* describe, in accordance with which the man lay shoeless, hatless, and ungirt upon the bare earth and ate bread and drank water only on alternate days.[4] It was believed in 1306 that none could survive these rigours,[5] and yet they were later to be made even harder as they developed into the *peine forte et dure*. In the end it seems that the accused lost his right to claim battle,[6] so the *peine* came to be a coercive measure applied to all who refused to plead.[7] It is one of the rare instances of the use of prison as an instrument of torture, in clear opposition to Bractonian doctrine.[8]

[1] *Bracton*, II, 402.

[2] Westm. I. c. 12. One version says he is to 'have' strong prison, another that he is to be 'sent back' to it.

[3] One version of *Placita Corone* (p. 24) says that the man is to be held in prison *en grant destresse*.

[4] *Fleta*, II, p. 85; *Britton*, I, 26–7. Cf. *Placita Corone*, 18. *Britton* adds that he should be 'ironed'.

[5] *Sel. Cases in K.B.* II, p. clv.

[6] *Court Baron* (Selden Soc. IV), 65. It seems to have been settled at a gaol delivery in 1304 that no homicide charge could proceed until a writ *de bono et malo* had been sued out; in its absence the prisoner was remanded: Coke, 2 *Instit.* (1671 ed.), 43.

[7] For the whole subject see Pollock and Maitland, *History of English Law*, II, 651–2, and works there cited. For a categorization of the circumstances in which the *peine*, as it then was, might be applied see *Fleta*, II, p. 85.

[8] See p. 17.

II

THE LATER USES OF IMPRISONMENT

ALTHOUGH the accession of Edward I marks a definable stage in the history of imprisonment, there is no strict cleavage between what happened before his time and what happened after it. Naturally enough, the circumstances that had led to prisonment in the past could still lead to it. Thus, in or about 1318 a man was imprisoned because he imputed perjury to a jury and did not prosecute his claim.[1] A man who about 1311 sued out a writ to have execution of the land of a tenant already deceased earned imprisonment for his deceit.[2] What makes the 1270s a watershed is that imprisonments now begin to multiply greatly.

This was partly due to the ever-growing popularity, already indeed evident,[3] of the action of trespass, which, developing out of actions started by writs *quare*, had become common by the time of Henry III's death. What distinguished trespass from the earlier forms of action was the allegation by the plaintiff that the defendant had acted against the king's peace, with or without *vis et arma*, but to a growing extent with that allegation added.[4] Thus what had once been actions in tort developed into semi-criminal indictable actions. When proved against the defendant such actions often resulted both in imprisonment, to expiate the criminal features of the charge, and in damages, to expiate its civil content.[5] The multiple nature of the punishment had indeed already been expressed by Bracton.[6]

Among the commoner trespasses to be punished by imprison-

---

[1] *Cal. Close R.* 1318–23, 27.

[2] *Yr. Bk. 5 Edw. II* (Selden Soc. LXIII), 263.   [3] See pp. 19–20.

[4] For a case where a man was imprisoned for trespass without the allegation *vi et armis* see *Yr. Bk. 32 & 33 Edw. I* (R.S.), 258.

[5] T. F. T. Plucknett, *A concise history of the common law* (5th ed. London, 1956), 366–7, 456–7; cf. Pollock and Maitland, *History of English law*, II, 166.

[6] See p. 20.

ment were assault, breach of close, false imprisonment,[1] asportation of chattels, and—what was close to the last—petty larceny. Only a few examples can be cited now, all coming from the fourteenth century. Cases of beating and wounding resulting in imprisonment and also in damages are found in 1302[2] and 1345.[3] Cases of close breach resulting in imprisonment are found in 1305,[4] and of asportation of timber in 1304,[5] of wine and cups in 1305,[6] and of barley in 1310.[7] The last of these incidents resulted also in damages. By the time of Edward I's death larceny was being punished at the rate of one week's incarceration for every penny stolen.[8] In 1327 a man taken with the mainour of a coat and hood was imprisoned eight days.[9] Next year another man convicted of stealing a coat was, for no evident reason, given a sentence five times that length.[10] These two sentences were inflicted by London courts. No doubt many such actions were adjudged in urban courts. The punishment there inflicted, however, was not always imprisonment; a Nottingham larcener in 1312 was sent to the pillory.[11]

By no means less important than trespass actions as the efficient cause of imprisonment were the numerous imprisonments that were created by statute. Up to the closing years of Henry III's reign there are comparatively few documents declaratory of the uses of imprisonment and most of what is known about the subject has had to be deduced from the records of pleas. In Edward I's time this situation changes. Even a somewhat cursory examination of the statutes of the realm from Edward I to the eve of the Reformation parliament reveals at least 180 instances of the imposition of imprisonment as a punishment, a threat, or a means

---

[1] See p. 216.   [2] *Yr. Bk. 30 & 31 Edw. I* (R.S.), 106–10.
[3] *Sel. Cases in K.B.* VI, pp. 39–41. The imprisonment is said to be 'against the statute', but what the statute is is not apparent: nor does the editor offer an explanation.   [4] *Cal. Close R.* 1302–7, 244.
[5] *Yr. Bk. 32 & 33 Edw. I* (R.S.), 258.
[6] *Cal. of Mayor's Ct. R. London*, 175.
[7] *Yr. Bk. 3 Edw. II* (S.S.), 41.
[8] Plucknett, *A concise history of the common law*, 457.
[9] *Cal. Plea & Mem. R.* 1323–64, 49.
[10] Ibid. 50.   [11] *Recs. of Nottingham*, I. 74.

of coercion. Moreover, as is shown elsewhere,[1] the statutory
provisions are to some degree paralleled by regulations framed
by municipalities or universities.

The statutes or clauses in statutes which provide for imprisonment vary a good deal in form. Too much, however, must not
be read into this variety. Differences between one phrase and
another which might seem to a modern observer to be substantial
may well have struck a contemporary as immaterial. Nevertheless,
that caution given, it will be useful to try to analyse roughly the
forms that statutory imprisonment assumed. For the purpose of
analysis it is prudent to divide the long period of 250 years or so
into five, inevitably arbitrary, sub-periods. They are 1275–1325,
1330–76, 1377–1421, 1422–83, 1485–1523. The third of these
was the most fertile in the creation of new statutory imprisonments or confirmation of existing ones and the fourth the least
so.[2]

The first distinction to be drawn, at certain points an indefinite
one, is between the coercive and penal. For the present, however,
imprisonment which seems to be wholly or primarily coercive
will be ignored. Imprisonments wholly or primarily punitive
divide themselves into (A) those which were coupled with a fine
or 'ransom' or with both and (B) those that were not. In each of
these broad categories there will be found (i) imprisonments for
a defined term and (ii) imprisonments of indefinite duration, and
each of these subordinate categories may again be split into those
imprisonments (*a*) that were and (*b*) that were not coupled with
some additional penalty or requirement, such as loss of office,
the restitution of property, or the payment of damages. (B) is a
somewhat larger category than (A), both absolutely and also in
all sub-periods except the third. Ignoring the distinction between
(A) and (B) and simply inquiring into the relationship between
defined and indefinite imprisonments we find that (i) and (ii)
are equally numerous over the whole period but that (i) is less
numerous than (ii) in the second and fifth sub-periods. Ignoring

[1] See pp. 42–3, 51.
[2] The analysis is based on *Stat. Realm* and *Rot. Parl.*

next the distinction between both (A) and (B) and also between (i) and (ii) we find that (*b*) is both absolutely and in all periods more numerous than (*a*). Expressed less schematically the truth would seem to be that over the whole 250 years the commonest form of statutory penal imprisonment was one for an indefinite term that required the payment of a fine or 'ransom' but not the performance of any other additional act (Aii*b*), and that this was fairly closely followed by imprisonment for a defined term without fine or 'ransom' but with other requirements (Bi*a*). After this comes imprisonment for an indefinite term not coupled either with a fine or with any other requirement (Bii*b*). Next come—and they are of approximately the same frequency—imprisonment for a defined term coupled with a 'ransom' but no other requirement (Ai*b*) and imprisonment for a defined term not coupled with a 'ransom' but coupled with other requirements (Bi*b*). The remaining three types (Aii*a*, Bii*a*, and Ai*a*) are all comparatively uncommon.

If we analyse the frequency of the types by period we shall find that what was commonest over the whole period (Aii*b*) was also commonest in the third sub-period, second commonest in the first and second sub-periods, third commonest in the fifth sub-period, and fourth commonest in the fourth sub-period. The type, however, that was found with the second degree of frequency over the whole period (Bi*a*) occupied first place in the fourth sub-period, second place in the first and third sub-periods, third place in the second sub-period, and fifth place in the fifth sub-period. Again, the type (Bii*b*) that was found with the third degree of frequency over the whole period occupied the first place in the first, second, and fifth sub-periods, and the fourth place in the third sub-period, and was not represented in the fourth sub-period at all. It cannot therefore be said that over the whole period, that is, between *c.* 1272 and *c.* 1523, there was any consistent ascension or declension in the popularity of one type of imprisonment over another.

Where the duration of imprisonment was expressly limited, the most frequent term both absolutely and in all sub-periods was a year or a year and a day[1]—terms which in the rare instances where there is any evidence to go upon had been characteristic of earlier times.[2] Such terms are followed over the whole period by terms of under a year. It perhaps deserves to be noticed in passing that the lenten term of forty days, which was prevalent under the Anglo-Saxon kings,[3] recurs not only in the legislation of Edward I[4] and in the labour legislation of the later fourteenth century[5] but even as late as 1495.[6] Terms of two years or, in two instances, of two years as a minimum,[7] form the next most common category. There are three instances of three-year terms under Edward I and one each in the second and fourth sub-periods. The figures therefore suggest a tendency towards a reduction in the length of defined terms. There is no positive evidence of a term longer than three years,[8] though by Westminster II (1285) kidnappers might in certain circumstances be imprisoned 'perpetually'.[9] In a few instances under Edward I statutes provide that if on the completion of a term the culprit cannot pay his fine or 'ransom' his imprisonment shall be prolonged.[10] Another clause provides that salmon-fishers using nets in the close season shall have three months' imprisonment for a second offence, a year's imprisonment for a third, and so on in geometrical progression.[11]

In the preceding chapter the point whether penal imprisonment was solely or almost solely intended as a means of coercing a prisoner into paying a fine or 'ransom' to the crown was discussed.[12] The conclusion was reached that it was not, and that the imprisonment was often real even if not always at all lengthy. But even if that conclusion be exaggerated, the reality of fining and imprison-

[1] The year-and-a-day sentences will be found in Westm. I. c. 29 (1275); *Rot. Parl.* I. 286, one of the Ordinances of 1311; and 11 Hen. VII, c. 17, s. 2 (1495).
[2] See p. 23.   [3] See p. 2.   [4] Westm. I. c. 31.
[5] See p. 39.   [6] 11 Hen. VII, c. 23.
[7] 25 Edw. III, St. III, c. 3 (1351); 34 Edw. III, c. 22 (1361).
[8] C. 9 of Westm. I (1275) provides that if a royal officer who has concealed felonies and has been imprisoned for a year, as the statute requires, cannot pay his fine on release, he is to be imprisoned for a further term, which some MSS declare to be three and others four years: *Stat. Realm*, I. 29.
[9] Westm. II. c. 35 (1285). The alternative was abjuration.
[10] E.g. Westm. I. cc. 9, 13 (1275).   [11] Westm. II. c. 47 (1285).
[12] See pp. 15–16.

ment as a combined punishment is abundantly proved by the statutes from Edward I's time onwards, as is also the reality of irredeemable imprisonment. Imprisonment followed by a fine or 'ransom' is provided for in several of Edward I's statutes[1] and is no less evident in those of the late fifteenth century.[2] Imprisonment without the option of a fine,[3] irredeemable imprisonment,[4] or imprisonment without mainprise are expressly provided for in statutes of the fourteenth century. It is true that there are other statutes promulgated in the fourteenth century, and also in the fifteenth, which provide expressly for imprisonment until a fine or 'ransom', or a fine and 'ransom', shall have been paid,[5] and there is also a mass of statutes the terms of which are loose enough to make the student think that an immediate payment could almost have bought off the imprisonment. But that the parliaments throughout the period often intended that some sentences should actually be worked out does not admit of question. Among these may be numbered a few statutes, coming from all sub-periods, which provide for imprisonment if offenders are too poor to make cash payments by way of fine or damages. These also inevitably make the imprisonment a punishment. There are also some statutes which impose fines for first or for first and second offences, but imprisonment for repetitions. By these also real imprisonments must have been intended. Congruent with the philosophy of the statutes, judges might insist on making imprisonment a reality. In 1310 a defendant was sentenced to prison, whereupon his attorney petitioned for bail. Hervey de Staunton insisted that the client had behaved so ill that he should remain in prison until he was 'well chastised'.[6]

---

[1] E.g. Westm. I. c. 9 (1275); Westm. II. c. 34 (1285).

[2] E.g. 11 Hen. VII, c. 7 (1495), which provides that convicted rioters shall be imprisoned as long as the justices of the peace shall deem reasonable and shall then depart on payment of a fine to be assessed by the justices.

[3] 34 Edw. III, c. 8 (1361).

[4] 5 Ric. II, St. 1, c. 2 (1381).

[5] E.g. 15 Ric. II, c. 2 (1391); 6 Hen. IV, c. 3 (1404); 2 Hen. V, St. 1, c. 6 (1414); *Rot. Parl.* VI. 423, 439 (1488, 1489).

[6] *Yr. Bk. 3 & 4 Edw. II* (S.S.), 194–5.

It would be quite impracticable to catalogue all the offences to which penal imprisonment was statutorily imposed within our period. The most that can conveniently be done is to group some of the offences into roughly constructed categories. Before that is attempted, however, it should be noticed that the fixed terms of imprisonment for poaching, which had begun to be imposed under Henry III and are one of the earliest instances of penal imprisonment, continue into a later age and are sometimes severe. By Westminster I[1] poachers in parks and fishponds were to be imprisoned for three years, pay a fine, and find surety. By a statute of 1361 the taking of hawks was to be punished by a two-year sentence, prolonged beyond that term if the value of the hawk could not be restored to the owner,[2] and by another of 1495 the taking of hawks' and swans' eggs by a year and a day's imprisonment and a fine.[3] Owners of hunting dogs, not having a sufficient estate in cash, were by a statute of 1390 to be imprisoned for a year.[4]

It is next to be noticed that some of the non-statutory imprisonments of the twelfth and thirteenth centuries now come to be clothed in a statutory dress. One of the most notable grounds for imprisonment in the earlier period was the corrupt and deceitful prosecution of suits or the tendering false evidence about deeds.[5] This now becomes a not uncommon statutory ground. Westminster I awarded a year's term to serjeants and pleaders who deceived a court,[6] Westminster II the same sentence (coupled in these instances with damages to the aggrieved party) to those who maliciously procured appeals of felony[7] or alleged false exceptions in bar of an assize of novel disseisin.[8] By a statute of 1306 the second of these was extended to a tenant who maliciously claimed a joint tenancy, but in this case a fine was substituted for damages.[9] In the next reign the Ordinances of 1311 imposed the same term of imprisonment for deceitfully pleading the king's protection,[10]

[1] C. 20. [2] 34 Edw. III, c. 22. [3] 11 Hen. VII, c. 17.
[4] 13 Ric. II, St. 1, c. 13. [5] See pp. 9, 11. [6] C. 29.
[7] C. 12. [8] C. 25.
[9] Statute of Joint Tenancies: *Stat. Realm*, 1. 146.
[10] *Rot. Parl.* 1. 286.

and for making or abetting a false appeal.[1] In 1331 jurors accepting bribes were ordered to be imprisoned indefinitely but 'ransomed',[2] and in 1361 the sentence was stiffened by precluding the option of a fine.[3] Statutes of 1419[4] and 1421[5] awarded punishment to those who laid indictments and appeals in non-existent places.

We saw that Bracton was familiar with forcible disseisin and was satisfied that among other things it deserved penal imprisonment.[6] Edward I was of the same mind, for by Westminster I (1275) he provided that a forcible disseisor, whether or not additionally a robber, must be imprisoned and also fined.[7] *Britton* glossed this by declaring that the disseisor's accomplices must be punished in the same way.[8] These provisions were enforced[9] and continued to form part of the penal tradition, for a statute of 1381 required that forcible entry should be punished by imprisonment and 'ransom'.[10] The procedure was elaborated upon in 1391 when justices of the peace, on discovering such entries, were authorized to imprison the offenders until they had been fined and 'ransomed'.[11] After this the offence comes to be assimilated to riotous assembly. A statute of 1394[12] refers back to the immediately preceding one, and provides for the arrest of rioters. By a statute of 1402 forcible entry is to be punished by a year's imprisonment and double damages to the deforced party.[13] The next step was a statute of 1411 imposing upon convicted rioters the punishments of the statutes of 1391 and 1394.[14] After this, by a statute of 1414, those who created major disturbances were to have a minimum imprisonment of a year, without bail, and to pay a fine.[15] In 1429 the statute of 1391 was extended to forcible detainers, in apparent ignorance of the fact that the punishment which that statute

---

[1] Ibid. For an actual instance, occurring about 1332, see *East Anglian*, III (1869), 149.

[2] 5 Edw. III, c. 10.   [3] 34 Edw. III, c. 8.   [4] 7 Hen. V, c. 1.

[5] 9 Hen. V, St. 1, c. 1.   [6] See p. 20.   [7] C. 37.

[8] *Britton*, I, 354–5. *Britton* says, too, that peaceable disseisin is to be punished only by amercement.

[9] *Yr. Bk. 6 Edw. II* (Selden Soc. xxxiv), 37 (1312–13).

[10] 5 Ric. II, St. 1, c. 7.   [11] 15 Ric. II, c. 2.   [12] 17 Ric. II, c. 8.

[13] 4 Hen. IV, c. 8.   [14] 13 Hen. IV, c. 7.   [15] 2 Hen. V, St. 1, c. 8.

provided had been altered.[1] Finally in 1495 the ringleaders in
riotous and unlawful assemblies were to suffer imprisonment for
a term to be fixed by the justices of the peace, who were also to
set upon the perpetrators a fine of their own assessing.[2]

Not far removed from the deceits of private individuals are the
corrupt and negligent acts of officials of all degrees. Those who
were the king's greater servants must at all times expect arbitrary
imprisonment, but something approaching regulated imprisonment was already the fate of lesser officials under Henry III.[3]
Now a whole flood of statutes engulfs such defaulters. By Westminster I franchise-bailiffs who do not pursue felons[4] or who
release the unbailable[5] and royal officers who conceal felonies or
fail to arrest suspects[6] are awarded terms of imprisonment, a year
in the first and third instances and three years in the second, and are
also to be fined. By Westminster II sheriffs' bailiffs who corruptly
fail to execute process are to be imprisoned,[7] and by statute of 1292
justices of gaol delivery who deliver prisoners corruptly or ignore
the terms of their commissions are to be imprisoned and 'ransomed'.[8] Thereafter the statutes are too numerous to recite individually. They impose imprisonment, either for a term or
indefinitely and with or without other penalties, on forest wardens
refusing bail to men suspected of forest offences (1327)[9] or
sheriffs who let hundreds and wapentakes at rents above the
customary farm (1340)[10] or who make improper returns to parliament (1429);[11] on alnagers who deceitfully seal cloth (1380);[12] on
the king's butler and his deputies when they take excessive prise
or receive bribes (1352, 1369),[13] on corrupt wine gaugers (1353);[14]
on Exchequer clerks who claim debts already discharged (1377),[15]
on customers who depute their duties to others or act fraudulently
(1410),[16] on tax commissioners who corruptly excuse men from

[1] 8 Hen. VI, c. 9.   [2] 11 Hen. VII, c. 7.   [3] See p. 22.
[4] C. 9.   [5] C. 15.   [6] C. 9.   [7] C. 39.   [8] *Rot. Parl.* I. 86.
[9] 1 Edw. III, St. I, c. 8. This provision had been incorporated in one of the
Ordinances of 1311: *Rot. Parl.* I. 283.
[10] 14 Edw. III, St. I, c. 9.   [11] 8 Hen. VI, c. 7.   [12] 3 Ric. II, c. 2.
[13] 25 Edw. III, St. v, c. 21; 43 Edw. III, c. 3.
[14] 27 Edw. III, St. I, c. 8.   [15] 1 Ric. II, c. 5.   [16] *Rot. Parl.* III. 626.

acting as tax collectors (1488, 1489),[1] and on tax collectors who disobey the orders of their superiors (1523).[2]

Not far removed from these officials and perhaps almost to be grouped with them are real or reputed king's purveyors. Such men, if they acted contrary to a defined course of conduct, might be imprisoned as well as punished in other ways. Such punishment may be traced from Westminster I[3] and the *Articuli super Cartas* (1300),[4] and its imposition is confirmed in 1330.[5] Other purveying offences were imprisonable by statutes of 1352,[6] 1362,[7] and 1445.[8] The imprisonment in cases of undue purveyance was normally indefinite. The statute of 1362, however, provided for a two-year term, followed by 'ransom', forfeiture of office, and damages to the injured party, and the clause in Westminster I mentioned above, which prohibited the improper requisitioning of horses and carts,[9] inflicted treble damages and forty days' imprisonment. The butler and his lieutenants, whose case has been referred to[10], were of course also purveyors.

Inevitably new crimes and misdemeanours are created as society grows more sophisticated. *Pari passu* new imprisonments are created to punish new offences. Only a few of these can be mentioned. The statute *de falsa moneta* (1299) had awarded imprisonment at the king's pleasure to importers of bad money.[11] Conversely imprisonment, fine, and 'ransom' were meted out in 1394 to those who exported English money to Scotland.[12] Other currency offences were also imprisonable. In 1335 it was decreed that those who melted down specie should be imprisoned until they had surrendered half what was molten.[13] This was reaffirmed in 1394

---

[1] Ibid. VI. 423, 439.   [2] 14 & 15 Hen. VIII, c. 16, s. 12.

[3] C. 32 (the improper appropriation of transport). Another part of the same chapter ordained imprisonment for purveyors withholding just payment from creditors, if their lands and goods could not be distrained upon in satisfaction of the sum due. This, however, is really a coercive measure.

[4] C. 2.   [5] 4 Edw. III, c. 4.   [6] 25 Edw. III, St. v, c. 6.

[7] 36 Edw. III, St. I, c. 3.   [8] 23 Hen. VI, c. 1, confirming the foregoing.

[9] For an imprisonment (1300) under this section of c. 32 see *Sel. Cases in Exchq. of Pleas*, p. 186.

[10] See p. 34.   [11] *Stat. Realm*, I. 132.

[12] 17 Ric. II, c. 1.   [13] 9 Edw. III, St. II, c. 3.

and at the same time imprisonment, fine, and 'ransom' were awarded to those who retained foreign currency instead of surrendering it to the melting-pot.[1]

Turning somewhat abruptly to an entirely different legislative field we note that the first Statute of Provisors (1351) had imposed no penal imprisonment but had simply laid it down that provisors should be held in prison until they had been fined and 'ransomed', paid damages to the party prejudicially affected, and given surety that they would not violate the statute again.[2] To this was added, by the second statute (1390), that those of lesser estate than that of a lord spiritual or temporal who sought to sue out provisions at the Roman *curia* should be imprisoned for a year and forfeit the value of the benefice in question.[3] By the first Statute of Praemunire (1353) men suing in the *curia* for matters cognizable in the king's court were, on failure to answer a summons for such contempt, to be outlawed, to lose their lands and goods, and to be imprisoned.[4] The conjunction of outlawry and imprisonment is strange and possibly unparalleled. The second statute (1393)[5] omitted express imprisonment but provided for attachment and summons before the council, an outcome which may sometimes have ended the same way. Even a casual inspection of the evidence shows that imprisonment under both Provisors[6] and Praemunire was no dead letter.[7]

Imprisonment was also incorporated as a punishment in the statutes of livery and maintenance, although to a considerable extent those statutes relied on fines for their enforcement. This began in 1377 when two statutes were enacted, the one prohibiting lesser royal officers and other royal servants from sustaining 'quarrels' by maintenance,[8] on pain of imprisonment and 'ransom', the other, by a similar penalty, forbidding anyone to give a livery with the object of maintaining a 'quarrel'.[9] The

---

[1] 17 Ric. II, c. 1.   [2] 25 Edw. III, St. IV.
[3] 13 Ric. II, St. II, c. 2.   [4] 27 Edw. III, St. I, c. 1.
[5] 16 Ric. II, c. 5.   [6] *Cal. Close R.* 1349–54, 443.
[7] *Hemingby's Register* (Wiltshire Archaeological Society, Records Branch, XVIII), 241.
[8] 1 Ric. II, c. 4.   [9] 1 Ric. II, c. 7.

principal Statute of Maintenance of 1390 made imprisonment one of several possible punishments for wearing 'livery of company' against the Act.[1] By a further statute of 1399 yeomen wearing liveries were, subject to certain provisos, to be imprisoned, fined, and 'ransomed'.[2] By yet another statute of 1429 those who wore 'liveries' which had been provided at their own cost for the purposes of maintenance were to be imprisoned and were also required to pay the fines that former statutes had imposed.[3] Yet another Act, of 1504, reaffirming the earlier code, imposed imprisonment as well as fines.[4]

From Edward III's early days numerous statutes provided for the imprisonment of those who disrupted the proper channels of trade. One of 1335 declared in general terms that imprisonment, 'ransom', and damages were to be the punishment for anyone who interfered with friendly merchants in their exchanges;[5] another, of 1353, inflicted imprisonment and damages on municipal officers who obstructed imports by foreign merchants;[6] a third, of 1378, punished with a year's imprisonment and 'ransom' the 'disturbance' of merchants.[7] Three statutes of 1353,[8] 1429,[9] and 1463[10] imposed either indefinite imprisonment or imprisonment for two years on those exporting wool, hides, or woolfells elsewhere than to the staple of Calais, and another of 1429 a year's imprisonment on the import into Scotland of merchandise of the Calais staple.[11] The statutes, however, of Edward IV's earlier years visited export outside the staple with nothing worse than fines and forfeitures, though later on, in 1472, such export was made a felony.[12] It may be added that in 1369, at a time when the Calais staple had been temporarily closed and staples in England substituted, denizens who exported wool, hides, and woolfells were to suffer the loss of the merchandise and of the bottom in which it was conveyed, to be imprisoned for three years, and to be 'ransomed'.[13]

---

[1] 13 Ric. II, St. III. [2] 1 Hen. IV, c. 7. [3] 8 Hen. VI, c. 4.
[4] 19 Hen. VII, c. 14, s. 3. [5] 9 Edw. III, St. I, c. 1.
[6] 27 Edw. III, St. II, c. 26. [7] 2 Ric. II, St. I, c. 1.
[8] 27 Edw. III, St. II, c. 27. [9] 8 Hen. VI, c. 17. [10] 3 Edw. IV, c. 1.
[11] 8 Hen. VI, c. 21. [12] 12 Edw. IV, c. 5. [13] 43 Edw. III, c. 1.

Other statutes concerned with trade and industry also provided for imprisonment. Thus sentences of imprisonment, with or without other penalty, were imposed on those who did not use standard weights (1390).[1] In and after the fifteenth century certain manufacturing processes of which the crown disapproved also earned imprisonment as well as giving rise to fines, 'ransom', or damages. Such practices were: making arrows with unsuitable points (1406),[2] gilding metal other than silver and silvering objects other than those specially excepted (1420),[3] exporting wool that had been bearded or clacked (1429),[4] or selling bad leather in London (1512).[5]

No statutes, however, which bear upon economic life are more closely interwoven with imprisonments than those which regulated or sought to regulate the labour market. They perhaps deserve a rather full exposition. The first Statute of Labourers (1349) decreed that all agricultural day-labourers who took higher wages than those ruling in 1346–7, or, on average, in the six years before, should be coercively imprisoned until they should find surety to accept them, and all workers in manufacturing industries similarly trespassing should be imprisoned, no terms of release being specified in the second case. If an agricultural labourer left his master's service before an agreed term, or if any master received such a person into his service, the defaulting labourer and master were to be imprisoned, as must also be any man who gave alms to those who disobeyed the statute.[6] By the second statute (1350) agricultural workers were to be put in the stocks for three days and sent to gaol until they found surety to comply with the stipulated rates. It also provided for the custodial imprisonment of those who evaded the requirements of the law by migrating from one county to another.[7] The statute of 1361 empowered the 'lords of towns' to imprison for fifteen days, presumably in the stocks, labourers who disobeyed its terms. If this pressure did not do the trick, the labourers were to be sent

[1] 13 Ric. II, St. I, c. 9.
[2] 7 Hen. IV, c. 7.
[3] 8 Hen. V, c. 3.
[4] 8 Hen. VI, c. 22.
[5] 3 Hen. VIII, c. 10.
[6] 23 Edw. III, cc. 1, 2, 5, 7.
[7] 25 Edw. III, St. II, cc. 2, 7.

to a common gaol *quousque*.[1] Further powers were bestowed on 'lords' by the statute of 1377 to imprison villeins who sought to evade their services by alleging on the testimony of Domesday Book that they were tenants in ancient demesne. Such evaders were to be held summarily pending investigation and if convicted were not to be released until they had paid a fine and then only with the lord's assent.[2] The Statute of Cambridge (1388) required the wage-earner who took more than a stipulated rate to pay the excess (or, on a second or third conviction, double or treble the excess, as the case might be) or in default to go to prison for 40 days.[3] Another clause prohibited artificers from leaving their usual abodes without a certificate showing the reason for that departure and the time at which they would return on pain of the stocks. If they forged such certificates, they were to be imprisoned for at least 40 days and for a longer term if before the end of that time they should not have found security for their return.[4]

A statute of 1383 had provided that justices of assize and the peace should round up vagrants, compel them to find surety for good behaviour, or, in default, commit them to gaol until the next gaol delivery.[5] Some of these vagrants were no doubt potential criminals, indeed the statute specifies sneak-thieves and 'roberdsmen', but others were presumably common labourers fugitive from their normal occupations. The Statute of Cambridge sought to control such vagrants by declaring that those who wandered without certificates of the same kind as those described above were to be treated like labourers who prematurely abandoned their employment and consequently were to be put in the stocks.[6] A statute of 1406,[7] confirming earlier Statutes of Labourers, added the penalty of a year's imprisonment with fine and 'ransom' for any parent, whose worldly inheritance was below a specified figure, who put his child to any craft or other work within a town when he might be working on the land. Rural labourers who refused to take statutory wages were to be put into the stocks for a brief period and then sent to gaol (no doubt, though the statute

---

[1] 34 Edw. III, c. 9.   [2] 1 Ric. II, c. 6.   [3] C. 3.   [4] C. 4.
[5] 7 Ric. II, c. 5.   [6] C. 8.   [7] 7 Hen. IV, c. 17.

does not say so, until they should make surety to behave henceforth). A statute of 1423 stipulated a month's imprisonment for masters who paid and for labourers who took wages 'in excess of law' and for artificers and victuallers who sold above the rates fixed by justices of the peace.[1] The Act of 1427,[2] reissued in 1429,[3] extended the term to forty days for labourers. By an Act of 1425 combinations of masons seeking to avoid the Statute of Labourers were to be punished by both imprisonment and fine.[4] In 1445 the injunction of 1349 on agricultural workers who left their service before an agreed term was repeated, again under pain of imprisonment.[5]

A statute of 1495, declaring that experience had shown the insufficiency of the statute of 1445, imposed a month's imprisonment and a specific fine upon those who left their employment prematurely, thus making positive what had formerly been indefinite.[6] Another statute, however, of the same year, dealt more leniently with vagrants, who were to be imprisoned in the stocks alone for no more than three days,[7] a term which was reduced to one day in 1504.[8] Finally, a statute of 1515 authorized the imprisonment of labourers who would not work for prescribed rates until they should have found security to do so.[9]

Two examples, both drawn from the records of London courts, must suffice to illustrate the operation of these laws. In 1349 some journeymen cordwainers were imprisoned in Newgate for conspiring to upset the rules of trade contrived by their masters. They were committed for an indefinite term but released on promising to serve at their original wages.[10] In 1364 a hurer's apprentice was also imprisoned, apparently indefinitely, for leaving his master's service.[11]

Notwithstanding the extraordinary multiplication of imprisonments which the statutes bespeak, no effort was made during the period covered by this book to apply that punishment to any

[1] 2 Hen. VI, c. 18. [2] 6 Hen. VI, c. 3. [3] 8 Hen. VI, c. 8.
[4] 3 Hen. VI, c. 1. [5] 23 Hen. VI, c. 12. [6] 11 Hen. VII, c. 22, s. 2.
[7] 11 Hen. VII, c. 2, s. 1. [8] 19 Hen. VII, c. 12, s. 1.
[9] 6 Hen. VIII, c. 3, s. 3.
[10] *Cal. Plea & Mem. R.* 1323–64, 231–2. [11] Ibid. 276.

species of felony. That offence remained capital in law, though, by means of benefit of clergy[1] and the free use of pardons, the rigour of the law was mitigated. Pardoning seems at first sight to represent a complete evasion of punishment. This, however, is a superficial view. The purchase of a pardon was probably at all times somewhat costly. By 1390 the price was coming to be held insufficient. A statute of that year[2] regulates the whole procedure, barring from pardon some felonies entirely, and providing for the others a new and stiffer tariff graded according to the offender's rank. The higher ranks paid what were in effect very heavy fines, but clerks, bachelors, or those of lesser degree need pay only 200 marks. They were, however, also to spend a year in prison— a curious anticipation of the future. The mention of clerks is arresting. The statute seems to have provided for them, if they were rich enough, an escape from the perpetual imprisonment which would have ensued upon an unsuccessful purgation. It would be valuable if we knew what use was made of this statute.

The chief purpose of the foregoing survey will have been to point out the variety of uses to which statutory penal imprisonment was put and the frequency with which it was imposed. It must, however, be admitted that it takes comparatively little account of the way in which particular imprisonments were or might be abolished by subsequent legislation or converted into punishments of greater or less severity. Still less does it relate particular types of sentence to the changing moods and the changing economic state of society, to which penal imprisonment, which is after all only one form of social punishment, must inevitably respond. Practices severely reprobated in one period are condoned in another and punishments fitted to an affluent society will not do in a poor one. A fascinating investigation awaits the student who will take a much shorter period of time than that covered by this book and try to determine the philosophy favoured by contemporaries in imposing social punishment.

There is much evidence for the infliction of imprisonment by the courts or urban communities, and the custumals of some such

[1] See p. 49. [2] 13 Ric. II, St. II, c. 1.

communities contain regulations about it. Many of the regulations, it is true, merely authorize coercive imprisonment pending the payment of damages and fines or the finding of surety of the peace,[1] but others are of a penal kind. Thus men of Waterford (*c.* 1300) who raised the hue needlessly and could not pay an amercement were to be imprisoned forty days.[2] At Cork (*c.* 1339) deforcers were to be imprisoned.[3] A London ordinance of 1345 stipulated that the collection of excessive toll on merchandise by city officers should result in eight days' imprisonment.[4] The fifteenth-century custumals of Fordwich, Sandwich, and other places provide for short-term imprisonment for theft and similar wrongs[5] and the Lydd custumal of the same century empowers the authorities to imprison false appellors for a year and a day.[6] At Winchelsea and Hastings at the same time, men who had been bound over and failed to keep the peace thereafter might be summarily imprisoned for 40 days.[7] Apart from what was codified it is quite clear that mayors and other chief officers exercised wide powers of imprisoning the unruly on their own authority.[8]

A good deal of recorded municipal imprisonment, whether resting upon statute or codified custom or springing from the exercise of mayoral authority, was concerned with vagrancy, sometimes aggravated by other offences such as threatening the peace or at least enjoying an evil reputation. London furnishes several instances. The lock-up there called the Tun was, as will be shown, established for offenders such as these.[9] In 1320 a woman was committed to it for straying in the city with a bundle of cloth,[10] a man for pure vagrancy,[11] and a chaplain for endangering the peace of the city by night.[12] The third of these was subsequently sent to Newgate because he was going about armed and violating the city proclamation against vagrancy and arms-bearing. In 1338

[1] E.g. Dover (fifteenth century), Romney (1352): *Borough Cust.* I, 85, 86.
[2] Ibid. 1.   [3] Ibid. 96, 257.
[4] *Cal. Plea & Mem. R.* 1323–64, 217.
[5] *Borough Cust.* i. 6 n.   [6] Ibid. 87.   [7] Ibid. 4.
[8] Cf. Bristol ordinance of 1370: *Little Red Book of Bristol*, ed. F. B. Bickley (Bristol, 1908), II, 55.   [9] See p. 112.
[10] *Cal. Lr. Bks. E*, 136.   [11] Ibid. 120.   [12] Ibid. 130–1.

some 'incorrigible' persons were sent to Newgate to prevent them from doing further mischief,[1] as in the next year were some other disorderly persons and nightwalkers.[2] In 1364 some men and women were imprisoned for creating a disturbance and for being common scolds and brawlers.[3]

Akin to such offences were trespasses against public morals. In London the Tun was being used for such persons from its establishment.[4] By city ordinances of the late fourteenth century whoremongers and bawds upon a second conviction were, among other punishments, to suffer a term of ten days' irredeemable imprisonment. By the same code adulterers and adulteresses and women found with priests were to be imprisoned for unspecified periods terminable at the discretion of the mayor and aldermen.[5] An actual instance of the imprisonment of a chaplain and his lover is found in 1389. They spent the night in the Tun but their later fate is unrecorded.[6] In 1510 the city officers were directed to settle the destinies of a group of people who were in prison for 'bawdry and other mysrule of their bodyes'.[7] In 1338 a Londoner convicted of keeping a brothel was imprisoned for two months.[8]

Among the other common faults of a minor order that resulted in short terms of punitive imprisonment in towns and cities must be reckoned that of uttering what are usually called 'opprobrious words'. Imprisonment for this kind of offence is very common from the sixteenth century but it is certainly much earlier than that. As usual the earlier instances come from London. Even as early as 1299 a scavenger was imprisoned for a period terminable at the mayor's discretion because he scandalized an alderman by his remarks.[9] From the later fourteenth century London instances are more numerous. In 1364 a saddler who threatened a coroner was committed to Newgate.[10] In 1382 a fishmonger who had insulted the mayor,[11] in 1388 the gate-keeper of one of the Counters

---

[1] *Cal. Plea & Mem. R.* 1323–64, 168.
[2] Ibid. 108–9. [3] Ibid. 277. [4] See p. 112.
[5] *Mun. Gild.* I. 457–60. [6] *Cal. Lr. Bks. H*, 339.
[7] Rep. 2, f. 96. [8] *Cal. Plea & Mem. R.* 1323–64, 167.
[9] *Cal. Lr. Bks. B*, 85–6. [10] *Cal. Plea & Mem. R.* 1323–64, 272.
[11] *Cal. Lr. Bks. H*, 203–4.

who had insulted an alderman,[1] were each committed for a year. In both cases the sentence was remitted, the fishmonger's after about three weeks. In 1386 a man aggravated his default of appearance by abusing a serjeant and for both offences was committed for the same term as the saddler and fishmonger.[2] In 1417 a man was, perhaps more reasonably, imprisoned for a year and a day for unjustly accusing the mayor. On apologizing he was fined in lieu and in the end the fine itself was released.[3] In 1447 the keeper of Newgate, partly for failing to remove the corpse of a dead prisoner and partly because of shameful words spoken by his wife, was committed for nine days.[4] In 1417 the corporation of Winchester ordained imprisonment and a fine for those who blasphemed or who slandered the mayor, a bailiff, the recorder or other senior officers.[5] The ordinance was still being enforced in the early sixteenth century, when a bailiff abusing another bailiff was imprisoned for four days.[6] It was no doubt mainly to accommodate such minor delinquents that urban prisons multiplied and the crown gave the towns themselves the right to keep prisons not only for the 'custody' but for the 'correction' or punishment of such persons. Such phrases are inserted in many charters, as in those granted to Hull in 1299,[7] Berwick-upon-Tweed in 1302,[8] Stafford in 1315,[9] Coventry in 1344,[10] and Chester in 1506.[11]

The area occupied by coercive imprisonment, already extensive under Henry III, was considerably enlarged in and after the reign of his son. It has already been made plain[12] that the coercive imprisonment of crown accountants continued for many generations

[1] *Cal. Lr. Bks. H*, 329.
[2] *Memorials of Lond. and Lond. Life*, 506–7.
[3] Jorn. 1, f. 9*b*.
[4] Jorn. 4, f. 172.
[5] C. Bailey (ed.), *Transcripts from the municipal archives of Winchester* (Winchester, 1856), 49, 50.
[6] *Sel. Cases in Star Chamber* [i], 275–8.
[7] *Cal. Chart. R.* 1257–1300, 475.   [8] Ibid. 1300–26, 28.
[9] Ibid. 279, where the year is wrongly printed.
[10] Ibid. 1341–1417, 36.
[11] R. H. Morris, *Chester in the Plantagenet and Tudor reigns* (Eccleston, 1895), 529.   [12] See p. 8.

if not for many centuries after the *Dialogus*, in which it is first described, was drafted. In fact it continued indefinitely as a prerogative right[1] and by the late fifteenth century was beginning to acquire a statutory foundation as well. Commissioners for collecting the benevolence of 1495[2] and the General Surveyors after the statutory establishment of their office in 1515[3] were authorized to imprison accountants *quousque* who refused to account or were dilatory in so doing.

But of much more profound effect upon the state of the prisons than any measures limited to crown accountants were those statutes that affected the recovery of debts by private creditors. The first of these was the Statute of Acton Burnell (1283),[4] which authorized merchants to require their debtors to acknowledge their debts before the mayor of a town, stating at the same time the day on which payment fell due. If the debtor defaulted, the creditor might distrain, and if the debtor lacked goods on which distraint might be made, he might be arrested and imprisoned until he or his friends had made satisfaction. The Statute of Merchants passed two years later[5] strengthened the creditor's powers by authorizing immediate imprisonment of the debtor on proof being offered that the debtor had defaulted on his day. The statute, however, did not replace Acton Burnell, which continued to furnish an alternative procedure.[6]

A measure somewhat similar in character was incorporated in Westminster II (1285).[7] This authorized the imprisonment of receivers and other servants of lords who, after auditors had been assigned, were in arrear in their accounts, until the arrears should have been paid. The imprisonment might be effected on the testimony of the auditors, but the accountant might appeal to be heard before the Barons of the Exchequer. Thus was created the statutory action of account. It is not hard to find instances of its effectiveness. Cases of appeal to the Exchequer are, for example,

---

[1] See e.g. *Cal. Close R.* 1349–54, 413 (1352); *Sel. Cases in K.B.* VI, pp. 115–16 (1357).   [2] 11 Hen. VII, c. 10, s. 1.
[3] 6 Hen. VIII, c. 24, s. 9; cf. 14 & 15 Hen. VIII, c. 15, s. 7 (1523).
[4] *Stat. Realm*, I. 54.   [5] Ibid. 99.
[6] See e.g. *Cal. Close R.* 1302–7, 111.   [7] C. 11.

recorded in 1287[1] and 1310,[2] and another, where the accountant escaped from prison before making that appeal, in 1394.[3]

No piece of fourteenth-century legislation, however, played a more important part in the history of imprisonment than the seventeenth clause of the Statute of 1352 which extended from the action of account to the actions of debt and detinue process against the person of the debtor or detainer, in cases where there had been no prior acknowledgement of the debt before a mayor or his clerk.[4] This placed the common creditor in the same position as the crown and gave him the power of imprisoning his debtor's body until the debt in dispute should have been settled. From this statute sprang all the imprisonings for debt, all the debtors' prisons or debtors' wards, and all the lamentations which they brought in their train.

Statutes of the fourteenth and fifteenth centuries also imposed coercive imprisonment either to secure that offenders were bound over to observe those statutes or, more generally, to keep the peace or be of good behaviour. By the Ordinance of Money (1283–4)[5] men found with false or clipped coin were to be imprisoned until they found surety. Men so detected were in prison in 1295[6] and 1373.[7] The labour legislation outlined above[8] furnishes several illustrations of binding over as well as of penal imprisonment. The first Statute of Provisors (1351) provides for such imprisonment to secure both binding over and the payment of fines and damages.[9] Imprisonment until fines and damages had been paid was also enforced under a statute of 1365 directed against those who falsely suggested that others were being falsely imprisoned.[10] Imprisonment to secure the payment of fines and 'ransoms' alone is mentioned in a statute of 1404 directed against fraudulent royal accountants[11] and one of 1421 against falsifiers of weights,[12] and

[1] *Sel. Cases in Exchq. of Pleas*, pp. 121–2.
[2] *Yr. Bk. 3 Edw. II* (S.S.), 92. [3] *Cal. Close R.* 1392–6, 287.
[4] 25 Edw. III, St. v. c. 17; cf. T. F. T. Plucknett, *Legislation of Edward I* (Oxford, 1949), 149 and n. [5] *Stat. Realm*, I. 219.
[6] *Sel. Cases before King's Council*, 15. [7] *Sel. Cases in K.B.* VI, 165.
[8] See p. 38. [9] See p. 36. [10] 38 Edw. III, St. I, c. 9.
[11] 6 Hen. IV, c 3. [12] 9 Hen. V, St. II, c. 8.

to secure the payment of damages alone by one of 1397 against those guilty of taking horses without the consent of the owners on the false ground that they were needed for the king's service.[1] A somewhat similar statute of 1445 directed the imprisonment of purveyors of the duke of Gloucester or other lords who took food, horsemeat, and carts without authority. In this case, however, the specific restitution of the thing taken and not the payment of damages in cash was the object aimed at.[2] By a statute of 1439 alien merchants who would not place themselves or remain under a native 'host' were to be imprisoned until they would agree to do so.[3]

Such coercion was not always embodied in statutes. It might rest on nothing more than a patent issued in favour of some particular community. Thus a patent of 1385 authorized the mayor and bailiffs of Winchester to imprison those who failed to contribute towards the repair of the city walls until the crown should otherwise order,[4] and another of 1465 empowered the bailiff of Havering to commit to prison any trespassers at Havering fair until they might find security.[5]

[1] 20 Ric. II, c. 5. This is a modification of Westm. I. c. 32.
[2] 23 Hen. VI, c. 13.   [3] 18 Hen. VI, c. 4.
[4] *Cal. Pat. R.* 1381–5, 556.   [5] *Cal. Chart. R.* 1427–1516, 205.

III

THE IMPRISONMENT OF CLERKS, SERFS, AND JEWS

IN medieval England clerks, or those who were deemed to be clerks, were controlled by a system of law separate from that which regulated the conduct of laymen, and imprisonment affected the two estates or classes in different ways.[1] Serfs and Jews also formed distinct classes who, when generalizations are framed, have to be wholly or partially excepted.

Before their trial, clerks, when charged with felony, were not treated very differently from laymen. They might even be imprisoned in lay prisons. But whether they were in such prisons or in 'bishops'' prisons[2] it was the duty of the ordinary to ensure their appearance in the lay court. Once in court they might either plead their clergy at once and if convicted on the facts be thereupon redelivered to the ordinary; alternatively they might stand their trial as laymen and plead their clergy if convicted. The former method was much the more common in the thirteenth century; the latter gained ground in the fourteenth. Once delivered or redelivered to the ordinary, the clerk, unless he openly admitted his offences, had to undergo the process called compurgation, which involved the convocation of oath-helpers. If he succeeded in thus purging himself, he naturally went free. If he failed he was or might be degraded[3] from his orders and be assigned a 'penance'. This 'penance' was life imprisonment,[4] the most severe or almost the most severe punishment available to the

---

[1] The subject of clerical imprisonment is considered in Leona C. Gabel, *Benefit of clergy in England in the later middle ages* (Northampton, Mass. 1928–9) and by C. R. Cheney, 'The punishment of felonous clerks', *E.H.R.* LI, 215. Unless otherwise stated the ensuing paragraphs are based upon those sources.

[2] See p. 134.

[3] R. M. Haines, *The administration of the diocese of Worcester in the first half of the fourteenth century* (London, 1965), 185.

[4] F. M. Powicke and C. R. Cheney (eds.), *Councils and synods*, II (1), 684.

church.[1] Purgation, however, did not necessarily ensue immediately upon the clerk's surrender. The delay might indeed be no more than two months, but periods of two and four years were not unknown in the fourteenth century and in the fifteenth there was even one of fourteen years. These prolonged imprisonments were not necessarily the result of mere dilatoriness; Archbishop Peccham had decreed (1279 × 1292) that clerks should not be lightly purged but should have their cases rigorously investigated.[2] Perhaps it was often felt that the clerk would be likely to succeed in his purgation, but was in fact a disreputable character and might be all the better for the enforced restraint upon his liberty.

Indeed it is a fact that most purgations, when eventually conducted, succeeded. Aware of this, the lay courts tended increasingly to restrict purgation, either by forbidding the ordinary in particular instances to proceed with it at all or by allowing him to do so only upon the king's special order. Nor were ordinaries unwilling to comply with the wishes of lay authority. The Statute *pro clero* of 1352 was issued as a result of a bargain whereby the clergy, in return for certain concessions to themselves, undertook to make clerical imprisonment more severe.[3] Thus perpetual penance came to be the statutory punishment for unpurged clerks. Archbishop Islip at once issued appropriate instructions to his suffragans in 1352.[4] These measures were later supplemented. In 1377 the crown instructed the bishops to abstain from purging notorious felons,[5] thus expressing in general terms prohibitions which had hitherto been particular.

Up to the sixteenth century the categories of persons admitted to be 'clerks' were progressively extended from all those in full orders through all those who were tonsured to all those who were literate. This enlargement of benefit of clergy, which at first glance looks like a rather dubious legal fiction, had both advantageous and disadvantageous features. Its advantage lay in the

[1] Pollock and Maitland, *History of English law*, I, 444.
[2] Powicke and Cheney, op. cit. II (2), 1122. [3] 25 Edw. III, St. VI, c. 4.
[4] D. Wilkins (ed.), *Concilia Magnae Britanniae et Hiberniae*, III. 13–14.
[5] *Rot. Parl.* III. 23.

fact that it furnished a means of mitigating the severity of the law by substituting for an even larger section of the population guilty of felony the punishment of imprisonment instead of death. Its disadvantage was that an increasing number of disreputable or desperate characters were kept for very long periods in insecure custody.

Because of the disadvantages, the crown was not very well disposed towards benefit of clergy. It not only took the steps already described but it imposed heavy fines upon those who allowed clerks convict to escape.[1] Moreover, it did nothing to enlarge the categories of offence to which the benefit might be applied. Thus it never admitted that high treason could be clergy-able[2] and in 1402 the clergy themselves seem to have acquiesced.[3] The same instrument that excluded treason from purgation also excluded 'common theft', by which, perhaps, petty larceny is meant. Nor were misdemeanours clergyable; from the late thirteenth century a small London lock-up was, despite initial protests from both crown and clergy, largely occupied by disreputable chaplains.[4] Clerks guilty of contempt were in the same condition for, as we have already seen,[5] they were imprisoned like any layman. Clerical debtors under the Statute of Acton Burnell were not exempt from imprisonment, though by the Statute of Merchants, which complemented Acton Burnell, they escaped it.[6] Finally, clerks were only to a very limited degree spared the imprisonment imposed by the forest law. In the mid-thirteenth century they were so treated if they were condemned by the forest eyre. It was, however, possible for the bishop to claim

[1] See p. 237.
[2] Pollock and Maitland, op. cit. II, 500; Plucknett, *A concise history of the common law* (1956 ed.), 443. For a statement of the crown's case see *Rot. Parl.* II. 244.
[3] 4 Hen. IV, c. 3.   [4] See p. 112.
[5] See pp. 12–13 for the imprisonment of the abbot of Gloucester, presumably a clerk. In 1222 a clerk who had been intruded into a royal benefice by judges delegate was imprisoned: *Bracton's note book*, II, no. 187.
[6] It was presumably the protection of this statute that the bishop of Worcester was claiming when he complained to the crown in 1313 that a clerk had been committed to Warwick gaol for debt: *Register of Walter Reynolds, bishop of Worcester* (Worcestershire Historical Society XXXIX), 65.

them as *convicti et aperti malefactores*. If they were so claimed they might be surrendered and possibly were liberated, but they were not thereby excused their fines. Nor does it seem that claim and surrender were automatic and, according to the clergy themselves, they were not surrendered until they had lain in prison.[1] In the next century there is not even any evidence that such surrenders took place at all.[2]

The way in which the crown in parliament fortified the bishops in exercising their powers of imprisonment has already been referred to. It was, however, not only when the clerks had been guilty of felony that that support was forthcoming. A statute of 1401 confirmed the rights of diocesans to keep in prison, for terms to be settled by the diocesans themselves, the teachers of heretical doctrine.[3] Another statute (1485) empowered diocesans to imprison priests guilty of 'flesshely incontinency' for periods of their own determination.[4]

No attempt has been made to examine how far bishops and their clerical subordinates imprisoned men and women guilty of offences less grave than felony. It must, however, be here recorded that the powers which the chancellors and vice-chancellors of the universities derived from the bishops included that of punishing by imprisonment not only academical clerks but also the townsmen of the university towns. Those powers were being exercised at Oxford by 1313,[5] if not well before, and were still enjoyed in the mid-fifteenth century.[6] At Cambridge by 1327 the chancellor or his deputy was fixing the terms of imprisonment for prostitutes.[7]

Just as the imprisonment of clerks by their bishops requires to

---

[1] *Sel. Pleas of Forest*, pp. lxxxvii–xciii. The editor there quotes in extenso the clergy's complaint (1257) that clerical forest trespassers could not be surrendered until they had suffered imprisonment in a lay prison. He interprets this as meaning custodial imprisonment before trial. It seems more likely that it was penal imprisonment after trial. [2] Ibid. p. xcii. But cf. p. xciii.

[3] 2 Hen. IV, c. 15. [4] 1 Hen. VII, c. 4.

[5] *Mun. Acad. Oxon.* I. 94. Cf. I. 18 and II. 466. These references come from the *liber cancellarii et procuratorum*.

[6] Ibid. II. 505, 527, 539, 665 (clerks); 556 (laymen). These references come from *acta curie cancellarie*. [7] *Cal. Pat. R.* 1327–30, 183–4.

be treated apart, so does the imprisonment of serfs by their lords. Its history is long. The first observed instance of it comes from 1196[1] and it is still acknowledged in the sixteenth century.

Servile status, of course, implied the complete subjection of serf to lord, and imprisonment was but one way, and perhaps not the most disagreeable way, in which the lord's rights might be exercised. In exactly what circumstances the lord took advantage of his power is not known, but it may be said that among the declared objects of such imprisonment in early times were the observance of villein customs,[2] the proof of villeinage,[3] and the avoidance of prosecution,[4] and in later times the enforcement of payment for manumission.[5]

Our information about the practice comes from the records of the central courts. Cases reached those courts in various ways, but often did so on pleas or writs of false imprisonment. The plaintiff would allege that he had been arbitrarily imprisoned by another man; the defendant would answer that the plaintiff was not a free man but his own serf, subject to all the incidents of serfdom. The issue of neifty would then be tried. If successfully averred, the plaintiff was presumably surrendered to the defendant's court. In an exceptional instance the issue of neifty could be tried by an assize appointed to determine whether a set of tenants were villeins and consequently owed specified services.[6] If convicted as villeins they were to be committed to gaol. The king's court never seems to have cavilled at imprisonment if neifty could be proved,[7] and Bracton positively states that the plea that a man had been imprisoned as his lord's neif is good in an appeal of false imprisonment.[8] It was no doubt to ensure that

[1] *Cur. Reg. R.* I. 22.   [2] Ibid. XII, p. 13 (1225).
[3] Ibid. I. 45–6, 67 (1198). The brother of a serf claimed to have been imprisoned by a lord until he would join with the lord in proving the villein status of the family.
[4] Ibid. IV. 148, 305–6. An alleged serf sued his lord in the king's court.
[5] *Yr. Bk. 11 Ric. II* (Ames Foundation), 168 (1388). For enforced manumission see also E. Lipson, *Introduction to the economic history of England* (7th ed. London, 1937), I, 131.
[6] *Cur. Reg. R.* XII, pp. 209–10 (1225).   [7] *Fleta*, II, p. 98.
[8] *Bracton*, II, 411.

this should be so that the thirty-ninth clause of Magna Carta was limited so expressly to 'free men'.[1]

But though such detention was admitted to be lawful, the form that it might take under the law was open to doubt. In the mid-thirteenth century a justice held that detention in the stocks was permissible, but not detention in prison,[2] and *Fleta* implies that detention might never go beyond the stocks.[3] The author of the *Mirror*, however, declared that lords might use stocks, irons, or 'prison' to hold the bodies of their serfs.[4] The records do not distinguish between the various possible methods, and some show that they were used in combination.[5] Certainly there is no evidence of the lapse of a suit because a lord had used a wrong one.

It is reasonable to suppose that at least until the earlier fourteenth century this sort of imprisonment was a not uncommon feature of rural life, though the records of only a small number of cases have survived. No doubt it was partly to facilitate such imprisonment that the network of small manorial prisons[6] was maintained and the customary service of guarding prisoners enforced.[7] How frequently it was resorted to cannot in the circumstances be measured. It may, however, be presumed that its use varied greatly not only from lord to lord, but from time to time. One might indeed have supposed that it should have lapsed entirely after the enactment of the statute of 1331 which defined the *liber homo* of clause 39 of Magna Carta simply as *homme*, or, at all events, after the statute of 1350 in which that phrase is rendered 'homme de quel estate ou condicion il soit'.[8] But whatever may have been the intention or temporary effect of those

---

[1] W. S. McKechnie, *Magna Carta* (2nd ed. Glasgow, 1914), 386.

[2] *Casus Placitorum*, 4. The 'rule' (*aprise*) based upon this judgement is rather different. It states that a lord may put his villein in the stocks but not in irons (*firges*). This 'rule' is followed in *Brevia Placitata*, 124, no. 23.

[3] *Fleta*, II, p. 98.   [4] *Mirror*, 79.

[5] *Cur. Reg. R.* I. 264: a case of imprisonment in rings (1200); *Sel. Cases in Star Chamber*, [i] 120: a case of imprisonment in stocks and irons (1500).

[6] See pp. 88, 250.   [7] See p. 260.

[8] H. E. Malden (ed.), *Magna Carta commemoration essays* (Aberdeen, 1917), 82.

liberalizing translations, the practice is found recurring in the years immediately following the Peasants' Revolt.[1] Indeed it might be said that such an imprisonment was one of the minor proximate causes of the revolt itself, for in 1381 the commons of Kent took up the case of a man whom Sir Simon de Burley claimed as his neif and imprisoned at Rochester; the populace eventually broke into the castle and released the man.[2] Such imprisonment was also resorted to in the fifteenth century,[3] though in none of the cases occurring at that time is there evidence that the lord's plea of neifty was successful and in three of the four it certainly failed. Yet even in 1527 the duchess of Buckingham was imprisoning her bondmen and refusing, because they were bondmen, to answer in the king's courts.[4] The almost contemporary treatise called 'Surveyinge', attributed to John Fitzherbert, includes among the lord's powers that of 'having the rule' of his bondman's body,[5] by which imprisonment could, among other things, be meant. When, by the end of the sixteenth century, manumission had become universal the custom of course disappeared.

The recorded durations of imprisonment are very varied. About 1275 a Cambridgeshire villein was imprisoned for three days.[6] About 1308 a Norfolk villein claimed gigantic damages for detention that lasted only a few hours.[7] Ten years later the prior of Ely is alleged to have kept a man in prison for two years.[8] The most notorious case, which comes from a much later period, was that of a south Wiltshire gentleman who claimed to have been im-

---

[1] *Yr. Bk. 11 Ric. II* (Ames Foundation), 168, 247. Nine cases have been noticed in the Yr. Bks. of Edw. III. For a case of 1394 see *Sel. Cases before King's Council*, 82–5.

[2] *Anonimalle Chron.* 136.

[3] A. E. Bland, P. A. Brown, and R. H. Tawney (eds.), *English economic history: select documents* (London, 1914), 98–102 (a Wiltshire case, 1447, and a Hants case); *Sel. Cases in Star Chamber*, [i] 118 (a Wiltshire case, 1500); G. F. Farnham, *Leicestershire medieval village notes* (privately printed, Leicester, 1929–31), III, 263, v, 420–1 (Leicestershire cases, 1432, 1435).

[4] *Law Quarterly Review*, IX (1893), 364. [5] C. 13.

[6] C 144/14/35.

[7] *Yr. Bk. 1 & 2 Edw. II* (S.S.), 13.

[8] *Yr. Bk. 11 Edw. II* (S.S.), 292–3.

prisoned, on grounds of neifty, by Humphrey duke of Gloucester in a most brutal manner for over seven years.[1]

From the imprisonment of neifs by their lords it is logical to proceed to the imprisonment of Jews by the king. A Jew was certainly a species of bondman[2] and whether he was at liberty or in confinement was rather a matter of expediency than of justice. Jews were, of course, often coercively imprisoned to secure the payment of tallages either by themselves or by other members of their communities.[3] They were, however, as often imprisoned penally for specifically Jewish offences, true or imagined, or taken into custody to await the king's pleasure. Thus the Jews of Norwich were imprisoned in 1234 for circumcising a Christian boy,[4] London Jews in 1239 on an imputation of murdering a Christian,[5] and Lincoln Jews in 1255 in the belief that they were implicated in the death of 'Little' St Hugh.[6] In 1247 a relapsed Christianized Jew was sent to the Tower.[7] After the statute *de Judaismo* had been promulgated in 1275 many of the poorer Jews, denied their customary means of livelihood, took to coin-clipping and this became so scandalous as to lead in 1278 to wholesale imprisonment. It is said that nearly 700 were sent to the Tower at this time.[8] Finally in 1287, on the eve of the expulsion, all Jews in the kingdom were imprisoned.[9]

It is to be imagined that Jews so imprisoned were seldom if ever fairly tried, though we may hear of them being removed from prison to hear judgement.[10] No doubt, so long as they remained prosperous, they could purchase their liberty. Once or twice, indeed, we hear of their release without any mention of a ransom. Thus in 1252 two Jews were discharged by royal fiat, one of them because he had been over-long in gaol.[11] The period and circumstances of detention must have varied greatly with the particular policy which the crown was pursuing at the time. But

---

[1] *English economic history: select documents*, 98, quoting patent roll.
[2] So called in the statute *de Judaismo*: *Stat. Realm*, I. 221.
[3] C. Roth, *A history of the Jews in England* (3rd ed. London, 1964), 45, 67.
[4] *Close R.* 1234–7, 17. [5] Roth, op. cit. 55. [6] Ibid. 57
[7] *Cal. Lib. R.* 1245–51, 133. [8] Roth, op. cit. 75. [9] Ibid. 79.
[10] *Cal. Lib. R.* 1240–5, 242. [11] *Close R.* 1251–3, 67, 131.

the risk of prison cannot ever have been far from the thoughts of the thirteenth-century Jew.[1] When the Jewish community was mortgaged to the lord Edward in 1262 he was specifically granted a prison for the distraint and punishment of Jews and others.[2] It is significant that the word 'custodire' does not occur in the grant.

[1] Roth, op. cit. 47–8. [2] *Close R.* 1261–4, 80.

IV

COUNTY GAOLS

IT has already been concluded that there were prisons in pre-Conquest England, designed for that purpose, and that they survived the Conquest.[1] It is also very evident that castles were used for custody or torment in the early Norman period.[2] The castles are often named, but the names are hardly worth recording here. It may be assumed that they were but seldom structurally adapted at this time for custodial use, though in 1140 Brian FitzCount built a cell called 'Cloere Brien' in Wallingford castle for the reception of William Martel.[3] The first true prison of which we have any account was the baulk house in Winchester High Street in which, as it is said, thieves used to be imprisoned. By 1115 this seems to have been no longer open.[4] Whether it had been some kind of 'national' prison surviving from the time when Winchester was the centre of government or whether it had merely been the prison of the sheriff of Hampshire cannot now be ascertained.

The responsibility of the sheriffs for guarding suspect felons has already been explained, and the way in which they gradually provided special buildings for the purpose.[5] It was these sheriffs' prisons, distributed throughout England, that formed historically the ground-work of our prison system, and under the name of county gaols remained in being until 1878. This is the first class of prison to be discussed.

Gaols and gaolers are not mentioned in the Pipe Roll of 1130, and they were probably few in number. This is attested by the

---

[1] See p. 1.   [2] See p. 3.
[3] Matthew Paris, *Chronica Majora* (R.S.), II. 174.
[4] The prison is mentioned in the Winchester Domesday which Round assigned to 1103 × 1115 and probably rather late in that period: *V.C.H. Hants*, I, 527–8. It is called 'lebalche regis ubi latrones ponebantur inprisone': *Domesday Bk. Additamenta* (Rec. Com.), 532. Cf. G. W. Kitchen, *Winchester* (London, 1891), 75.   [5] See pp. 3–4.

legend of Bricstan recorded in Henry I's reign. Convicted in the county court of Huntingdon, Bricstan had to be brought as far as London to be imprisoned.[1] When, however, the Pipe Roll series is resumed at the opening of Henry II's reign references to both appear at once. In 1155–6 the Fleet was mended,[2] but that prison does not fall historically into this class. In 1157–8 gaolers were paid out of the issues of Hampshire[3] and in 1158–9 works were done upon a gaol in Wiltshire.[4] There was a gaol in Norfolk by 1162–3[5] and in Suffolk by the following year.[6]

Two years after the sheriff of Suffolk was working on his gaol at Ipswich, general instructions were issued about gaol provision.[7] They stipulated that gaols should be built in counties where no gaols existed and were promptly obeyed. In the year of publication expenses were incurred in eighteen different counties, among them four which probably already had gaols.[8] Five other sheriffs severally made provision in 1166–7,[9] 1167–8,[10] 1169–70,[11] 1182–3,[12] and 1183–4.[13] In 1185 three did so.[14] By 1188 London, which previously, perhaps, had used the Fleet, had been furnished with a prison of its own,[15] and in the same year a gaol was built in Lancashire.[16] In 1194[17] and 1198[18] three further counties severally laid out money for this purpose, in 1206–7 two more[19] and in

[1] *Liber Eliensis* (Camden 3rd ser. xcii), 267.
[2] *Pipe R.* 1155–6 (Rec. Com.), 4. See p. 114.   [3] Ibid. 172.
[4] Ibid. 1159 (P.R.S. i), 38.   [5] Ibid. 1163 (P.R.S. vi), 29.
[6] Ibid. 1164 (P.R.S. vii), 33.
[7] Stubbs, *Charters*, 9th ed. 171. See p. 4.
[8] *Pipe R.* 1166 (P.R.S. ix), 11, 17, 36, 64, 67, 72, 75, 84, 93, 105, 111, 117, 123. The fourteen new counties were Beds., Bucks., Cambs., Devon, Essex, Herts., Hunts., Kent, Leics., Northants., Northumb., Oxon., Warws. and Yorks. For the nature of Hants prison see p. 79.
[9] Somerset: *Pipe R.* 1167 (P.R.S. xi), 149.
[10] Lincs.: ibid. 1168 (P.R.S. xii), 61.
[11] Notts.: ibid. 1170 (P.R.S. xv), 80.
[12] Berks.: ibid. 1183 (P.R.S. xxxii), 134, 137.
[13] Derbys.: ibid. 1184 (P.R.S. xxxiii), 99.
[14] Cornwall, Glos., Staffs.: ibid. 1185 (P.R.S. xxxiv), 200, 144, 164.
[15] For the history of Newgate see p. 103.
[16] *Pipe R.* 1188 (P.R.S. xxxviii), 6.
[17] Cumb.: ibid. 1194 (P.R.S. n.s. v), 120.
[18] Sussex: ibid. 1198 (P.R.S. n.s. ix), 225.
[19] Salop., Surrey: ibid. 1207 (P.R.S. n.s. xxii), 5, 64.

1213–14 a sixth.[1] Thus by the accession of Henry III there were only five counties for which no gaol is known to have existed. Two of these, Chester and Durham, were regalities, where the nature of the records, sparser than those of the kingdom, makes it hard to ascertain the facts. The other three were Herefordshire, Rutland, and Westmorland, two of them very small counties and the third remote and ill-developed.

The sheriffs had been told in 1166 that they must site their gaols in one of the king's boroughs or castles. They were given no further guidance and they were not expressly told how many buildings to provide. Where a county possessed a single fixed administrative centre, a county town, that centre was the obvious site. Gloucestershire, centred on Gloucester, provides a perfect example of this type of county. There were, however, several counties which had no single nucleus and here the choice of site was more uncertain. Berkshire, Somerset, and Wiltshire are counties of this sort.

In many counties, if not indeed in most, the sheriff had or claimed control of the castle in the county town. Here he often had his offices and here a gaol could often conveniently be planted. The curtain wall of the castle provided additional security and this was no doubt one reason why castles had been suggested as gaol sites in 1166. In some counties, however, the castle was not available to the sheriff or, owing to the exigencies of warfare or some other cause, was only available intermittently. In such counties it was necessary either to construct a separate building in the county town, as was done at Warwick, or to place the gaol in a town other than the original county town, as was done at Aylesbury.

During the middle ages there were twenty counties which for shorter or longer periods were grouped together in pairs, each pair being entrusted to a single sheriff.[2] Bedfordshire and Buckinghamshire, Cambridgeshire and Huntingdonshire, Derbyshire and Nottinghamshire, Norfolk and Suffolk were so linked

---

[1] Worcs.: ibid. 1214 (P.R.S. n.s. xxxv), 107.
[2] For the details see P.R.O. *List of sheriffs*.

throughout the period covered by this book, as, except for very short intervals, were Dorset and Somerset, Essex and Hertford-shire, and Leicestershire and Warwickshire. Berkshire and Ox-fordshire were linked from 1248 and so continued except in the years 1255–8. Surrey and Sussex were linked from 1242, Shrop-shire and Staffordshire, the only pair to be divorced before the later sixteenth century, from 1204 to 1344. In some instances these unions affected the arrangements that the sheriffs made for the custody of prisoners. Apart from franchise and municipal gaols there were in some counties royal castles, other than those located at the seat of government, which were sometimes brought into use as supplementary prisons. The numerous complexities and qualifications make it impossible to describe in general terms the arrangements made by sheriffs over several centuries. The only convenient course, therefore, is to survey developments in each county, beginning with those counties whose bailiwicks were united, turning next to the unitary bailiwicks, and closing with the two counties palatine.

In 1165–6, and therefore before his county was joined to Berkshire, the sheriff of Oxfordshire began to build a gaol in Oxford.[1] That it was in the castle from the outset dare not be asserted, but it was clearly there by 1230[2] and remains there to this day. Occasionally the sheriff lost custody of the castle[3] and it is not always clear what he did with his prisoners during these intervals. Sometimes they were in Berkshire prisons.[4] So far as is known, however, no other common gaol was ever planted in the county.

The Berkshire story is as complicated as the Oxfordshire one is simple. The sheriff made no early attempt to construct a gaol himself. Instead he relied upon the farmer of Windsor to furnish him with accommodation in the castle. Accordingly we find the

---

[1] *Pipe R.* 1166, 117. [2] *Close R.* 1227–30, 460.
[3] *C.* 1303–6. W. A. Morris, *The medieval English sheriff to 1300* (Manchester, 1927), 186. The immediately preceding keeper had been Amaury de St Amand (*Peerage*, s.v. St Amand). About 1280 the castle had been out of the sheriff's custody. James Cok, from whom the sheriff received it in 1281, was not a sheriff: *Cal. Close R.* 1279–88, 146. [4] See pp. 62, 64.

farmer (or constable) supporting approvers in 1179–80[1] and mending the castle gaol in 1184–5[2] and 1233–4.[3] But long before the last of these dates had been reached, the sheriff had begun to build a prison at Faringdon at a cost roughly equal to that which his Oxfordshire colleague had incurred at Oxford.[4] This was repaired in 1196–7,[5] but it did not again become a charge upon the issues of Berkshire. A prison at Faringdon did indeed remain in use until 1241, but it was probably the borough prison.[6]

In 1221,[7] if not indeed in 1216,[8] mention begins to be made of a prison at Wallingford. Like Windsor Wallingford was at this time a royal town with a castle inside it, and it is tempting to believe that the sheriff took the castle over as a prison rather than maintain Faringdon. It was ordered to be delivered in 1228.[9] The castle, however, a *caput honoris*, was granted to Richard, earl of Cornwall, by Henry III,[10] and much of the prison business from 1229, though not all of it, was conducted through him, as constable. That the grant to the earl of Cornwall was not, at least at first, meant to interfere with the use of a part of the castle as a prison is clear enough from a writ of that year which instructed the constable to receive prisoners from the sheriff as had been customary before Richard received the custody.[11] It also continued to be delivered.

Deliveries ceased for a while with that of 1244–5,[12] and in 1246 Wallingford was being called *prisona R. comitis Cornub' apud Walingeford'*.[13] Perhaps thenceforth it should be looked upon rather as a franchise prison than a common gaol. At all events for some years to come, years which coincide with the unification

---

[1] *Pipe R.* 1180 (P.R.S. xxix), 42.   [2] Ibid. 1185, 25.

[3] W. H. St J. Hope, *Windsor Castle, an architectural history* (London, 1913), I, 59.

[4] *Pipe R.* 1183, 134, 137.   [5] Ibid. 1197 (P.R.S. n.s. viii), 183.

[6] *Close R.* 1237–42, 311. Cf. p. 98.   [7] *Rot. Litt. Claus.* I. 470.

[8] *Rot. Litt. Pat.* 179.

[9] *Pat. R.* 1225–32, 223. The history of gaol delivery is traced in chapters xii–xiv.

[10] *V.C.H. Berks.* iii, 524. He was made constable in 1216 and was finally invested with the honor in 1231.

[11] *Close R.* 1227–31, 265.   [12] C 66/56 m. 3 d.

[13] *Close R.* 1242–7, 439.

of the counties under one sheriff, it becomes inconspicuous. In fact the transfer of an approver who was in the castle from the earl's bailiffs into the sheriff's hands[1] rather suggests that it was temporarily abandoned. In 1254, however, a woman was in prison there,[2] and later in the same year the sheriff was told to repair what is called the gaol outside Wallingford castle.[3] Probably this means that it lay within the outer bailey.[4] From this time Wallingford came back into use and remained a prison for many centuries.

One consequence of linking the two counties together in 1248 was that the delivery of all Berkshire gaols, and not Wallingford alone, ceased for a time. In fact no gaol in Berkshire was delivered between 1245–6, when there was a once-for-all delivery of Newbury,[5] and 1255–6[6] when the delivery of the franchise gaol of Reading was resumed after an interval of fourteen years. Oxford, however, was delivered continuously, and during the period of union housed Berkshire prisoners.[7]

It has been said[8] that in the late twelfth and early thirteenth centuries Windsor castle was used as a prison. There is, however, no evidence that this use continued into the middle years of the thirteenth century, and the military importance of the castle, especially during the civil war, would in any case have made it improbable.[9] That it was not available for venison trespassers in 1260 seems clear from the admission that there was then no gaol in Windsor forest and that such trespassers had to be sent into Surrey.[10] In the same year the bailiffs of the town were told to build a gaol in Windsor, so that prisoners need no longer be moved to London or Guildford as had then recently been cus-

---

[1] *Close R.* 1247–51, 28.

[2] Ibid. 1253–4, 126.   [3] *Cal. Lib. R.* 1251–60, 169.

[4] Cf. the position of one of the Salisbury castle gaols (*V.C.H. Wilts.* VI, 59) and the gaol at Sherborne castle (p. 66 n. 8).

[5] C 66/57 m. 2*d*.   [6] C 66/70 m. 20*d*.

[7] *Close R.* 1247–51, 25, 426–7.   [8] See pp. 60–1.

[9] *V.C.H. Berks.* III, 7–8.

[10] *Close R.* 1259–61, 26. For the confinement of a forest trespasser at Guildford in 1255 see ibid. 1254–6, 255. But Guildford was still used for such people even after the building of Windsor gaol: *Cal. Close R.* 1279–88, 455 (case of 1287).

tomary.[1] It was no doubt this prison, and not the castle, that was delivered for the first time in 1265–6.[2] Such deliveries became almost an annual event from 1271–2, and in 1277 it was decreed that Windsor should be the 'chief gaol' of Berkshire.[3] It does not seem, however, that the castle went completely out of use as a prison, for it was delivered in 1280–1[4] and 1284,[5] and in 1295–6 the gaol within it was mended.[6] At times it might be used for state prisoners.[7] But in the ordinary way, when Windsor gaol is referred to in the seventy-five years after 1260, it is probably not the castle that is intended.

The pre-eminence of Windsor did not prove popular in the county and in 1351 the commons of Berkshire complained about it in parliament. They said that the town of Windsor was remote and difficult of access, and was not stocked with food enough to nourish those who had to attend the sessions.[8] A commission was appointed to inquire into these allegations,[9] but its report is not known. In 1318–19 the commons complained again, alleging this time that the county gaol used to be at Wallingford and ought to be restored to that place.[10] Once again a commission was set up and once again nothing is known of the outcome. It is, however, possibly significant that after 1336 nearly all gaol delivery documents refer not to the gaol of Windsor but to that of Windsor castle.[11] It is therefore possible to argue that, after the complaints mentioned above, the main county gaol was moved to

[1] *Cal. Lib. R.* 1251–60, 531; *Close R.* 1259–61, 125.
[2] C 66/84 m. 4*d*.　　　　　　[3] *Cal. Chart. R.* 1257–1300, 203.
[4] *Cal. Pat. R.* 1272–81, 467 (a special commission).
[5] J.I. 1/44 mm. 19–20;/46 m. 24;/47 mm. 20, 44;/48 mm. 47–8.
[6] Hope, *Windsor Castle*, I, 89.
[7] E.g. imprisonment of John, earl of Moray, in 1336: *Cal. Close R.* 1333–7, 586.
[8] *Rot. Parl.* I. 300.　　　　　[9] *Cal. Pat. R.* 1313–17, 328–9.
[10] *Rot. Parl. hactenus inediti* (Camden 3rd ser. LI), 76; H. Cole (ed.), *Documents illustrative of English history in the thirteenth and fourteenth centuries, selected from the records of the department of the Queen's Remembrancer of the Exchequer* (Rec. Com.), p. 40.
[11] E.g. J.I. 3/130,/166; B.M. Add. MS 35205. A roll of 1380 (J.I. 3/4) is an exception. The cover of Add. MS 35205 contains a list of gaols by counties, followed by a list of gaol delivery justices arranged by circuits. The justices' names are those included in commissions of 1504 (*Cal. Pat. R.* 1494–1509, 361–3, etc.). This fact suggests the date for the list of gaols.

Wallingford, where a new prison is known to have been built in 1359;[1] that the Windsor gaol was then allowed to fall down; but that it was soon found that more gaol accommodation was needed in the county and that some area in Windsor castle was brought into use.

It will thus be seen that the reunification of Oxfordshire and Berkshire under one sheriff in 1259 did not mean that the gaols of one county were altogether suppressed. It is certain, however, that there was a good deal of mixing up of prisoners. A list of twenty-eight prisoners who died in Wallingford gaol in 1316 contains the names of at least ten Oxfordshire men,[2] and Oxfordshire prisoners were there again in the fifties and sixties.[3] Berkshire prisoners were found at Oxford not only in the later thirteenth century[4] but on various occasions between 1373 and 1422.[5] The castles of both Wallingford and Oxford were, of course, on the borderline between the two counties. Each therefore had two catchment areas.

Works were first done upon a gaol within the joint bailiwick of Derbyshire and Nottinghamshire in 1169–70,[6] but it is not stated where the building stood. In 1177–8, however, a gaol at Nottingham was repaired[7] and after that time a county gaol always existed in the town. It does not seem to have been originally in the castle, for in 1201 expenses were separately incurred upon 'the gaol' and the 'gaol within the castle'.[8] There are further references to the castle gaol in 1235[9] and 1248, and on the second of these occasions the keeper of the castle had custody of approvers.[10] In the mid-fourteenth century the constable or his lieutenant received or surrendered prisoners of state.[11] With one exception,[12] however, the fourteenth- and fifteenth-century building accounts refer to the county gaol simply as the gaol of Nottingham town

[1] *King's Works*, II, 851. [2] Berkshire Rec. Off. W/JC m. 1.
[3] J.I. 3/223/1. [4] See p. 62.
[5] J.I. 3/161,/172,/180,/189,/197. [6] *Pipe R.* 1170, 80.
[7] Ibid. 1178 (P.R.S. xxviii), 81. [8] Ibid. 1201 (P.R.S. n.s. xiv), 89.
[9] *Close R.* 1234–7, 143. [10] Ibid. 1247–51, 37.
[11] *Cal. Close R.* 1349–54, 225, 320; *Cal Pat. R.* 1370–4, 331; 1374–7, 417.
[12] In 1458–9: E 364/93 m. J.

and it seems unlikely that by that time the building was an integral part of the castle.

Attempts to plant a gaol in Derbyshire were somewhat ineffectual. In 1183–4 the sheriff mended what is called the gaol of the Peak[1] and in 1194–5 carried out some works upon a gaol at Chesterfield.[2] The removal of some prisoners from that place to the Peak in 1202[3] might possibly suggest that Chesterfield was being abandoned in its favour. Other suggestions, however, are also available. Both, for example, may have been forest prisons. A forest trespasser was in the Peak castle in 1281[4] but otherwise a prison there is not referred to further. A prison at Derby was delivered in 1278–9,[5] and prisoners are found there up to 1287.[6] Nevertheless at the same time there were Derbyshire prisoners at Nottingham.[7] The truth seems to be that from the eighties Nottingham served both counties. Indeed this may have been the case for many years before, since there was a Derbyshire prisoner in Nottingham in 1251.[8] The county was small and at this time probably barbarous. Derby gaol was indeed once delivered in the fourteenth century, in 1330–1.[9] After that it is not heard of any more.

While it is no doubt the case that Somerset grew out of Somerton and Dorset out of Dorchester, it would be rash to assert that in the mid-twelfth century those towns were the natural centres of the counties that took their names from them. At all events they did not then become gaol towns. Instead in 1166–7 the sheriff of the joint counties chose Ilchester as the place in which to put a gaol for the joint bailiwick,[10] and this remained in continuous use for over a century.[11]

The sheriff was slow to do anything about a prison for his other county. Sometimes, as in 1248[12] and 1252,[13] he kept Dorset

[1] *Pipe R.* 1184, 99.   [2] Ibid. 1195 (P.R.S. n.s. VI), 15–16.
[3] Ibid. 1202 (P.R.S. n.s. xv), 187.
[4] *Cal. Close R.* 1279–88, 99.   [5] *48 D.K. Rep.*, App., 55.
[6] *Cal. Close R.* 1279–88, 162, 272, 450.
[7] Ibid. 401, 458.   [8] *Close R.* 1247–51, 468–9.
[9] J.I. 1/169 mm. 41–6.   [10] *Pipe R.* 1167, 149.
[11] See below.
[12] *Close R.* 1247–51, 32, 68.   [13] Ibid. 1251–3, 140.

prisoners at Ilchester. He also once or twice used Corfe castle, for suspect felons were there between 1241 and 1251.[1] Corfe, however, was much in demand for 'political' prisoners, some of them aliens,[2] and probably, therefore, was rarely available for common ones. Sherborne castle was also sometimes used. It was perhaps the unnamed Dorset prison which justices were appointed to deliver in 1242,[3] and it was without any doubt once delivered about that time.[4] A man was imprisoned in it in 1259–60[5] and it was again ordered to be delivered in 1271–2[6] and 1275–6.[7] In 1279 a further step was taken when the constable was directed to make the outer bailey available to the sheriff for the custody of prisoners.[8] This order was evidently carried out, and Dorset prisoners were sent to Sherborne until 1289.[9] At length, in 1305, the commons of Dorset were authorized to build, at their own expense, a county gaol in Dorchester.[10] They promptly took advantage of this licence, for the prison was delivered almost at once,[11] and remained open for many centuries. A building which had been commissioned in 1269 for the receipt of the king's toll at Shaftesbury and the custody of his prisoners there never seems to have developed into a county gaol,[12] perhaps because it was too near the boundary.

While arrangements for a Dorset prison were thus at last completed, those in Somerset were undergoing an almost simultaneous change. In the 1280s the gaol in Ilchester was abandoned in favour of one at Somerton. The latter was in use by 1280[13] and its delivery was for the first time ordered in 1280–1.[14] Ilchester was ordered to be delivered for the last time for many years

---

[1] *Close R.* 1237–42, 382; 1242–7, 414; 1247–51, 514.

[2] See pp. 128–9.

[3] Commission to deliver the prisons of Somerset and Dorset: *Close R.* 1237–42, 442.

[4] *Somerset Pleas* [I] (Som. Rec. Soc. XI), 271–2.

[5] C 144/5/6.   [6] C 66/90 m. 7d.

[7] *45 D.K. Rep.*, App. II, 304.

[8] *Cal. Pat. R.* 1272–81, 356. Cf. Wallingford (p. 62) and Salisbury (*V.C.H. Wilts.* VI, 59).

[9] *Cal. Close R.* 1288–96, 6.   [10] *Cal. Pat. R.* 1301–7, 317.

[11] J.I. 3/16/1.   [12] *Cal. Lib. R.* 1267–72, p. 90.

[13] *Cal. Pat. R.* 1272–81, 395.   [14] *50 D.K. Rep.*, App., 207.

in 1281–2.[1] Somerton remained the county prison until about 1370,[2] when Ilchester was restored.[3] In 1366 it had been decided that Ilchester should once again become the meeting-place of county and assize courts, so as to relieve the economic depression of the town,[4] and doubtless the construction of a gaol was a complement to that decision. At Ilchester the county gaol remained until 1843.

In 1165–6 the sheriff for the combined counties of Essex and Hertfordshire laid out money on two gaols,[5] but their location is not stated. When in 1177–8 he incurred further expenses, the gaols were said to be at Newport and at Hertford.[6] It was at Hertford that the county gaol for Hertfordshire thenceforward stood, and it never seems to have fallen out of use or, if it did, not for long. It is true that in 1342 the crown threatened that, unless it was repaired, Hertfordshire prisoners would have to go to Colchester,[7] but, if this occurred, the gaol was again being delivered in 1358–60.[8] Although Hertford possessed a castle there is no evidence that it was used as a gaol,[9] except in 1493 when the gaol itself was out of repair.[10]

The early history of the Essex gaols is more complicated. The obvious place for the county gaol was the royal castle of Colchester which, strictly speaking, should have played the same role in the life of Essex as Cambridge castle did in that of Cambridgeshire and Salisbury castle in that of Wiltshire. Owing, however, partly to its military potentialities and partly to the fact that valuable lands belonged to or were customarily granted with it, the crown grudged it to the sheriff, who at first was consequently

---

[1] C 66/101 m. 20 *d*. In 1283 the crown was planning to give away the building materials: C 143/6/16.

[2] Apparently last delivered in 1370: J.I. 3/156.

[3] It was first certainly delivered in 1371: ibid. m. 26.

[4] *Cal. Pat. R.* 1364–7, 235.

[5] *Pipe R.* 1166, 123.

[6] Ibid. 1178 (P.R.S. xxvii), 33, 52.

[7] See p. 339.

[8] J.I. 3/22/5.

[9] It is called the castle gaol in a gaol delivery commission of 1525, but probably only by analogy with the other castle gaols mentioned in the same commission: *L. & P.* iv (1), 499.   [10] D.L. 37/62.

not at liberty to set up a prison within it.[1] Hence in early times the choice of Newport, a place which lying as it did on the borders of both counties could be useful to each of them. Newport gaol continued to be kept in repair until 1200–1.[2] Perhaps it even continued to enjoy a rudimentary existence until Edward I's reign, for it was delivered in 1276–8 and 1283,[3] in which years the sheriff did not enjoy the custody of Colchester.

Colchester castle, though of royal origin, was granted in fee by Henry I to Eudes the sewer and in his family it remained off and on until the outbreak of the civil war towards the end of John's reign. Its military importance then led to the appointment of military constables or keepers and the descendants of Eudes never recovered it for any length of time. In the thirteenth century these keepers were seldom the sheriffs; indeed until the very end of that century the sheriffs seem to have been in charge of the castle for little more than fifteen years in all, and never for more than five years at a stretch.[4] Notwithstanding this, the castle often contained a prison in that century. This was so by about 1226[5] and from 1232[6] the prison was constantly delivered. The king's gaol within the castle is expressly mentioned in 1236.[7] At those times, however, when a constable and not a sheriff was in charge, it was necessary to give express orders, as in the case of Berkshire castles,[8] for the admission of prisoners. Such orders for forest trespassers were issued in 1236[9] and 1260;[10] and in 1234,[11] 1236,[12] 1240,[13] and 1253[14] the constable was enjoined to receive prisoners from the sheriff or others. In August 1256 the sheriff, who had

---

[1] For the castle see [J. H. Round], *History and Antiquities of Colchester Castle* (Colchester, 1882).   [2] *Pipe R.* 1201, 59.   [3] J.I. 3/85.

[4] The keeper who surrendered the castle in November 1214 was sheriff at the time: *Rot. Litt. Pat.* 123. Richard de Muntfichet, who had been appointed constable in 1240 (*Close R.* 1237–42, 246), became sheriff in 1242. Other periods in Henry III's reign when the sheriffs are known to have been granted the castle were May–June 1251, June 1255–June 1256, July 1261 (or June 1262)–9 October 1266, April 1268–April 1272: *Cal. Pat. R., passim.* Cf. P.R.O. *List of sheriffs.*

[5] *Pat. R.* 1225–32, 37.

[6] First delivery commission: C 66/43 m. 9 d.

[7] *Close R.* 1234–7, 284.   [8] See p. 61.   [9] *Close R.* 1234–7, 295.

[10] Ibid. 1259–61, 21.   [11] Ibid. 1231–4, 499.   [12] Ibid. 1234–7, 284.

[13] Ibid. 1237–42, 251.   [14] Ibid. 1251–3, 307.

lost the castle in June, was told to use it *ex concessione* the constable.[1] Such arrangements cannot have been altogether convenient to either the constable or the sheriff. It is therefore not surprising that in 1234 and 1236[2] Essex prisoners were also being kept at Hertford. Indeed in 1259 during the civil war, when Colchester was in the earl marshal's custody, the sheriff was altogether denied access to it and was directed to send his prisoners to Newgate.[3]

After the long keepership of Richard of Holebrook (1276–c.1291)[4] had ended, a period of some fifty years ensued during which the sheriff seems to have had the custody of the castle more often than not.[5] At least the tradition seems to have been established that, other things being equal, he might expect to receive it with the counties. By 1344 things had gone so far that the sheriff of the day succeeded in securing the revocation of a grant to a royal retainer made in the preceding year and the castle was annexed to the shrievalty.[6] By 1350, however, the castle and shrievalty were again separated,[7] and after this, except in 1368–71,[8] were never reunited. By 1385 the commons of Essex seem to have accepted the fact that the castle was lost to the sheriff for good.[9]

Despite these alienations, whether temporary or permanent, a gaol seems to have been kept continuously in the castle throughout the fourteenth, fifteenth, and sixteenth centuries. The substitution of a constable for the sheriff made no difference. Constables on receiving the castle took with it the responsibility for guarding prisoners. Thus in 1343 the constable bound himself in Chancery to answer for escapes.[10] When in 1371 the castle was committed temporarily to the escheator, the prisoners were

[1] Ibid. 1254–6, 348–9. [2] Ibid. 1231–4, 408; 1234–7, 259.
[3] Ibid. 1256–9, 387.
[4] *Cal. Pat. R.* 1272–81, 141. He was dead by 27 February 1291: *Cal. Fine R.* 1272–1307, 290.
[5] Deduced from entries in *Cal. Pat. R.*, *Cal. Close R.*, and *Cal. Fine R.* But it cannot at present be said who had the custody in 1291–9, 1301–3, or 1304–13.
[6] *Cal. Pat. R.* 1343–5, 113, 157. The revocation had to be reiterated: *Cal. Fine R.* 1337–47, 397.
[7] *Cal. Fine R.* 1347–56, 235. [8] *Cal. Fine R., passim.*
[9] *Rot. Parl.* III. 211. [10] *Cal. Pat. R.* 1343–5, 113.

committed as well,[1] and after that time, as indeed before,[2] constables or the gaolers whom they appointed were pardoned like any sheriff or county gaoler for the escapes which they had suffered to occur.[3]

It has already been mentioned that in the earlier thirteenth century Essex prisoners were sometimes kept at Hertford. This was again true in 1388–98.[4] In Essex itself, moreover, the crown possessed another castle besides Colchester. This was at Rayleigh. The castle there does not seem to have been maintained in a defensive state much after the end of the twelfth century if at all.[5] The site, however, belonged to the crown, and a royal residence which stood upon it was still in use in 1301.[6] At Eastwood, an adjacent royal manor, a man was in custody in 1254–5[7] and a prison at Rayleigh itself was ordered to be delivered in 1256–7.[8] The prior of Prittlewell, who owned land in Rayleigh, was told to repair the prison in 1299–1301,[9] and it was frequently delivered until about 1346.[10] It was still being delivered in 1504.[11]

Within this bailiwick the crown also possessed the Hertfordshire castle of Berkhamsted. This was being used for prisoners in 1225,[12] the year in which it seems to have been granted to Richard, later earl of Cornwall. Like Wallingford castle, which Richard also owned,[13] Berkhamsted remained an appanage of the crown and seems to have served as a prison with even greater regularity than Wallingford. It was being delivered in 1225,[14] and still appears in an early sixteenth-century list of gaols.[15]

In 1165–6 the sheriff of Leicestershire and Warwickshire began to build gaols in each county, for Leicestershire at Rothley and for Warwickshire at Kineton.[16] The Kineton gaol is not heard of

---

[1] *Cal. Fine R.* 1377–83, 141.   [2] *Cal. Pat. R.* 1364–7, 55.
[3] Ibid. 1377–81, 267 (1378); 1452–61, 242, 645 (1455, 1460); 1485–94, 156 (1487).   [4] J.I. 3/217/3.
[5] *Transactions of the Archaeological Society of Essex*, n.s. XII, 151; *King's Works*, II, 804.   [6] Ibid. 152.
[7] C 144/4/24.   [8] C 66/72 m. 5 d.
[9] *V.C.H. Essex*, II, 139.   [10] J.I. 3/129.
[11] *Cal. Pat. R.* 1494–1509, 359.   [12] *Rot. Litt. Claus.* II. 21, 26.
[13] *V.C.H. Herts.* II, 166.   [14] *Rot. Litt. Claus.* II. 85.
[15] B.M. Add. MS 35205. See p. 63 n. 11.   [16] *Pipe R.* 1166, 67.

after 1192,[1] that at Rothley not after 1233.[2] But before Kineton had disappeared, another Warwickshire gaol was being maintained at Kenilworth. Money was spent upon it for the first time in 1185–6,[3] and it was first ordered to be delivered in 1229.[4] It continued to be delivered up to 1237–8,[5] and makes its last appearance in 1251, when it was the place of custody for a vivary trespasser.[6]

In 1199–1200 a site was bought for a gaol in Warwick itself and was at once covered by a building.[7] Apparently it began to be delivered in 1220[8] but between 1229 and 1233 it is not mentioned. It was perhaps ruinous. At all events the costs of repair were recovered in 1234–5.[9] In the interval, no doubt, Kenilworth took its place.[10] Orders to deliver Warwick were again issued in 1234[11] and after that the gaol always remained open.

A gaol existed in Leicester by 1208–9[12] and was repaired in 1210–11.[13] It appears then to have fallen out of use, for by 1234–5 orders had been given to buy a site in the town suitable for a 'strong and good gaol'.[14] A building was evidently erected and continues to be mentioned until 1284–5.[15] But for a part of that period, at least from 1261,[16] Warwick gaol was used for the prisoners of both counties, and after 1285 Leicester gaol was abandoned for a while. Before 1301, however, money was being collected in Leicestershire for the construction of a gaol, and in the parliament of that year Thomas of Lancaster granted that the crown should have a gaol in Leicester town, of which he was the lord,[17] so that Leicestershire prisoners need no longer be taken

---

[1] Ibid. 1191 and 1192 (P.R.S. n.s. II), 245.
[2] *Close R.* 1231–4, 215.   [3] *Pipe R.* 1186 (P.R.S. xxxvi), 126.
[4] *Close R.* 1227–31, 239.   [5] C 66/48 m. 10d.
[6] *Close R.* 1247–51, 413.
[7] *Pipe R.* 1200 (P.R.S. n.s. XII), 176, 250; 1201, 232.
[8] A commission was issued in that year for the delivery of the gaols of Warwickshire and Leicestershire: *Rot. Litt. Claus.* I. 413.
[9] *Close R.* 1227–31, 184; E 372/79 m. 12.
[10] R. B. Pugh, 'King's prisons before 1250' (*Trans. R. Hist. Soc.* 5th ser. v), 7.
[11] C 66/44 m. 5d.   [12] *Pipe R.* 1209 (P.R.S. n.s. XXIV), 21.
[13] Ibid. 1211 (P.R.S. n.s. XXVIII), 197.
[14] E 372/9 m. 12.   [15] C 66/104 m. 13d.
[16] *Close R.* 1259–61, 341.   [17] *Cal. Close R.* 1296–1302, 428.

out of the county to Warwick, as had been the former custom.[1] The prison took long to build and was not finished by 1306,[2] but it was being delivered by 1307,[3] and by 1309 the sheriff was being told not to send any more Leicestershire prisoners into Warwickshire.[4] From this time Warwick and Leicester remained the sites of the common gaols of the two counties in which they lay.

From the time of its early fourteenth-century reconstruction, however it may have been before, Leicester gaol was on a site remote from the castle, which indeed enclosed a franchise prison of its own. It is equally certain that at the beginning Warwick gaol was not inside the castle. Curiously enough, however, it is sometimes stated or implied from the fourteenth century that it was. Thus an inquiry into its physical state carried out in 1325 was entrusted not to the sheriff but to the constable,[5] commissions were issued in 1367 and 1368 to deliver the castle gaol,[6] and four more between 1497 and 1508,[7] and a financial document of 1449 expressly places the gaol within the castle. While scribal errors may account for some of these usages, it may be that the castle was indeed sometimes in use either as the sole or as a supplementary prison. For a part if not for the whole of the period 1497–1508, when one set of the above-mentioned commissions was issued, the castle was in the crown's hands[8] and possibly at this time the true gaol and the castle were used concurrently. Certainly in 1501, 1502, 1507, and 1508 commissions were also issued to deliver, in the conventional phrase, the 'gaol of Warwick'.[9] It is also a fact which is not open to dispute that by 1590 the castle was being used as a gaol,[10] and the precedent may have been set in an earlier day.

Before 1204, when Staffordshire and Shropshire began to be linked together, two gaols had been planted in Staffordshire. One

---

[1] *Cal. Pat. R.* 1301–7, 477.   [2] Ibid.
[3] J.I. 1/467 m. 14.   [4] *Cal. Close R.* 1307–13, 167.
[5] E 143/8/3/11/1.   [6] *Cal. Pat. R.* 1364–7, 352; 1367–70, 106.
[7] Ibid. 1494–1509, 145, 249, 286, 560.
[8] The evidence will be cited in the forthcoming *V.C.H. Warws.* VIII.
[9] *Cal. Pat. R.* 1494–1509, 285, 292, 295, 529, 561.
[10] *Hist. MSS. Com. Hatfield*, XI, 433, where it is said that the castle has been 'a common gaol these ten years'.

of these, on which money was first spent in 1185, was in Stafford itself;[1] the other was at Newcastle under Lyme, first mentioned as a prison site in 1198–9.[2] Both these gaols continued to be repaired until 1203–4,[3] the year of linkage. In 1205–6 the cost of work at 'the gaols' is accounted for under Staffordshire.[4] In the following year expenses for mending 'four gaols' appear in the Pipe Roll under Shropshire[5] and for mending 'one gaol' under Staffordshire.[6] In 1213–14 the cost of 'the gaols' is again to be found under Staffordshire.[7] During this period from 1204 to 1214 the only gaol named in either county is that at Newcastle, which was mended for the last recorded time in 1207–8.[8] It is not possible to interpret these references with any certainty, but it seems likely that the sheriff was at last beginning to provide Shropshire with a gaol or gaols, and it is possible that this or these were at Shrewsbury and Bridgnorth. At all events there was a gaol at Shrewsbury by 1221[9] and one at Bridgnorth by 1234–5.[10] Both Shropshire gaols began to be delivered soon after this, Bridgnorth in 1235 and Shrewsbury in 1232–3,[11] and delivery was frequent and regular thenceforward. Stafford had begun to be delivered in 1230[12] and was delivered on several later occasions up to 1241.[13] For many years after this, however, allusions to that prison are extremely rare and bail writs make it clear that by the middle years of the century Staffordshire prisoners were being kept in Shropshire prisons.[14] Commissions to deliver 'the gaols of Shropshire and Staffordshire', issued in 1261–2 and 1267–8,[15] suggest that a prison was open somewhere in Staffordshire, but in general the situation seems to be that Shropshire had taken over the custody of the prisoners of both counties, as Staffordshire had done in the twelfth century.

[1] *Pipe R.* 1185, 164.
[2] Ibid. 1199 (P.R.S. n.s. X), 163.
[3] Ibid. 1204 (P.R.S. n.s. XVIII), 209.
[4] Ibid. 1206 (P.R.S. n.s. XX), 112.
[5] Ibid. 1207 (P.R.S. n.s. XXII), 5.
[6] Ibid. 7.
[7] Ibid. 1214, 46.
[8] Ibid. 1212, 88.
[9] *Pat. R.* 1216–21, 321.
[10] C 66/45 m. 6*d.*
[11] C 66/43 m. 5*d.,*/45 m. 6*d.*
[12] *Close R.* 1227–31, 359.
[13] Evidence of *Pat. R.*
[14] E.g. *Close R.* 1247–51, 165, 289–90, 406; 1253–4, 28, 85.
[15] C 66/77 m. 19*d.*; /86 m. 9*d.*

Bridgnorth continued to be used[1] and to be delivered up to 1301.[2] It was, however, reported in 1281 that the original prison, which was in the barbican, had collapsed. In consequence prisoners had to be kept in the keep, which was felt to be less secure.[3] It was no doubt for this reason that Bridgnorth was abandoned as a place of detention. Stafford was restored and took its place. Orders to repair Stafford gaol, then threatening to fall, were issued in 1272,[4] and in 1285–6 its delivery was resumed.[5] Until 1293, however, references are few. It was ordered to be repaired in 1332[6] and 1350,[7] but by 1390 county prisoners were being kept in the town gates,[8] presumably because the gaol was again ruinous. It seems to have been then greatly altered, perhaps even rebuilt upon a new site.[9] It was repaired again in 1450.[10] After that it was kept in use until *c.* 1559,[11] when apparently it disappeared. There was then no gaol in Stafford until an entirely new one was built in 1617.[12] In the interval the sheriff seems to have used the borough gaol.[13]

Was Stafford gaol enclosed within a castle wall? There is hardly any reason to suppose that after 1102 there was a castle in Stafford town.[14] Yet the county gaol that was delivered in 1337–55 is said to be the gaol of Stafford castle,[15] and in 1437 further commissions to deliver the castle gaol begin to be encountered.[16] The phrase, which is not indeed confined to commissions,[17] continues to be used in commissions up to 1508.[18] After that it is very rare.[19] What this 'castle' was, if it was a castle, is a matter for topographical specu-

---

[1] C 144/29/26 and/38.
[2] C 66/104 m. 24*d.*; J.I. 3/100.
[3] *King's Works*, II, 577.
[4] *Cal. Lib. R.* 1267–72, 217.
[5] C 66/105 m. 6*d.*
[6] *Cal. Close R.* 1330–5, 508.
[7] Ibid. 1349–54, 253.
[8] Ibid. 1389–92, 215.
[9] E 101/587/8 and /9 (1391–4).
[10] E 101/587/10.
[11] 1 Eliz. I, private Act.
[12] W.S.L., D 1721/1/4, f. 28*b.*
[13] Ibid. f. 131.
[14] It is proposed to consider the evidence in a forthcoming volume of *V.C.H. Staffs.*
[15] J.I. 3/131.
[16] *Cal. Pat. R.* 1436–41, 145, 370.
[17] *Will. Salt Arch. Soc.* n.s. VI (1), 107.
[18] *Cal. Pat. R.* 1494–1509, 561.
[19] Evidence of *L. & P.* and *Cal. Pat. R.* After 1508 the only instances of the use of 'castle' gaol in gaol delivery commissions are C 66/633 m. 20*d.* (1519) and *L. & P.* XII (1), p. 143 (1537).

lation not relevant in the context. The omission, however, of the word 'castle' from documents about the gaol dated after 1508 and its inclusion in the period 1437–1507 are so very much the rule as to lead to the belief that omission or inclusion was deliberate. In any case the word 'castle' seems normally to have been abandoned about 1509.

There is nothing to suggest that the gaol in Shrewsbury, apparently located in the castle, ever fell out of use, and after 1344 it presumably served Shropshire alone. Deliveries were regular. In 1399, however, the commons of Shropshire complained that the castle gaol was ruinous and urged that it should be rebuilt.[1] It is not known whether it was. The castle itself was much in ruin by 1443[2] but the gaol seems to have been in it still in 1536, when the sheriff sought the corporation's leave to move it into the town.[3]

In comparison with their remoter neighbours, the adjacent 'home' counties of Surrey and Sussex were slow to provide themselves with gaols.[4] It is not at all unlikely that in early days their sheriffs used the gaols of London. At all events in 1172–3 Surrey contributed a tolerable sum towards building the Fleet, and this suggests that its sheriff was sharing both accommodation and expenses with his colleagues in London and Middlesex. Sussex never made such a contribution, but in 1191–2 it was paying for the movement of some prisoners from Lewes to Lambeth, possibly in order that, once they had crossed the river, they could be tried in London.

In 1197–9 works began to be done upon a gaol in Chichester castle and here for a time a Sussex gaol was established. The castle was demolished soon after 1217 and a gaol built upon the site on which it formerly had stood.[5] Meanwhile a gaol for Surrey

---

[1] *Rot. Parl.* III. 441.

[2] *King's Works*, II, 837.

[3] [H. Owen], *Ancient & present state of Shrewsbury* (Shrewsbury, 1808), 428.

[4] Except where otherwise stated the ensuing paragraphs are based upon my article, 'Medieval Sussex prisons', in *Sussex Archaeological Collections*, XCVII, 69–81, although I here depart slightly from some of its conclusions.

[5] *Rot. Litt. Claus.* I. 468.

makes its appearance. It was in Guildford, probably in the castle, and is first recorded in 1207. It remained in continuous use throughout the period.

When in 1242 the two counties, which had intermittently shared the same sheriff since 1226, were formally united, a sharing of prison accommodation resulted almost immediately. In 1242, and again in 1248, there is clear evidence for the custody of Sussex men at Guildford, and after 1248 it is extremely common. A gaol at Chichester is indeed mentioned in 1246, 1252, and 1268, and was probably the county gaol of 1221, but in 1269 Richard, earl of Cornwall, gave the site of that prison to the Grey Friars. After that the only prison in Chichester seems to have been the city prison, first clearly mentioned in 1271–2.[1]

For a part of the thirteenth century Hastings and Pevensey castles were at the crown's disposal and appear at those times to have supplemented the prison accommodation for the two counties. Common suspects were sent to Hastings in the period 1235–40 and to Pevensey rather later on. In Edward I's early years Hastings was delivered.

It is not hard to imagine that the removal of Sussex men into Surrey, as was so often necessary, was an inconvenience to the commons of Sussex. Nor may the arrival of such prisoners at Guildford have been altogether welcome in Surrey. At any rate in 1306 the gaoler of Guildford complained to the crown that his castle was too weak to hold as many prisoners as it then contained, and asked for their release by ransom or transportation to another place. The crown, however, refused to sanction releases, suggesting instead the strengthening or enlargement of the building or the closer confinement of the prisoners. In 1320 the commons of Sussex for their part complained that their county lacked both gaol and county offices. Their complaint went unheeded. A similar plea for the construction of a gaol at Chichester was uttered in 1347 and was likewise unsuccessful.

[1] C 66/90 m. 24*d.* (23*d.*). At all events a gaol in Chichester was then ordered to be delivered and if the county gaol had gone the city gaol must have been intended.

So matters remained until the Peasants' Revolt created great congestion in the London gaols, all of which had been broken into by the rebels.[1] Accordingly in 1381 the earl of Arundel was ordered to take prisoners into his castles at Arundel and Lewes because Guildford castle was not large enough to hold so great a throng. In the following year Lewes castle was formally constituted a felons' gaol for two years. Whether this was much used may be doubted, for apparently in 1383 a mob broke into it and damaged it severely.[2]

The ambition of Sussex to possess its own common gaol was not indeed satisfied until after 1487. A petition laid before parliament in that year for the establishment of a gaol at Lewes was granted, and two years after that the prison was delivered. In Lewes, which had already become the meeting-place of the county court, the county gaol remained until about 1541, when for a few decades it went to Horsham.[3]

The gaol of Bedfordshire was planted at Bedford in 1165–6[4] and remained continuously in use. It never seems to have been in the castle, which was in any case demolished in 1224.[5] The gaol of Buckinghamshire was planted at Aylesbury in the same year.[6] There was no castle there in which to put it and it probably stood on or near the site of the present County Hall.[7] There is no satisfactory evidence that the sheriff ever maintained any other gaol within the county.[8]

Gaols were started in Cambridgeshire and Huntingdonshire in 1165–6[9] and by 1171–2[10] and 1175–6[11] were respectively located at Cambridge and at Huntingdon. So far as is known, both remained uninterruptedly open. Cambridge gaol was inside the

---

[1] See p. 223.
[2] *Cal. Pat. R.* 1381 5, 259.
[3] See p. 345.
[4] *Pipe R.* 1166, 11.
[5] *King's Works*, 11, 559.
[6] *Pipe R.* 1166, 11.
[7] *V.C.H. Bucks.* 111, 1–2.
[8] The sheriff was charged to repair the gaol of Buckingham in 1261: *Cal. Lib. R.* 1260–7, 54. Though a gaol at Buckingham was ordered to be delivered in 1276–7 (*46 D.K. Rep.* App., 115) it is probable that the order of 1261 really refers to Aylesbury. The status of the prison at High Wycombe is considered on pp. 90–1.
[9] *Pipe R.* 1166, 84.
[10] Ibid. 1172 (P.R.S. xviii), 135.
[11] Ibid. 1176 (P.R.S. xxv), 70.

castle by 1260.[1] Probably it was there at a much earlier time, for
the castle had been of little strategic importance since 1215 and
the sheriff had his office there by about 1240.[2] Moreover, the construction and maintenance of the gaol between 1165–6 and 1210
were nearly four times less costly than that of Huntingdon[3] and
this might be attributed to the fact that it enjoyed the benefit of a
protecting curtain wall. Huntingdon castle was destroyed by
Henry II[4] and was not rebuilt. Between 1366 and 1387 the gaol
is called Huntingdon castle gaol.[5] This can only have been by
analogy or inadvertence,[6] unless the meaning simply is that the
gaol stood within the still existing earthen ramparts.

The sheriff of Norfolk and Suffolk had 'prepared' a gaol at
Thetford in 1162–3,[7] but, except for a delivery in 1262–3,[8] this is
not heard of again. He began to build one at Norwich in 1165–6.[9]
Norwich gaol may possibly have been in the castle from the
beginning and seems certainly to have been there by the later
fourteenth century.[10] At Ipswich, where there was no castle, a
gaol was being worked upon in 1163–4.[11] Each prison was kept
continuously open, except for a short period between 1314–16
and *c.* 1325 when Ipswich gaol seems to have fallen into ruin.[12]

Such was the history in outline of the county gaols in the
twenty linked counties. Of the seventeen unitary counties there
are five which have a gaol history sufficiently complicated to
warrant individual attention. The sheriff of Gloucestershire
started to lay out money on a gaol for his county a good deal
later than many of his colleagues, for it was not until 1184–5 that
he raised a charge.[13] The building then lay within Gloucester
castle. During the civil war the castle was not deemed a proper
place for prisoners,[14] and they were not admitted. Again in 1223

[1] W. M. Palmer (ed.), *The assizes held at Cambridge in A.D. 1260* (Linton, 1930), 2, 9. [2] *V.C.H. Cambs.* II, 116.
[3] *Pipe R., passim.* [4] *King's Works*, II, 682.
[5] J.I. 3/152, /158, /164. [6] See p. 67 n. 9.
[7] *Pipe R.* 1163, 29. [8] 'Thoford': C 66/79 m. 13 d.
[9] *Pipe R.* 1166, 17.
[10] E.g. *Cal. Inq. Misc.* III, p. 196 (1363); *Cal. Pat. R.* 1381–5, 45, 285, 287 (1381, 1383). [11] See p. 58. [12] *Rot. Parl.* I. 436.
[13] *Pipe R.* 1185, 144. [14] Maitland, *Glos. Pl.* p. 99.

prisoners were removed from the castle for a short while because Eleanor of Brittany, the king's kinswoman, was in prison there. The abbot of Cirencester lent his gaol during this interval.[1] At all other times the gaol seems to have been within the castle and to this day there is a prison adjacent to the ancient castle area.

Two other royal castles in the county supplemented Gloucester. Bristol castle was a prison in 1216[2] and seems to have continued in that use at least until the eighties of the thirteenth century. A Welshman, taken in war and confined in 1305,[3] and the third Hugh le Despenser[4] are among the last known prisoners.[5] St Briavels castle was also used in the thirteenth century,[6] though partly at least for forest trespassers.[7]

In Hampshire the early history of the county gaols is rather puzzling. It has already been noticed that by 1115 there was an abandoned prison in Winchester High Street,[8] and that in 1157–8 the issues of Hampshire were charged with a small payment for the support of 'gaolers'.[9] In 1165–6 some inconsiderable works upon 'the gaols', as they are called, were paid for out of the issues of Winchester.[10] Later on, in 1171–2 and 1199–1200, much larger sums of money were laid out upon the king's works in the city, including a gaol. In the earlier of the two years the gaol is said to be in the castle.[11] After this, up to 1233, the sheriff is five times ordered to repair Winchester gaol, which in 1226 is said to lie within the castle.[12] During the same period the reeves of Winchester spent on one occasion (1221) a fair sum on mending the gaol, and were allowed the costs out of the Exchequer.[13] It seems, therefore, that in the early years of Henry II there were two gaols in Winchester, one in the castle and one outside it, and that both

---

[1] *Rot. Litt. Claus.* I. 543, 556.   [2] Ibid. 288.
[3] *Cal. Close R.* 1302–7, 298.   [4] *Peerage*, IV, 272.
[5] For prisons in the borough see pp. 101–3.   [6] C 66/62 m. 5 d.
[7] *Cal. Close R.* 1279–88, 79, 86, 158–9, 202, 259.
[8] See p. 57.   [9] See p. 4.
[10] *Pipe R.* 1166, 105.   [11] Ibid. 1172, 84; 1200, 191.
[12] *Rot. Litt. Claus.* I. 506; II. 137; *Cal. Lib. R.* 1226–40, 33, 116, 207.
[13] *Rot. Litt. Claus.* I. 467.

continued in existence until the coming of age of his grandson.[1] In 1228, however, the sheriff is suddenly forbidden to imprison in the castle,[2] although only two years before he had been ordered to repair its gaol, which was full of prisoners.[3] Hampshire prisoners, he was told, should be imprisoned in 'Winchester gaol', as the crown had no wish to have any other prison in Hampshire than that in Winchester. The use of the castle by the sheriff had been irregular and he was only to revert to it on express instructions. Indeed the Chancery declared that Hampshire prisoners by custom always had been imprisoned in 'Winchester gaol'.[4]

What is meant at this time by 'Winchester gaol'? As will be mentioned later on,[5] the gaolership of Winchester was held in fee, and there is good ground for supposing that in the beginning the gaoler was in charge not only of the prisoners but of the castle gate. Since this was so, the gate was presumably the prison. Yet now the castle was not to be used as a prison. May it be that the gaolers in fee had moved the prison away from the castle, perhaps even to the site that it later occupied[6] in the north-west angle of the city wall? It seems safest to assume that they had done so, and that for the time being the castle was abandoned as a place of custody. On the few occasions during the remainder of the thirteenth century when prisoners in the castle are referred to, those prisoners seem to have been of a political sort;[7] probably they were received there only by special direction.

In 1299 the prison of Winchester city begins to be delivered.[8] Does this mean 'Winchester gaol' of 1228 or is it something new? We may only guess, but guessing leads us to conclude that it was the second of these and that the county gaol at this time was still the city gaol of 1228.

During the earlier fourteenth century the castle continued to be used for state and political prisoners and for vert and venison

---

[1] The existence of a municipal gaol in 1223 appears to be confirmed by *Cur. Reg. R.* XI. p. 160.
[2] *Close R.* 1227–31, 31.　　　[3] *Rot. Litt. Claus.* II. 137.
[4] *Close R.* 1227–31, 31.　　　[5] See p. 141.　　　[6] See p. 81.
[7] *Cal. Lib. R.* 1240–5, 159, 214; *Close R.* 1256–9, 339.
[8] J.I. 3/98.

trespassers.[1] It does, however, seem also to have been used for a less special type of prisoner. Thus in 1320 twenty-four men were there who had trespassed against a merchant,[2] and in 1350 orders went forth to send to the castle all labourers who were resisting the collection of their taxes.[3] In the same year the castle held some men who had committed what looks like highway robbery in the 'pass' of Alton.[4] Moreover, from the period 1336–48 the county gaol, when delivered, is normally called Winchester castle,[5] and this continues to be its style, as often as checks can be imposed, down to 1475.[6] It would naturally not have been at all impossible for the castle to have replaced the gaol of 1228 as the sole place of custody for county prisoners. Indeed this is the more probable explanation. It must, however, be objected that in Speed's time what is called the 'gail prisone' is on a site quite remote from the castle,[7] and the use of 'castle' simply as a conventional label for the county gaol cannot be ruled out.[8]

In 1165–6 the sheriff of Kent provided his county with two gaols, one at Canterbury and the other at Rochester.[9] The second of these was probably in Rochester castle from the beginning. It must, indeed, be admitted that up to 1215 the ownership of the castle was disputed between the crown and the archbishops of Canterbury, but it seems that the building was in the crown's hands at the time when the gaol was being planted.[10] At all events there was a castle gaoler by 1210,[11] though whether he was the nominee of the sheriff or the archbishop cannot be established. In 1175–7 and until at least the end of the twelfth century Canterbury gaol stood in Rose Lane in that city and was probably

[1] *Cal. Close R.* 1302–7, 410 (bishop of St Andrews); ibid. 1318–23, 594; ibid. 1323–7, 105, 438, 639; ibid. 1333–7, 586 (earl of Moray); ibid. 1337–9, 435 (vert trespassers); ibid. 1343–6, 39 (Spaniards); ibid. 162 (vert and venison trespassers); E 101/561/48 (forest trespassers).

[2] *Cal. Close R.* 1318–23, 267–8.   [3] *Cal. Pat. R.* 1348–50, 456.

[4] Ibid. 459.   [5] J.I. 3/130.

[6] *Proc. before J.P.s*, 201, 209, 229, 233, 237, 265.

[7] *V.C.H. Hants*, v, plate facing p. 2.

[8] Cf. Huntingdon, Stafford, and Warwick (pp. 72, 74, 78).

[9] *Pipe R.* 1166, 111.   [10] *King's Works*, II, 807.

[11] *Cur. Reg. R.* VI. 53.

purpose-built. By 1220, however, there was a gaol in the castle[1] and it seems likely that this eventually superseded the other building. In 1237 the crown stipulated that prisoners from the east of the county should go to Canterbury and those from the west to Rochester.[2] This corresponds to the long-lasting division between east Kent and west Kent, but whether this segregation was ever strictly observed is open to question.

The use of Canterbury seems to have been discontinued in 1260[3] and again in 1417,[4] when it was weak, and at these times Rochester took its place. Canterbury gaol was ordered to be repaired in the former year[5] but it was again being used in 1266–7.[6] How soon it was restored after 1417 is not known. With these exceptions Canterbury seems to have been normally open throughout the period and for long after.

The history of Rochester castle as a prison is less continuous. It was certainly in use and being delivered up to 1307–8,[7] but after that no records of delivery survive. In 1331–2 the archbishop of Canterbury was renting a house in Rochester to keep prisoners in,[8] a thing that he would hardly have done if the castle prison had been available. In general there are few fourteenth-century references to the prison. It was, however, certainly in use at the time of the Peasants' Revolt, for the rebels broke it open and rescued a prisoner.[9] The directions issued to the constable in 1417 to take over the prisoners at Canterbury are in a form that suggests that it was then not normally a place of custody.[10] Possibly it remained in use from that time. Certainly in 1452 it was being treated as a gaol of more or less equal status to Canterbury,[11] and it was again being delivered in 1504.[12]

The prison at Milton-next-Sittingbourne, which is traceable from the mid-thirteenth century,[13] ought possibly to be men-

---

[1] *Sel. Pleas of the Crown* (Selden Soc. 1), 134.
[2] *Close R.* 1234–7, 460.
[3] Ibid. 1259–61, 70.
[4] *Cal. Close R.* 1413–19, 409.
[5] *Cal. Lib. R.* 1251–60, 515.
[6] It was then delivered: C 66/85 m. 5 d.
[7] J.I. 3/109.
[8] Lambeth Palace MSS, C.R. 664.
[9] See p. 223.
[10] *Cal. Close R.* 1413–19, 409.
[11] *Cal. Pat. R.* 1452–61, 58.
[12] Ibid. 1494–1509, 438.
[13] C 66/54 m. 3 d.

tioned at this point. Milton was a royal manor with an appurtenant hundred and came to possess a separate system of local government.[1] Its prison, which was constantly delivered,[2] may at times be assumed to have supplemented the sheriff's prisons in the county. Since, however, the hundred or liberty was apt to be bestowed on queens consort or dowager as jointure or dower its prison must as often have been unavailable to the sheriff. Indeed it is at such times better to class the prison among the franchise prisons to which it will be necessary to refer later.[3]

The sheriff of Wiltshire, whose county was long and narrow, complied with the instructions of 1166 by 'repairing' the gaol of Salisbury in the year of promulgation and by building a wholly new one at Malmesbury.[4] Of Malmesbury nothing further is heard, though the abbot of that place had a franchise gaol between the twenties and the forties of the next century.[5] The Salisbury gaol lay within or closely adjacent to the castle of the old city, now known as Old Sarum. It remained there for many generations after the historic Salisbury had moved down the hill into the valley in and after 1220. Indeed it does not seem to have been abandoned finally until late in the fifteenth century.[6] But deliveries of the new city prison had been taking place from 1342[7] and none occurred at the old after 1414.[8] By 1485 the sheriff, who had until that time kept his offices in the castle, had moved them to Fisherton Anger, the western suburb of Salisbury,[9] and thither the county gaol followed.[10] It there remained, though not always on the same site, until it was closed in 1870.[11] By 1194 the king's castle of Marlborough was also being used as a prison,[12]

---

[1] *Kent keepers of the peace, 1316–17* (Kent Arch. Soc. Rec. Brch.), pp. xlviii–lv.

[2] It was still among the gaols in the early sixteenth century: B.M. Add. MS 35205. See p. 63 n. 11.

[3] See chapter v.   [4] *Pipe R.* 1166, 72.

[5] *Rot. Litt. Claus.* I. 427; *Cal. Lib. R.* 1226–40, 471.

[6] *V.C.H. Wilts.* v, 21–22; vi, 59.   [7] J.I. 3/130.

[8] *V.C.H. Wilts.* v, 40.   [9] Ibid. vi, 182.

[10] The last mention of Old Salisbury gaol occurs in 1508: ibid. 56.

[11] Ibid. 182.

[12] *Rolls of the King's Court 1194–5* (P.R.S. xiv), 88.

and it remained in use, both for suspect felons and for forest trespassers, for a full century.[1] Indeed in Edward I's earlier years it was at sundry times delivered.[2] It then seems to have been given up as a common gaol, though some Templars were in the constable's custody in 1309.[3] Strangely enough, it is included in the early sixteenth-century list of gaols already mentioned.[4]

Apart from the palatinates there remain twelve counties whose gaol history, so far as the sheriff is concerned, is relatively simple. The sheriff of Cornwall planted a gaol at Helston in 1184–5[5] and in the castle at Launceston in 1186–7.[6] The first only recurs in 1198–9, when it was repaired.[7] The second remained as the county gaol of Cornwall until, in the nineteenth century, Bodmin was preferred. The first Lancashire gaol was at Manchester, a strange choice since it was not *terra regis*. A small sum was laid out upon it in 1187–8.[8] After that, from 1196–7[9] the county gaol was seated at Lancaster. Northampton was the gaol town for Northampton-shire from the beginning and by 1210 the gaol was in the castle.[10] In the thirteenth century, however, it was supplemented by Rock-ingham castle, which was in use as a prison by 1213,[11] was delivered in 1247–8[12] and 1272–3,[13] and was full of venison trespassers in 1280–4.[14] The sheriff of Yorkshire constructed gaols at York and Tickhill, both castle towns, in 1165–6.[15] The second of these does not seem to have been maintained. The great castle at York re-mained the county gaol for the vast region that surrounded it, supplemented apparently from the mid-thirteenth to the mid-

---

[1] The last reference to its use for this purpose that has been noticed is dated 1294: *Cal. Close R.* 1288–96, 356.

[2] 1275–80: J.I. 3/71; 1283–4: C 66/103 m. 20d.

[3] *Cal. Close R.* 1307–13, 187.

[4] B.M. Add. MS 35205. Cf. p. 63 n. 11. [5] *Pipe R.* 1185, 200.

[6] Ibid. 1187 (P.R.S. xxxvii), 154. [7] Ibid. 1199, 182.

[8] Ibid. 1188, 6. [9] Ibid. 1197, 192.

[10] Ibid. 1210 (P.R.S. n.s. xxvi), 208. [11] *Rot. Litt. Pat.* 97.

[12] C 66/59 m. 5d. [13] *42 D.K. Rep.*, App., 642.

[14] *Cal. Close R.* 1279–88, 29, 91, 97, 198–200, 203, 205, 208, 255, 281.

[15] For a full history of York castle see *V.C.H. Yorks., City of York*, 521–8.

fourteenth century by the castle at Scarborough.[1] The other eight counties seem only to have had one county gaol apiece. Carlisle served Cumberland, Exeter Devon, Hereford Herefordshire, Lincoln Lincolnshire, Newcastle Northumberland, Oakham Rutland, Appleby Westmorland, and Worcester Worcestershire. Appleby is first mentioned in 1224[2] and Oakham in 1253.[3] All these gaols seem to have been placed in castles or castle areas. To be sure, Worcester castle hardly existed after 1216 but the prison seems to have stood upon a part of the former outer bailey.[4] Appleby castle is an unexpected site, for it belonged to the Cliffords after 1203.[5] Nevertheless, from 1334 gaol delivery documents use 'Appleby castle' in their title. There is of course the possibility, already mentioned,[6] that 'castle' has intruded itself into the documents through analogy, but in this case it is not a strong one.

The two counties palatine remain. The only county gaol for Cheshire appears to have been in Chester castle, where it was located by 1237–8.[7] The Durham story is a little more complicated. By 1237,[8] though no doubt from a much earlier time, the bishops of Durham, as earls palatine, kept their prison for county Durham in Durham castle. They also had a prison at Sadberge for the county of Sadberge.[9] No reference to it has, however, been traced before 1303, when it was stipulated that men taken in Sadberge 'wapentake', by which the county of Sadberge may be taken to be meant, should be imprisoned there, and those taken in the 'franchise' of Durham at Durham; there was to be no intermingling.[10] Deliveries of Sadberge were taking place by 1312[11] and

---

[1] It was delivered sporadically from 1254–5 (C 66/69 m. 5 *d*) until 1354–9 (J.I. 3/141 A and /141 B). Probably its military importance in the Hundred Years War prevented its continued use as a common prison.

[2] *Cur. Reg. R.* XI, p. 548.

[3] *Close R.* 1251–3, 318. The sheriff's prison is mentioned in 1250 but the location is not stated. *Cal. Lib. R.* 1245–51, 305.

[4] *King's Works*, II, 888.   [5] Ibid. 553.   [6] See p. 63 n. 11.

[7] *Cheshire in Pipe R.* (Lancs. & Ches. Rec. Soc. XCII), 37.

[8] *Close R.* 1234–7, 543.

[9] For Sadberge county see *V.C.H. Durham*, III, 192.

[10] *Cal. Close R.* 1302–7, 101.

[11] *Reg. Palatinum Dunelmense* (R.S.), II. 1171.

of Durham by 1314.[1] Both prisons were maintained and delivered until the end of the period.[2] In the first decade of the sixteenth century there were also gaols for Islandshire and Norhamshire, which were delivered by separate justices from those who acted at Durham and Sadberge.[3] There is no positive evidence that they existed before, nor is it known where they stood.

[1] *Reg. Pal. Dun.* II. 1258.   [2] *36 D.K. Rep.*, App. I. 98.
[3] Ibid. 60, 61, 81, 99.

V

MUNICIPAL AND FRANCHISE PRISONS

BY the late thirteenth century, if not before, the word 'prison' (*prisona*) had acquired a very extensive meaning. It could be applied to a county gaol maintained by a sheriff, like those that have just been described, to one of the few 'national' prisons, or to a franchise gaol owned by the lord of a liberty.[1] The third of these classes is naturally a very broad one, for it comprises prisons owned by leading ecclesiastics and lay barons and also those in borough ownership. For the sake of clarity, however, it seems convenient to call the second of these broad classes 'municipal' prisons, and to reserve them for separate consideration.

Ownership of a prison implied the right or duty to maintain the buildings and appoint the staff. The exercise of these prerogatives, however, did not completely separate franchise prisons from those under the sheriff's management. According to the doctrine that eventually prevailed, all prisons, or at any rate all prisons outside the palatinates, were the king's.[2] They were his because they were ancillary to his justice. Though a common person or a municipal community might own the building and appoint the keeper, the institution itself remained *prisona regis*. When this doctrine evolved has not been established, but the phrase *prisona regis* was certainly being applied by the Chancery in the earlier years of Henry III[3] to places of which the king's officers were in no sense custodians. Unfortunately for the modern student, however, the phrase was not used consistently. Even

[1] *Eyre of Kent*, I, p. lxv. Bolland classified the prisons of Kent in 1313–14 in much the same way, except that he formed hundred prisons into a fourth category.

[2] Edward Coke, 2 *Instit.* (1671 ed.), 589.

[3] For example, in 1234 the gaol in Bramber castle, which belonged to the Braoses, and that in Wallingford castle, which belonged to Richard, earl of Cornwall, are each called *prisona regis*: *Close R. 1234–7*, I, 17. Cf. *Suss. Arch. Coll.* XCVII, 74.

in 1279 it could still be used in pleas in the narrow sense of a prison directly maintained and managed by the crown.[1] Nor was this narrower usage confined to the clerks who drew up the rolls. It was also adopted by *Britton*, who, speaking with the king's mouth, differentiated between 'our' prison and 'the prison of another'.[2] Thus, while the phrase usually denotes any lawful prison, it may sometimes mean the converse of a franchise prison.

Franchise prisons were extremely varied, both in catchment area and physical appearance. They might serve an extensive group of estates, a single hundred, or a single manor. In form they might consist of a suite of rooms in a monastic gatehouse or in a baronial castle, or a mill, a dwelling-house, or a chamber in a house. Indeed the word 'prison' need, in certain contexts, mean nothing better than the stocks.[3]

If we give to the expression 'franchise prison' its broadest meaning we must conclude that the face of the landscape was closely pitted with such prisons. England certainly contained a mass of private courts which exercised a jurisdiction over various types of malefactor, and it is probable that every such court required some place of imprisonment. It is clear, however, that when thirteenth- and fourteenth-century lawyers argued about rights of prison or when the Chancery bestowed those rights by charter, the disputants and draftsmen were thinking of a right more fundamental than that of merely locking up a brawler or a vagabond to cool his heels. They were concerned with a substantial franchise, with the power to hold for a more or less protracted period a man suspected of grave ill-doing.

---

[1] *Suss. Arch. Coll.* xcvii, 75.   [2] *Britton*, I, 43.

[3] It is not clear how soon the stocks came to be reckoned as 'prison'. A document of 1232 implied that the two are equivalent: *Sel. Cases of Procedure without Writ*, 62. On the other hand the various late thirteenth-century authorities who expressed their views about the imprisonment of serfs seem to draw a distinction between the two: see p. 53. But whatever interpretation may be put upon those views it had by 1329 become possible for a man who extricated himself from the stocks to be deemed a prison-breaker: *Assoc. Archit. Soc. Rep. & Pap.* xxxii. 472. Sir M. Hale, *Historia Placitorum Coronae* (1800 London ed.), I, c. 51, observes that 'the stocks is the prison of the constable', but he does not date his doctrine.

Municipal and franchise prisons

In the earlier thirteenth century and indeed back to the Conquest the right to 'have' a prison in the sense thus defined was probably enjoyed widely by the greater lords. Express grants, however, were at that time most unusual. Perhaps the nearest we get to the equivalent of such a grant is the record of a payment to the crown by the abbot of Fécamp of a sum of money to have a prison at Winchelsea. This was in 1200.[1] Even express statements of claim are not very common and seldom come from an early time. Such claims were, however, advanced by the abbot of Cirencester in 1230–9 and 1249 in respect of his Gloucestershire hundreds of Rapsgate[2] and Bradley,[3] and by the abbot of Tewkesbury in 1273 in respect of Tewkesbury borough.[4] In both these cases the prisons seem to have been only for thieves or receivers of thieves. Other claimants were the abbot of Ramsey in 1274–5 in respect of his hundred of Clackclose,[5] the abbot of Peterborough throughout his liberty in 1275,[6] John Warrenne, earl of Surrey, for his prisons at Dorking, Reigate,[7] and Lewes[8] in 1279 and for a prison in Norfolk in 1285–6,[9] the archbishop of Canterbury for his prison at Maidstone in 1279,[10] the abbot of Byland in 1293–4,[11] and the archbishop of York in the same year for his prisons at Beverley, Hexham, and Ripon.[12] Claims first noticed in the next century are those of the abbot of Vale Royal for his prisons at Darnhall, Over, and Weaverham (1350),[13] and that of the lords of Cockermouth (1394).[14] The second of these was said to rest on immemorial antiquity.

It is not, of course, necessary to rely upon overt claims in order to gain an impression of the distribution of franchise prisons. There is reasonably certain evidence that in the thirteenth

[1] *Pipe R.* 1200 (P.R.S. n.s. XII), 248.
[2] W. Dugdale, *Monasticon Anglicanum* (1819 ed.), II, 83.
[3] C. D. Ross (ed.), *The cartulary of Cirencester Abbey, Gloucestershire* (London, 1964), I, pp. 215, 218.   [4] Ibid. p. 222.
[5] W. O. Ault, *Private jurisdiction in England* (New Haven, Conn. 1923), 97–8.
[6] *Chron. Petroburgense* (Camden o. s. XLVII), 21–2.
[7] *Plac. de Quo Warr.* 745.   [8] Ibid. 751.
[9] *Arch. Rev.* II, 209.   [10] J.I. 1/921 m. 8.
[11] *Plac. de Quo Warr.* 223.   [12] Ibid. 221–2, 591.
[13] Ault, op. cit. 245, 260.   [14] *Cal. Inq. Misc.* VI, p. 23.

century the archbishop of Canterbury possessed rights of prison
not only at Maidstone but also in Sussex,[1] the bishop of Ely in the
Isle, Norfolk, and Suffolk,[2] the earl of Gloucester in Bedfordshire[3]
and Kent,[4] the earls of Cornwall in Berkshire,[5] Gloucestershire,[6]
Hertfordshire,[7] Middlesex,[8] and Sussex,[9] the Warrennes not only
in Surrey, as has been already mentioned, but also in Sussex[10] and
perhaps Norfolk,[11] Peter of Savoy in Cambridgeshire,[12] Essex,[13]
and Sussex.[14] Presumably in all these instances the franchise-
holders enjoyed the right not only in the counties named but
throughout their lands. The abbot of St Albans had a prison by
1220,[15] the abbot of Waltham by 1236.[16]

There are other instances where there is presumptive but not
conclusive evidence: the many commissions to deliver gaols in
places which are not likely to have been within the sheriff's control. These prisons may often have been franchisal but they could
also have been municipal. For example, it is known that on many
occasions in the later thirteenth century a prison at High Wycombe was ordered to be delivered.[17] Are we to look upon this as
the franchise prison of Alan Basset, lord of Bassets Bury in High
Wycombe, who had a prison in the town about 1227,[18] or is it the

[1] At North Berstead, South Malling, and Pagham (1266–7) (*Suss. Arch. Coll.*
xcvii, 72); and at Uckfield (*Close R.* 1259–61, 163).
[2] At Ely and Wisbech for the Isle, at East Dereham for Norfolk, and at Melton
for Suffolk: E. Miller, *The abbey and bishopric of Ely; the social history of an
ecclesiastical estate from the tenth century to the early fourteenth century* (Cambridge,
1951), 205; *V.C.H. Cambs.* iv, 252; *Close R.* 1251–3, 221.
[3] At Southoe (*c.* 1267): *Beds. Coroners' R.* (Beds. Hist. Rec. Soc. xli), 8.
[4] Tonbridge (1226): *Rot. Litt. Claus.* ii. 108.
[5] Wallingford, see p. 61.
[6] Lechlade (1273–4): *Rot. Hund.* i. 166.   [7] Berkhamsted: see p. 70.
[8] Isleworth (1274): *V.C.H. Middx.* iii, 119.
[9] *Suss. Arch. Coll.* xcvii, 76.
[10] Lewes (1279): *Plac. de Quo Warr.* 751.
[11] Gimingham (1285–6): *Norf. Ant. Misc.* ii, 180.
[12] Bassingbourn (1252): *Close R.* 1251–3, 62. Cf. p. 250.
[13] Finchingfield (1252): *Close R.* 1251–3, 205–6.
[14] Hastings, Pevensey: *Suss. Arch. Coll.* xcvii, 71–2, 74.
[15] *Cur. Reg. R.* viii. 273.   [16] *Close R.* 1234–7, 235, 268.
[17] E.g. the deliveries that took place in 1257–8, 1269–70, 1273–5, 1277–8,
1279–81, 1284–5.
[18] *Rolls of justices in eyre* [for Bucks.], *1227* (Bucks. Rec. Soc. vi), 50.

Municipal and franchise prisons

municipal prison of High Wycombe for which there is a good deal of later evidence?[1] The bishop of Salisbury's prison in New Salisbury (1246)[2] and the prison of the bishop of Norwich in King's Lynn (1291)[3] provide other instances of the same uncertainty. Doubts of a rather different sort attach themselves to the prison at Wimbotsham. The abbots of Ramsey owned both the hundred of Clackclose, in which Wimbotsham lies, and also one of the manors in Wimbotsham.[4] They enjoyed rights of prison both at Ramsey[5] and in Clackclose Hundred[6] and therefore presumably throughout their lands. The Warrenne family, however, also owned a manor in Wimbotsham,[7] and, as we have seen, they enjoyed rights of prison elsewhere in Norfolk.[8] When the franchise prison at Wimbotsham is mentioned are we to assume that Ramsey abbey or the Warrenne family was the owner? It would be easy to multiply the ambiguities, which are so numerous as to make it quite impossible to construct a reliable list either of franchise prisons or of franchise-prison owners.

It was said above that before the fourteenth century express grants of prison seem to be unknown. Claimants accordingly had not much to go upon when their claims were challenged. The abbot of Peterborough when seeking to establish his right to a prison in 1275 pointed vaguely to his charters.[9] His charters, however, when examined, convey no right of prison. *Soc* and *sac*, *tol* and *team*, *infangthief* and *outfangthief* they do indeed convey, but nothing more specific.[10] Evidently the crown was not satisfied with the abbot's plea and the issue had to be tried before the Council. Though judgement went in the abbot's favour, it had to be confirmed in parliament. The abbot of Byland, when challenged in 1293–4,[11] rested his claim upon a clause in a charter

[1] It is thought to have stood in the High Street: *V.C.H. Bucks.* III, 113.
[2] *V.C.H. Wilts.* VI, 95–6.
[3] *Sel. Cases in K.B.* II, 34–5.   [4] *Feud. Aids*, III, 451.
[5] Ault, *Private jurisdiction in England*, 118.
[6] See p. 89.
[7] Although in the fourteenth century in service: *Feud. Aids*, III, 401, 510.
[8] See p. 90.   [9] *Chron. Petroburgense*, 22.
[10] See the charter of 1200 and that of 1270 inspecting one of 1253: *Rot. Cart.* 82; *Cal. Chart. R.* 1257–1300, 142. And cf. p. 1.   [11] *Plac. de Quo Warr.* 223.

of 1247, inspected in 1271. This conveyed *infangthief* and *out-fangthief* and also the right to have causes tried at the abbey's manor of Sutton under Whitstone Cliffe, when the eyre came into Yorkshire.[1] Presumably if trials were to take place at Sutton, there must have been a prison there in which to hold the suspects.

If we had to rely exclusively upon deduction we might feel ourselves on very unsure ground in our search for a foundation for such claims. Deduction is, however, fortified by the doctrines about prison-keeping enunciated by Bracton. According to Bracton suspect felons could only be held in the prison of a man who had power to try the felonies (*qui tales posset in curia sua judicare*).[2] This implied, in Bracton's opinion, a precedent grant of the six jingling liberties associated, as already mentioned, with the abbot of Peterborough and naturally with many other lords.[3] Whether Bracton's doctrines coloured the views of later generations of jurors, or whether the doctrines were based on the views prevailing in and before his time must remain uncertain. It is, however, the case that a Northamptonshire jury of 1353 thought that the prison that had once belonged to Yardley Hastings manor and Wymersley hundred owed its existence to the fact that its lord had enjoyed the privileges of *infangthief* and *outfangthief*.[4] Likewise the verdict upon the liberties of Cockermouth, already referred to, is so phrased as to make it clear that the possession of a prison is the logical consequence of the cognizance of felonies by the lord's ministers.[5] While, however, it might be possible to show that many other owners of prisons either enjoyed the twin jingles, as did the abbot of Vale Royal,[6] or else had power to try the felonies with which the suspects in their prisons stood charged,

---

[1] *Cal. Chart. R.* 1226–57, 314. The abbot also claimed (*Plac. de Quo Warr.* 223) that his charter of 1271 enabled him to have causes tried in eyre at his manor of Clifton, with the implicit corollary that he had a prison there also. Clifton is not mentioned in the charter (C 53/39 m. 10) though J. Burton (*Monasticon Eboracense*, I, 329), possibly relying on a lost original, states that it was.

[2] *Bracton*, II, 345–6.   [3] *Ibid.* 346.

[4] *Cal. Inq. Misc.* III, pp. 50–1.   [5] *Ibid.* VI. p. 23.

[6] Dugdale, *Monasticon Anglicanum*, V, 709.

there must have been others who could point to nothing more definite than a phrase such as that recorded in the Conqueror's charter to Battle which declared that that abbey should have 'all dignities and royal customs'.[1]

The trial of suspects in their prisons was perhaps in early times normally conducted by the officials of the franchise-owner himself. Gradually, however, the crown assumed, in most instances, the functions of those officials by issuing commissions for the delivery of those prisons. Increasingly from Henry III's middle years justices were appointed to deliver franchise prisons in common with the gaols of counties and the prisons of urban communities. This policy prevented the franchise-holder from setting up a private criminal jurisdiction and thus making his prison a base from which to terrorize his neighbours.[2] Indeed, almost at the beginning of Henry III's reign opposition to keeping suspects in private castles can be discerned. At the Somerset eyre of 1225 it was reported that two reputed evil-doers had been shut up in Taunton castle by the bishop of Winchester's bailiffs. One of the bailiffs was asked why he did not surrender the prisoners to the sheriff to be kept *in prisona regis* and was nonplussed. He was not prosecuted for his act, but the justices evidently thought it of doubtful propriety.[3]

As time went on, other devices were adopted which had the effect of reducing the importance of franchise prisons. If *Britton* may be believed, it had, by Edward I's time, ceased to be a felony to allow a prisoner to escape from such a prison.[4] The corollary perhaps was that appellants would seek to prevent appellees from being sent thither. But more significant than this prohibition was the general limitation upon the time during which suspects might be kept in franchise prisons. Once again *Britton* is a witness. He says that no one claiming custody of a prison may hold either an approver or anyone taken for a felony for more than a day and a night. Instead he is to send such people on to a *prisona regis*,

---

[1] *Suss. Arch. Coll.* xcviii, 45, quoting *Plac. de Quo Warr.*
[2] For the delivery of franchise gaols see chapter xiv.
[3] *Somerset Pleas* [1] (Som. Rec. Soc. xi), 1, 33.   [4] *Britton*, 1, 43.

using that term in the narrower sense.[1] These time limits are not
mentioned by Bracton and it is possible that they grew up between his day and *Britton*'s. By 1273–4 the earl of Cornwall's
prison rights in Gloucestershire, lawful in themselves, seem to
have been confined to keeping prisoners at Lechlade for one night
only.[2] In 1279 the sheriff of Sussex asserted that no one ought to
be kept beyond three nights in any place in his county apart from
the royal castle of Pevensey.[3] The whole county agreed that this
was a true statement of the law and that the constable of Bramber
who had imprisoned a man for a fortnight in that castle had acted
unlawfully.

At the same eyre during the course of which the constable of
Bramber's conduct was investigated, John de Warrenne, earl of
Surrey, was summoned to substantiate his claim to have a prison
in the rape of Lewes. In his answer he did not claim for this right,
as he did for some others which were challenged at the same time,
immemorial antiquity, but said that it was customary for all who
were taken in the rape for felony 'or other trespass' to be first
led to his prison at Lewes and there kept for three days. If they
were taken with the mainour or if they could be appealed in an
action justiciable in his own court they were to remain at Lewes
pending trial. Otherwise they were to be taken to the county gaol
at Guildford, apparently by his own officers. A jury was thereupon empanelled to consider the claim, and they found very much
in accordance with what Warrenne had said. According to the
verdict the immemorial custom was that all those taken upon
suspicion or indictment, those taken without the mainour, and
those prosecuted by a party without immediate suit (*secta incontinenti*) ought to be reported to the sheriff. Thereupon the sheriff
ought, within three days, to come to Lewes to collect the prisoners. If he did not do so the earl should send them under the
charge of his own officers to Guildford. If, however, they were
taken with the mainour or were prosecuted by a party with im-

---

[1] *Britton*, I, 47, 80. The words used at the first citation are 'a nostre prisoun
qe serra en nostre meyn'.   [2] *Rot. Hund.* I. 166.
[3] *Suss. Arch. Coll.* XCVII, 75. For Pevensey see p. 76.

mediate suit (*secta incontinenti*), they should be tried in the earl's court, *sicut est in curia baronum*. The court decided to accept the verdict,[1] and the Warrennes continued to claim the right of custody for three days and nights for another half-century at least.[2] These statements of the law, as they were recorded in Sussex, do not always correspond with what we know to have happened at this time. In Sussex and elsewhere men stayed in franchise prisons for longer terms than those limited. Nevertheless, when combined with other evidence, they appear to represent a strong desire to restrict rather than to extend the right to 'have' a prison.

After the end of the thirteenth century gaol delivery was re-modelled. Justices began to travel on well-defined circuits and in their peregrinations delivered not only county and municipal gaols but also the prisons of the lords of liberties.[3] But the lords whose prisons were delivered in the fourteenth, fifteenth, and sixteenth centuries were with rare exceptions the lords of ecclesiastical liberties and particularly abbots and priors. Although as late as 1404 the rights of all owners of franchise prisons were saved by statute,[4] the crown was more tender towards ecclesiastics than towards the laity. Accordingly it was the ecclesiastical franchise prisons that descended into modern times, while those in lay ownership withered away.

By Edward I's time the doctrine appears to have been evolved that a prison to be lawful required express sanction from the crown. As *Britton* puts it, a prison is 'a place limited by us within certain bounds for the keeping of the bodies of men'.[5] It is very doubtful whether this doctrine was rigidly enforced, but certainly during the fourteenth and fifteenth centuries ecclesiastics were granted by charter the right to 'have' a prison. So, as we shall see, were municipalities. Some of the ecclesiastics are not known to have enjoyed the privilege before; others seem to have been converting a vague or questionable right into a certain one. Grants

---

[1] *Plac. de Quo Warr.* 751.
[2] *Yr. Bk. Liber Assisarum* (Vulg.), 27 Ass. 27 (pp. 135–6). This refers actually to their prison at Reigate (Surrey).
[3] See chapter XIII.   [4] 5 Hen. IV, c. 10.   [5] *Britton*, I, 43.

of the former class include the bishop of Durham (1448) for the liberties of Howdenshire and Allertonshire[1] and the abbot of St Mary, York (1448) for an abbey gaol.[2] The second class includes Cirencester abbey (1343) in respect of Cirencester with Minety and with what are called 'the seven hundreds',[3] Westminster abbey (1399) for its lands in six counties,[4] Christ Church, Canterbury (1447),[5] and the archbishop of York (1462) for his prisons at Beverley and Ripon.[6] The abbot of St Albans is supposed to have had a grant by 1406–7,[7] but the text has not been traced. A third type of grant merely gave the grantee the power to commit to prison. The rector of Wigan was so privileged in 1350,[8] St Augustine's, Canterbury, in 1446,[9] and Syon abbey in 1448.[10] It is probable, however, that such grants, although more restrictively drawn, were also meant to bestow the right to erect and maintain a prison on the grantee's land.

In Queen Anne's reign it was laid down that none could possess the franchise of a prison unless that prison were delivered.[11] Such a doctrine would probably not have been valid during our period. Some of the prisons conceded to be lawful in the charters mentioned in the preceding paragraph are not known to have been deliverable. Nevertheless the eighteenth-century doctrine was perhaps rooted in our period, for those prisons that ceased to be delivered seem to disappear.

Franchise prisons represented a diminution of royal authority and, in a measure, of royal patronage.[12] Perhaps, too, they were slightly less secure than county gaols, and if it was not felony to escape from them that insecurity was magnified. On the other

[1] *Cal. Chart. R.* 1427–1516, 105. [2] Ibid. 110.
[3] Ibid. 1341–1417, 23.
[4] Ibid. 379–80, 404. The counties were Beds., Berks., Middlesex, Oxon., Wilts., Worcs.
[5] Ibid. 1427–1516, 80. [6] Ibid. 154.
[7] Coke, 2 *Instit.* (1671 ed.), 43. The date is deduced from a marginal, which appears to refer to a year book. The reference, however, has not been traced.
[8] *Cal. Chart. R.* 1341–1417, 122.
[9] Ibid. 1427–1516, 58. [10] Ibid. 92.
[11] 7 *Mod.* 31: Holt C.J.'s judgement of 1702.
[12] For the usurpation of the sheriff's patronage over gaolers see p. 149.

The Tun at Bristol (upper half of letter). See p. 113

Gruffydd ap Llywelyn falling
from the Tower of London.
See p. 221

Early fourteenth-century stocks. See p. 370

hand there was a chronic shortage of prison space and the existence of a set of supplementary prisons which the crown had no obligation to m͏ ͏ ͏tain was an obvious asset. Nor was the crown anxious to ant͏͏ ͏onize the franchise-holders by robbing them of prerogatives which they valued for reasons of patronage and prestige. Hence their elimination was not systematically aimed at. Their owners, however, were watched and sometimes punished for abuse. *Britton* said that wardens in fee, among whom the owners of franchise prisons must presumably be numbered, ought to lose their franchises if prisoners escaped.[1] In 1406–7 the abbot of St Albans temporarily forfeited his rights through failure to deliver speedily and in 1480 the abbot of Crowland was similarly punished because he would not release acquitted prisoners until they had paid fees.[2]

The history of franchise prisons might perhaps be summed up as follows. In the earliest times lords both great and small imprisoned men freely even when the offences charged against the prisoners were heinous. Later the theory prevailed that the right to 'have' a prison was confined to those who had the power to try serious offenders. Finally, that right was limited to those who had an express grant or who submitted their prisons to periodical delivery.

There cannot be much reasonable doubt that by the end of our period most municipal communities, whether boroughs or not, had prisons of their own which they governed and maintained and to which they committed offenders convicted in their courts. It would, however, be a matter of the greatest difficulty to construct a list of them that would be in the least complete. Nor can the origins of those that are known to have existed be safely dated in most cases. Though it is true that by 1256 the practice of granting the inhabitants the right to have a prison had begun, and that over thirty such grants may be counted up, it is not to be supposed that such grants were essential to the constitution of a prison; many such prisons, like the franchise prisons just

[1] *Britton*, I, 43. [2] Coke, 2 *Instit.* (1671 ed.), 43. Cf. p. 96 n. 7.

examined, rested on prescription only. Nor would it be right to assume that a grant of prison, even if, on the surface, it looks like a constituting grant, was anything more than the formal sanction to do something that had already long been done.

Although no list can confidently be constructed, it may be useful to name those towns that are known to have had prisons by 1250, adding in each case the date of first occurrence. We may perhaps begin by excluding the Fleet,[1] which, though it was at first called the gaol of London, was certainly not lastingly a municipal prison. That exclusion made, the first occurrence of such a prison seems to be at Winchester, though the evidence for its existence is perplexing.[2] Next comes Southampton in 1182–3,[3] and thereafter Newgate, built or enlarged in 1188.[4] There follow Preston (1200),[5] Great Yarmouth (1213),[6] Kingston upon Thames (1220),[7] Gloucester (1221),[8] Cambridge (1224),[9] Oxford[10] and Worcester[11] (1231), Faringdon (1238),[12] Bristol (1240),[13] Wallingford (1241–2),[14] Taunton (1243),[15] Orford (1244),[16] and Wilton (1249).[17] York (1248)[18] may possibly need to be added. There were also prisons at Winchelsea (1200)[19] and King's Lynn (1212),[20] but there is no proof in those cases that they were under the management of officers appointed by the municipal community and it might be better to class them as franchise gaols.

The prison at Southampton, which has been singled out as one of the very earliest municipal prisons in the provinces, has a somewhat curious history. Expensive works were begun upon it in 1182–3 and were paid for out of the borough farm,[21] and it was

---

[1] See p. 114.
[2] See p. 79.
[3] See below.
[4] See p. 103.
[5] *Cur. Reg. R.* I. 224; cf. *Pipe R.* 1201 (P.R.S. n.s. XIV), 272; *Rot. de Ob. et Fin.* 115.
[6] *Rot. Litt. Pat.* 102.
[7] *Cur. Reg. R.* IX. 309.
[8] Maitland, *Glos. Pl.* pp. 107, 109.
[9] *V.C.H. Cambs.* III, 120.
[10] *Close R.* 1227–31, 469.   [11] Ibid. 567.   [12] Ibid. 1237–42, 69.
[13] *Borough Cust.* I, 64.
[14] C 66/51 m. 3 d.
[15] *Somerset Pleas* [I]. 296.
[16] *Close R.* 1242–7, 346.
[17] *Crown Pleas of the Wilts. Eyre, 1249*, pp. 171–2.
[18] *V.C.H. Yorks., City of York*, 491.
[19] *Suss. Arch. Coll.* XCVII, 72.
[20] *Cur. Reg. R.* VI. 216.
[21] *Pipe R.* 1183 (P.R.S. XXXII), 148.

kept in repair out of those issues until 1208–9.[1] In 1222[2] and again in 1239[3] the bailiffs were ordered to repair it, and it began to be delivered in 1234–5.[4] After this, however, it is not mentioned again for over thirty years. It is extremely unusual for the crown to allow a borough to meet the costs of a municipal gaol in this way or to issue orders for its repair. Indeed, apart from London[5] and possibly Winchester, the only town known to have been treated in this way is Cambridge, where in 1238 the burgesses were allowed to charge the issues with the purchase of a new gaol building.[6] It will be recalled that in 1165–6 the gaol at Winchester had been mended out of the issues of that city and that in the later twelfth and earlier thirteenth centuries there seems to have been a municipal gaol there as well as a county gaol.[7] May it be that Hampshire was one of the counties, like Essex, Warwickshire, and Wiltshire, where, at the beginning, several gaols were planted, but that in this case, in distinction to the others, the secondary gaols were planted in towns which were self-governing communities? As the gaols were serving a county and not a purely municipal purpose the crown helped those communities financially to maintain them. The prison in Southampton naturally continues,[8] but after the mid-thirteenth century does not seem to have enjoyed any unusual status.

In the next half-century, stretching up to 1300, the crown began the practice of making express grants of prison to boroughs. The towns so privileged were Canterbury (1256), Great Yarmouth (1261), Bakewell (1286), Kirkham (1296), Kingston upon Hull and Ravenser Odd (1299), and Chester (1300).[9] Of these Great Yarmouth figures in the earlier list and Canterbury had had a prison for at least four years before the charter issued,[10] and merely received from the crown authority to imprison in the city gaol, and there alone, men taken in the city and portsoken. In addition

---

[1] Ibid. 1209 (P.R.S. n.s. XXIV), 172.
[2] *Rot. Litt. Claus.* I. 522.   [3] *Cal. Lib. R.* 1226–40, 401.
[4] C 66/45 m. 9d.   [5] See p. 338.
[6] *V.C.H. Cambs.* III, 120.   [7] See p. 79.   [8] See p. 103.
[9] A. Ballard and J. Tait (eds.), *British borough charters, 1216–1307* (Cambridge, 1923), 168–71.   [10] *Close R.* 1251–3, 60.

Shrewsbury claimed a prison by charter of Henry III[1] and Edmund Crouchback's charter to Leicester of 1277 implied a grant
of prison to that place.[2] Besides the towns whose prisons were
chartered in this period the following town prisons now emerge:
Faversham[3] and Lincoln (1254),[4] Chichester (1271–2),[5] Colchester[6] and Norwich (1274–5),[7] Bridgnorth (1284–5),[8] St Albans (1285–6),[9] Ipswich (1291),[10] Exeter (1296),[11] and Hereford
(1300).[12] Prisons also appear in Grimsby (1260),[13] Bath (1275–6),[14]
and Portsmouth (1278–9)[15] which were probably but rather less
certainly municipal. The prisons at High Wycombe, Stamford,
and Leominster, of which little is at this time known, could as
well have been the franchise gaols of the Bassets, the Warrennes,
and the abbot of Reading as municipal prisons.[16] For the present,
at least, their status must be left unsettled.

It is not necessary to proceed with the analysis. Prisons continued to be granted by charter to the end of the period and well
beyond, and they also continued to spring up spontaneously.
The grants usually do no more than empower the inhabitants to
'have' a prison.[17] At least twenty towns received grants in this
form, and six others received the right to imprison or to commit
to prison, which is another way of saying the same thing. Three
charters declare that men taken within the town and its liberties
shall be imprisoned only in the town prison. A few charters
expressly grant to the officers of the town the right to keep the
prison, that is, to appoint the staff, and one (Canterbury, 1453) is
concerned with that point exclusively.[18] Twelve towns received
their right of prison in a form which authorized them to hold

[1] Confirmed in 1341: *Cal. Chart. R. 1341–1417*, 2.
[2] Mary Bateson (ed.), *Records of the borough of Leicester, 1103–1603*, 3 vols.
(London, 1899–1905), I, pp. xxv–xxvi.
[3] *Borough Cust.* I, 65.
[4] *Cal. Inq. Misc.* I, pp. 560–1.
[5] C 66/90 m. 24d (23d).
[6] *Rot. Hund.* I. 140.
[7] *Recs. of Norwich*, I, 218–19.
[8] C 66/104 m. 29d.
[9] C 66/105 m. 3d.
[10] *Borough Cust.* I, 83.
[11] *Yr. Bk. 5 Edw. II* (Selden Soc. LXIII), 9–10.
[12] J.I. 3/99.
[13] C 144/5/20.
[14] *45 D.K. Rep.*, App. II, 88.
[15] *48 D.K. Rep.*, App., 151.
[16] See p. 90.
[17] This paragraph is founded on the enrolments digested in *Cal. Chart. R.*
[18] *Cal. Chart. R. 1427–1516*, 124.

suspected felons until delivery. This might imply that the towns
need not send their prisoners to another gaol for the execution of
that process. But of these twelve prisons there are seven which
are not known to have been delivered after the charters had issued,
even though one of these excepted seven, Grimsby, was told in
1318 that the king would send his gaol delivery justices to that
place.[1] The implication might, therefore, merely be that they
might hold suspects in their prisons pending trial elsewhere.

By the fifteenth century some quite insignificant towns had
prisons. Wenlock, for example, was granted one in 1468,[2] West-
bury (Wilts.) had one by 1460,[3] Steyning by 1477–8.[4] How far
did this go? In the latter half of the next century, when borough
records become so much more abundant, a prison seems to be a
natural part of the equipment of every town. It is at present
impossible to prove that this was the situation in the preceding
century or before, but quite possibly it was. If lock-ups were as
common as they seem to have been in early thirteenth-century
villages, some kind of prison seems likely to have been tucked
away in the cellar or attic of every fifteenth-century guildhall.

It is well established that several medieval towns enclosed im-
munities, fees, or sokes, that were not subject to borough government. Some of these fees had prisons of their own. The earl of
Lancaster had a prison in Leicester castle in the late thirteenth
century[5] which continued to exist until 1361.[6] In 1285 Sir Thomas
Berkeley had a prison on his fee in the suburb of Redcliffe and
Sir Richard Arthur a prison on his fee elsewhere within the city.[7]
It is not unlikely that in early times there were also such prisons
in London as concomitants of *infangthief* and *outfangthief*, to
which some city soke-owners were laying claim as late as 1321.

---

[1] Ibid. 1300–26, 411. Grimsby had, however, been delivered in 1276–7:
46 D.K. Rep., App. II, 174. In 1327 the Crown also promised to send justices to
Derby (*Cal. Chart. R.* 1327–41, 51) and did so from 1328 (J.I. 3/123).
[2] *Cal. Chart. R.* 1427–1516, 232. [3] Ibid. 1427–1516, 137.
[4] S.C. 6/1100/17.
[5] C. J. Billson, *Medieval Leicester* (Leicester, 1920), 42.
[6] *John of Gaunt's Register* [1371–5], II (Camden 3rd Ser. XXI), 348.
[7] *Great Red Book of Bristol*, I (Bristol Rec. Soc. II), 107; *Trans. Bristol and
Glos. Arch. Soc.* XXII, 162.

Nothing was done, however, to protect those claims, which were no doubt already obsolete.[1] Nor is there any certain evidence for the existence of the prisons, although a 'cage' in the parish of St Michael Bassishaw, disposed of by will in 1370,[2] may represent one of them.

By the fourteenth century the citizens of London were arguing, apparently with success, that they alone could have a lawful prison within the walls or bars. When in 1326 the bishop of Hereford imprisoned Robert Baldock, who was his clerk, in his house in St Mary Mounthaw, the citizens dragged the chancellor thence to Newgate saying that the bishop had no prison in the city and could not have.[3] In 1377 a man who had defamed John of Gaunt and was consequently imprisoned in Lord Percy's London house was removed by the citizens to Newgate for like reasons.[4] In general all urban enclave prisons, so far as they were in lay hands, had probably disappeared before the fourteenth century ended.[5] This was not so true of those belonging to ecclesiastics. Even in London the bishop kept a 'bishop's' prison in St Paul's[6] and 'Peter prison' in York survived into the nineteenth century.[7]

As boroughs planted upon mesne estates grew in number and their burgesses in power, they tended by a well-known process to wrest authority from their lords. A part of this process was the partial transformation of the franchise prisons of those lords into municipal prisons. This happened at New Salisbury[8] and no doubt also at King's Lynn.

Some towns contained more municipal prisons than one. Leicester, for instance, seems in the fourteenth century to have had its main prison in the High Street[9] and by the middle of the fifteenth to have had another in the Tolbooth.[10] Bristol in 1285 owned Monkbridge prison within the walls and the market prison

---

[1] *Cal. of Mayor's Ct. R. London*, p. xiii n.   [2] *Hust. Wills*, II, 140.
[3] See p. 106.
[4] *Anonimalle Chron.* 104.
[5] Leicester castle prison was perhaps extinguished by John of Gaunt in 1375: *Leicester Borough Records*, II, 150.   [6] See p. 136.
[7] *V.C.H. Yorks., City of York*, 497.   [8] Ibid. *Wilts.* VI, 95–6.
[9] *Leicester Borough Records*, I, 342 (1323).
[10] Ibid. II, 275 (c. 1462, but the prison was not then in use).

outside.[1] How long these coexisted and which of them became the Newgate of Bristol[2] is at present uncertain. In the fifteenth century there seem to have been two prisons in Southampton, one forming part of Bargate[3] and the other in Fish Street.[4] By 1398 York seems to have had two prisons, the Kidcotes, one managed by the sheriff and the other by the mayor. There may even have been more, for by 1435 a further distinction is drawn between Kidcotes for men and for women.[5] All, however, may have been enclosed within the same boundary walls.

Not unexpectedly, the town which had most municipal prisons in it was London, and of these Newgate was both the earliest and the greatest. Newgate was, of course, primarily a gatehouse. Roman in origin, it was perhaps rebuilt, not necessarily for the first time, in the earlier twelfth century.[6] How soon it came to be used as a prison is not precisely known, but in 1187–8 some land was bought beside the gate as a gaol site and in that year and the next quite a substantial sum was laid out in building a gaol upon the land.[7] Whether this building was an enlargement of a prison that already existed in the gatehouse or whether it was something quite distinct from the gatehouse cannot be determined. At all events, from this time until 1219[8] there are constant references to works and repairs upon and to 'the gaol of Newgate', whatever that phrase may precisely have implied. By 1236 it eventually becomes obvious that the gatehouse was in use as a prison, for a

[1] *Great Red Book of Bristol*, I, 107.

[2] First noticed under that name in 1483: *Somerset Medieval Wills* [1st series] (Somerset Rec. Soc. XVI), 244.

[3] *Stewards' Bks.* (Southampton Rec. Soc. [XVIII]), II, 95; *Oak Bk.* (ibid. [III]) II, p. xxviii; *Assize of Bread* (ibid. [XIII]), 17.

[4] *Stewards' Bks.* (Southampton Rec. Soc. [XVIII]), I, 2; J. S. Davies, *History of Southampton* (Southampton, privately printed 1883), 391–2.

[5] *V.C.H. Yorks., City of York*, 491–2.

[6] For the origin of the gate itself together with a history of the gaol see Margery Bassett, 'Newgate prison in the middle ages', *Speculum*, XVIII (1943), esp. p. 233.

[7] *Pipe R.* 1188 (P.R.S. XXXVIII), 18; ibid. 1189 (Rec. Com.), 223.

[8] *Pipe R.* 1193 (P.R.S. n.s. III), 159; 1195 (P.R.S. n.s. VI), 113; 1200 (P.R.S. n.s. XII), 150; 1202 (P.R.S. n.s. XV), 284; 1204 (P.R.S. n.s. XVIII), 93; 1206 (P.R.S. n.s. XX), 55; 1214 (P.R.S. n.s. XXXV), 79; 1215 (P.R.S. n.s. XXXVII), 33; *Rot. Litt. Claus.* I. 398.

fairly large sum, just under £100, was then spent on fitting out one of its turrets for that purpose.[1] As will be later shown,[2] the Fleet had originally been 'the gaol of London', but it lost that name when Newgate was first built or enlarged. After 1219, when there are signs that the crown wished to improve the security of Newgate,[3] it seems as though the Fleet received, for a while, fewer building grants than Newgate. At all events, by the mid-thirteenth century Newgate was firmly established as a prison. Its fame or notoriety spread throughout the world, and prisons in Bristol, in Dublin, and near Simsbury in the state of Connecticut took its name. It did not close until 1902–4.

The prison was regularly maintained during the thirteenth century and somewhat expensively repaired in 1281–2.[4] In the first thirty years of the next century pressure to maintain was exerted by the crown.[5] There is no reason to conclude, as has been done,[6] that this pressure was not ultimately successful; most medieval sheriffs had to be chivvied into carrying out such work. The repairs, if effected, do not seem to have amounted to alterations, but in 1406 an extension southwards from the gate was authorized.[7] In 1423–32 the old gate and gaol were pulled down and a completely new building put up at the cost of the executors of Sir Richard Whittington (d. 1423), who had left money for the purpose.[8] It has been conjectured[9] that rebuilding was precipitated by the unfortunate consequences of closing Ludgate in 1419 and removing the prisoners to Newgate,[10] since the congestion so caused spread disease and death among the prisoners.

[1] *Trans. R. Hist. Soc.* 5th ser. v, 12, as corrected by *Cal. Lib. R.* 1226–40, 396.
[2] See p. 114.
[3] Further expenditure authorized by the crown, 'so that our prisoners may be safely kept': *Rot. Litt. Claus.* I. 398.
[4] About £66 spent: E 101/467/11.
[5] *Cal. Pat. R.* 1313–17, 270, 295; *Cal. Close R.* 1313–18, 278; 1327–30, 483; 1330–3, I, 47.
[6] *Speculum*, XVIII, 236.   [7] *Cal. Lr. Bks. I*, 49.
[8] Ibid. *K*, 19, 39, 140. The petition to rebuild was lodged on or before 12 May 1423. By January 1425 the prisoners had been transferred to other prisons. By January 1432 the new prison was finished: *Cal. Lr. Bks. K*, 140. The *Gt. Chron. of Lond.* (p. 128) states that the executors began the rebuilding in 1423.
[9] *Speculum*, XVIII, 239.   [10] See p. 108.

In origin Newgate was nothing but a municipal prison, meant to confine the citizens of London and the men of rural Middlesex until their trials took place. A very early list of prisoners (1214) tried *coram rege* bears this out.[1] Very soon, however, Newgate acquired a much wider importance. From the very early years of Henry III writs enrolled in Chancery show how frequently it was used for the safe custody of approvers brought from many different parts of England.[2] Out of more than 130 writs issued between 1221 and 1273 and requiring the keeper of Newgate to receive 'foreign' prisoners nearly sixty concern approvers. Among other classes fifteen concern robbers and thirteen forgers. Somewhat unexpectedly, perhaps, homicides are comparatively rare. With the approvers there often came the men whom they had appealed. It was not uncommon for the crown to require the senders to provide an escort,[3] and in two instances the escorts seem to have been strong ones.[4] The conclusion that one is bound to draw is that the crown ordered into Newgate many of those men and women from accessible prisons whom it thought to be particularly dangerous to itself or to society and whom it wished accordingly to try carefully either *coram rege* or at a Newgate gaol delivery.[5]

Several of the prisons from which prisoners were drawn were those of liberties in the home counties, where the custodial arrangements may well have been inadequate. Thus on three occasions the bailiffs of Havering-atte-Bower[6] were so accommodated, and once each the bailiffs of Uxbridge,[7] of Holy Trinity, Aldgate,[8] and of the archbishop of Canterbury at Harrow.[9] The

[1] *Cur. Reg. R.* VII. 241. The marginal reads 'Middlesex'.

[2] The writs abstracted in the *Calendar of Liberate Rolls* have been carefully examined, and those printed in the *Close Rolls* up to 1254.

[3] The earliest example noticed is dated 1233: *Cal. Lib. R.* 1226–40, 210.

[4] E.g. in 1242 the sheriff of Oxfordshire was to go in person with his own escort and with one of 6 serjeants drawn from the Windsor garrison in order to take Roger de Clare: ibid. 1240–5, 166. In 1261 5 horses and ten men were needed to convey a suspect thief and his brothers from Norwich: ibid. 1260–7, 21.

[5] For the delivery of Newgate see p. 290.

[6] *Close R.* 1237–42, 300 (1241); ibid. 1242–7, 283 (1245); ibid. 1247–51, 512 (1251).

[7] Ibid. 1251–3, 105–6.   [8] Ibid. 1253–4, 44.   [9] Ibid. 1251–3, 417.

abbot of Waltham was ordered to send in his prisoners on four occasions.[1] But several of the greater prisons were also drawn upon, especially Oxford and Northampton. Rather naturally, it was much less common to treat the remoter bailiwicks in this way. No prisoners came from Devon or Cornwall, from Northumberland, Westmorland, or Lancashire, and only one each from Herefordshire, Dorset, and Somerset.

Once in the thirteenth century, in 1259, the prison was put at the disposal of the sheriff of Essex, because, it was said, he had no prison in his own county.[2] Twice commissioners acting in quite distant counties were ordered to collect suspects and bring them to Newgate. The first group were to search Warwickshire, Gloucestershire, and Oxfordshire in 1255 and bring in those who had plundered and burnt the houses of a Warwickshire gentleman.[3] The second was appointed in 1271 to sweep up various malefactors in Lincolnshire.[4]

While Newgate thus established itself as a gaol for men on serious criminal charges drawn from all over England, it had various other uses. From the late thirteenth century debtors under the Statute of Merchants[5] or otherwise,[6] defaulting accountants[7] until they had fulfilled their obligations and, to an increasing degree, those who fell foul of the municipal authorities for breaking the peace or violating local economic regulations were detained or punished there.[8] Newgate also occasionally held state prisoners and prisoners of war. Alan *Alemannus,* called the king's prisoner, who was sent there in 1237,[9] looks like an early instance of such a person. In 1326 the chancellor, Robert Baldock, a fellow victim with his sovereign, was dragged from the bishop of Hereford's house and thrust into Newgate,[10] where he was tormented to death. In the 1380s divers suspected spies were kept

---

[1] *Close R.* 1234–7, 235, 268 (1236); ibid. 1247–51, 66 (1252); ibid. 1251–3, 66 (1252), 337 (1253).

[2] Ibid. 1256–9, 387.   [4] *Cal. Pat. R.* 1247–58, 431.

[3] Ibid. 1266–72, 543.   [5] E.g. *Cal. Lr. Bks. C,* 215 (1308).

[6] *Rot. Parl.* I. 323 (1314, an action of account).

[7] *Cal. Close R.* 1279–88, 497 (1287); 1307–13, 293 (1310).

[8] *Speculum,* XVIII, 233 and n.   [9] *Close R.* 1234–7, 428.

[10] *Chrons. Edw. I and II,* I. 320–1.

there,[1] and in 1397 a glover who had said that since the king's accession there had been 'no peace or love in England'.[2] Such people formed a treasonable or alien element in the prison population, and to traitors and enemy aliens the gates of Newgate stood for ever open. In 1404, 59 Welshmen,[3] adherents of Glendower, were sent there and, in 1495, 42 Flemings, 'Dutchmen',[4] and others, who were adherents of Perkin Warbeck. In each case the Tower and Newgate shared the burden, though the Tower took the bulk of the Welshmen and Newgate the bulk of the 'Dutchmen'.

A notable change in the uses of Newgate took place in 1383, a year or two after Ludgate was converted into a prison.[5] As will be shown, Ludgate became the prison for freemen of the city who were held on such charges as debt, trespass, or contempt. In theory the only freemen who were sent henceforth to Newgate were those charged with felony and maiming. This provision might, however, be circumvented by the simple process of depriving a freeman of his franchise and sending him in ignominy to Newgate. Of this procedure instances occur in 1402 and 1413.[6] The Counters, which make their appearance at about the same time as Ludgate,[7] also drew lesser offenders away from Newgate. But while these developments reduced the non-criminal element in the Newgate population they by no means removed it. Alien debtors and debtors not belonging to London could still be sent there without question. Such was the fate of a Genoese merchant in 1395[8] and a man who in 1474–5 represented a Wiltshire borough in parliament.[9] Nor, whatever the theory might be, were freemen of London kept out for long, for the regulations of 1431[10] and 1488[11] expressly mention them.

We have just seen that from very early times Newgate had

---

[1] *Cal. Inq. Misc.* IV, pp. 89, 187; *Cal. Plea & Mem. R.* 1381–1412, 90–1.

[2] *Cal. Plea & Mem. R.* 1381–1412, 248.

[3] *Cal. Close R.* 1402–5, 252.

[4] *Gt. Chron. of Lond.* 259; *Chrons. of London,* 206.   [5] See p. 108.

[6] *Cal. Lr. Bks. I,* 19, 118.   [7] See p. 109.

[8] *Cal. Plea & Mem. R.* 1381–1412, 233.   [9] *Rot. Parl.* VI. 160.

[10] *Cal. Lr. Bks. K,* 124 ff.   [11] Jorn. 9, fos. 170*b* ff.

been at least as much a national as a municipal prison. This fact, coupled with a growing desire to segregate the felon from the debtor, the citizen or burgess from the foreigner and, even in confinement, the patrician from the hind, led to the establishment of a free or freeman's prison in London, distinct from the royal prisons of the Tower, the Fleet, and the Marshalseas, and the ancient gaol of Newgate. The site chosen was Ludgate, perhaps after a short-term experiment had been made with Temple Bar.[1] The custody of Ludgate, with the rooms or buildings above it, was conveyed in 1378 to two serjeants of the city chamber, on condition that, if the gate should become a temporary prison, the keepers should ensure that it was equipped with gear at the city's expense.[2]

Stow took the year 1378 to be that of the foundation of the prison, and said that foundation was confirmed in 1382.[3] However this may be, the prison was recognizable as such in 1383, when it was decided that all freemen of the city committed for civil offences should be sent there and all those suspected of felony and maiming to Newgate.[4] By 1384 testators were beginning to bequeath alms to the prisoners,[5] so the prison must by then have been completely open.

Although the arrangements of 1378 appear to have been intended as temporary ones, the prison in fact continued in existence. It was, however, closed in 1419 because debtors, 'more willing to keep up their abode there...than to pay their debts', were using it as a lodging-house and as a base for conspiracies. Accordingly the prisoners were transferred to Newgate. The congestion, however, became so great in Newgate that Ludgate was re-opened after a few months and its prisoners restored.[6] Ludgate was again closed for a brief period in 1431,[7] and in 1453–4 the

<hr/>

[1] Bequests were made to prisoners there in wills dated 1349 (*Hust. Wills*, I, 653, II, 3). It is not mentioned again.
[2] *Cal. Lr. Bks. H*, 97.
[3] C. L. Kingsford (ed.), J. Stow, *A survey of London* (Oxford, 1908), I, 39.
[4] *Cal. Lr. Bks. H*, 213.
[5] *Hust. Wills*, II, 242.
[6] *Memorials of Lond. and Lond. Life*, 673–4, 677.
[7] *Chrons. of London*, 97, 134.

prisoners were temporarily transferred to Newgate because the smoke from a neighbouring fire was almost suffocating them.[1] Later it was enlarged by Agnes, the widow of Stephen Forster, a fishmonger. The new work, which consisted of a tower, was incorporated with the original building in 1463.[2]

The prison was meant originally for the exclusive use of freemen and women of the city so that they might there find an easier lodging than in Newgate.[3] Others, however, soon began to use it. Thus John Slake, dean of the king's chapel, and some Westminster monks, none of whom can have been citizens, were sent there in 1398–9,[4] and in 1419 the prison was expressly said to be available not merely to freemen but to others charged with light offences.[5] This extension was possibly due to the growing congestion in all London prisons, but in 1463[6] the original limitation was reintroduced, and confirmed in 1488.[7] In 1419 the prison seems to have been open to suspect traitors, for a man who was thought to have betrayed Harfleur to the enemy was then housed in it.[8] In 1488, however, men charged with treason were required to go to Newgate.[9] In the sixteenth century the efforts that have already been noticed to keep it exclusive to freemen of the city were resumed. In 1502 a prohibition was issued against the removal of 'foreign' prisoners from the Counters to Ludgate.[10] It had to be repeated in 1527.[11]

The sheriffs of London and Middlesex exercised jurisdiction in courts of their own, sitting ultimately at the Guildhall. As a complement to these courts they needed offices and prisons. The buildings which housed both were called Compters or, more suitably, Counters. They are somewhat late in making their appearance, in fact the first reference to them comes from

---

[1] R. Flenley, *Six town chronicles of England* (Oxford, 1911), 108 n., citing Stow's *Survey*. Cf. Jorn. 5, f. 153.
[2] *Cal. Lr. Bks. L*, 40–1; Jorn. 7, f. 62.
[3] *Cal. Lr. Bks. L*, 250; Riley, op. cit. 673.
[4] *Chrons. of London*, 19.
[5] *Cal. Lr. Bks. I*, 215.
[6] Jorn. 7, f. 45.   [7] *Cal. Lr. Bks. L*, 250.
[8] Ibid. *I*, 230.   [9] Ibid. *L*, 250.
[10] Rep. 1, f. 100*b*.   [11] Jorn. 13, f. 21*b*.

1381.[1] In earlier times the sheriffs used their own houses both as prisons and as courts,[2] and they continued to use them as prisons even after the Counters became available.[3]

By 1412 the Counters had begun to have fixed locations. In that year, we are told, the 'brokenseld', opposite the Standard in Cheapside, had been turned into a Counter.[4] The building was actually on the west side of Bread Street, wedged in between well-built merchants' houses and inns for travellers.[5] It was moved across Cheapside into Wood Street in 1555 and into Gilt-spur Street in 1791.[6] In 1555 it was its keeper's private house[7] and had probably been so from the beginning. Nevertheless, both Counters were large and secure enough to house a fair quantity of prisoners, some of whom were dangerous. In 1425 the prisoners in Newgate were removed there, while that prison was being altered,[8] and in 1431 the buildings were also used for some of the Ludgate prisoners during a short emergency.[9] The other Counter, which stood in the Poultry, can be traced from 1441.[10] It may have been there long before—Stow did not know its origin[11]—and there it remained until its demolition in 1815.[12] Unlike the other Counter it fell early into the city's hands, by bequest of 1477.[13]

In the fourteenth and fifteenth centuries the Counters con-tained many different classes of prisoner. Thus they were one of the places assigned *c.* 1383 for the preliminary custody of adul-teresses and fornicatrixes.[14] Prisoners at the suit of a party are found there in 1386[15] and 1474–5,[16] Lord Strange of Knockyn after

---

[1] *The Brut,* II (E.E.T.S. cxxxvi), 337. It should, however, be remembered that the text of this chronicle dates from the mid-fifteenth century. The first docu-mentary reference comes from 1383: *Cal. Lr. Bks. H,* 209.

[2] B.M. Add. Chart. 5153 m. 15 *d*(1254–5); *Cal. of Mayor's Ct. R.* London, p. xv.

[3] *Mun. Gild.* I. 215.   [4] *Cal. Lr. Bks. I,* 109.

[5] Stow, *Survey of London,* I, 350.   [6] *Gt. Chron. of Lond.* 430.

[7] Stow, *Survey of London,* I, 351.

[8] *Cal. Lr. Bks. K,* 19, 39. In 1425 the Counters, instead of Newgate, were ordered to be delivered. Cf. *Cal. Pat. R.* 1429–36, 35 for a delivery of *c.* 1428.

[9] *Gt. Chron. of Lond.* 156; *Chrons. of London,* 97, 134.

[10] Stow, *Survey of London,* II, 330.   [11] Ibid. I, 263.

[12] *Gt. Chron. of Lond.* 430.   [13] Stow, *Survey of London,* II, 330.

[14] *Mun. Gild.* I. 460; and see p. 112.   [15] *Cal. Lr. Bks. H,* 294.

[16] *Rot. Parl.* VI. 160.

a brawl in 1416,[1] the keeper of Newgate in 1447 because of his own contumacy and his wife's abusive language[2] and in 1449 after he had violated a female prisoner.[3] The Counters also held a man who had stabbed a Lombard in 1455,[4] some of Simnel's supporters in 1493–4,[5] and some of the youths who burst into xenophobia on the eve of Evil May Day 1517.[6]

At the outset the Counters were perhaps meant for temporary confinement,[7] but regulations drawn up in 1393 made it possible for them to become places in which prisoners might stay for longer periods, provided that there was no charge of treason or felony. As the above examples, together with other evidence, show, this proviso was not adhered to after the mid-fifteenth century. The prisons seem to have been regarded as more comfortable than Newgate or Ludgate. But those who sought this ease must pay for it, and the same regulations lay down a tariff for permanent residents.[8] Later on, in 1419, it was decreed that condemned prisoners who were put into custody as a punishment should not be lodged there,[9] and later still that poor prisoners should not stay there for more than a day and a night, but should pass on to Newgate. This was in 1431, after that prison had been expanded.[10] Nevertheless, the Counters had by this time become places where certain prisoners might stay for fairly long periods, and accordingly testators, who had not remembered them before, started to leave alms for the relief of their inmates.[11]

It is probable that most larger towns had, in addition to their ordinary prisons, lock-ups for the temporary custody of minor

---

[1] *Gt. Chron. of Lond.* 96.

[2] Jorn. 4, f. 172. He could hardly have been imprisoned in his own prison.

[3] Jorn. 5, f. 16.   [4] *Gt. Chron. of Lond.* 188.

[5] *Chrons. of London*, 198–9.

[6] E. Hall, *Chronicle* (1809 ed.), 588–9.

[7] E.g. a prisoner failing to appear after due summons and who, when eventually encountered, used abusive words was first sent to a Counter and then sentenced to a year's imprisonment in Newgate: *Cal. Lr. Bks. H*, 292.

[8] *Mun. Gild.* I. 523. For the date see *Cal. Lr. Bks. H*, 402 n.

[9] Jorn. 1, f. 66b.   [10] *Cal. Lr. Bks. K*, 124–5.

[11] The first bequest noted is in the earl of Salisbury's will made in or before 1427: *Reg. of Hen. Chichele* (Cant. & York Soc. XLII), II, 392.

offenders and, as required by thirteenth-century legislation, vagrant strangers.[1] Perhaps the most notable of these was the London Tun on Cornhill. Built by the order of Henry le Waleys, mayor, in 1282[2] and taking its name from its rotundity, this little lock-up was primarily intended for 'night walkers',[3] by which is meant not only prostitutes, but anyone found wandering in the streets after curfew. The city of London at once took advantage of its existence to imprison in it clerks suspected of illicit relations with women. In 1297 the crown tried to restrain its use for that purpose,[4] though how successfully is not apparent. Later it was used for quite different offenders. Thus a scavenger who uttered scandalous words was put there in 1299,[5] and a man who had wounded another in 1339.[6] It was also used at the same time for others considered to be of bad character.[7] By regulations issued in Richard II's reign, according to Stow in 1383, it was again ordered to be used for the correction of moral delinquents. Priests found with women and adulterers were to be sent there, immediately upon detection. Adulteresses and fornicatrixes found with priests, and also adulteresses found with married men were to be sent there after a preliminary detention in Newgate or a Counter.[8] There is evidence that these regulations were not merely promulgated but enforced.[9]

In 1401 the lock-up was turned into a conduit fed by pipes from Tyburn. An adjacent well, which had no doubt served the prisoners, was boarded in.[10] A 'cage', with stocks, was placed on top of it, and above the 'cage' a pillory. These structures seem to have lasted until 1546, when Sir Martin Bowes, then mayor, covered the spring with a pump and moved the pillory west-

---

[1] See p. 194.

[2] *Gt. Chron. of Lond.* 17, 399, 400. The *Chronicle* gives 1286 as the date. This was corrected by Stow, *Survey of London*, I, 189.

[3] *Gt. Chron. of Lond.* 17; *Mun. Gild.* I. 275–6. Cf. *Cal. Lr. Bks. A*, 213.

[4] *Mun. Gild.* II (1), 213–14 (*Liber Albus*).

[5] *Cal. Lr. Bks. B*, 85.   [6] *Cal. Plea & Mem. R.* 1323–64, 109–10.

[7] *Cal. Lr. Bks. D*, 277 (1312).

[8] *Mun. Gild.* I. 457–60. These regulations were assigned by Stow to 1383: op. cit. I, 189.

[9] *Cal. Lr. Bks. H*, 339.   [10] Stow, op. cit. I, 191.

Manor Offices, Hexham
(probable prison). See p. 378

Durham Chapter House:
prison for light offences.
See p. 364

ward.[1] Apparently these measures marked the death of the Tun. Naturally, however, it was not the end of London lock-ups. Details are hard to gather but in 1503–4 the mayor had 'small howsis' built in all the wards and stocks put inside them to punish 'sterk beggars and vagabundys'. The 'houses' were grated and secured and the keys entrusted to the ward beadles.[2] The 'cage' in Fenchurch Street, referred to in 1518, was one of these.[3]

By charter of 1347 the townsmen of Bristol were authorized to build, or possibly to rebuild, a 'Tun' of their own, modelled upon the London Tun and likewise primarily intended for the custody of night walkers.[4] The picture of this little building, appearing in the illuminated initial letter of the charter,[5] is the only realistic portrait of a medieval English prison. Other towns were similarly equipped: York in the later years of the sixteenth century,[6] Leicester in 1531–2.[7] Examples could easily be multiplied.

---

[1] Stow, *Survey of London*, I, 192.
[2] *Gt. Chron. of Lond.* 328.
[3] Rep. 3, f. 245 *b*.
[4] *Bristol Chart.* 109.
[5] *Little Red Book of Bristol*, ed. F. B. Bickley (Bristol, 1908), II, plate facing p. 33. See also plate facing p. 96.
[6] *V.C.H. Yorks., City of York*, 493.
[7] *Leicester Borough Records*, III, 32.

VI

'NATIONAL', 'BISHOPS'', AND OTHER SPECIAL PRISONS

THE prison called the Fleet, which through later literature enjoys an international reputation, is of uncertain but of very great antiquity. A member of the Leaveland family, then its hereditary wardens, claimed in 1196–7[1] that their ancestors had enjoyed its custody from the Conquest. While this may not be literally any more veracious than other claims of the same sort, there seems little doubt that the prison existed in 1130.[2] It was being mended in 1155–6[3] and was being called 'the gaol of London' in 1172–3.[4] In 1196–7 it begins to be called 'the Fleet'[5] but the Exchequer did not at first use that name consistently. The adoption of a new title had probably something to do with the establishment of Newgate as a prison in 1187–8 or at any rate the enlargement of that prison at that time.[6] Newgate was in truth London's very own prison and, for clarity's sake, men may have felt that the king's own prison to the west of it should no longer bear so ambiguous a name.

The Fleet stood in what is today Farringdon Street just north of Ludgate Circus and therefore not far from the mouth of the Fleet river. It was by the twelfth century a stone building[7] and carefully contrived.[8] It was surrounded by a moat which may have been as old as the mid-thirteenth century.[9] However this may be, it is clear that a moat, 10 feet wide, with tree-clad banks, was either dug or redug about 1335. Whether the west channel

---

[1] *Pipe R.* 1197 (P.R.S. n.s. VIII), 167.　　[2] See p. 157.
[3] See p. 58.　　[4] *Pipe R.* 1173 (P.R.S. XIX), 91.
[5] Ibid. 1197, 167.　　[6] See p. 103.
[7] *Trans. R. Hist. Soc.* 5th ser. V, 13.
[8] The building operations undertaken in 1172–3, 1184–6, were viewed by Alnod the engineer: *Pipe R.* 1173, 91; 1185 (P.R.S. XXXIV), 44; 1186 (P.R.S. XXXVI), 198.　　[9] *London Top. Rec.* XIX, 39 and n.

of the moat was the river itself, or whether it was connected with the river by a cut running at right angles to it, is uncertain. The latter is probably the better opinion. The moat framed both the prison proper and the close or precinct in which stood other buildings.[1] By late 1356 the ditch had been encroached upon and partly stopped up and this was again its condition in 1502. It has been suggested that it was because of such abuse that the ditch had been covered in by Stow's time.[2] We have no early impression of the prison building itself. Large sums were spent upon it in 1184–90,[3] and about 1335 it was rebuilt or very substantially altered.[4] In or about 1357 it was subjected to something more than routine repairs.[5]

Such evidence as there is suggests that the Fleet was originally the only gaol in London and was used for all prisoners whom the king wished to have tried there. Indeed its content remained very miscellaneous at least until the mid-fourteenth century. It was being used for approvers in 1198–9[6] and at sundry other times right up to 1231.[7] Until as late as 1270 suspect homicides were being sent there,[8] though there is sometimes evidence that they were not quite the common run of felons but people in whose prosecution the king had a direct interest.[9] Once, in 1241–2, a special delivery of a single prisoner was ordered.[10] To an increasing degree, however, as the thirteenth century wore on, the sort of persons who are found in the Fleet are trespassers in parks or

[1] Ibid. In 1303 five people who had robbed the Treasury at Westminster met together with other 'ribalds' at a house within the close: *Cal. Lr. Bks. C*, 125–6.
[2] For the topography of the Fleet see Marjorie B. Honeybourne in *London Top. Rec.* XIX. For the trees on the banks of the moat see *Cal. Lr. Bks. G*, 49–50.
[3] *Pipe R.* 1185, 44; 1186, 198; 1190 (P.R.S. n.s. I), 156.
[4] *Toronto Law Jnl*, V, 389, 393–4. Stones from the 'old' prison were being carried away by 1337: *Cal. Close R.* 1337–9, 156–7.
[5] E 101/471/20; E 101/472/24. Structural defects were reported in 1355: *Toronto Law Jnl*, V, 390.
[6] *Pipe R.* 1199 (P.R.S. n.s. X), 129.
[7] *Rot. Litt. Claus.* I. 395, 472; *Close R.* 1227–31, 529; *Cur. Reg. R.* XI, p. 102.
[8] E.g. *Rot. Litt. Pat.* 125 (1214); *Close R.* 1234–7, 12 (1234); *Cal. Lib. R.* 1240–5, 52 (1241); *Cal. Pat. R.* 1266–72, 435.
[9] E.g. a Jew in 1178–9: *Pipe R.* 1179 (P.R.S. XXVIII), 126; a murderer of the king's servants in 1228: *Close R.* 1227–31, 48.   [10] C 66/50 m. 13*d*.

forests[1] and persons guilty of contempt or of frustrating the course of justice.[2] They were presumably undergoing penal or at least coercive detention. There were also a few quasi-political prisoners. In 1242 some men, taken in Lundy with William Marsh the buccaneer, were sent there as well as to Newgate[3] and two years later a member of Gruffydd ap Llywelyn's household.[4] They represented the less dangerous participants in revolt or treason. Gradually, and particularly after its enlargement in 1236, Newgate supplemented it as a place of custody for approvers and felons. After the organization of Newgate gaol deliveries on a substantial scale under Edward I it was very convenient to keep London felons there, while the increasing use of coercive or penal imprisonment for debtors, defaulters, and the like kept the older prison full enough.

With the opening of Edward I's reign the Fleet became pre-eminently the gaol attached to the courts of Common Pleas and Exchequer, both of them courts which remained at rest at Westminster and did not travel like the King's Bench. Crown accountants in arrears with their payments[5] and other crown debtors[6] were frequent inmates. So were those private accountants who, thinking that they were too hard pressed by their principals, caused their suits to be removed into the Exchequer. To the latter class the Fleet was statutorily assigned by Westminster II (1285),[7] and there such accountants stayed, in theory at least, while awaiting their trials—and after them if they were not discharged.[8] If we were to trust the statistics of fees collected in 1337–40[9] and

---

[1] *Cal. Lib. R.* 1245–51, 84 (1246); *Close R.* 1247–51, 232 (1249); 1251–3, 372–3 (1253).

[2] E.g. jurors who made false oaths: *Cur. Reg. R.* IX. 265 (1220); receivers of malefactors: *Close R.* 1237–42, 310 (1241); trespassing before the justices: ibid. 1247–51, 181 (1249).

[3] F. M. Powicke, *King Henry III and the Lord Edward: the community of the realm in the thirteenth century*, 2 vols. (Oxford, 1947) II, 753.

[4] *Cal. Lib. R.* 1240–5, 228.

[5] *Fleta*, II, p. 133; T. Madox, *The history and antiquities of the Exchequer* (London, 1769), II, 234, 238, 241.

[6] E.g. *Cal. Close R.* 1349–54, 93–4 (1349); ibid. 350 (1351).

[7] C. 11.

[8] E.g. *Yr. Bk. 3 Edw. II* (S.S.), 92.   [9] E 372/184 m. 49.

1350¹ we should conclude that all prisoners received were committed by one or other of the two courts. By the late fourteenth century, however, the Fleet was also used by the Council and the Chancery,² neither of which ever built up prisons of their own, as did the King's Bench and the household.³

The reasons which might lead to detention in the Fleet in the late fourteenth and fifteenth centuries were naturally very varied. To slander the archbishop of Canterbury (1391),⁴ to make, if a sheriff, an 'undue' parliamentary return (1404),⁵ to assault the Spanish envoys in the streets of London (1430)⁶—all these enormities led or could lead the culprit to that prison. Unexpectedly, some men accused of felony were, if caught, ordered to be sent there in 1453.⁷ In the second decade of the sixteenth century it was used for prisoners of war⁸ and for numerous state prisoners, even so great a subject as the earl of Northumberland.⁹

In the 1380s and perhaps over a much longer period it was the prison to which outlaws were to be sent when they had been hunted down and arrested by local commissioners.¹⁰ The prison was indeed the place frequently assigned for the surrender of outlaws, who were often conditionally pardoned upon so doing.¹¹ But while it was a prison much used by the crown for holding or punishing men and women who, though neither traitors nor felons, had fallen foul of the government, it was also the home of very many private debtors, particularly, no doubt, after the statute of 1352¹² had been passed. By way of example, instances may be cited of two people who about 1428 failed¹³ to pay damages and of a Welshman who about 1444 defaulted on a statute staple recognizance.¹⁴

¹ E 101/508/13.   ² *Sel. Cases before King's Council*, p. xlv.
³ See pp. 118–21.   ⁴ *Rot. Parl.* III. 288–9.
⁵ Ibid. 530.   ⁶ *The Brut*, II (E.E.T.S. cxxxvi), 456.
⁷ *Rot. Parl.* v. 270.   ⁸ *L. & P.* I (2), pp. 1078, 1223, 1423 (1513–14).
⁹ Ibid. II (1), pp. 524, 546–7.
¹⁰ The counties in which the commissioners operated included Essex, Hereford, Lincoln, Norfolk and Suffolk: *Cal. Pat. R.* 1381–5, 132–3, 250, 258, 593.
¹¹ Over 230 such pardons were issued between 3 May 1381 and 21 June 1385: *Cal. Pat. R.* 1381–5 passim.   ¹² See p. 46.
¹³ *Sel. Cases in Exchq. Chamber* (Selden Soc. LI), I. 38–48.   ¹⁴ *Rot. Parl.* v. 106.

From the later fourteenth century the Fleet was accounted a comfortable prison, at least for those who could afford to pay for the better accommodation it contained.[1] The privilege of going about the town in a baston's company was widely enjoyed,[2] regulations were not restrictive,[3] and in the later fifteenth century visiting was easy,[4] as it was in Pickwick's time. At Christmas 1523 games, in which the warden joined in person, were being played there.[5]

By ancient custom the marshals of England, predecessors of the earl marshal of today, claimed the custody of prisoners awaiting trial in the king's central courts or condemned by such a court to coercive or punitive imprisonment. So far as is known, their plea was first voiced in 1253 by Roger Bigod, who declared that sheriffs and other Exchequer accountants were, on arrest, being sent to the Fleet instead of being committed to the under-marshal in the Exchequer, who was his own representative.[6] The plea was successful, as was a like one made in 1260 for custody of prisoners found guilty before the king himself or his chief justice.[7] The effective custody was naturally in the hands of deputies or under-marshals who, in a manner familiar to all students of medieval administration, often assumed the title of their principals and were called 'marshals'. These in turn sometimes appointed keepers of prisoners to serve under them.[8] There seems, however, little doubt that at least until the mid-fourteenth century the earl marshal himself, when the office was filled, formally bore the final responsibility for custody.

The marshal in the Exchequer does not seem to have persisted, although in 1344, when the marshalsea of England was taken in hand, there is a passing reference to him.[9] The reference was probably inserted *pro majori cautela*. The customary place of custody for prisoners committed by or awaiting trial in the

---

[1] For the grading of prison accommodation see p. 351 and for lodging charges p. 175.   [2] *Toronto Law Jnl*, v, 397–8, and see p. 336.   [3] Ibid. 398.
[4] Ibid. 399.   [5] *L. & P.* v (1), p. 170.   [6] *Close R.* 1253–4, 196.
[7] *Sel. Cases in K.B.* I, pp. lxxxix–xc; *Trans. R. Hist. Soc.* 4th ser. v, 61.
[8] E.g. in 1328 and in 1344: *Sel. Cases in K.B.* v, pp. xxiv, xxv, cxxii.
[9] *Cal. Fine R.* 1337–42, 375.

Exchequer, despite Bigod's claim, continued to be the Fleet,[1] whose interests were, no doubt, strongly protected by its warden, who was a man of position.[2] Similarly there seems to have been a marshalsea of the Common Pleas in 1307.[3] This is also not heard of again, except in 1344, and doubtless disappeared for the same reason as the Exchequer office. Thus, so far as the ancient courts are concerned, the under-marshal comes to mean the person who guarded King's Bench prisoners. On the other hand, in Edward II's reign we begin to hear of the marshal of the king's household, who was the custodial officer of the marshalsea court and imprisoned trespassers falling within that jurisdiction.[4]

The King's Bench marshalsea seems originally to have been a form of custody rather than a place. When, later on, it was given an address it was not a fixed one. Prisoners, when in London, were kept in the under-marshal's house or in that of one of his deputies. Thus in 1309 the prisoners were in Lime Street,[5] in 1342 and 1344 in West Smithfield, and from 1347 until apparently 1353 at Holborn Bridge in Farringdon Without.[6] When the court was in the provinces the marshal was required by statute to hire accommodation for prisoners, after the court had settled what towns were to be visited in the ensuing term.[7] Such provincial marshalseas are mentioned at Lincoln in 1331[8] and at York in 1362.[9]

The prison of the marshalsea of the household seems to have been recognized as a building, as distinct from a custody, from the outset.[10] Its metropolitan home was at first at Westminster. It may have been there in 1332[11] and certainly was there in 1371.[12] In 1373 the men of Southwark were licensed to build, in what is now Borough High Street, a house 40 by 30 feet in size, to accommodate the court of the marshalsea of the household and its

[1] See p. 116.   [2] See p. 157.
[3] *Cal. Pat. R.* 1307–13, 1: appointment of a marshal of 'the bench'.
[5] J. C. Davies, *The baronial opposition to Edward II: its character and policy* (Cambridge, 1918), 202.   [5] *Cal. Inq. Misc.* II, p. 21.
[6] *Cal. Pat. R.* 1343–5, 399; *Sel. Cases in K.B.* II, p. cxv n.: ibid. p. xxvi; ibid. p. xliv.   [7] 5 Edw. III, c. 8.   [8] *Sel. Cases in K.B.* v. 57–8.
[9] Ibid. p. cxvi.   [10] E.g. *Cal. Pat. R.* 1307–13, 538.
[11] *Cal. Plea & Mem. R.* 1323–64, 94.   [12] *Hust. Wills*, II, 151.

prisoners when in town 'and to hold other the king's courts'.[1] The building was to be completed within the year. This was probably done and by 1375 bequests to the inmates begin.[2] In 1377 a man awaiting his trial in the court of the household in Southwark seems to have been imprisoned in a building, presumably the prison, adjacent to the court.[3]

It is very possible that the King's Bench prison migrated to Southwark shortly before. It was there in 1368,[4] and by 1378 bequests are being made to it as though it had a fixed location.[5] By 1381 when, like the other marshalsea, it was broken by the rebels, it was certainly in the borough.[6] In the borough the two prisons remained, side by side, until the nineteenth century. Or rather Southwark was their headquarters, for they continued for a while to peregrinate. In 1392 the gaol of the household marshalsea was at Uppingham,[7] and throughout most of the fourteenth century it was one of the duties of the keeper of the King's Bench marshalsea to furnish carts to take his prisoners to the different parts of the country in which the court was sitting.[8]

At first there is some care to distinguish between the prison of the marshalsea of the king's house and that of the marshalsea of the King's Bench;[9] or reference is made to 'the two marshalseas'.[10] From the beginning of the fifteenth century, however, as many wills testify, the two prisons seem to have been distinguished in current speech by the respective names of the 'marshalsea' and the King's Bench prisons. It may be doubted whether there was the same clarity of distinction in the fourteenth century, and in official documents it is often most difficult to be quite certain to which prison or custody reference is being made.

In Edward II's time the prison of the marshalsea of the household seems to have been a good deal used for the detention of

---

[1] *Cal. Pat. R.* 1370–4, 265.　　[2] *Hust. Wills,* II, 187.
[3] *Chronicon Anglie ... auctore monacho ... S. Albani* (R.S.), 138.
[4] *Sel. Cases in K.B.* VI. 155.　　[5] *Hust. Wills,* II, 203.
[6] *Cal. Pat. R.* 1381–5, 409.　　[7] *Sess. of Peace in Lincs.* I (XLIX), 26–7.
[8] *Sel. Cases in K.B.* V, p. xxvi.　　[9] *Hust. Wills,* II, 224, 329 (1381, 1397).
[10] Ibid. 294, 335 (1391, 1397).

men who, falsely claiming to be members of the household, were requisitioning provisions for themselves in the king's name.[1] That apart, there is little to suggest that the use of either prison was limited to particular types of prisoner. Somewhat surprisingly, a forest trespasser was in 'the marshalsea prison' in 1320[2] and debtors are to be found in both custodies from the early fourteenth century.[3] This mixture continued, at least in the King's Bench, for when that prison was broken in 1381[4] and in 1472[5] it contained both 'debtors' and 'felons'. In the latter year there were also prisoners held coercively. There was a statute staple debtor in the Marshalsea in 1533.[6] In the fourteenth and fifteenth centuries the 'Marshalsea' or the 'Marshalsea of the King's Bench' was greatly used by outlaws surrendering in anticipation of pardon.[7] By this the King's Bench prison is presumably always intended.

At the beginning of the sixteenth century both marshalseas seem to have been used as common gaols by the sheriff of Surrey and Sussex, and there is evidence that one or other of them was being so treated in 1452.[8] This practice was forbidden by statute in 1503.[9] Nevertheless it continued, for in 1533 two men entered into a recognizance with the sheriff for the safe keeping of a prisoner[10] and in 1559 an outgoing sheriff handed over 22 prisoners there to his successor.[11] Shortly after this it seems to have been replaced as the northern Surrey county gaol by the 'White Lion'.[12] In 1513 a commission was issued for delivery of a Surrey gaol in Southwark.[13] Which 'marshalsea' it was that was thus used has not been established.

---

[1] Davies, *Baronial opposition to Edward II*, 202; *Cal. Pat. R.* 1317–21, 56, 67. Cf. *Cal. Pat. R.* 1327–30, 211.

[2] *Cal. Close R.* 1318–23, 275.

[3] Ibid. 1302–7, 111; Davies, op. cit. 202.

[4] *Anonimalle Chron.* 140.   [5] *Rot. Parl.* VI. 49–50.

[6] Guildford Castle Arch. Loseley MSS 963/1.

[7] E.g. *Cal. Pat. R.* 1340–5, 1381–5, 1446–52 *passim*.

[8] Ibid. 1452–61, 58.   [9] 19 Hen. VII, c. 10, s.4.

[10] Guildford Castle Arch. Loseley MSS 963/1.   [11] Ibid. 969/2.

[12] C. L. Kingsford (ed.), J. Stow, *A Survey of London* (Oxford, 1908), II, 60.

[13] *L. & P.* I (2), p. 1102.

Imprisonment in medieval England

From the days of Rannulf Flambard (d. 1128),[1] its first known prisoner, the Tower of London has held a multitude of prisoners.[2] Many of them have been state prisoners, at variance with the powers that be, but others have enjoyed no public prominence. In fact no English prison has been put to more varied uses.

The popularity of the Tower for prisoners of every type is attributable to the great strength of the fortress, to its proximity to the king's person, whether at Westminster or in the Tower itself, and to its comparative remoteness from the urban mob. Besides this the building, until very recent times, was always garrisoned and the garrison formed a supplementary prison guard, far more effective than the average staff of medieval gaolers. Furthermore, by Henry III's time the Tower had become relatively spacious and even comfortable, and thus could afford a fitting shelter for those men of rank or eminence for whom secure but honourable custody was needed.

It would be tedious and barely useful to list the many men of rank who were shut up in the Tower within the period covered by this book. It is only necessary here to recall that they included Richard II, Henry VI, and Edward V, kings of England, and Margaret of Anjou. Henry VI and Edward V died within its walls. Among the many alien hostages or prisoners of war of varying degrees may be mentioned three kings of Scots—John (Balliol) (1297–9) though only after his abdication, David II (1346–7), and James I (1406, 1413).[3] To them must be added John II, king of France (1360), and his son Philip (1357–60), taken after Poitiers, and the dukes of Bourbon and Orléans, taken at Agincourt. The experiences of these royal or princely inmates, as of

[1] A. le Prévost, *Orderici Vitalis . . . historiae ecclesiasticae* (Paris, 1838–55), IV, 107–9.

[2] There is no satisfactory history of the Tower. J. W. Bayley's *History and antiquities of the Tower*, 2 vols. (London, 1821–5), is still useful. Vol. II contains the best available list of medieval prisoners, and has been used for this account, wherever it seemed reliable. Cf. also Lord Ronald Gower, *Tower of London*, 2 vols. (London, 1901–2) and R. Davey, *Tower of London* (London, 1910). For the buildings see *King's Works*.

[3] His captivity in England has been carefully worked out in E. W. M. Balfour-Melville, *James I, King of Scots* (London, 1936). For his stay in the Tower see ibid. pp. 38, 55, 57, 66.

many native Englishmen in prominent positions, cannot here be told.

More important is it to recall, for it is a fact too seldom mentioned, that in the thirteenth century the Tower was a prison for common felons. Thus between 1220 and 1235 it held at least three suspect homicides,[1] and another one in 1286.[2] There were robbers in 1223[3] and 1259–60,[4] and in 1252 there was even an approver.[5] That suspects of this sort were not merely chance inhabitants seems to be proved by the fact that in the middle years of the century the Tower prison was formally delivered. The first reference to justices to deliver it occurs in 1252,[6] though no instrument appointing them has been found. General commissions were appointed in 1269–70,[7] 1275–6,[8] and 1282–3,[9] four in the second year and two in the third, and there are records of such deliveries within the period 1276–93.[10] There were further deliveries in 1302–3[11] and both before and after it is not hard to find special ones.[12] How long this type of prisoner was housed in the Tower has not been established. In 1336 and 1337[13] it could still be designated as a place to which to send suspects rounded up in certain provincial areas by commissioners specially appointed for that purpose. It is, however, probable that it was not normally regarded as the place for felons after Edward I's reign. This was partly because Newgate had come to be organized as the leading criminal prison in the kingdom,[14] and partly because surer methods of delivering provincial prisons were coming into being.[15]

---

[1] *Rot. Litt. Claus.* I. 424 and *Cur. Reg. R.* IX. 167–8 (1220); *Rot. Litt. Claus.* I. 515 (1222); *Close R.* 1234–7, 154.

[2] *Cal. Chart. R.* 1427–1516, 288.   [3] *Rot. Litt. Claus.* I. 555.

[4] *Cal. Lib. R.* 1260–7, 189.   [5] Ibid. 1251–60, 76.

[6] *Close R.* 1251–3, 277.   [7] C 66/85 m. 28Bd.

[8] *45 D.K. Rep.*, App. II, 233, 259. The fourth of these is a commission to deliver Newgate also.   [9] C 66/102 m. 22d.

[10] J.I. 3/35B, /36/1, /36/2, /85, /87. These rolls include deliveries of Newgate and in two instances other prisons as well. Cf. also *Sel. Cases in K.B.* II. 31.

[11] *Cal. Close R.* 1302–7, 486. The year is that of the shrievalty of Hugh Pourte.

[12] E.g. 1278–9, coin-clippers: *48 D.K. Rep.*, App., 116; 1318, forger: *Cal. Pat. R.* 1317–21, 169; 1319: J.I. 3/41/2; 1384, the notorious John of Northampton and his associates: *Cal. Lr. Bks. H*, 264.

[13] *Cal. Pat. R.* 1334–8, 357, 448.   [14] See p. 105.

[15] See chapter XIII.

Imprisonment in medieval England

So long as Jews remained in England the Tower was a much-favoured place for confining them. Individual imprisonments are traceable from 1234[1] at least and are frequent from that time.[2] Jews who failed to meet demands for tallages in 1240 and 1271 were imprisoned there in some number, as were many others of their creed charged in 1278 with clipping and defacing the coinage.[3] Jews formed a precious category requiring abundant security; and since they were the peculiar property of the king it was to be expected that they would be imprisoned close to his person.

From the mid-thirteenth century the Tower was also used, like the Fleet, as a place of confinement for defaulting crown accountants. The first case to be noticed comes from 1251, when a sheriff was imprisoned there for arrears of his accounts.[4] Several other instances can be cited from the early fourteenth century,[5] and in the middle of that century a corrupt escheator.[6] For such persons the Tower must often have been chosen because the Fleet did not provide adequate security, a reason which is once or twice adduced or implied.[7] Trespassers in parks or forests were also to be found there in the later thirteenth and in the fourteenth centuries,[8] and in both the fourteenth and the fifteenth centuries there are examples of prisoners held for various contempts.[9]

Apart from the mass imprisonment of Jews in 1278 the Tower witnessed other mass imprisonments. Templars who belonged to the more southerly preceptories were sent there upon their arrest in 1308, and by the next year there were 43 of them together.[10] There were many Lollard prisoners in 1421.[11] There were supporters of Simnel in 1493[12] and of Warbeck in 1495,[13] and in 1517

---

[1] *Close R.* 1231–4, 502; 1234–7, 17, 39.   [2] Ibid. 1237–42 *passim*.
[3] C. Roth, *A history of the Jews in England* (3rd ed. London, 1964), 45, 67, 75.   [4] *Close R.* 1247–51, 397–8.
[5] Madox, *History of the Exchequer* (1769 ed.), II, 234, 238.
[6] *Sel. Cases before King's Council*, 37.
[7] *Sel. Cases in Exchq. of Pleas*, p. 141 (1292); *Close R.* 1337–9, 577 (1338).
[8] *Cal. Pat. R.* 1281–92, 445 (1291); *Cal. Close R.* 1279–88, 99, 155, 197 (1281–2); 1302–7, 298 (1305); 1343–6, 62 (1343).
[9] *Rot. Parl.* II. 448–9 (1340); III. 288, 489.   [10] *E.H.R.* XXIV, 434.
[11] *Rot. Parl.* IV. 174.   [12] *Chrons. of London*, 198–9.
[13] Ibid. 205–6; *Gt. Chron. of Lond.* 259.

many rioters who had got themselves mixed up in the rising of London apprentices known as 'Evil May Day'.[1] Perhaps it may be suggested that the comparative spaciousness of the Tower made it a useful place to which to send comparatively large bodies of men whose arrest and imprisonment had to be hastily arranged and whom it was expedient to keep together.

The Tower was a place in which there were many horrible dungeons, to which prisoners of no public esteem might be sent in order that the crown might exhibit to them and to the world its detestation of their reputed offences. An example of this attitude occurs in 1430 when a London ostler assaulted the Spanish ambassadors in Fenchurch Street. The man was arrested and sent first to a Counter and then to the Fleet. There was a strong feeling that he should proceed thence to the Tower, because of the enormity of his offence, namely, violating the king's safe conduct. Only the intervention of the Spanish embassy prevented this from being done and the man remained in the Fleet.[2] This incident seems to show that where the crown's interest was very strong the Tower was the place for the culprit.

But while the Tower could be a very hateful or a very secure prison, it could also be an honourable one. Thus it was felt in the later thirteenth century that men who were untainted with felony might reasonably be expected to be housed there rather than in Newgate. That view was taken in 1264 for the benefit of certain men implicated in the civil war,[3] and in 1269 when a Florentine suspected of homicide was removed to the Tower by the king's grace.[4] Presumably in later times Newgate, with other prisons of the like sort, came to furnish its own superior accommodation, its own *libera prisona*. Nevertheless, though there are some examples to the contrary, it is unlikely that in the fourteenth or fifteenth century many men of rank, provided always that they were also men of wealth, lay for long among thieves.

It seems probable that in very early times the Tower contained

[1] E. Hall, *Chronicle* (1809 ed.), 589.
[2] *The Brut*, II (E.E.T.S. cxxxvi), 456.   [3] *Close R.* 1261–4, 410.
[4] Ibid. 1268–72, 164.

a purpose-built prison-house. A reference (1182–3) to the door of the Tower gaol[1] suggests that this was so. What looks like a special prison room is mentioned in 1295,[2] and in a commission of as late a date as 1307 'the gaol of the Tower' occurs.[3] But it is most likely that the White Tower itself was being used equally early, at least for exalted prisoners, for in 1249 its middle and upper stories were housing hostages.[4] It is a reasonable assumption that the original keep could not have held many prisoners over a long period without detriment to the other activities centred upon the Tower. A special prison-house would therefore most probably have been necessary. When, however, the inner curtain wall had been built by Henry III, and still more after Edward I had completed it and constructed the outer curtain, there was ample space in the bastions of the inner curtains for prisoners. The Beauchamp and Martin towers are known to have been much favoured for the purpose. The White Tower, however, was not permanently abandoned. In 1360 it was fitted up for John II[5] and, if a well-known picture may be trusted,[6] Charles duke of Orléans was also lodged within it.

Although the Tower was the chief place of custody for state prisoners and prisoners of war, it was not the only one by any means. Some of those common gaols which were located in castles, like Wallingford,[7] Nottingham, and Chester, were also used. Thus Welsh prisoners were sent to Nottingham in 1287,[8] William Douglas and other Scottish hostages in 1350–1,[9] two sons of Charles of Blois in 1373,[10] one of John of Northampton's supporters in 1384,[11] and a group of Frenchmen in 1422.[12] At Chester throughout the thirteenth century Welsh prisoners of

[1] *Pipe R.* 1183 (P.R.S. xxxii), 161.
[2] *Sel. Cases before King's Council*, 15.   [3] *Cal. Close R.* 1302–7, 486.
[4] *Close R.* 1247–51, 241–3.   [5] *Cal. Close R.* 1360–4, 24.
[6] B.M. Royal, 16. F ii, f. 73.
[7] In 1264 its owner, the earl of Cornwall, was imprisoned in it in the lord Edward's company: *Chrons. Edw. I and II*, 1. 64. For other prisoners see *V.C.H. Berks.* III, 526–8.
[8] *Cal. Close R.* 1279–88, 464.   [9] Ibid. 1349–54, 225, 320.
[10] *Cal. Pat. R.* 1370–4, 331.
[11] *Cal. Lr. Bks. H*, 266 n., quoting Higden.   [12] *Cal. Pat. R.* 1422–9, 35.

war and hostages abounded[1] and, at the end of the century, Scotsmen as well.[2] In later times the castle was the prison of King Richard II, Janice d'Artois, and Eleanor Cobham.[3] Windsor[4] and Winchester[5] castles were also much in use for such prisoners, but whether they enjoyed the status of county gaols uninterruptedly is, as has been said, not altogether certain. Whether a county castle gaol was a fit place for this purpose no doubt depended on a number of different factors. Security was essential, and not all county gaols were secure. Sometimes, too, accessibility to London was important, if the prisoners in question were state prisoners whose interrogation or trial needed to be arranged. Not all such gaols were accessible. It is also to be supposed that a relatively high degree of comfort was often needed, for the prisoners might be of noble lineage or knightly rank. Not all such prisons possessed the needful amenities.

There are several royal castles which appear to have played no continuous part in the ordinary administration of justice and were never delivered, which were none the less pressed into service on occasion for such prisoners as these. Devizes is a fair example. Its use for suspect felons and venison trespassers is most rare, but it is widely renowned as the prison of Robert of Normandy[6] and Hubert de Burgh (1233).[7] Later on, in the reign of Edward I, it housed Scotsmen,[8] and, later still, the two sons of Charles of Blois both before and after they were at Nottingham.[9] Portchester, though used occasionally for suspect felons in the early thirteenth century[10] and for forest trespassers in 1253,[11] was the place of custody for soldiers taken on Sark in 1215,[12] for a prisoner

[1] *Cheshire in Pipe R.* (Lancs. & Ches. Rec. Soc. xcii), 77 (1244–5), 149 (1283), 164 (1284–1300); *Cal. Lib. R.* 1240–5, 252; 1245–51, 76.

[2] *Cheshire in Pipe R.* 165, 176, 181 (1296–9).

[3] R. H. Morris, *Chester in the Plantagenet and Tudor reigns* (Eccleston, 1895), 99.

[4] See p. 63. For its prisoners see *V.C.H. Berks.* iii, 8–11.

[5] See p. 80.   [6] Orderic Vitalis, *Hist. Eccl.* iv. 486.

[7] Powicke, *Henry III and the Lord Edward*, i, 138–40.

[8] *Cal. Close R.* 1288–96, 483; 1307–13, 17, 371, 463.

[9] *Cal. Pat. R.* 1370–4, 325, 331; 1374–7, 417–18.

[10] *Rot. Litt. Pat.* 97, 102; *Close R.* 1227–31, 360.

[11] *Close R.* 1251–3, 397.   [12] *Rot. Litt. Pat.* 133.

honourably confined in 1254,[1] and for the bishop of Glasgow in 1306.[2] John king of France was imprisoned at Somerton (Lincolnshire) in 1359–60[3] and Frenchmen taken at Agincourt at Melbourne (Derbyshire) in 1415.[4] In 1371 six prisoners, of unknown status, were sent in honourable custody to Queenborough.[5] These last three castles have no other known prison history. Some duchy of Lancaster castles were similarly used after the merger of the duchy with the crown. Thus James I of Scotland was twice in Pontefract, as were some Scottish hostages in 1424.[6]

One royal castle of this type seems to deserve a paragraph to itself. The castle of Corfe, at once remote from large centres of population and so sited as to make escaping difficult, was for long a favourite place of detention. In John's reign it was used for Frenchmen taken at Mirebeau[7] and later for men captured in the civil war.[8] One scholar, writing of that period, has called it 'a contemporary Bastille'.[9] Gascon prisoners of war were there, apparently in some numbers, in 1254–5.[10] A Poitevin knight was there in 1276[11] and Scotsmen in 1296.[12] During the troubles with the Despensers it was used for rebels[13] and, with the reversal of their fortunes, the king himself was shut up in it for a brief period on his way from Kenilworth to Bristol.[14] Three years after his death rumour had it that he was still within its walls.[15] In 1346 it was used for six Luccan merchants detained as hostages to secure the release of some London merchants shut up in a Pisan prison.[16]

---

[1] *Close R.* 1253–4, 64, Vivian of Egremont. He was eventually released from Corfe in 1256, by which time he had satisfied the king for his trespasses: *Cal. Pat. R.* 1247–58, 469.

[2] *Cal. Close R.* 1302–7, 410.   [3] *King's Works*, II, 838–9.

[4] Ibid. 739.

[5] They were taken there from Winchester castle: E 101/561/48.

[6] Balfour-Melville, *James I*, 66, 84, 103. It had already been used before the merger, e.g. in 1327: *Chrons. Edw. I and II*, I. 337.

[7] A. L. Poole, *From Domesday Book to Magna Carta* (Oxford, 1951), 382.

[8] *Chrons. Edw. I and II*, I. 17.   [9] *King's Works*, I, 68 n.

[10] *Close R.* 1253–4, 233–4, 254; *Cal. Lib. R.* 1251–60, 231; *Cal. Pat. R.* 1247–58, 420–1.

[11] *45 D.K. Rep.*, App. II, 283.   [12] *Cal. Close R.* 1288–96, 483.

[13] *Cal. Close R.* 1323–7, 438; *Chrons. Edw. I and II*, I. 311.

[14] *Chron. Murimuth Contin.* 52; *Chrons. Edw. I and II*, II. 315.

[15] *Sel. Cases in K.B.* V, 43.   [16] *Cal. Close R.* 1346–9, 136–7.

In 1384 John of Northampton, after raising an insurrection in the city of London, was sent to Corfe pending his first trial, together with two of his associates, and after a second trial another associate, Richard Norbury, lay there in penal detention for ten years.[1] In addition to this, the castle sometimes held forest trespassers, as it did in 1283[2] and 1305,[3] but apart from two mid-thirteenth-century instances[4] it was never the home of suspect felons.

To catalogue all the castles that were pressed into service as temporary prisons in times of emergency would be a most laborious operation and one that would be out of proportion to any advantage that might be gained. The truth is that in all probability most castles had some kind of prison accommodation which could be used at comparatively short notice. It is instructive to see how such accommodation was quickly made available in the autumn of 1325 when it became necessary to distribute a group of the king's adversaries, described as rebels. These men were in prison in Berkhamsted castle and thence, in October and November, were transferred in small parties to Pevensey, Colchester, Sandal, Exeter, Kenilworth, and Nottingham.[5] Others, who were in the Tower, were sent to Corfe, Winchester, and Barnard castles;[6] others again, who were at Scarborough, were taken thence to Corfe.[7] There is also reason to think that Windsor, Hereford, Rochester, and Dover played their part in the same decanting operation, as did Berkeley and Warwick.[8] We have here a mixture of castles of all types—county gaols, royal castles which were not county gaols, and private castles. Sandal, Kenilworth, Barnard, Berkeley, and Warwick are examples of the last type.

There is one other royal castle which may conveniently be mentioned here, though it does not fall readily into any category. It is Dover, which was freely used as a prison from at least 1191.[9] After the middle of the thirteenth century, when the constableship

---

[1] *Cal. Lr. Bks. H*, 229, 232, 264; cf. ibid. 246 n. and 266 n., quoting Higden.
[2] *Cal. Close R. 1279–88*, 199. [3] *Mem. de Parl.* 120–1.
[4] See p. 66. [5] *Cal. Close R. 1323–7*, 422–3.
[6] Ibid. 438. [7] Ibid. 417. [8] Ibid. 479.
[9] Poole, *From Domesday Book to Magna Carta*, 356. The prisoner was Geoffrey, archbishop of York (d. 1212).

was permanently linked with the wardenship of the Cinque Ports,[1] the castle served as the prison for the various courts over which the warden presided.[2] It was in exercise of the warden's jurisdiction that in 1302 the abbot of Faversham was imprisoned in it. This, it was said, was for trespass and damage to the king's crown and dignity.[3] Persons suspected of maritime offences, whether awaiting trial in Cinque Port courts or not, were also to be found there: two pirates who had attacked merchants of Dieppe in 1251,[4] and a mariner, who seems to have been a privateer, in 1435.[5] It was perhaps to deal with such offenders that the delivery of the castle was ordered in 1251–2 and 1258–9.[6] It was also an obvious place in which to lodge Englishmen who were arrested at the moment when they landed from the Continent. A man who had been outlawed while overseas was ordered to surrender to it in 1290,[7] and another man, who returned from France in 1305, would have been put there had he not been rescued.[8] But it was not used exclusively for maritime offenders and Cinque Port prisoners, for a man thought to have been implicated in the murder of the prior of Campagne (Landes) was sent there in 1253.[9] There were reputed forgers there in the late thirteenth century[10] and several supporters of de Montfort in 1266.[11] There were supporters of the Mortimers in 1321.[12] De Montfort's men held the castle against the warden and had to be reduced by the king and the lord Edward.

In early times, when the forest law was strenuously enforced, efforts were made in some regions to construct special forest prisons. The gaol in Kinver forest in Staffordshire, built in 1195–6,[13] was one of these. So was the prison of Galtres forest, otherwise

---

[1] Katherine M. E. Murray, *The constitutional history of the Cinque Ports* (Manchester, 1935), 77–8.
[2] For its use by the warden in the sixteenth and seventeenth centuries see Murray, op. cit. 111, 125, 129.

[3] Ibid. 69.   [4] *Close R.* 1247–51, 476.
[5] *Rot. Parl.* IV. 489.   [6] C 66/63 m. 8*d.*;/73 m. 14*d.*
[7] *Rot. Parl.* I. 57.   [8] Ibid. 181.
[9] *Cal. Lib. R.* 1251–60, 135. The prisoner was John of Frome, see p. 232.
[10] Murray, op. cit. 100.   [11] *Flor. Hist.* III. 8.
[12] Ibid. 202.   [13] *Chanc. R.* 1196 (P.R.S. n.s. VII), 81.

called the prison of the larder, which stood by 1216 in Davygate in York.[1] It has been argued that the gaol at Writtle, in Essex, the seat in the twelfth century of one of the king's houses, was also a forest prison.[2] The first of these survived as Stourton castle until 1360;[3] the second continued in use until the fifteenth century; the third was maintained from 1196[4] until 1223.[5]

By no means all wardens of forests, however, had prisons, and sheriffs often had to lend accommodation in the county gaol, just as they lent it to prisonless diocesans.[6] Thus in 1236 the constable of Colchester castle was told to take over such trespassers from the Essex forester in fee, because that officer had no prison of his own.[7] Two years earlier the sheriff of Northamptonshire was somewhat similarly required to receive such prisoners from the bailiff of the forest between the bridges of Stamford and Oxford.[8] In 1260 the sheriff of Surrey had to find space in Guildford gaol for trespassers in Windsor forest.[9] It could presumably have been argued that it was not part of the sheriff's duty to accommodate forest trespassers, since the enforcement of forest law and the punishment of those who infringed it did not fall to him. But if that was the original theory it did not prevail. Not only do we find many forest trespassers in county gaols mixed up with other prisoners,[10] but on one occasion, namely at the Rutland forest eyre of 1269, it was positively laid down that there should be but one gaol in Rutland for every type of prisoner. This was to be in Oakham castle, and the prison at Allexton in Leicestershire, which the warden of the forest had been using, was implicitly

---

[1] For its history see *V.C.H. Yorks., City of York*, 494–6.
[2] *King's Works*, II, 1019.   [3] *Cal. Close R.* 1360–4, 74.
[4] *Chanc. R.* 1196, 111.   [5] *Rot. Litt. Claus.* I. 542.   [6] See p. 135.
[7] *Close R.* 1234–7, 295.   [8] Ibid. 1231–4, 499.
[9] Ibid. 1259–61, 26. Cf. p. 62.
[10] For example in 1251 two suspect homicides and one suspect forest trespasser were bailed out of York: *Close R.* 1247–51, 440, 457, 467. In 1285 four suspect homicides and one suspect forest trespasser were bailed out of Somerton: *Cal. Close R.* 1279–88, 311, 313, 318, 338, 381. Cf. also J. C. Cox, *The royal forests of England* (London, 1905), 269–70, for forest trespassers in the custody of the sheriff of Cambridgeshire and Huntingdonshire (*c.* 1255).

condemned to extinction.[1] A little later, about 1292–3, the forester of Newcastle under Lyme appears to have had a prison rather like the one at Allexton. He kept a man in it for a few days but then, uneasy at the probable irregularity of so doing, he sent the prisoner elsewhere.[2]

Notwithstanding such facts as these, new forest prisons of a kind continue to appear. A prison is known to have been built at Lyndhurst as part of the king's hunting lodge in 1358–61 and to have been repaired ten years later,[3] and another royal hunting lodge, that at Moor End in Northamptonshire, which was acquired in 1363, is thought to have contained a prison.[4] By 1445–6 a prison was attached to Clarendon palace, for poachers in the park,[5] and by 1485 there were gaols 'above' and 'under' the wood in the forest of Dean.[6] It is thus clear that forest prisons were never absent from the medieval scene. It is equally clear that forest trespassers were often to be found in other gaols. They were also put in castles and other buildings that were seldom[7] if ever used for other types of prisoner. We should have said, for instance, that Queenborough castle was never used as a prison did we not know that in 1371 six forest trespassers were sent there from the castle at Winchester,[8] which was itself not then a common gaol.[9] Nor should we have suspected that there was any kind of prison at Brill, were it not that some venison trespassers were confined there in 1291, presumably in the king's palace.[10] Many forests were committed to keepers with an adjacent castle, and where this occurred the castle was the natural seat of forest courts and the resting-place of forest prisoners.

The stannaries also had their prisons, which by charters of 1305 were declared to lie in Lydford and Lostwithiel for Devon and Cornwall respectively.[11] The building at Lydford was the same as

[1] *Sel. Pleas of Forest,* 52–3.
[2] *Sel. Bills in Eyre,* 51–2.
[3] *King's Works,* II, 989.
[4] Ibid. I, 236.
[5] Ibid. II, 918.
[6] *Cal. Pat. R.* 1485–94, 5, 18.
[7] For the use of Devizes and Portchester castles see p. 127.
[8] E 101/561/48.
[9] See p. 80.
[10] *Cal. Close R.* 1288–96, 220.
[11] *Cal. Chart. R.* 1300–26, 54.

that which is now called Lydford castle.[1] It has an uncertain ancestry but seems to derive from the 'strong house' (*domus firma*) erected out of the issues of both counties in 1194–5 with the express object of housing prisoners.[2] Under the name Lydford castle it was expensively provisioned in 1198–9[3] and was under repair twenty years later.[4] Presumably it served many purposes, of which the prison was but one, but was not primarily a fortress; at all events this must have been the case after it was rebuilt in the mid-thirteenth century. Whether it was at the outset a stannary prison, the prison of Dartmoor forest, or both cannot now be said. The attraction of Cornish issues, however, to meet the initial cost—and they were used more abundantly than Devon issues—suggests that it was always a stannary prison in part; Cornwall has no kinship with Dartmoor. Its erection, too, is almost contemporary with the first appointment of a warden of the stannaries.[5]

Lydford's Cornish counterpart was a block of offices with a prison, which Edmund, earl of Cornwall, built at Lostwithiel about 1290. This was taken over by the Black Prince and kept in repair until the sixteenth century.[6] Perhaps before its establishment Cornish tinners had been kept at Lydford.

In 1307 the warden of the stannaries claimed custody of all tinners by virtue of his charter. So large a claim was disputed in the King's Bench and finally in parliament and it was found that the charter did not extend to pleas of life and limb.[7] Notwithstanding this judgement the warden continued to keep suspect homicides as well as other prisoners, a practice which gave rise in 1376 to complaints in parliament.[8] An inquiry was ordered but

---

[1] It remained in use as a prison until the early nineteenth century. For the general and building history of the castle see *Lydford Castle* (Min. of Public Bdg. and Works, Guide, 1964) and p. 364.

[2] *Pipe R.* 1195 (P.R.S. n.s. VI), 126, 132.

[3] Ibid. 1199 (P.R.S. n.s. x), 242. Cf. *Mem. R.* 1199–1200 (P.R.S. n.s. XXI), 51.

[4] *Pipe R.* 1209 (P.R.S. n.s. XXIV), 88.

[5] G. R. Lewis, *The stannaries: a study of the English tin mines* (London, 1908), 35.   [6] *King's Works*, II, 982–3.

[7] *Sel. Cases in K.B.* III, pp. cxciv, 158–61.   [8] *Rot. Parl.* II. 344–5.

its findings are not known. Both Lydford and Lostwithiel were subsequently delivered,[1] so the conclusion seems to be that formal judgement went in favour of the warden or that the crown thought fit to leave matters as they were.

The power to punish merchants who contravened the ordinance of the staple is at least as old as 1313.[2] Imprisonment, however, is not expressly included among those punishments until 1353. It then became possible for the mayor and constables of the staple to imprison and it was further enacted that to that end a prison of the staple should be established in each staple town.[3] Whether such prisons were in fact brought into being has not yet been proved.

Secular clerks could not properly suffer penal imprisonment for felony in lay prisons and ultimately did not await trial in them.[4] Diocesans accordingly needed prisons for those purposes. These came to be called 'bishops'' prisons, a term which covered the prisons and parts of prisons kept for this purpose by archbishops and by those abbots who enjoyed an episcopal or quasi-episcopal jurisdiction.[5] Among the abbots those of Westminster and St Albans must be numbered.[6]

Archbishops and bishops, of course, possessed lay estates and often rights of prison within them. The bishop of Salisbury had such a prison by 1200,[7] the first episcopal prison so far noticed. By 1216–18 the bishop of Worcester kept a prison in which a

---

[1] B.M. Add. MS 35205, cover. There are rolls for Lostwithiel gaol deliveries, the latest (J.I. 3/9/5) being for 1410.

[2] *Cal. Pat. R.* 1307–13, 591.   [3] 27 Edw. III, St. II, c. 21.

[4] For an enunciation of the doctrine of 1328 see *Sel. Cases in K.B.* II, pp. cxlviii–cxlix.

[5] The comprehensiveness of the phrase is illustrated in a will made in 1371 (*Hust. Wills*, II, 152, checked with MS) whereby money is left to the prisoners *in prisonis episcoporum* at Westminster and Canterbury as well as (e.g.) Salisbury. The English phrase the 'bysshope prison' applied to the bishop of London's prison at Bishop's Stortford is found by 1430: *Cal. Pat. R.* 1429–36, 35. A similar phrase applied to the archbishop of York's prison in York is found by 1529: *Test. Ebor.* v. 271.

[6] For Westminster see the preceding note and p. 238; for St Albans see *Chron. Monast. S. Albani* IV (3) (Walsingham), 48–9; for the jurisdiction in general see D. Knowles, *The religious orders in England* (Cambridge, 1948), II, 281.

[7] *Cur. Reg. R.* i. 264.

clerk was confined.[1] This could perhaps be classed as the first
known 'bishop's' prison in the more exclusive sense defined
above. In the earlier thirteenth century, however, some bishops
seem to have lacked the necessary accommodation and the crown
provided it for them. Thus in 1232 the sheriff of Herefordshire
had to lend the county gaol to the bishop of Hereford[2] and in
1235 the sheriff of Nottinghamshire was required to do a like service for the archbishop of York.[3] In 1236 the bishop of Chichester
drew upon the accommodation of the sheriff of Sussex.[4] In 1242
the sheriff of Essex was directed to lend Colchester gaol to the
archdeacon of Colchester for the custody of a clerk.[5] In or
about 1254 the bishop of London begged the city to lend him
Newgate because he had no fit prison for a clerk who was suspected of murder.[6] Such arrangements, acknowledged by Bracton
to be in no way exceptional,[7] were no doubt meant to be temporary. At all events, of those mentioned above the bishop of
Hereford had his own prison at least for laymen in 1244.[8]

In 1261 the Constitutions of Archbishop Boniface were promulgated and these imposed upon every diocesan the obligation
to have one or two such prisons in his diocese.[9] Presumably in
course of time this order was universally obeyed, though by 1274
some bishops still lacked prisons for their lay fees[10] and therefore,
we may suppose, for their criminous clerks as well. The evidence for
the location of the clerical prisons, however, is often sparse and
sometimes even dubious. In some dioceses, particularly those that
spread themselves over several counties, there was more than one
prison. Thus in the thirteenth century the bishop of Norwich
had prisons at Norwich,[11] North Elmham,[12] and Thetford;[13] the
bishop of London kept his clerks at Bishop's Stortford[14] and

---

[1] Maitland, *Glos. Pl.* pp. 71–2.   [2] *Close R.* 1231–4, 174.
[3] Ibid. 1234–7, 143.   [4] Ibid. 282.   [5] Ibid. 1237–42, 480.
[6] *Flor. Hist.* II. 406–7. The clerk was John of Frome, see p. 232.
[7] *Bracton*, II, 348–9.   [8] *Close R.* 1242–7, 226.
[9] *Councils and Synods*, ed. F. M. Powicke and C. R. Cheney, II (1), 684.
[10] Ibid. II (2), 812.   [11] *Close R.* 1251–3, 398.
[12] *Arch. Rev.* II, 209.   [13] Ibid.
[14] *Registrum Roberti Winchelsey Cantuariensis Archiepiscopi* (Cant. & York Soc. LII), II. 788.

perhaps at Chelmsford too.[1] By the sixteenth century at the latest there was also a London episcopal prison in a tower of St Paul's.[2] The bishop of Worcester had prisons at both Worcester[3] and Gloucester,[4] presumably but not certainly coexistent. As benefit of clergy extended itself, the need to expand such accommodation became the greater and lasted until that benefit began to be restricted by Tudor legislation.

A 'bishop's' prison and the prison of an episcopal lay fee might well be one, or at least might well form part of the same building. Sometimes, perhaps, the lay prison faded out, leaving only the 'bishop's' prison, which was in its turn extinguished in the sixteenth century. In other cases the two types of custody continued to coexist. The prison at New Salisbury, for example, seems always to have been both a 'bishop's' prison and the prison of the city.[5] In 1276 the bishop of Lincoln seems to have had both a lay and a 'bishop's' prison at Spaldwick in Huntingdonshire.[6] Maidstone contained both clerks and laymen in 1279–80 and, less certainly, in 1299–1300,[7] and long remained a laymen's gaol. As late as 1447 the bishop of Rochester secured authority to commit laymen to his prison,[8] and as late as 1541–2 clerks and laymen lay side by side in the bishop of Coventry and Lichfield's castle at Eccleshall.[9] A strange example of mixing is to be found at Westminster, where the abbey gatehouse served partly as the abbot's prison for his lay fee and partly as the prison for the bishop of London's clerks taken within the liberty of Westminster.[10] By 1282–3 the abbot was claiming the right by charter to

---

[1] There was a prison here by 1253–4 (C 66/67 m. 2*d*.) but no proof that there was a 'bishop's' prison there, then or later, is as yet forthcoming.

[2] W. Sparrow Simpson, *Chapters in the history of old St. Paul's* (London, 1881), 113–26.

[3] Probably by 1220 (*Cur. Reg. R.* ix. 353–4); certainly by 1463 (*Cal. Pat. R.* 1461–7, 263).

[4] By 1317–21: Leona C. Gabel, *Benefit of clergy in England in the later middle ages* (Northampton, Mass. 1928–9), 110.

[5] *V.C.H. Wilts.* VI, 95–6.

[6] *Beds. Coroners' R.* 95.

[7] Lambeth Palace MSS, C.R. 656, 658.

[8] *Cal. Chart. R.* 1427–1516, 87.

[9] W.S.L., D 1734 J./1949 mm. 20*d*.–21.

[10] J. Stow, *Survey of London*, II, 122.

imprison such clerks[1] and in later times was addressed as the ordinary.[2]

Bishops who had castles sometimes used them for the criminous clerks. Thus the bishop of Lincoln used Banbury,[3] Newark,[4] and Sleaford,[5] the bishop of Chichester Amberley,[6] and the bishop of Coventry and Lichfield Eccleshall.[7] Some also used their metropolitan palaces: Chichester,[8] Wells,[9] Wolvesley,[10] Worcester,[11] and York.[12] To these Lambeth may be added.[13] But the distinction between a 'castle' and a 'palace' is somewhat unreal. Mere manor houses were also brought into service. The bishop of Lincoln's house at Woburn[14] was presumably no more than that. The bishop of Hereford used his manor house at Ross-on-Wye, where a rocky prison chamber was found in 1837.[15]

Although clerks could not normally be kept in lay prisons, an exception was made in the case of academical clerks. In fact in both the university towns the lay arm was positively enjoined to provide accommodation for them. In Oxford it was the borough upon which the responsibility was first fixed. By a writ issued in 1231 the mayor and bailiffs were to put their prison at the disposal of the chancellor of the university for the custody of delinquent clerks.[16] Five years later, in 1236, the constable of Oxford castle was likewise directed to let the chancellor have accommodation

---

[1] Gabel, *Benefit of clergy*, 52 n.   [2] *Cal. Pat. R.* 1467–77, 340.

[3] From at least 1276: *Rot. Hund.* II. 33.

[4] From at least 1342–7: Lincoln Muniments Room, Episcopal register VII, fos. 107–13.

[5] From at least the same time: ibid.   [6] *Cal. Pat. R.* 1413–16, 198.

[7] Ibid. 1364–7, 135, where, however, it is called a palace. It was in fact a castle: P. and M. Spufford, *Eccleshall* (Department of extra-mural studies, University of Keele, 1964), 12, 36; and cf. p. 152.   [8] *Cal. Pat. R.* 1436–41, 492.

[9] T. S. Holmes, *Wells & Glastonbury, Historical Account* (London, 1908), 48; *Register of John Stafford, bishop of Bath & Wells* (Som. Rec. Soc. XXXI), II. 233.

[10] Gabel, *Benefit of clergy*, 109 (1317–21).

[11] *Cal. Pat. R.* 1461–7, 263.

[12] *V.C.H. Yorks., City of York*, 497.

[13] Dorothy Gardiner, *Story of Lambeth Palace* (London, 1930), 145–8.

[14] S. R. Cattley (ed.), John Foxe, *acts and monuments* (London, 1837–41), IV, 124–5.

[15] *Record of household expenses of Richard de Swinfield, bishop of Hereford* (Camd. Soc. O.S. XLII), pp. cxlvi, cxlvii.   [16] *Close R.* 1227–31, 469–70.

for the coercion of those rebellious scholars who would not suffer the chancellor to do justice upon them.[1] These instructions were evidently obeyed, for in 1244 certain clerks who were charged with robbery in the borough Jewry were distributed between the two prisons.[2] Neither the borough officers nor the sheriff were to do more than act as custodians and were without question to surrender their prisoners to the chancellor or to the representatives of the bishop of Lincoln on request. Later, however, in 1254, other clerks whom the sheriff had imprisoned were only to be handed over if they were free of the taint of homicide or of any other offence which, if they had been laymen, would have required the judgement of a court.[3] Such measures made it unnecessary for the chancellor of Oxford to furnish himself with a special prison. In this respect Oxford followed Paris, her exemplar in so many directions. The chancellor of Paris had indeed once had a prison of his own, but it was denied him by a bull of 1219 and denied him once for all in the great charter of that university, the bull *Parens Scientiarum* of 1231.[4] The respective responsibilities towards Oxford clerks of the borough and the sheriff were delimited by the university's charter of 1255. It was there clearly stated that clerks charged with grave offences were to go to the castle and those charged with lighter ones to the town prison.[5] How long this distinction lasted is not known. In 1331 it was still the theory that grave offenders should go to the castle, though it was said that the sheriffs and keepers had been resisting their admittance.[6] It is probable that in the end all were imprisoned by the town.

At Cambridge the town prison was being used by members of the university by 1242 and it was then established that, if the burgesses were unable or unwilling to take custody of a prisoner, the sheriff must do so by default.[7] Until 1431, at least in theory,

---

[1] *Close R.* 1234–7, 514. [2] Ibid. 1242–7, 181, 241–2. [3] Ibid. 1253–4, 46, 50.
[4] F. M. Powicke and A. B. Emden (eds.), H. Rashdall, *The universities of Europe in the middle ages* (Oxford, 1936), I, 304–5, 338.
[5] *Medieval archives of University of Oxford* (Oxf. Hist. Soc. LXX), I. 20.
[6] Ibid. 120–1.
[7] C. H. Cooper, *Annals of Cambridge* (Cambridge, 1842–1908), I, 44.

both town and county gaols were still available to clerks,[1] though it seems that the responsibility mainly rested with the borough.[2] There is little sign that there was ever the same correlation between the town gaol and light offences and the county gaol and severe ones that prevailed in earlier times at Oxford, though the terms of a patent of 1317[3] suggest that at that time the castle was deemed best for serious delinquents. Neither sheriff nor burgesses could evade the responsibility of receiving men committed by the chancellor and holding them until his instructions for release were received,[4] though neither discharged that duty very well.[5] In the end at Cambridge, as at Oxford, the castle was no doubt cut out. The use of the borough gaol had likewise been discontinued by 1535, for the borough corporation was denying it to the university. Cromwell, newly elected as chancellor, protested at this denial and begged the borough to rescind the prohibition.[6] How successful his appeal was is not known. In the end the borough prison disappeared and was replaced by a house of correction, called the Spinning House, jointly maintained by town and gown.[7]

[1] *Rot. Parl.* v. 425–33.
[2] *Cal. Pat. R.* 1266–72, 195; *Cal. Chart. R.* 1300–26, 332; ibid. 1327–41, 57.
[3] *Cal. Pat. R.* 1313–17, 665.
[4] *Rot. Parl.* v. 425; *Cal. Chart. R.* 1327–41, 57; *Cal. Close R.* 1333–7, 559–60; 1389–92, 428.
[5] Cooper, *Annals of Cambridge*, I, 67, quoting T. Madox, *Firma Burgi* (London, 1726); *Rot. Parl.* I. 381; *Cal. Close R.* 1333–7, 559.
[6] R. B. Merriman, *Life and letters of Thomas Cromwell* (Oxford, 1902), I, 431–2.
[7] *V.C.H. Cambs.* III, 78.

VII

THE CUSTODY OF PRISONS
AND PRISONERS

FROM 1166, and indeed before, county gaols were normally in the charge of sheriffs, who built or mended them, equipped them with the needful gear, and accepted, if unwillingly, a responsibility for securing the inmates. The day-to-day work of guarding the prisoners was actually deputed to common gaolers who, in the twelfth and thirteenth centuries, if not in later times, were sometimes paid out of the county farm. In a few cases, however, the sheriffs in those centuries were wholly or partly relieved even of the ultimate responsibility and this relief continued, nominally at all events, into the centuries that followed.

It seems possible to distinguish two systems of affording them this relief. One was to sell the 'custody' of the gaol temporarily to someone willing to purchase it, the other to grant the gaoler-ship in fee with land to support it. Of the first system there are two early examples. In 1198–9 Walter son of Aubrey paid the first instalment of £5 for having the custody of Salisbury gaol.[1] He was still in debt to the crown in 1201–2,[2] and never seems to have cleared his debt. In 1199 Warin the porter paid £2 for keeping the gate and prison of Lancaster.[3] Both of these men are quickly lost to sight. In neither case does the gaoler seem to have borne the cost of maintaining the buildings, for shortly after each purchase the sheriff was granted an allowance for doing so him-self.[4] By such bargains each side profited, the purchaser drawing an income from fees and perquisites and the vendor making a capital gain and relieving himself of the wages of gaolers. About the other system there is more to be said. Outside London the

---

[1] *Pipe R.* 1199 (P.R.S. n.s. x), 177.
[2] Ibid. 1202 (P.R.S. n.s. xv), 122.   [3] *Rot. de Ob. et Fin.* 33.
[4] *Pipe R.* 1201 (P.R.S. n.s. xiv), 75; 1202, 159.

most noteworthy example of its operation is to be found at Winchester. The story of the custody of that gaol can be traced with some assurance from the late twelfth century and less certainly from Domesday.[1] The earliest positive evidence shows that some time before 1197–8 the constable of Winchester castle had conveyed the custody of 'the gaol of Winchester' to Alan of Bramdean[2] and that Richard I had given the same custody, with some land in Bramdean, to William of Hoo.[3] Alan, whose date of death is unknown, left a brother,[4] and in 1197–8 Henry of Bramdean, that brother's son, claimed by writ of mort d'ancestor the serjeanty of keeping the gaol.[5] The conflict between the rival claimants was tried in 1200, and the jurors found, not necessarily correctly, that Alan had been seised *ut custos* only and not in fee.[6]

After this judgement William of Hoo presumably remained in possession. In 1204, however, Matthew of Wallop replaced him by purchasing the custody of the gaol together with the custody of the castle gate and some other castle buildings. To these custodies lands in the Hampshire parishes of Bramdean and Preston Candover were annexed.[7] These annexed lands approximately correspond to two estates in the county held in 1086 by Miles the porter (*portarius*). The first of these estates consisted of the manor of Bramdean, which may be equated with the later manor of Woodcote, together with a haw in Winchester; the second was made up of 2½ virgates in Bermondspit hundred and can be identified with a complex of land and rent in Preston Candover and Oakhanger.[8] For some time after the grant to Matthew of Wallop these lands are associated with the custody of the gaol and the castle buildings, though the connection between them and the custody of the gate seems to have been severed. It seems a very fair deduction that Miles the porter

[1] For what is meant by 'Winchester gaol' see p. 80.
[2] *Cur. Reg. R.* I. 117. For the date see *Pipe R.* 1198 (P.R.S. n.s. IX), 26.
[3] *Cur. Reg. R.* I. 117; *Rot. de Ob. et Fin.* 18; F. W. Maitland (ed.), *Bracton's note book* (London, 1887), III, p. 315.   [4] *Cur. Reg. R.* I. 117.
[5] *Pipe R.* 1198, 26.   [6] *Cur. Reg. R.* I. 117.
[7] *Rot. Cart.* 126; *Pipe R.* 1204 (P.R.S. n.s. XVIII), 129.
[8] *V.C.H. Hants*, I, 431, 503.

received his cognomen because he kept the castle gate and that he received the lands in return for keeping it together with the prisoners that it contained. Of such an association between gate-keeping and gaol-keeping there are several other examples.[1] If the argument is sound, the gaolership in fee of Winchester is as early as any on record.

Matthew of Wallop was treated as keeper until 1217.[2] He then surrendered the custody[3] in circumstances that are unexplained. Henry of Bramdean may have been installed in his place but, if he was, he did not enjoy the office long; in fact he was not holding it in 1219,[4] though both he and Matthew still had claims upon it in that year.[5] His own claim he then traced back to the Conquest. Though such a claim must always be treated with great reserve, it does at least suggest that there was some popular belief that a gaolership in fee had been created at a very early date.

It looks as though the crown kept the gaol in hand from 1219 until 1227 and then committed its custody, with some of the lands, to Warin son of Geoffrey, called 'le Paneter', first during pleasure and then for life.[6] Matthew of Wallop died about this time[7] and Warin enjoyed the custody, albeit intermittently, until late in 1232.[8] The crown then entrusted the gaol to Thomas de Blanc-muster first *ut custos*[9] and by January 1233 during pleasure.[10] Later in 1233 William of Hoo, possibly not the same as Richard I's grantee, was substituted for Thomas, apparently as gaoler in fee.[11]

[1] *Trans. R. Hist. Soc.* 5th. ser. v, 21.
[2] He was still in office in Michaelmas Term: *Bracton's note book*, III, p. 315.
[3] He had been disseised by 1219: *Cur. Reg. R.* VIII. 35.
[4] It was then in hand: ibid.
[5] *Bk. of Fees*, I. 259. The statement in *Cur. Reg. R.* (see preceding note) is to be preferred to the statement in the feodary, which somewhat disparages Henry's title.
[6] *Rot. Litt. Claus.* II. 168 (pleasure); *Pat. R.* 1225–32, 112 (life). The suffix 'le Paneter' is used in 1230: *Close R.* 1227–31, 362.
[7] Before 25 January 1227: *Rot. Litt. Claus.* II. 168.
[8] The custody was restored to Warin in July 1230, June 1231, and October 1232. On the first two occasions it had been taken in hand because of the escape of prisoners: *Close R.* 1227–31, 362, 516. On the third occasion the seizure was unauthorized: ibid. 1231–4, 124.
[9] *Cal. Lib. R.* 1226–40, 214.   [10] *Close R.* 1231–4, 184.
[11] Ibid. 282–3, 349. The William who had been keeper in John's time claimed against Matthew of Wallop in 1217: *Bracton's note book*, III, p. 315.

William's rights evidently descended to Robert of Hoo, who was keeper in 1241–2.[1] Since, however, the sheriff had charge of the prisoners in 1244[2] and 1245,[3] Robert may very soon after have forfeited the custody, and if he did so it was because of the escape of prisoners.[4]

Robert was restored and thereafter gave the gaol and gaol lands to Niel son of Robert of Winchester,[5] otherwise Bekke or Beket, and that gift the crown confirmed in 1246.[6] Whether the gift was made outright is uncertain, for when some prisoners escaped in October 1247 both Niel and Robert of Hoo were pardoned.[7] It was, however, to Robert that the gaol was restored in December of that year, after it had been taken in hand for a short time.[8] The effect of this restoration, however, is not clear, for in 1249 Niel was in a position to make Robert his tenant for life.[9] How uninterrupted was his tenure is likewise far from clear, for the sheriff seems to have had charge of the prisoners in 1251,[10] and in 1252 Robert was himself in prison.[11] Be this as it may, the custody eventually returned to Niel, who died seised of it in or about 1270.[12]

So far as is known, the Bekke family continued to hold the manor of Woodcote by the same serjeanty until in 1360 it was taken in hand.[13] This was done because Alice, Valentine Bekke's widow, and her second husband were declared to have allowed some prisoners to escape.[14] In 1363 the custody was released to William, one of Valentine's sons.[15] He was succeeded by John Bekke, apparently his brother, who conveyed the manor, at approximately the same serjeanty, to John and Agatha Marshall in 1367.[16] Marshall was fined in 1372 for allowing escapes to occur[17] and an

[1] H. L. Cannon (ed.), *Pipe R. 1242* (New Haven, Conn. 1918), 270.
[2] *Cal. Lib. R. 1240–5*, 225.   [3] *Close R. 1242–7*, 289.
[4] He owed or had paid £10 for escapes in 1241–2. As there is a blank in the MS, we do not know which: *Pipe R. 1242*, 270.
[5] *V.C.H. Hants*, III, 47.   [6] *Cal. Chart. R. 1226–57*, 295.
[7] *Cal. Pat. R. 1232–47*, 510; *Close R. 1247–51*, 19–20.
[8] *Close R. 1247–51*, 20.   [9] *V.C.H. Hants*, III, 47.
[10] *Close R. 1251–3*, 4, 183.   [11] Ibid. 270.
[12] *Cal. Inq. p.m.* I, p. 230.   [13] *V.C.H. Hants*, III, 47.
[14] *Cal. Fine R. 1356–68*, 130.   [15] Ibid. 263.
[16] *V.C.H. Hants*, III, 48.   [17] Ibid.

Edmund Marshall was pardoned for the same offence in 1414.[1] After Edmund's death in 1427 the manor of Woodcote passed to the Framptons and from them to one John Thornes,[2] who was regarded by the Chancery as keeper of the gaol in 1441.[3] He settled it upon his daughter and her husband John Quidhampton, who on his death in 1489 held it by the customary serjeanty.[4] Even after this the serjeanty was not extinguished, for it can be traced until 1628.[5]

In the first forty years of the thirteenth century the Chancery addressed the keeper direct, requiring him, and not the sheriff, to release,[6] remove,[7] or receive prisoners.[8] This practice does not appear to have been followed in the forties and fifties of that century. It would, however, be a mistake to assume that it had been wholly abandoned for, as we have seen, it is not always certain in those decades precisely when the gaol was in the possession of a keeper and when it was in hand. Later the situation is more confused. When Niel Bekke died *c.* 1290 it was said that he was obliged to keep the gaol 'at his own cost and peril'.[9] At the minimum this meant in practice that he, like his predecessors and successors in fee, was accountable for escapes. There is in fact no instance of a sheriff of Hampshire being held accountable for escapes when a keeper in fee was seised. The maintenance of the fabric had not originally been the responsibility of the gaoler in fee, for in 1199–1200 and in 1227–33, during the respective custodies of William of Hoo and Warin son of Geoffrey, the sheriff repaired it.[10] Why this should have been so is not clear. Possibly in 1200 it was so much in doubt who the actual keeper was that no responsibility could have been effectively devolved, while it seems evident that shortly before Warin's appointment the gaol lands had been reduced in extent and therefore might have been thought inadequate to meet the cost. Later on, the crown considered that liability rested upon the keeper, for in 1358, after

---

[1] *Cal. Pat. R.* 1413–16, 198. [2] *V.C.H. Hants*, III, 48.
[3] *Cal. Pat. R.* 1436–41, 489. [4] *Cal. Inq. p.m.* I, pp. 254–5.
[5] *V.C.H. Hants*, III, 48. [6] *Rot. Litt. Pat.* 73. [7] Ibid. 129.
[8] *Close R.* 1234–7, 280. [9] *Cal. Inq. p.m.* I, p. 230.
[10] *Pipe R.* 1200 (P.R.S. n.s. XII), 191; *Cal. Lib. R.* 1226–40, 33, 116, 207.

he had failed to repair, Bramdean manor was taken in hand and the issues used to meet the costs.[1] A jury took the same view of liability in 1367.[2] But by the fifteenth century the view had changed. By 1455 it was even uncertain who owned the site of the gaol and an inquiry was instituted to establish the facts.[3] In pursuance of this it was found in 1458 that the prison stood on the king's ground and that the buildings had always been repairable by the crown, and they were accordingly so repaired in 1462.[4] In all other respects the sheriff appears to have replaced the keeper in fee as the effective custodian well before the fourteenth century had begun, for it is to him and not to the keeper that orders for the reception or enlargement of prisoners are addressed.

Although the keepership of Winchester gaol is unquestionably to be classed as a keepership in fee, it has been shown that its feudal character was not quite unbroken. The gaol of Exeter, on the other hand, was held in fee continuously over a long period. This gaol was given by Henry I to the ancestors of John the porter (*janitor*), together with lands in Bicton which they held by the service of keeping it.[5] John was holding it in 1212 and was succeeded by his brother William, but he soon forfeited the gaol and lands for felony.[6] The gaol was then granted, in 1226, to Ralph le Petit or the Norman, a crossbowman, during pleasure.[7] In 1227 this grant was converted into a custody in fee and the gaol lands, which had been temporarily withheld from him, were added.[8] Ralph's descendants, who by 1266 had assumed the surname Arblaster,[9] thereafter enjoyed the serjeanty until 1347,[10] though about 1318–19 the sheriff tried to eject the Arblaster of the day.[11] In 1355 Joel son of William of Bicton, upon whom Richard

---

[1] *Cal. Inq. Misc.* III, pp. 160–1.   [2] *V.C.H. Hants*, III, 48.
[3] *Cal. Pat. R.* 1452–61, 223.   [4] E 101/563/1.
[5] *Bk. of Fees* I. 96.
[6] John had died and William had forfeited before 26 December 1226: *Rot. Litt. Claus.* II. 163.   [7] Ibid. 161.
[8] Ibid. 193. The gaol lands had been held a few months before this gift by John's widow, in dower: ibid. 172.
[9] *Cal. Pat. R.* 1258–66, 594 and thereafter.   [10] *Cal. Inq. p.m.* IX, p. 19.
[11] H. Cole (ed.), *Documents...from the records of...the Queen's Remembrancer of the Exchequer* (Rec. Com.), 21, 25.

Arblaster had settled the gaol in tail remainder in 1331,[1] died seised of it.[2] After this time the serjeanty appears to have lapsed. By 1356 the gaol was nominally in the sheriff's custody,[3] and in the next year in the effective custody of a man who had no known connection with the Arblasters.[4] Nevertheless, the fact that its custody reposed in 1393 upon one Ralph Sackville and his wife Joan[5] might suggest that the serjeanty had been continued in the female line, since it is otherwise hard to account for a woman as joint custodian; nor does any patent survive appointing the Sackvilles, although they appear to have enjoyed full responsibility. The descent of the serjeanty has not been traced beyond this point. Whether John Rolle Walter, who in 1777 held the 'high gaol' by grant from the duchy of Cornwall,[6] was a descendant of the Sackvilles must for the moment remain an open question.

There is nothing to suggest that the hereditary keepers, while they lasted, were ever required to repair the gaol. On the contrary, the sheriff did so five times between 1227 and 1241 and on the second of these occasions, in 1229, seems actually to have rebuilt it. At the same time he found the keeper irons.[7] The keeper, however, was responsible for escapes.[8]

To other keepers of county gaols in fee there are only passing references. At the Worcester eyre of 1221 Michael the porter was keeper of Worcester gaol in fee,[9] and at the Wiltshire eyre of 1249 William the Champion was, according to one account, gaoler in fee of Salisbury castle gaol.[10] Both were answerable for escapes. In the twelfth and thirteenth centuries such keeperships

---

[1] *Cal. Pat. R.* 1330–4, 225.

[2] *Cal. Inq. p.m.* x, pp. 206–7; *Cal. Close R.* 1346–9, 353. Three inquisitions were taken after Joel's death: they record different findings about its date and his heir.

[3] *Cal. Pat. R.* 1354–8, 373.   [4] Ibid. 609–10.

[5] Ibid. 1391–6, 194.

[6] J. Howard, *The state of the prisons in England and Wales* (Warrington, 1780), 371.

[7] *Cal. Lib. R.* 1226–40, 14, 122, 161, 305; 1240–5, 52.

[8] *Close R.* 1237–42, 56; *Cal. Pat. R.* 1258–66, 594.

[9] *Rolls of justices in eyre for Lincolnshire and Worcestershire* (Selden Society, LIII), 542–3, 610.

[10] *Crown Pleas of the Wilts. Eyre, 1249*, pp. 155, 171.

in fee were perhaps more numerous than the preceding paragraphs imply. At all events they were sufficiently widespread to justify a statement in *Britton*[1] that it was one of the duties of the eyre to investigate the validity of claims to them.

We have seen[2] that many county gaols were placed within the castles of county towns and that sometimes those castles, with their complement of prisoners, were removed from the sheriff's hands and entrusted to specially appointed constables or keepers. Many, if not most, of such constables were removable officers. Lincoln, however, was an exception, for its constableship early became hereditary in the family of la Haye. From them it passed by marriage to Henry de Lacy (d. 1311) and from him, through his wife Alice, to another Henry de Lacy (d. 1361), later created duke of Lancaster.[3] In 1311 the custody of the prison was said to be annexed to it.[4] In 1323, however, Alice de Lacy surrendered her interest in the prison.[5] Notwithstanding that, it was declared at her death in 1348 that she held the castle by the service of keeping the gaol.[6] Whatever this may mean, there does not seem to be any evidence that the constables were effectively in charge of prisoners at the time that either of the *post mortem* claims were made on behalf of the Lacys. Indeed, apart from these claims, there is no known connection between the constables and the prison after 1280.[7]

Where county gaols were not kept by tenants in serjeanty, the sheriff, who consequently remained in charge of them, deputed the daily work to common gaolers. In the earlier thirteenth century we find the crown sanctioning payments to such subordinates out of the county farm, and by the forties payments were being made to working gaolers in ten counties. These ten included Yorkshire where, by 1226, two gaolers were employed.[8] We also know that by 1225 there were gaolers in two other counties

[1] *Britton*, I, 75.   [2] See p. 59.
[3] J. W. F. Hill, *Medieval Lincoln* (Cambridge, 1948), 87–90.
[4] *Cal. Inq. p.m.* v, p. 153.
[5] Exemplification (1377) of deed of 1323: *Cal. Pat. R.* 1377–81, 83.
[6] *Cal. Inq. p.m.* IX, p. 97; *Cal. Fine R.* 1347–56, 97.
[7] *Cal. Close R.* 1279–88, 4.   [8] *Trans. R. Hist. Soc.* 5th. ser. v, 20–1.

besides these ten, though we lack evidence about their wages.[1] There is no doubt that gaolers and their assistants formed a well-recognized profession at this time. Mostly they were simple men, known by their occupational names, which have left their traces in the still current but none too common surnames of Galer, Gayler, Gaylor, and Jailler, and of Gale and Gayle.[2] When paid by thirteenth-century sheriffs, their wages were not high.[3] An Oxford gaoler, however, very early in that century, was rich enough to buy three houses,[4] and by 1226 Eudes de la Jayle was keeper of a Gloucestershire manor.[5] There were, of course, many opportunities, to be later described,[6] for making money 'on the side'. So far as it is possible to determine, the 'working' gaolers of the fourteenth and fifteenth centuries were also for the most part rather simple men.[7] As we shall shortly see, a good many were or had been menial royal officials. But there are some exceptions. In the middle years of the century the 'underkeeper' at Aylesbury owned five houses and forty-five acres of land and meadow.[8] In 1305 the keeper of Oxford castle gaol rather unexpectedly declared himself to be a clerk.[9]

We must suppose that originally the sheriff was unfettered in making such appointments and that gaolerships were consequently a useful piece of patronage for him. From the later thirteenth

---

[1] Somerset: *Rot. Litt. Claus.* II. 13–14. Devon: ibid. 25. The assumption has been made that the gaoler here referred to was not the gaoler in fee described above but a predecessor appointed by the sheriff. The gaoler of Rochester castle is mentioned, not by name, in 1210: *Cur. Reg. R.* VI. 53.

[2] P. H. Reaney, *A dictionary of British surnames* (London, 1958), s.v. Gale, Galer. The earliest relevant form for Gale that Reaney records is Philip de la Jaille (1208, Hants). A William Gaoler or le Gaoler was acting for the king in Gascony in 1228: *Pat. R.* 1225–32, 186, 193. Gale and Gayle have of course other roots. In March 1966 the London telephone directory recorded 16 Gayles, 12 Galers, 21 Gaylers, 11 Gaylors, and 2 Jaillers. The Manhattan telephone directory for 1963–4 contained 21 Gayles, 1 Galer, 1 Gayler, 7 Gaylors, and no Jailler. [3] See p. 165.

[4] *Cart. of Oseney* (Oxford Hist. Soc. XC), II, 395. The extreme dates of the document are 1184–1205.

[5] *Cur. Reg. R.* XII, p. 495. [6] See chapter VIII.

[7] The keeper of Stafford gaol in 1414 was a weaver: *Will Salt. Arch. Soc.* XVII, 27.

[8] *Cal. Inq. Misc.* III, p. 47. [9] *Abbrev. Plac.* 253.

century, however, and throughout the fourteenth and fifteenth centuries, the crown strove continuously, though not always successfully, to deprive him of this perquisite. How early it had begun to make direct appointments is not certainly known, but in 1259 there seems to have been a keeper of Guildford gaol, distinct from the sheriff, to whom the Chancery addressed a writ.[1] For this, however, the civil war might be enough to account. The sheriff seems to have recovered custody by 1295,[2] but a keeper is heard of again in 1306 when he petitioned the king in parliament to provide him with ampler accommodation.[3] In the same year the sheriff of Oxfordshire persuaded the crown to grant him compensation because for the past three years he had been deprived of Oxford castle and had thus lost the profit of the gaol.[4] While this loss might well deserve a recompense the sheriff was at least relieved of the responsibility, for it was the keeper of the gaol and castle who in the preceding year was held accountable for an escape.[5] Likewise the sheriff of Essex was on many occasions deprived of the custody of Colchester castle.[6]

Of these appointments no formal record has been traced. Such letters of appointment, however, now begin to come to notice. In 1301 the king appointed Peter Burtet, described as one of his yeomen, to be keeper of Launceston castle and gaol, and directed the sheriff to pay him out of the issues of Cornwall.[7] Similar appointments were made to Stafford gaol in 1315[8] and to Warwick gaol in 1327.[9] Thus began, if it had not begun already, the practice of using gaolerships as a means of providing for minor civil servants to the detriment of local patronage. It was a practice not of course confined to gaolerships but one which extended to many other lesser offices under provincial government.[10]

A vaguely worded statute of 1336 appears to forbid the crown to

---

[1] *Close R.* 1256–9, 367.

[2] *Surrey Pipe R. for 1295* (Surrey Rec. Soc. [VII], 28).

[3] *Rot. Parl.* I. 193.

[4] W. A. Morris, *The medieval English sheriff to 1300* (Manchester, 1927), 186, quoting Lord Treasurer's Remembrancer, Memoranda Roll.

[5] *Abbrev. Plac.* 253.   [6] See p. 68.

[7] *Cal. Pat. R.* 1292–1301, 573.   [8] Ibid. 1313–17, 366.

[9] Ibid. 1327–30, 165.   [10] *E.H.R.* LXXVIII, 367.

deprive sheriffs in this way. Gaols appendant to sheriffdoms, it says, are to be kept as they were wont to be kept. If their keeping has been alienated they are to be taken back 'by writs' and delivered to those who ought to have them.[1] A further statute of 1340 repeated this injunction more clearly, expressly authorizing sheriffs to put in keepers for whom they were to answer.[2] The crown, however, repeatedly ignored these statutes. It continued, for example, to fill the gaolerships at Stafford and Warwick with royal nominees. It began to do the like at York in 1339,[3] at Ilchester in 1371,[4] and at Nottingham and Salisbury in 1382.[5] In five of these six instances the appointments continue to be made until well on into the fifteenth century.[6] In Stafford, the excepted instance, they appear to have been discontinued after 1360,[7] but perhaps only because the gaol was temporarily closed about that time.[8] At this time, too, Guildford gaol is again treated similarly. From at least 1359 until 1365–6 its castle with the gaol had been in the hands of a keeper,[9] who was also keeper of the town.[10] The town was then granted to the townsmen in fee farm,[11] but the castle with the gaol was reserved, and in 1367 was committed to the sheriff.[12] A century later, however, the crown was again intruding its own servants,[13] and the survival of a writ of mainprise addressed to the keeper in 1413 suggests that that process may have begun even sooner.[14]

It is not at present known how widely crown nominees were scattered over the county gaols of England but at least it may be said that, apart from those already mentioned, the gaolerships at Cambridge[15] and Norwich[16] were so filled in 1381, at Newcastle

[1] 10 Edw. III, St. II.
[2] 14 Edw. III, St. I, c. 10.
[3] *Cal. Pat. R.* 1338–40, 344.
[4] Ibid. 1370–4, 114.
[5] *V.C.H. Wilts.* v, 22.
[6] The crown nominee was still held responsible for repairing York gaol in 1446: *V.C.H. Yorks., City of York*, 524. The sheriff, however, repaired it in 1454: E 364/89 m. D.
[7] *Cal. Pat. R.* 1358–61, 487.
[8] See p. 74.
[9] *Cal. Pat. R.* 1358–61, 296; 1364–7, 161.
[10] *Cal. Chart. R.* 1341–1417, 195.
[11] Ibid.
[12] *Cal. Pat. R.* 1367–70, 15.
[13] Ibid. 1461–7, 43, 211, 328; 1467–77, 513.
[14] *Cal. Close R.* 1413–19, 30.
[15] *Cal. Pat. R.* 1381–5, 47, 389.
[16] Ibid. 45.

upon Tyne in 1383,[1] at Oakham about 1393 and in 1412,[2] and at Carlisle in 1400–1.[3] These may represent more or less isolated appointments or part of a longer or shorter succession. The gaolership at Exeter, after the lapse (perhaps only a temporary one) of the gaolership in fee,[4] was thus filled only once (1399), and that at Guildford (1461, 1475) only twice.[5] Where the terms of appointment are stated, life grants preponderated, but there were also a number of grants during pleasure, and a few during good behaviour. Two grants during pleasure, those at Cambridge and Norwich in 1381, were converted into life grants shortly afterwards. The York gaoler appointed for life in 1362 alienated his office without leave and the alienee in turn alienated.[6] That the office could pass completely out of the crown's control and could be held by a person whose very name might be unknown to the Chancery seems today a strange proceeding. Nevertheless, when the last of the three alienees above referred to was dead, the crown once again made a grant for life, with its attendant risks, and even added the power of deputation.[7]

By a third statute, made in 1504, the practice was once again forbidden; sheriffs were to have the keeping of all common gaols, except those held in fee, and all patents to the contrary were to be voided.[8] This evidently had some lasting effect, for there survive from the sixteenth century, as indeed from an earlier time, a number of indentures transferring prisoners in the gaol from outgoing to incoming sheriffs and others between sheriff and sheriff, gaoler and gaoler, conveying and accepting the gaoler's office.[9] The sheriff's triumph, however, was not complete, for in 1541 the

[1] Ibid. 300.
[2] Ibid. 1391–6, 259; 1408–13, 404. The first reference bears witness to the surrender of a patent.
[3] Ibid. 1399–1401, 38, 396, 424.   [4] Ibid. 130.
[5] Ibid. 1461–7, 43, 211; 1467–77, 513.
[6] *Cal. Inq. Misc.* III, p. 407.
[7] *Cal. Pat. R.* 1377–81, 27. Ilchester gaolers were also authorized to appoint deputies: ibid. 1429–36, 59; 1446–52, 73; 1452–61, 427.
[8] 19 Hen. VIII, c. 10.
[9] E.g. W. M. Palmer, *Cambridge castle* (Cambridge, 1928), 33–4 (Cambridge, 1580, 1598); *Cat. Anc. D.* VI. C 7243 (Notts. and Derbys., 1537); Guildford Castle

crown resumed the practice of nominating the gaoler of York castle and maintained it, despite the sheriff's protests, until the interregnum.[1]

In essence a franchise-holder possessing a prison was like a sheriff. At any rate his responsibilities were akin. There is little enough to be collected about the way in which he chose and appointed his gaolers but, like the crown, he sometimes created gaolerships in fee. In 1279 the porter of Lewes castle, which belonged to the Warrennes, so held the gaolership,[2] and in 1306 a man was holding land in Skipton by the serjeanty of keeping the castle gate, guarding the prisoners, and finding 'irons' for them.[3] By 1306 Skipton was in the hands of the crown, but it seems most probable that the serjeanty had been created by the de Forz family, who held the honor of Skipton until 1274, if not by their predecessors.[4] Somewhat unexpectedly, the keeper of Arundel castle gaol, c. 1269–c. 1274, was a knight, who subsequently became a county coroner.[5]

In the sixteenth century the nominal responsibility for at least one 'bishop's' prison in the diocese of London rested upon the bishop's chancellor.[6] Whether this was true of earlier periods and other dioceses is most uncertain. Twice, at widely spaced intervals in time, we find the manager of an episcopal manor serving as the nominal custodian of the gaol within it. In 1332 the keeper of the gaol at Hexham was also 'serjeant' of the manor and town[7] and in 1541–2 the bailiff of the manor of Eccleshall kept the castle

Arch. Loseley MSS 962/1, 962/2 (Surrey, 1532–3); W. Alberry, *A millennium of facts in the history of Horsham* (privately printed, 1947), 333–7 (Sussex, 1589); B.M. Add. MS 18291 (Wiltshire, 1547). An indenture between an outgoing and incoming sheriff of Kent exists for 1378 (*Arch. Cant.* LXXI. 206). A standard fee for drawing such an indenture was laid down in Bristol in 1518: *Sel. Cases in Star Chamber*, II. 165.

[1] *V.C.H. Yorks., City of York*, 524–5.
[2] *Suss. Arch. Coll.* LXI, 88. [3] *Cal. Inq. p.m.* IV, pp. 235–6.
[4] For the descent of the honor see W. Farrer, *Early Yorkshire Charters* (Yorks. Arch. Soc. Rec. Ser., extra ser. VI), VII.
[5] *Suss. Arch. Coll.* XCVIII, 56.
[6] A. Ogle, *The tragedy of the Lollards' Tower* (Oxford, 1949), 12.
[7] *History of Northumberland* [Northumberland County History Committee], III, *Hexhamshire*, 1, 226 n.

there and the gaol within it.[1] In 1402[2] and 1439[3] the gaoler at Wells was also the bishop's park-keeper. Bishops like kings also appointed household servants, past or present, as gaolers. The bishop of Durham did so in 1317[4] and the bishops of Salisbury in the fifteenth and sixteenth centuries.[5] The keeper of Hexham gaol, mentioned above, was a barber. The keeper of the bishop's gaol in Chichester in 1477–9 became bailiff of the city and a Sussex county coroner.[6] He was, therefore, of somewhat better station than some of his brethren.

In cities and boroughs that were counties in their own right the sheriffs were responsible for the prisons and presumably in all ordinary circumstances appointed the gaolers. This was certainly the case with Newgate in earlier times. The disputes that took place in 1254[7] and 1318[8] over the responsibility for suffering escapes from that prison seem to leave no doubt that the keeper of that gaol was at those times directly subordinate to the sheriffs. Later the *Liber Albus* expressly calls the gaoler and the gaoler's clerk the sheriff's servants, and makes it clear that the sheriffs were to see to it that fit gaolers were appointed.[9]

Rather naturally, too, the sheriffs appointed the gatekeepers[10] or porters[11] of the Counters, as the gaolers of those institutions were called, for the Counters were peculiarly their own and at the outset bore their names.[12] The keepership of Ludgate, on the other hand, seems on sundry occasions between 1378 and 1414 to have been filled by the mayor and aldermen or by the mayor, aldermen, and common council.[13] The sheriffs were not excluded from

[1] W.S.L., D 1734 J/1949 m. 20d.
[2] *Register of Walter Giffard and Henry Bowett* (Som. Rec. Soc. XIII), pp. 28, 29; cf. Registrum Bowett episcopi Badon. et Wellen. f. 13 b.
[3] *Register of John of Stafford* (Som. Rec. Soc. XXXII) II. p. 233.
[4] *Cal. Pat. R.* 1321–4, 417 (royal confirmation of 1324). The gaoler also kept the castle gate, which was in fact the prison.
[5] Registrum Blythe episcopi Sar. f. 36; C 3/27/45.
[6] *Suss. Arch. Coll.* XCVIII, 65.　　　[7] See p. 252.　　　[8] See p. 253.
[9] *Mun. Gild.* I. 45–7.　　　[10] *Cal. Lr. Bks. H*, 329.
[11] So called by 1383: ibid. 209. Cf. ibid. 402; *Mun. Gild.* I. 523.
[12] See pp. 109–10.
[13] *Cal. Lr. Bks. H*, 97 (1378), 253 (1384), 292 (1386); *I*, 123 (1414). Sometimes two keepers held office jointly.

control of that prison for, when they left office, they handed over the prisoners to their successors,[1] just as they would have done at Newgate.[2] The governing assemblies, however, at the time when Ludgate was being opened, were beginning to take a serious interest in prison security and discipline, and they perhaps felt it wisest to keep the gaoler's office effectively in their own hands. Indeed, where discipline required it, they were apt to take direct action against the keepers of other prisons. Thus it was apparently by a collective decision that the keeper of Newgate was removed in 1341 for extortion[3] and a porter of Sheriff Venour's Counter in 1388 for insulting an alderman.[4] In 1449 the common council imprisoned a former keeper of Newgate,[5] apparently for an offence committed while in office. In the next year it dismissed his successor[6] and later forbade any future sheriff to employ him.[7] It is perfectly clear that by 1441 the keeper of Ludgate was removable by the common council.[8] Perhaps the best opinion is that by the fifteenth century, if not somewhat before, the keepers of the city prisons were felt to be a part of the civic bureaucracy, controlled, and even subject to dismissal, by the common council, but that when vacancies occurred the sheriffs of the day might exercise the patronage. Such a view is supported by the fact that in 1440 it was decided that the sheriffs should 'provide' the keepers of Newgate and Ludgate and that the keepers should be responsible to the sheriffs.[9] While the context makes it plain that on this occasion these 'keepers' were primarily gatekeepers, the oath of the keeper of Newgate of only a few years later, and indeed other evidence, shows that that officer was at this period in charge of both the gate and the prison.[10]

There is little evidence that outsiders were successfully intruded into the keepership of London prisons as they were into those of prisons in the counties. Edmund le Lorimer, keeper of Newgate in 1319 was possibly an exception for, though a Londoner and a

[1] *Cal. Lr. Bks. I*, 76 (1409).
[2] *Mun. Gild.* 1. 45–6.
[3] *Cal. Plea & Mem. R.* 1323–64, 135.
[4] *Cal. Lr. Bks. H*, 329.
[5] Jorn. 5, f. 16.
[6] Jorn. 5, f. 48.
[7] Jorn. 5, f. 51.
[8] Jorn. 3, f. 82*b*.
[9] Jorn. 3, f. 55*b*; *Cal. Lr. Bks. K*, 243.
[10] See p. 185.

warden of his craft, he seems to have owed his preferment to Despenser. He did not in any case last long, but he was convicted of extortion and deprived.[1]

In 1343 the city was twice summoned to show cause why it would not commit Newgate to one of the king's larderers to hold as two former crown nominees had held it.[2] No returns to these writs have been discovered and it is possible that the crown's allegation was false. Alternatively, one at least of the earlier nominees may have been appointed when the city was in hand between 1285 and 1298. In 1509 Edmund Dudley, to the great scandal of the city, appointed one of the sheriff's serjeants to the portership of the Poultry Counter. The appointment, however, was quickly quashed.[3]

We know little of the quality of these London gaolers. In the earlier thirteenth century the crown habitually addressed writs direct to the keeper of Newgate, a practice most rarely followed in the case of other prisons apart from the Fleet.[4] This suggests a status rather above that of most other gaolers. The joint keepers of Ludgate in 1378 were serjeants of the city chamber.[5] A man appointed to the same prison in 1431 was a tailor.[6] In the early sixteenth century the porter of the Poulty Counter could make an income large enough to 'live like a gentleman',[7] presumably because by that time it was possible to charge good rates for chamber hire. In 1509 the former keeper of Ludgate, who then received a pardon, could be described as a merchant or haberdasher.[8]

Outside London the story is inevitably very patchy. The earliest town gaoler known by name is Walter Longshanks (*longus*), who was keeper of the gaol of Gloucester town in 1221.[9] It would hardly be possible to name more than a score of others. At Wallingford in the earlier thirteenth century the town serjeant[10]

[1] *Speculum*, XVIII, 236–7.   [2] *Cal. Lr. Bks. F*, 90–1.
[3] *Gt. Chron. of Lond.* 349, 454.
[4] *Trans. R. Hist. Soc.* 5th ser. v, 17. For early examples of such writs see *Cal. Lib. R.* 1226–40, 210 (1233) and *Close R.* 1234–7, 39 (1235).
[5] *Cal. Lr. Bks. H*, 97.   [6] *Chrons. of London*, 134, 300.
[7] *Gt. Chron. of Lond.* 349.
[8] *L. & P.* I (1), p. 243; cf. Rep. 2, fos. 29*b*, 72.
[9] Maitland, *Glos. Pl.*, p. 107.
[10] Berks. Rec. Off. W/JB a.3 (*c.* 1230); W/JB a.9 (1237).

and later in the century the under-bailiff, presumably the same officer, was the effective custodian.[1] At other towns, too, the town serjeants, who were usually peace officers, seem to have acted as gaolers, at Hull in or shortly before 1348,[2] and at Newcastle under Lyme[3] and Salisbury[4] in the fifteenth century. At Southampton one of the two serjeants looked after the felons and the other the debtors. The gaoler at Norwich in 1506 was also serjeant of the mace,[5] a similar office. Who appointed these gaolers is seldom stated. It was being argued at Exeter in 1311 whether the keeper of the city prison was removable by the mayor alone or only by the mayor and four bailiffs together.[6] About 1518 the sheriffs of Bristol were authorized to let the city prison, presumably the Newgate of Bristol,[7] to farm, an action that had been forbidden in the fourteenth century to the sheriffs of London and Middlesex.[8] In 1382 the keeper of Monkbridge prison in the same city, a former groom of the scullery, was a crown nominee, as apparently his predecessor, Edmund del Ewerye, had been.[9] About 1484 the keepers of Nottingham town gaol were apparently appointed in the same way.[10]

Having dealt above with the custody of county, franchise, and urban prisons, it is time to speak of the custody of so-called 'national' prisons and of the prisons of the forest. Of these the Fleet deserves the leading place. The history of its custody, however, has thrice been carefully traced in recent times,[11] so a summary account will here suffice. In 1130 the keepership was being

---

[1] Berks. Rec. Off. W/JC f. 1 (1294); W/JB a. 30 (1294).
[3] *Cal. Pat. R.* 1348–50, 185.   [2] *V.C.H. Staffs.* VIII, 40.
[4] *Reg. of Henry Chichele* (Cant. and York Soc. XLII), II. 826.
[5] *Recs. of Norwich*, II, 368.   [6] *Yr. Bk. 5 Edw. II* (Selden Soc. LXII), 9–11.
[7] *Sel. cases in Star Chamber*, II. 63.   [8] *Cal. Lr. Bks. G*, 74.
[9] *Cal. Pat. R.* 1381–5, 110.
[10] Ibid. 1477–85, 513, 528–9. This is on the assumption that Randle Franke, who appears to have been in office before this year, was keeper of the town gaol and not of the county gaol. What is meant by the gaol within the town of Nottingham is not always clear.
[11] 'The keepership of the Old Palace at Westminster', *E.H.R.* LIX, 1; 'The Fleet and its neighbourhood in early times', *London Top. Rec.* XIX, 13; 'The Fleet prison in the middle ages', *Toronto Law Jnl*, V, 383. Except where otherwise stated, this and the next three paragraphs are based on these articles.

held by a Ralph *arborarius*[1] and remained in his descendants until at least 1163. Thereafter its holders are unknown until in 1189 it was granted by Richard I to Osbert, the brother of William Longchamp. In 1197 it was successfully claimed in hereditary right by Nathaniel of Leaveland (Kent) and his son Robert, who were presumably blood relatives of Ralph *arborarius*. It is worth recalling that a parallel conflict between a hereditary keeper and one who was declared not to be hereditary took place at almost the same time over the custody of Winchester gaol.[2] The respective rights of the claimants are harder to disentangle in Winchester's case, but it is tempting to believe that in both instances the crown was trying to break the continuity of a gaolership in fee, no doubt because freeholders were hard to keep in control.

In the Leaveland family the custody of the Fleet remained until the accession of Elizabeth I though, as the descent was often in the female line, the connection with the Leavelands is eventually obscured. Thus the owners of the serjeanty, as it was being called by 1204, were from 1293 to 1361 various members of the Sench family, and from then until 1434 of the Sapperton family. William Venour, who had married Elizabeth Sapperton, enjoyed it until 1461, when he died leaving Elizabeth a childless widow. In the following year she married Robert Worth and the succession to the serjeanty was thereupon disputed between him and William Babington, who had married into the Sapperton family. The upshot was that after Elizabeth's death the serjeanty passed to another William Babington and with the Babington family it remained until 1558. The custody then passed for ever from its ancient owners.

Although over the long period of four hundred years the Leaveland line never lost its connection with the Fleet, its members were often effectively relieved of responsibility during minorities, when guardians drew the profits and bore the burdens.

---

[1] The word may possibly mean 'maker of stocks for cross-bows'. If it does, there may be an affinity with the Exeter gaolership in fee which, as shown above (p. 145), was acquired by a crossbowman in 1226 and long remained in the Arblaster family.

[2] See p. 141.

Also, as in many other prisons, deputies were from time to time appointed, and this practice was particularly common after 1480.

The wardens of the Fleet were also hereditary keepers of the 'king's houses', or old palace, at Westminster. In return for the custody of both prison and palace they enjoyed from some uncertain date certain lands in London and Middlesex. This property consisted of the prison-house itself in which the wardens were entitled to live, a dwelling in the precinct of Westminster palace, which perhaps they later used more often, and rents from houses in Fleet Street, Thames Street, and elsewhere in the city and suburbs. When first particularized in 1332 these lands were valued at £6 18s. 5d.[1] and at slightly lower rates in 1466[2] and 1498.[3] From 1130 the wardens also received as keepers of the prison 5d. a day out of the issues of London and Middlesex, a considerable sum at the time when it was first enjoyed.[4] The wage was still being paid in 1559,[5] and perhaps for long after.

In the thirteenth century the 'marshals' or under-marshals of the benches and in the Exchequer were the nominees of the marshal of England.[6] This, however, did not prevent the crown from dismissing them, as was done in 1293 when the under-marshal in the King's Bench was temporarily removed for misconduct.[7] When Roger Bigod died in 1306, the marshalsea of England, which since 1302 he had held only for life, reverted to the crown[8] and the king in 1307 appointed an under-marshal in the King's Bench.[9] A new marshal, though not an earl, was appointed a few weeks later with power of deputation, but he and his successor held the office only during pleasure.[10] In 1316, however, a new earl marshal was created in the person of Thomas of Brotherton, the king's brother, to hold in tail male. Thence-

[1] *Cal. Inq. p.m.* VII, p. 331. The statement about the location of the property in *Toronto Law Jnl*, V, 384, based upon Elizabeth G. Kimball, *Serjeanty tenure in medieval England* (New Haven, 1936) is not correct.
[2] City of London Rec. Off., Hust. R. 196, 8.   [3] *Cal. Inq. p.m.* II, p. 30.
[4] In 1332 the wage is wrongly stated to be 6d. a day: *Cal. Inq. p.m.* VII, p. 331.
[5] Hust. R. 250, 54.   [6] See p. 118.
[7] *Sel. Cases in K.B.* II, 149–51.
[8] *Peerage,* s.v. Norfolk, and vol. II, App. D.
[9] *Cal. Pat. R.* 1307–13, 1.   [10] Ibid. 6, 51.

forth, for the next twenty years or so, there ensues a period during which sometimes the earl marshal with the king's confirmation and sometimes the king alone, because the marshalship had been confiscated for mismanagement, filled the under-marshalship.[1] This period ends in 1338 when Walter de Mauny who, with royal confirmation, had been appointed under-marshal by the earl of Norfolk in 1331, was deprived by William Montagu, earl of Salisbury, Norfolk's successor. When Thomas Beauchamp, earl of Warwick, succeeded Salisbury in 1344, Mauny was reinstated and held office for ten years. After this time, at least until 1391,[2] the crown appointed the under-marshals for life and so deprived the marshals of their patronage in much the same way as it filled the gaolerships of counties over the sheriff's head. It is not at present known what happened afterwards, but by the later fifteenth century the responsibility of the dukes of Norfolk as earls marshal had, at least for a season, been restored. Thomas Mowbray, the duke who died in 1461, is found removing a man from the office of under-marshal and, by his patent enrolled in court, appointing another in his place.[3] The next duke (d. 1476) was in his own estimation so far the ultimate custodian that when, in or about 1470, the under-marshal allowed some prisoners to escape he thought it necessary to procure an Act of Indemnity to protect himself from prosecution.[4]

In course of time the under-marshalship undoubtedly became a profitable office, for the man appointed in 1361 was willing to sacrifice an annuity of £10 a year in order to secure it.[5] The more profitable it grew the more appropriately could some of its duties be devolved, and accordingly we find the under-marshals appointing deputies of their own. Such men are traceable from 1328 to 1361.[6] But at least until 1381 the under-marshal himself remained in close contact with his prison, for at the time of his

[1] The story of the under-marshalship is traced in *Sel. Cases in K.B.* v, pp. xxii–xxiv and vi, pp. xlii–xliii.
[2] *Cal. Pat. R.* 1388–92, 489.
[3] *Yr. Bk. 39 Hen. VI* (Vulg.), pp. 32–3.
[4] *Rot. Parl.* vi. 49–50; and see p. 250.   [5] *Cal. Pat. R.* 1361–4, 82.
[6] For these deputies see *Sel. Cases in K.B.* vi, p. xliii.

death in that year he seems to have lived in or near it[1] and had certainly earned a reputation for cruelty for his treatment of his charges.[2]

Appointments to the office of under-marshal of the other marshalsea can only be traced with great difficulty. Two have been recovered, however, for the early fourteenth century,[3] and it is also known that in 1504 they were, like appointments to the other under-marshalship, made by crown patent.[4]

Of the custody of most forest prisons little enough is known. The prison of the forest of Galtres, however, is an exception. By 1219 the keepership was in the hands of David the larderer, whose ancestors, for almost a century before that time, had exercised the function of stocking the king's larder in York with game and domestic animals. David himself, the second of that name, and some of his descendants had the additional duty of selling beasts taken in distraint for payment of the king's debts. David's family continued to keep the prison, which was in Davy Hall in York, until, apparently in the fifteenth century, the buildings fell down. From the early years of Henry III the keepers received payment for their trouble both in cash and lands. The lands, and therefore, we may suppose, the custody, descended through the female line successively to the families of Leek, Clifton, Thornton, and Thwaites. By 1519 they had reached the Fairfaxes who were still holding them in the later seventeenth century.[5] The keeperships of the prisons in the forest of Dean were granted by crown patent and in two instances in 1492 were bestowed on just that type of minor royal official who occupied the gaolerships of so many counties.[6]

The number of people employed as subordinate prison staff in particular gaols inevitably varied a good deal with circumstances. But even in quite small gaols there must often have been more than one man in charge of prisoners. The 'bailiffs of the gaol' of

[1] *Anonimalle Chron.* 140. [2] See p. 283.
[3] *Sel. Cases in K.B.* v, xxi n. [4] 19 Hen. VII, c. 10, s. 4.
[5] *V.C.H. Yorks., City of York*, 494–6.
[6] *Cal. Pat. R.* 1485–94, 406, 421. Cf. p. 149.

Hereford are mentioned in 1224.[1] The gaoler of Oxford had a *garcio* in 1305[2] and in the same year the assistant to the keeper of the earl of Lancaster's prison fell down and broke his neck.[3] By 1352 the bailiff of Romney, who was the town gaoler, employed a 'serjeant'.[4] About 1384 the under-keeper of Salisbury castle gaol employed a gate-keeper,[5] and in 1394 we have the names of the *ministri gaole* who formed part of a jury there empanelled.[6] We read of the under-gaoler of York in 1441[7] and of a servant of the keeper of the county gaol at Nottingham in 1442,[8] though the second of these could have been a personal servant rather than a prison officer. A servant of the gaoler of Winchester about 1441 was responsible for searching the prisoners daily.[9]

That there should have been a staff of assistant gaolers in the London prisons is natural enough. In 1292 the deputy warden of the Fleet employed a deputy keeper and a *garcio*,[10] each of whom was then being used as an escort. Two servants of the warden of that prison are mentioned in 1381 as having charge of a single prisoner.[11] In 1467 the warden had a staff of six.[12] In 1509 he had a deputy, described as a 'gentleman', and the deputy had a servant.[13] About 1320 the under-marshal in the King's Bench had a servant (*serviens*)[14] and his colleague in the household a yeoman (*vallett'*).[15] In the King's Bench prison in 1351 the under-marshal's deputy had a deputy of his own and also a servant.[16] By 1393 clerks were being employed in the Counters to assess the lodging fees of prisoners.[17] At about the same time the keeper of Ludgate had a clerk and various other servants and officers,[18] some of whom were

---

[1] *Cur. Reg. R.* XI, p. 381.   [2] *Abbrev. Plac.* 253.
[3] *Leicester Borough Records*, I, 368.
[4] *Borough Cust.* I, 5.   [5] *V.C.H. Wilts.* V, 22.
[6] Ibid.   [7] *Cal. Pat. R.* 1441–6, 25.
[8] Ibid. 91.   [9] Ibid. 1436–41, 489.
[10] *Sel. Cases in K.B.* II, p. cliv; *Sel. Cases in Exchq. of Pleas*, pp. 141–2. That the chief officer of the Fleet was deputy warden is shown in *Toronto Law Jnl*, V, 388.
[11] *Rot. Parl.* III. 128.   [12] *Toronto Law Jnl*, V, 385 n.
[13] *L. & P.* I (1), p. 229.   [14] *Rot. Parl.* I. 365.
[15] T. F. Tout, *The place of the reign of Edward II in English history* (Manchester, 1936), 279.   [16] *Sel. Cases in K.B.* VI, 77–8.
[17] *Mun. Gild.* I. 523. For the date see *Cal. Lr. Bks. H*, 402 n.
[18] *Cal. Plea & Mem. R.* 1381–1412, 159.

needed as the personal escorts of prisoners who had licence to walk the city. Such a personal 'keeper' is mentioned in 1474–5.[1]

State prisoners, whose security was of prime importance, could not always be entrusted to the gaoler and his servants and had to be provided with personal guards. Thus in 1225, Richard Fitz-Niel, a prisoner in the Fleet, was put in charge of five crossbow-men.[2] When Piers Gaveston surrendered to the earl of Warwick in 1312 he was handed over to four keepers,[3] and in 1323 the younger Roger Mortimer escaped from the custody of his body-guard in the Tower.[4] Such guards, however, can hardly be reckoned a part of the prison staff.

Up to the present attention has been concentrated upon systems of custody under which the responsibility for guarding prisoners was entrusted to a single individual acting either in person or by deputy and with or without assistants. Custody, however, might also be collective. In the early twelfth century it was occasionally undertaken by a frankpledge tithing.[5] More often, however, the burden was borne by a township, a group of townships, or a class within a township. Thus in 1235–6 the task of guarding and conveying prisoners taken in Sadberge wapentake in Durham fell upon all the men of the 'borough' of Sadberge and of three or four adjacent townships.[6] Often the responsibility fell upon some particular class of men within a village, usually cottars or small tenants.[7] Evidence of this custom comes from all parts of the country: Blackwell and Newnham (Worcs.) in 1240,[8] Barton (Beds.) in 1255,[9] Pocklington (Yorks.) in 1260,[10] Isleworth

[1] *Gt. Chron. of Lond.* p. 222.
[2] *Rot. Litt. Claus.* II. 84–5. FitzNiel, according to his own account, had been approached by three men, who had asked him to join them in a plan to poison the king: *Cur. Reg. R.* XII, p. 215. He instituted an appeal against them and consequently was a kind of approver.
[3] *Chrons. Edw. I and II,* I. 207.   [4] *Abbrev. Plac.* 343.
[5] Maitland, *Glos. Pl.* p. 66.
[6] *Miscellanea* II (Surtees Soc. CXXVII), 77, 86. More than one inquiry was held to establish the facts, and the findings are not in complete agreement.
[7] H. S. Bennett, *Life on the English manor: a study of peasant conditions, 1150–1400* (Cambridge, 1937), 70.
[8] *Registr. Priorat. Wigorn.* 15 a, 66 b.   [9] *Cart. Mon. de Rameseia,* I. 484.
[10] *Yorks. Inq. Hen. III & Edw. I,* I (Yorks. Arch. Soc. Rec. Ser. XII), 75.

(Middx.) in 1274,[1] the Kentish townships of Hernhill (in Teynham), Graveney, and Grain in 1283–5,[2] Hadleigh (Suffolk) in 1305,[3] Godalming in 1317–18,[4] Banstead (Surrey) in 1325[5] and Writtle (Essex) in 1328.[6] The men of the three Kentish places were also upon the lord's direction to take their prisoners to a gaol. Similarly certain custumals discovered in 1381 declared it to be the custom for the men of Corfe to furnish the constable of Corfe castle with an escort whenever prisoners were sent to him at the king's command; they were to go to Wareham bridge to receive the prisoners and were to return them to that place if they were ordered to another prison.[7]

A curious variation of these arrangements is sometimes discernible: different groups within the same town were responsible for custody by night and by day. Thus, while all the men of Faversham were to keep thieves by night, only the tenants of the abbey mill were responsible by day. This is laid down in a custumal of 1254.[8] Somewhat later, in 1278–9, it was declared to be the custom of York that the butchers of that city should keep prisoners by night and the city bailiffs in the day-time.[9] In 1282 the men of Greywell must guard those who were imprisoned at Odiham every third night,[10] others no doubt being liable for daylight custody and custody on other nights. In 1283–5 the heirs of certain named persons, tenants of mills, were to be the night-time keepers of strangers taken within the archbishop of Canterbury's lands, and the miller of Westgate, Canterbury, the day-time keeper.[11] In 1306–7 it was the custom of Havering for

---

[1] C 135/95/14*d*; Syon House MS A XIV 1*a*, fos. 9–11.

[2] F. R. H. Du Boulay, *The lordship of Canterbury: an essay on medieval society* (London, 1966), 309.

[3] *Proc. Suffolk Institute of Archaeology*, III, 244.　　[4] *V.C.H. Surrey*, III, 29.

[5] H. C. M. Lambert, *The history of Banstead* (Oxford, 1912), 54.

[6] Essex Rec. Off. D/DP M 540. In this case the class of tenants bearing the burden were called *foremanni*.

[7] *Cal. Inq. Misc.* IV, pp. 86–7.　　　　[8] *Borough Cust.* I, 65.

[9] J.I. 1/1057 mm. 55*d*, 58, 58*d*. The butchers' liability is mentioned again in 1282: *Cal. Fine R. 1272–1307*, 161.

[10] *Cal. Inq. p.m.* II, p. 250.

[11] Du Boulay, *Lordship of Canterbury*, 309–10.

each cotman's house to be used in turn as a prison and for the cotmen themselves to guard the prisoners by day; by night they were to be in charge of all the tenants and under-tenants, apart from the cotmen.[1] As might be expected, it is the larger, or the more responsible, group that is burdened with the weightier duty of nocturnal custody.

As time passed and the manor changed, custodial duties by status sometimes transformed themselves into custodial duties by contract. Thus it was a Kentish practice to assign a mill to a tenant on the understanding that he would guard prisoners inside it. That such duties were enjoined upon the tenants of Faversham abbey mill has already been mentioned. A little later, in 1285, it is recorded that the custody of strangers in Kent devolved upon the tenants of sundry Kentish mills.[2] Later still, about 1313–14, South Mill, which was the prison of Milton hundred, and perhaps another mill in the same hundred, were held by the serjeanty of keeping prisoners.[3]

[1] Bland, Brown, and Tawney (eds.), *English economic history, select documents*, 61.

[2] D. & C. Canterbury MS E 24, f. 23 *b*.

[3] *Eyre of Kent*, I, pp. lxvi–lxvii, 147. 'Luth Mill' of the Year Book is almost certainly a misreading for South Mill. The Hadleigh cotmen, mentioned above, were required to keep their prisoners in the lord's mill, but it is not said that they were tenants of it.

VIII

THE GAOLER'S REMUNERATION
AND CONDUCT

IT has been explained that in the thirteenth century and possibly at other times some sheriffs employed working gaolers to take effective charge of county gaols.[1] The rates at which these men were employed varied from place to place and from generation to generation. Between 1235–6 and 1241–2 the gaoler of Warwick was paid about 10½d. a week[2] and in 1237–8 his colleague at Chester at almost exactly the same rate.[3] The Chester gaoler, however, was also a castle gate-keeper. The weekly rate at Stafford in 1230[4] and 1241–2[5] was a little over 9d.; that at York between 1225–6 and 1229–30 was 7d.[6] The York rate was apparently the same as that prevailing at Chichester in the earlier year.[7] At Bedford and Aylesbury in 1238–9 the wage was almost exactly 6d.[8] and it had been very close to that figure at Nottingham in 1203.[9] It was 5d. at Durham in 1238.[10] This was not particularly good pay. In the forties the bodyguard of a Welsh hostage might draw a weekly wage of 1s. 2d.[11] A century before, the wage of the warden of the Fleet, then, no doubt, a working gaoler, was set at 2s. 11d.[12]

At York these payments can be traced for more than thirty years (1225–61), at Stafford for a decade. At other prisons they

---

[1] For these arrangements see p. 147.

[2] *Pipe R.* 1242, ed. H. L. Cannon, 177.

[3] *Cheshire in Pipe R.* (Lancs & Ches. Rec. Soc. XCII), 37; *Cal. Lib. R.* 1226–40, 348.

[4] *Pipe R.* 1230 (P.R.S. n.s. IV), 232.   [5] Ibid. 1242, 9.

[6] C. P. Cooper, *History of the castle of York* (London, 1911), 91–2.

[7] *Rot. Litt. Claus.* II. 127; *Cal. Lib. R.* 1226–40, 20. This is on the assumption that there were at Chichester, as at York, two gaolers. The cost to the Exchequer, in respect of each place, was exactly equal in 1225–6.

[8] *Cal. Lib. R.* 1226–40, 420.

[9] *Pipe R.* 1203 (P.R.S. n.s. III), 164.   [10] *Cal. Lib. R.* 1226–40, 369.

[11] Ibid. 1240–5, 177–8.   [12] See p. 158.

seem to have been made for only a single year. For this reason, if for no other, it does not seem at all unlikely that, even in the thirteenth century, they were an exceptional rather than a regular method of providing gaolers with a livelihood. In later times references to such deductions from the county farm are hard to find. It is indeed the case that in 1346 the gaoler at Guildford was allowed 4*d.* a day,[1] and the crown nominees who filled that post more than a century later seem to have looked confidently to a 'fee' out of the county issues.[2] In Wiltshire, too, in 1389 and again in 1491 the gaoler was receiving £5 a year or about 2*s.* a week,[3] a rate which falls a little short of that applied at Guildford in the mid-fourteenth century. Much more commonly, however, crown nominees, when granted their patents, were simply told that they would receive the 'customary' wages and fees. Such phrases ominously suggest that the receipt of wages was uncertain. The gaoler appointed to Oakham in 1412 was indeed told that he might draw 3*d.* a day at the Exchequer, but it is significantly added that no precedent was to be thereby established.[4] By the mid-sixteenth century all memory of stipends for 'keepers' seems to have vanished.[5]

Much more important sources of revenue than payments at the Exchequer or by the hands of sheriffs were the various fees which gaolers collected from their prisoners. These fees were of great antiquity. They are first mentioned in the *Leis Willelme*, a compilation which appears to combine both pre-Conquest and post-Conquest customs. It is there laid down as the custom of Mercia that if a thief escape irrecoverably from his surety, the surety shall, after compurgation, forfeit certain sums. These sums include 4*d.* to the gaoler (*ceper*) who would have had charge of the

[1] E 372/191 m. 40.
[2] A grant of 6 September 1461 comprises the 'accustomed' fees: *Cal. Pat. R.* 1461–7, 43; on 24 October 1462 the terms were improved, for he was to receive the fees at the sheriff's hands: ibid. 211. On 12 April 1475 a successor was appointed with fees secured upon the issues of Cambridgeshire and Huntingdonshire: ibid. 1467–77, 513.
[3] *V.C.H. Wilts.* v, 22.   [4] *Cal. Pat. R.* 1408–13, 404.
[5] *Henry Brinklow's complaint of Roderyck Mors* (E.E.T.S., extra ser. XXII), 28.

prisoner if he had remained in custody and while in custody had been acquitted.[1] This fourpence is extremely like the release fee of later times. By the thirteenth century evidence for the practice of fee-collecting multiplies. In 1237 the constable of Oxford castle was instructed to ensure that neither the keeper of the gaol nor the porter of the castle gate should collect any fee from a certain clerk who was sent to him to guard.[2] The writ is so phrased as to imply that but for that prohibition fees would have been taken as a matter of course. Prisoners delivered in eyre, and in the custody of the marshal during their trial, had to pay a fee to the marshal before their release. This fee was made statutory in 1285,[3] and was being exacted in practice at least by 1272.[4] In 1283 some men arrested and put into the countess of Aumale's franchise prison at Carisbrooke had to pay for their release because such a payment was traditional and belonged to the liberty of the prison.[5] From this time examples of fee-paying are too common to be worth enumerating. Indeed the system of fee-paying expanded, rather than contracted, and remained in full vigour until in the later eighteenth century it came under the censure of Howard.[6]

In their simplest form these fees appear to have represented a contribution towards the costs of custody and were paid on release. Payment on release was, for example, the practice at Newgate by 1319,[7] at the town gaol of Romney by 1352,[8] and at the abbot of Crowland's gaol in 1480–1.[9] In 1323 it was declared to be lawful in regulations governing the marshalsea of Ireland.[10] It could, however, also happen that fees were collected on admission. In 1315 the sheriff of Norfolk received a fee for every

---

[1] *Leis Wl.* 51: Agnes J. Robertson, *Laws of the kings of England from Edmund to Henry I* (Cambridge, 1925), 255.

[2] *Close R.* 1234–7, 519.

[3] Westm. ii. c. 44. Ushers and vergers also collected fees.

[4] Helen M. Cam, *Liberties and communities in medieval England: collected studies in local administration and topography* (Cambridge, 1944), 145.

[5] *Sel. Cases in K.B.* i, 125.

[6] J. Howard, *The state of the prisons in England and Wales* (Warrington, 1780), 36.

[7] *Speculum,* xviii, 236. [8] *Borough Cust.* i, 5.

[9] Coke, 2 *Instit.* (1671 ed.), 43. [10] *Cal. Pat. R.* 1321–4, 363.

prisoner brought into Norwich castle from King's Lynn,[1] in 1358 the keeper of Winchester gaol benefited from a similar custom,[2] and in 1512 the keeper of Nottingham borough gaol collected a comprehensive fee for admission and 'irons'.[3] There was, of course, every inducement for the gaoler to collect his fee at the earliest rather than the latest moment. If the prisoner escaped from custody the gaoler lost the fee besides incurring a fine for the escape, and he also lost it, we must suppose, if the prisoner was hanged. The exaction of admission fees, however, was barely in the public interest since it tended to frustrate the ends of justice. Such fees were, in fact, closely akin to the fines or 'ransoms' levied upon prisoners on their admission to custody or upon the escorts who accompanied them.[4] *Britton* condemned them[5] and, less surprisingly, the author of the *Mirror*.[6] One of the grounds of complaint against Edmund le Lorimer, when he was dismissed from Newgate in 1319, was that he charged admission fees.[7]

Some prisons, as we shall see, possessed or could be equipped with several types of accommodation, the comfort of which varied.[8] Prisoners of high rank or charged only with light offences might hope to secure as of right a foothold in more luxurious apartments. Others might purchase that right. Within the period 1275–8 several Jews, imprisoned in the Tower, paid the substantial sum of 40s. or 50s. *pro bona prisona* or *pro libera prisona*.[9] Such payments presumably began in the form of bargains between prisoner and gaoler and could perhaps be stigmatized as bribes paid by the first to the second. By the fourteenth century, however, they had been regularized and dignified by the name of fees *pro sueta* or *pro suavitate prisone*.[10] One form of *suavitas*, or 'suet', though not the only one, which such fees might purchase was the removal of 'irons', a phrase to be explained below.[11]

[1] *Cal. Chart. R.* 1300–26, 284.   [2] *Cal. Inq. Misc.* III, p. 160.
[3] *Recs. of Nottingham*, III. 118.
[4] See p. 195.   [5] *Britton*, I, 46.   [6] See p. 169.   [7] See pp. 154–5.
[8] For the various forms of accommodation see p. 351.
[9] E 101/249/22.
[10] For a more careful discussion of the subject see *E.H.R.* LXXVI, 633. Cf. ibid. XXIV, 506; XXV, 307.   [11] See pp. 177–9.

Gaoler's remuneration and conduct

There is no doubt that the practice of collecting fees from prisoners in any circumstances made some moralists and legislators uneasy. The more moderate opinion of the later thirteenth century is that expressed in *Britton*, namely, that none should take more from a prisoner 'pur sa garde' than 4*d.*, that 'the poor' should pay nothing, and that imprisonment should not be prolonged because the prisoner could not meet his obligations.[1] The author of the *Mirror*, in a characteristic outburst, declared all fee-gathering to be an abuse.[2] Such radicalism cut little ice, though twice in the later fourteenth century the collection of fees was actually forbidden by statute. By the Statute of Labourers of 1361 sheriffs and gaolers were instructed to receive in county prisons without fee all labourers offending against the statute if those labourers should be transferred into that custody from the prisons of their lords. This prohibition was made to extend to both release and admission fees.[3] The effectiveness of this statute may well be doubted, for its provisions in this respect had to be reiterated in the Statute of Cambridge.[4] Neither the crown nor parliament, however, normally interfered with fee-collecting or, except in the case of the 'national' prisons, sought to regulate it. It is not until 1444 that there is any legislation beyond vague statutory denunciations of extortionate conduct. A statute of that year limited fees in all prisons, apart from the Fleet, to 4*d.* a prisoner,[5] but probably by this time such a fee was unrealistically low.

The governing bodies of certain towns took the matter more seriously. The charter granted to Swansea in 1306, which no doubt embodies the practice prevailing in certain towns in England, declares that only suspect felons shall pay fees and then only if they spend a night in prison. The fee is limited to 4*d.* a head. If a prisoner were bailed, surrendered to his bail, and returned to custody, the fee was not to be collected a second time.[6] The practice at the Northgate prison in Chester in 1340–1 was

---

[1] *Britton*, I, 46–7.   [2] *Mirror*, 160.
[3] 34 Edw. III, c. 9.   [4] 12 Ric. II, c. 9.   [5] 23 Hen. VI, c. 9.
[6] *British borough charters, 1216–1307*, ed. A. Ballard and J. Tait (Cambridge, 1923), 225.

169

somewhat similar. The fee was the same and could only be collected from suspect felons. Such suspects, moreover, must have
been kept in custody for more: han one night.[1] At Bristol it was
enacted that those sentenced to penal imprisonment by the mayor
were to be quit of fees.[2] By a new prison code for Coventry
issued in 1515, prisoners held for treason and felony were to pay
on delivery only 4*d.* to the keeper, 1*d.* to the under-keeper, and
2*d.* for 'irons'. A prisoner arrested 'for mater...under the some
of 40*d.*' was to pay nothing. Taking what was called a 'double fee'
was interdicted except for 'urgent causes openly known'.[3]

Regulation of fees began in London in 1346, when the keeper
of Newgate was limited to collecting 4*d.* from each prisoner
delivered.[4] In 1393 penal detainees in Newgate and Ludgate were
exempted from fees.[5] In 1431 prisoners charged with offences
less serious than felony were to pay a maximum fee of 8*d.* and
those charged with felony three times that sum.[6] This was reiterated in April 1488. At the same time the maximum fee at
Ludgate was fixed at 8*d.* and at the Counters at 4*d.*, and penal
detainees at all four prisons were exempted from paying them.[7]
A few years before, in 1476, a prison official at one of the Counters
had attempted to charge double that fee and had been punished
for so doing.[8]

These municipal regulations seem to have several features in
common. First, fees are to be reasonable and related to a fixed
scale. Secondly, suspect felons are to be treated less leniently,
penal detainees more leniently, than other types of prisoner.
Thirdly, there must be a genuine incarceration. Prisoners who
merely entered an appearance at a prison and were released the
same day on bail or for other cause presumably caused the gaoler
no expense and therefore earned him no reward. Such committals without pernoctation were no doubt quite common. Of

[1] R. H. Morris, *Chester in the Plantagenet and Tudor reigns* (Eccleston, 1895),
232–3.
[2] *Little Red Book of Bristol*, ed. F. B. Bickley (Bristol, 1908), II, 55.
[3] *Coventry Leet Bk.* II, 643–4.
[4] *Cal. Lr. Bks. G*, 74.
[5] *Mun. Gild.* I. 524.
[6] *Cal. Lr. Bks. K*, 126.
[7] Jorn. 9, fos. 172, 176*b*, 179.
[8] Jorn. 8, f. 123*b*.

the ten persons committed to the Fleet between 7 October and 8 November 1350 seven are said to have been released without pernoctation, although the warden, unlike some of the municipal gaolers mentioned above, was entitled to his fee.[1] The lack of indulgence shown to suspect felons may reflect the feeling, noticeable elsewhere, that suspects, even if unconvicted, were tainted with crime. The exemption of penal detainees may have more explanations than one. The most likely explanation is, however, that the governing body of the town hoped to extort a fine from the detainee and liberate him on its payment, and did not wish to discourage such a payment by making the imprisonment costly in itself.

While the king's government meddled very little with the payment of fees in county gaols and municipal prisons, it sought to control the fees taken in 'national' prisons, that is to say by the marshals and by the warden of the Fleet. In 1307, just after the marshalsea of England had been taken into the king's hand on the death of Roger Bigod, earl of Norfolk,[2] an agreement about fees was drawn up between the crown and Bigod's successor. Every knight, man of religion, royal bailiff, or tenant (*renter*) of the church who was in the marshal's custody was to pay $\frac{1}{2}$ mark and every prisoner of any other degree $4d$.[3] Thus we find creeping into the fee system an element of discrimination between classes or income groups. This tariff system also prevailed in contemporary France[4] and was common in England in later times.[5] How long the marshal's scale endured cannot at present be said, or whether it was ultimately operative in the King's Bench prison. In 1401 fees were prescribed for prisoners committed to the other marshalsea, the marshalsea of the household. None was to pay more than $4d$.[6]

The warden of the Fleet customarily received a fee of $2s$. $4d$. from each prisoner committed to his charge. This he was receiving

---

[1] E 101/508/13.   [2] See p. 158.
[3] *Sel. Cases in K.B.* I, p. cxlix.
[4] *Toronto Law Jnl*, V, 394–5 and n.
[5] Allardyce Nicoll (ed.), *Shakespeare in his own age* (Cambridge, 1964), 94.
[6] *Rot. Parl.* III. 469.

by 1337[1] and, as has been said,[2] he collected it even from prisoners who did not pernoctate. By 1561 this fee had become the discharge fee for the virtually destitute; men of greater substance paid far more.[3] Before that year the Fleet fees are not known to have been the subject of any published act or ordinance, although in 1401 the council, with the chancellor and other judges in attendance, were ordered to inquire into them.[4] When the release fee for common gaols was settled statutorily in 1444, the right of the warden of the Fleet to take higher fees than those that the statute sanctioned was protected.[5]

In all that has preceded, the assumption has been made that fees of all kinds were paid directly by the prisoner to the gaoler and that the gaoler pocketed them. This was no doubt the eventual arrangement everywhere and perhaps in some prisons the only arrangement that ever was in force. It was, however, sometimes the case that the fees were payable directly to the crown or constituted an allowance to a sheriff when accounting at the Exchequer. The fees collected at Guildford were thus accounted for, at least in 1295[6] and 1346.[7] Fees for 'suet' of prison taken in fourteenth-century Cheshire by the officers of hundreds[8] and in the fourteenth-century duchy of Lancaster by forest officers,[9] and fines or fees levied in the same century in the great sessions of South Wales accrued to the crown likewise.[10] Perhaps the various itinerant courts struck more bargains with prisoners *pro sueta* than we have yet the means to estimate. At all events, in or about 1274, the eyre in Buckinghamshire accepted a fine from a woman to enable her to lie more comfortably in prison. The payment on this occasion, though reduced from its original assessment, was a heavy one, too heavy to allow us to equate it with an ordinary 'suet'.[11] Like the 'suets', however, that were collected

[1] E 372/184 m. 49. The same payments were being made in 1350: E 372/194 m. 45 [46]; E 101/508/13.   [2] See p. 171.
[3] *Toronto Law Jnl*, v, 396.   [4] *Rot. Parl.* III. 469.
[5] 23 Hen. VI c. 9.
[6] *Surrey Pipe R. for 1295* (Surrey Rec. Soc. [VII]), 28.
[7] E 372/191 m. 40.   [8] *E.H.R.* XXIV, 506.
[9] *John of Gaunt's Register 1379–83* (Camden 3rd ser. LVII), II, p. 297.
[10] S.C. 6/1158/10 m. 2.   [11] *Cal. Close R.* 1272–9, 103.

in the great sessions of South Wales, it was a payment to the crown direct.

Where the custody of a county gaol was withheld absolutely or effectively from a sheriff and entrusted to the keeper of a castle or to a crown pensioner, it was, of course, that keeper or that pensioner who received the fees. This was one of the reasons why those sheriffs who claimed possession of castles so much deplored their alienation.[1] The prison fees that they collected, when they did collect them, though possibly including some surplus for themselves, were basically an appropriation in aid of their farms. If another man was collecting the fees, the sheriff could not show any receipts from that source in his account. The Barons of the Exchequer did not always accept that situation with equanimity. In 1336–7 they tried to charge the sheriff of Shropshire and Staffordshire with fees from Stafford gaol, although the custody was in the hands of a crown nominee. On this occasion the king intervened and the sheriff appears to have successfuly craved allowance.[2] At Norwich in 1383 the situation was reversed. The sheriff appears to have claimed the fees which the keeper of the castle and gaol considered to be his due. This time the crown intervened to protect the keeper, but with what success is not recorded.[3]

Whatever might be done to limit or control the payment of fees, the fact remains that in most circumstances payment was unavoidable. Consequently there must always have been a band of needy prisoners who, cleared by judgement of the court or for other reasons no longer liable to imprisonment, could nevertheless not be enlarged because they were in debt to their gaolers. Here private charity might come to the rescue. From the later fourteenth century testators, besides relieving prisoners in other ways, began to make provision for redemption. The first observed example of this practice comes from a will of 1384.[4] Some such bequests, it is true, were designed wholly or partly for debtors and trespassers who were held in custody not because

[1] See p. 149.   [2] *Cal. Close R.* 1337–9, 299.
[3] *Cal. Pat. R.* 1381–5, 285, 287.   [4] *Hust. Wills,* II. 242.

they owed money to their gaolers, or not wholly for that reason, but because they could not pay their debts or fines.[1] This form of redemption was overwhelmingly popular with testators from the early years of Queen Elizabeth I.[2] But in earlier times the objects were more mixed. Cardinal Beaufort in his will of 1447 mentions those who lie both for crimes and for debt.[3] Though some wills vaguely state that money is left so that 'hit helpe nede men oute of pryson',[4] it was possible, as in a will of 1534,[5] or in the foundation indentures of Henry VII's chapel at Westminster,[6] expressly to limit the object to the payment of fees. Such payments for release were no doubt also made as gifts *inter vivos*. Among other charges lodged against him in 1389 the keeper of Ludgate was apparently accused of withholding from his prisoners the alms contributed for their release.[7]

Since the late eighteenth century all fee-paying as a means of financing government has been under condemnation in Britain, and it is hard for us now to put ourselves back into an age when the practice was a normal one. Besides this, anything that may be loosely termed 'extortion' by officials is peculiarly repugnant to our modes of thought. Yet such fee-paying and, indeed, extortion are still well recognized in certain emergent countries and are perhaps an ineluctable feature of a certain stage of man's development. Even in more sophisticated societies it is necessary to pay persons who are not officials and at prices that are not regulated for goods and services which the citizen is forced to purchase in order to keep within the law, and the margin between the just

[1] *Reg. of Hen. Chichele* (Cant. and York Soc. XLII), II. 52 (1415, debtors owing not more than 20s.); *Some Oxford Wills* (Oxford Rec. Soc. [XXXIX]), 48 (1492, debtors and trespassers); *Journal of ecclesiastical history*, XVI, 185 (1405, 1505, small debtors).   [2] See p. 213.
[3] *Testam. Vetusta*, I, 250 (will proved 1447).
[4] *Fifty earliest English wills* (E.E.T.S. LXXVIII), 23.
[5] *Testam. Vetusta*, II, 667.
[6] The indentures provide for a requiem mass at the king's death which a number of great officials are expected to attend. On attendance they are to receive varying sums of money totalling £7. If they fail to attend, the money is to be paid to prisoners who lie for fees only. The prisoners are to be selected by the two chief justices: *Cal. Close R.* 1500–9, pp. 143–4.
[7] *Cal. Plea & Mem. R.* 1381–1412, 158.

and 'extortionate' price for such services is hard to draw in theory and seldom attempted in practice. These reflections may make us pause before condemning outright the system that has been described. At least it may be said in defence of the system that, though it bore upon the prisoner with ever-increasing weight, it was *pari passu* subjected to mitigatory regulation. If fees became heavier and more numerous as time went on, they also became, at least in theory, less arbitrary.

Besides the various wages and fees that have been described above, the gaoler might enjoy another source of revenue. This was the sale to the prisoner of various goods and services. The most notable of these services was the leasing of accommodation or 'chamber hire'. Naked chambers, however, offer cold comfort, and many prisoners sought and in fact purchased from their gaolers food, drink, fuel, light, beds, and bedding. Outside the prisons of the cities of London and Coventry information about such charges is not abundant. It is known, however, that by 1307 board-and-lodging charges for prisoners in the custody of the marshal of the Exchequer had been fixed. They amounted to ½ mark daily for each prisoner, whether the prisoner were a sheriff or some other bailiff,[1] and in 1351 the same charge seems to have been levied by the marshals serving the King's Bench and the Exchequer in Ireland. It was then severely reduced, to ½ mark a term.[2] This reduction was no doubt provoked by Ireland's relative poverty, but the reduced rate may possibly correspond to what it was thought to be reasonable to charge in the minor prisons of England. Such scraps of evidence about lodging charges as have survived from the next century present a very variable picture. In 1468 the deputy keeper of the King's Bench prison charged a London merchant in his custody 20s. a week for boarding him in his house. This was perhaps a top price for the best accommodation. Weekly rates in East Anglian prisons, where the accommodation was probably mediocre, varied from 1s. 8d. to 2s. a week.[3] In 1534 complaint was made against the

[1] *Sel. Cases in K.B.* I, p. cl.   [2] *Cal. Close R.* 1349–54, 292.
[3] *Toronto Law Jnl*, V, 396 and n.

gaoler of Norwich Guildhall that he sold ale to prisoners at 3*d.*
and 4*d.* a gallon, whereas in city alehouses the best ale could be
had for 2*d.*[1] Brinkelow, writing at about the same time, complained that for commons and a bed a prisoner must pay four
times more than at the dearest inn.[2] This, however, is perhaps a
jaundiced view.

By the later sixteenth century particulars about lodging charges
begin to grow abundant. In the Fleet, according to a document of
1561, there was graded accommodation, varying in price from
room to room. By this time, too, the warden ran a kitchen and
bar, where prices were likewise adjusted to the prisoner's rank.[3]
For the late sixteenth and early seventeenth centuries there is
indeed much detail about the provision of food in London prisons,
and evidence that prison-keepers tried to create a monopoly by
making the importation of food difficult. There is evidence, too,
of the segregation of prisoners in messes, distinguished from one
another by the social standing or wealth of prisoners.[4] It is not
possible here to trace all this in detail. It is, however, reasonable
to conclude that many of the practices of those later days were
not merely established but widespread in the later middle ages.
Indeed we know for certain that in both London and Coventry
charges for lodging and diet were regulated from the fourteenth
and fifteenth centuries as part of a general system for introducing
good government into the prisons of those cities. The details are
deferred for later exposition.[5]

Fees, 'suets', rents, profits from victuals and drink, all these
were at some time, if not at all times, a form of revenue which
authority was prepared to recognize. But outside these regulated
exactions there was much scope for the crudest extortion, and such
extortion was probably practised widely. But what is 'extortion'?
The distinction between an illegal act and a tolerated irregularity
is even today not an easy one to draw and was drawn within our

[1] *Recs. of Norwich*, ii, 165.   [2] *Complaint of Roderyck Mors*, 27–8.
[3] *Toronto Law Jnl*, v, 395–6.
[4] Nicoll (ed.), *Shakespeare in his own age*, pp. 87–100, esp. p. 96.
[5] See pp. 188–91.

period far less readily. Not only within that period but for long afterwards few would have doubted that gaolers, who had no adequate wages and sometimes no wages at all, were entitled to look upon their prisoners as a source of profit. It was not exploitation of prisoners that was in doubt but the lengths to which exploitation might be carried.

Having thus established the nature of the gaoler's reward, we may now consider how justly he merited it. Had he a good name among his contemporaries or a bad? It must be said at the outset that charges of misconduct against prison-keepers, whether those keepers were sheriffs or other 'principals', or common gaolers or other 'agents', are extremely common and derive from all periods. Such misconduct might have one of two effects: it might prejudice the course of justice by interrupting or altogether preventing the imprisonment, or it might damage the prisoner's health or estate. Refusal to admit a prisoner, either at all or before an extortionate payment had been made by his escort, negligent custody resulting in an escape or unauthorized release—all these might have the former effect. Duress of prison, including the needless or excessive use of 'irons', withholding the 'alms' contributed towards the prisoner's support,[1] obstructing confessions,[2] rejecting bail where bail was legitimate, raising lawful or customary fees to an extortionate point—all these illustrate misconduct of the other sort. Some of these activities will be more carefully examined when the story of admission and bail, release and escape has been reached. Others will be more completely understood when the nature of prisoners' alms[3] and of hard prison[4] is explained. There is, however, no better place than this in which to examine the practice of 'ironing'.

'Irons'—a comprehensive term used to cover chains, fetters, manacles, rings, and collars—were a regular part of the equipment

[1] The fifteenth-century oath of the keeper of Newgate includes a promise that the keeper will not do this: Jorn. 4, f. 166*b*.
[2] Keepers who obstructed confessions were in 1268 denied canonical burial: *Councils & synods*, ed. F. M. Powicke and C. R. Cheney, II (2), 750; cf. ibid. 994–5 (Exeter Stats. of 1287).
[3] See pp. 320 ff.   [4] See p. 180.

of a gaol, whether in a county[1] or a town,[2] and were handed on from sheriff to sheriff or from gaoler to gaoler.[3] Their moderate use for suspect felons was sanctioned, particularly if there was a risk of escapes.[4] For defaulting accountants their imposition was expressly enjoined by statute,[5] and *Britton* said that it was permissible to fix them upon those imprisoned for trespasses in parks and vivaries.[6] They might be fastened to prisoners on their transfer from one prison to another.[7] Bracton would have it that prisoners, when actually on trial, should not have their hands tied, though their feet might sometimes be shackled (*aliquando compeditas*) to guard against escapes.[8] One text of *Britton* declares that all fettering in court is wrong, another that it is permissible but must be light.[9] At all events shackling in court seems to have been the custom by 1293.[10] 'Irons', therefore, were meant in theory to secure the prisoner and not to make his imprisonment harder or more painful. Bracton deplored their immoderate use[11] and the author of the *Mirror* condemned the loading of unconvicted persons with 'iron' and declared that irons ought never to weigh more than 12 oz.[12] It was certainly in no way in keeping with a doctrine so relatively mild that a servant of the keeper of Newgate should in 1289–90 have bound a man so tightly with irons that his neck and spine were broken.[13] Nor was the action of the mayor of Exeter to be condoned when in 1495 he fastened a woman's legs in irons weighing 30 lb. and also chained her.[14]

Like so much else in prison life 'irons' and freedom from

---

[1] For an early instance see *Pipe R.* 1164 (P.R.S. VII), 4.

[2] Cf. the requirements that the first keepers of Ludgate (1378) should provide manacles and chains: *Cal. Lr. Bks. H*, 97.

[3] E.g. *Arch. Cant.* LXXXI, 211 (Kent, 1378); *Cat. Anc. D.* VI C 7243 (Nottinghamshire and Derbyshire, 1537).

[4] *Fleta*, II, p. 68.   [5] Westm. II. c. 11.   [6] *Britton*, I, 44.

[7] *Sel. Cases in K.B.* II, 149–51 (1293). The petitioner in this case objected that a criminal was allowed to wander about without 'irons', implying that 'irons' in such circumstances would have been normal. The gaoler replied that his prisoner, who had to be moved from London into Kent, could not walk in 'irons'.

[8] *Bracton*, II, 385.   [9] *Britton*, I, 35 and n.   [10] *Rot. Parl.* I. 95.
[11] *Bracton*, II, 299.   [12] *Mirror*, 52, 160.   [13] C 144/30/16.
[14] *Sel. Cases in Star Chamber*, [I.], pp. cxxxvi, 52.

'irons' came to be connected with payments by the prisoner to the gaoler. It is evident that prisoners, who could afford to do so, were accustomed to purchase quittance from 'irons' or perhaps sometimes the exchange of onerous bonds for lighter ones. If such freedom or such alleviation was permissible at all, it is not unreasonable that it should have been paid for, since the payment constituted an insurance entered into by the gaoler against the consequences of an escape. Such indulgence on the gaoler's part, though risky, was always humane and often reasonable. It was, however, but a short step from humanity and reason to what seems today neither reasonable nor humane: the deliberate 'ironing' of prisoners who did not need it, in order to secure a fee for the remission of irons. This practice, however much it may have been disliked, was incapable of prohibition, and the only step that authority could take was to limit the fee charged. The process may be traced in the prisons of the city of London.

The first set of London prison regulations, those issued in 1356 for the control of Newgate, forbade the exaction of fines or 'extortionate' charges for putting on irons or taking them off.[1] When new regulations were drawn up in 1393, and extended to Ludgate, a sum of £5 was sanctioned as a removal fee.[2] In 1431 after Newgate had been rebuilt and was consequently stronger, the 'ironing' of freemen in that prison, if charged with light offences, was altogether prohibited but, where the charges were graver, 'irons' might be affixed and removed in return for a reasonable 'suet'.[3] This was reiterated in April 1488 and extended to the other three prisons.[4] In 1530 a set of detailed rules about 'ironing' in the Counters was drawn up and rates fixed according to the scale of the debt or damages assessed were set for striking off 'irons'.[5]

Information is available about 'ironing' fees in other places but is less specific. In 1358 the keeper of Winchester gaol was accustomed to take from each prisoner delivered 5*d*. 'for his irons'.[6] As has been said, the gaoler of Nottingham town was

---

[1] *Mun. Gild.* I. 47.   [2] Ibid. 524.   [3] *Cal. Lr. Bks. K*, 126.
[4] Jorn. 9, fos. 170*b* ff.   [5] Jorn. 13, fos. 212*b*, 213.
[6] *Cal. Inq. Misc.* III, pp. 160–1.

12-2

collecting something on this account by 1512.[1] Regulations made in Coventry in 1515 permitted the collection of a small fee for 'irons' at the time of a prisoner's delivery.[2] In 1533 a man at Ilchester was giving the keeper of the county gaol of Somerset as much as 1s. a week to go without 'irons'.[3] Such payments became customary and continued into Howard's day.[4]

'Ironing' was only one form of duress to which a prisoner might be subjected. Placing him in the depths of the gaol, when neither his suspected offences nor status in society warranted such confinement, was another. A complaint that this had been done was lodged against the keeper of Newgate in 1314[5] and no doubt many others could be found. The variability in the rates charged for better or worse accommodation, which has already been referred to,[6] was in essence no more than a respectable cloak for the practice of shutting up or threatening to shut up prisoners in dark and damp vaults and liberating them from that accommodation or the threat of it in return for bribes. Duress indeed could exhibit itself in many horrible ways. Reynold of Coldingham has collected for posterity several twelfth-century instances of exceptional brutality.[7] In 1260–1 William de Braose's bailiff in the honor of Bramber was convicted of keeping a man whom he had imprisoned in a tower of Bramber castle naked by day and forcing him by night to stand or sit in a pool of cold water so that his feet rotted away.[8] It seems that the keeper of Rutland forest acted rather similarly about 1269, for he thrust several trespassers into a gaol at Allexton (Leicestershire) which was full of water at the bottom.[9] In 1274 the gaoler of York is said to have tied a prisoner naked to a post and kept him starving;[10] the feet of a prisoner in a Norfolk prison c. 1285–6 were so 'putrified' by his hard usage that he could not walk;[11] and in 1288 the constable of Exeter castle, who seems at that time to have had control

[1] See p. 168. [2] *Coventry Leet Bk.* II, 644. [3] *L. & P.* VI, p. 392.
[4] Howard, *State of the Prisons* (1780 ed.), 17, 18.
[5] *Cal. Pat. R.* 1313–17, 237. [6] See p. 175.
[7] *Reginaldis Monachi Dunelm. Libellus* (Surtees Soc. I), esp. p. 42.
[8] J.I. 1/911 m. 8. [9] *Sel. Pleas of Forest*, 50, 52.
[10] *Rot. Hund.* I. III. [11] *Arch. Rev.* II, 210.

of Exeter gaol, threw a defaulting accountant head first down a staircase and kept him chained and without food.[1] Chancellor Robert Baldock is reputed to have died in Newgate of his torments.[2] The keeper of Oxford town gaol in 1369 was rumoured to be beating one of his prisoners inhumanly and was reproved by the crown for so doing.[3] Accusations brought against John Bottisham, keeper of Ludgate, in 1389 included that of procuring prisoners to beat another prisoner in bed.[4] In 1449 the keeper of Newgate was committed to a Counter because *horribiliter violavit* a woman in his custody.[5] These specific charges support the credibility of more general ones, made by *Fleta* in the late thirteenth century, that gaolers were wont to hang their prisoners up by their feet or tear off their nails.[6]

Duress of prison was applied particularly, though not of course exclusively, as a means of inducing men already in prison to turn approver and appeal other men not in prison and not necessarily otherwise suspected. From the men thus brought within their power sheriffs and gaolers could secure either the normal fees and lodging charges or bribes for release. Such conduct was attributed to the gaoler of York castle in 1274,[7] to the sheriff of Nottinghamshire in 1291,[8] and to the gaoler of Stafford in 1293.[9] *Britton* numbered it among the abuses into which the eyre should particularly inquire,[10] though it never seems to have formed one of the 'chapters', and it remained such a common offence that it had to be expressly condemned by statute in 1327 on petition to the crown and brought within the purview of the justices of gaol delivery.[11] The statute did not check the practice and had to be re-enacted in 1340.[12] Even after that complaints continued. They

---

[1] *State Trials of Edward I* (Camden 3rd ser. IX), 51.
[2] *Chrons. Edw. I and II*, I. 334.
[3] *Mun. Civitatis Oxonie* (Oxf. Hist. Soc. [LXXI]), 144.
[4] *Cal. Plea & Mem. R.* 1381–1412, 157.   [5] Jorn. 5, f. 16.
[6] *Fleta*, II, p. 68.   [7] *Rot. Hund.* I. 115.   [8] *Sel. Cases in K.B.* II, 53.
[9] *Will. Salt Arch. Soc.* VI (1), 267–8.
[10] *Britton*, I, 87. He refers also to the opposite practice of hindering approvers from appealing the guilty.
[11] 1 Edw. III, St. I, c. 7; *Rot. Parl.* II. 9, 12.
[12] 14 Edw. III, St. I, c. 10.

are to be found on the rolls of parliament in 1343[1] and were among the offences imputed to a gaoler of York castle in 1388.[2] In 1355 it was alleged that sheriffs, constables, and gaolers had themselves put on commissions of oyer and terminer so that they might indict and, in consequence of indictment, imprison innocent persons until those persons should make fine with the gaolers for 'suet' of prison and with the sheriffs for bail. The inclusion of the officials in such commissions seems thereupon to have been forbidden.[3] In 1376 it was alleged that sheriffs, under-sheriffs, and gaolers were putting themselves into commissions of the peace and similarly indicting the innocent. The victims were thereupon forced to pay fines or fees for admission to the gaol, for 'suet' of prison, for bail, for their trial, and eventually, after acquittal, for their enlargement. From these commissions likewise, sheriffs and gaolers were excluded.[4]

It must not be overlooked that most of the atrocity stories which have been recited come from men and women who were already tainted with criminality and who were set against authority. Prison-keepers are seldom heard in their own defence. When they are, they naturally tell a different tale. Thus the constable of Exeter, accused, as we have seen, of enormities, merely said in answer to the charges that the prisoner in question was arrested for the arrears of his account and held in prison until bailed.[5]

Nor would it be in the least just to minimize the prison-keeper's difficulties. First, he lacked, as we have seen, an adequate or stable income, which led him, not without public approval, to make money 'on the side'. Secondly, although authority would not openly condone bad conduct, it was no less hot against escapes, and bitterly complained if prisoners, whether 'felons' or 'debtors', got loose.[6] Thirdly, the work which gaolers had to do was, as it is still, dangerous. Lawlessness and violence were endemic in England, and the violent did not cease from violence

[1] *Rot. Parl.* II. 141.   [2] *Cal. Pat. R.* 1385–9, 551.
[3] *Rot. Parl.* II. 265.   [4] Ibid. 335.
[5] *State Trials of Edw. I*, 52; and see pp. 180–1.   [6] See chapters X and XI.

upon confinement. Prisoners were always trying to break prison and this exposed the gaolers not only to legal punishment but to death or injury. About 1287 the gaoler of Bristol was killed by prisoners,[1] and so in 1325 was the gate-keeper of Newgate prison.[2] Sir Robert de Walkefare, with his companions, escaping from Corfe castle in 1326, killed the keeper on the way out.[3] Next year some prisoners at Pontefract, egged on by the Dominican Thomas of Dunheved, likewise killed the keeper but failed to escape.[4] In 1346 and 1349 two successive gaolers of Cambridge met their death in the same way, the second of them stabbed with his own knife.[5] About 1441, some prisoners in Winchester gaol severely beat the gaoler's servant with their own fetters and chains, as he was leaning over the stocks in which they were confined to search them.[6] The warden of the Marshalsea was described just before his murder in 1381 as 'a tormentor without pity',[7] and the keeper of Maidstone was numbered among the 'great extortioners' of Kent in Cade's proclamation.[8] They were perhaps typical of their class. At least we have yet to find in medieval art or literature a prison-keeper worthy to stand at the Judgement Seat beside Dr Primrose's gaoler[9] or Dr Johnson's friend Richard Akerman.[10]

It has been said that to a degree prisoners were protected from hard usage at common law.[11] More specifically, if death ensued from cruel forms of imprisonment, the gaoler was deemed guilty of homicide, and in theory a coroner's jury could return such a verdict.[12] No such verdict against a common gaoler has indeed been traced. A Trumpington landholder, however, who about

[1] *Trans. Bristol and Glos. Arch. Soc.* XXII, 163.
[2] *Cal. of City Coroners' R.* 121–2.
[3] *Chrons. Edw. I and II,* I. 311.   [4] Ibid. 337.
[5] W. M. Palmer, *Cambridge castle* (Cambridge, 1928), 19.
[6] *Cal. Pat. R.* 1436–41, 489.
[7] C. Oman, *The great revolt of 1381* (Oxford, 1906), 199.
[8] *Documents illustrative of medieval Kentish society* (Kent Arch. Soc. Rec. Brch. XVIII), 221 and n.
[9] *Vicar of Wakefield,* chapter xxv.
[10] *Boswell's life of Johnson,* s.a. 1777, 1780.   [11] See p. 178.
[12] R. F. Hunnisett, *The medieval coroner* (Cambridge, 1961), 35–6.

1260 caused a thief to be maltreated and hanged in his private prison, was condemned,[1] and the gaoler of Newgate's servant who in 1289–90 caused the death of a prisoner by duress of prison was hanged.[2] In another way, too, the gaoler was prohibited from doing his prisoner an injury. If the prisoner was too sick to travel without incurring the risk of death, the gaoler need not send him. This appears to have been settled law by 1320 at the latest,[3] and was still a possible plea in extenuation of the non-appearance of a prisoner in 1470.[4] Statute law at certain points also protected the prisoner. In 1285 debtors and defaulting accountants who were injured by over-rigorous imprisonment were given an action of trespass against the gaoler responsible.[5] The creation of false approvers by sheriffs and gaolers was, as has been said,[6] likewise condemned.

By the fourteenth century we begin to see signs, in some quarters at least, that positive steps were being taken to find men of responsible character to act as gaolers. London began to set an example in 1356 when it was ordained that Newgate should not be let to farm and that only men of good character should be appointed keepers of it. The keepers were to swear that they would not act extortionately.[7] By regulations of a slightly later date the sheriffs were required to promise that they would not sell the keepership.[8] A few years after this, Ludgate prison appears upon the scene and in 1386 it was ordained that its keepers should forfeit their offices for proved extortion.[9] The Counters appear as prisons at almost the same moment as Ludgate. In 1393 the

---

[1] W. M. Palmer (ed.), *The assizes held at Cambridge in A.D. 1260* (Linton, 1930), p. 32.

[2] J.I. 1/547 A m. 6*d*; for the inquest upon the victim see p. 178 n. 13.

[3] *Sel. Cases in K.B.* IV, 103.

[4] *Yr. Bk. 10 Edw. IV & 49 Hen. VI* (S.S.), 44.   [5] Westm. II. c. 11.

[6] See p. 181.   [7] *Cal. Lr. Bks. G*, 74.

[8] *Mun. Gild.* I. 46–7. These regulations seem to be an expansion of those of 1356 (see preceding note) and therefore of later date. They also seem to be later than 1370 since there is embodied in them an extension of the regulations of that date upon a different subject (see p. 185 n. 1). On the other hand, since they do not mention Ludgate or the Counters they are probably earlier than *c.* 1380 (see pp. 108, 110).

[9] *Cal. Lr. Bks. H*, 292.

farming of those prisons to their porters, a practice which had formerly prevailed, was interdicted.[1] In 1421 it was decreed that the keeperships of none of the city prisons should be sold, a prohibition which, in this respect, put Ludgate and the Counters on the same footing as Newgate.[2] As a further safeguard the corporation decided in 1431 that the keeper of Newgate should be annually chosen, which meant, no doubt, that he should be annually confirmed in his office, and that he should give security not only for keeping the prisoners safely but also for carrying out his duties faithfully.[3] In April 1488 these requirements were extended to the other three prisons,[4] and there is evidence that, so far as Newgate was concerned, security was being enforced in 1519.[5] At Newgate the regulations of 1431 were supplemented soon after by a more specific form of oath, administered to the keeper in English, whereby he swore to keep his prisoners well and truly, not to withhold from them their alms and 'provents', and to observe the city ordinances controlling the gate and prison.[6]

Other steps were taken in the later fourteenth century which were designed to elevate the conduct of the city gaolers. In or about 1370 the officers of Newgate were included in a prohibition against engaging in such 'degrading' mercantile pursuits as brewing and baking.[7] The prohibition applied primarily to the mayor, aldermen, and sheriffs, and the comprehension of the officers of Newgate with it perhaps attests the enhanced respectability of those persons. A little later such activities as haulage, regrating victuals, and retailing ale were added to the list of 'degrading' trades.[8] In 1383 the porters of the Counters were subjected to the same prohibition.[9] A safeguard against possible misconduct of a different sort was provided in 1378 when it was

---

[1] *Mun. Gild.* I. 522. For the date see *Cal. Lr. Bks. H*, 402.

[2] *Cal. Lr. Bks. I*, 262.   [3] Ibid. *K*, 127.

[4] Jorn. 9, fos. 178, 179 *b*. It had already been decided in 1419 that the keeper of Ludgate should give security to keep his prisoners: *Memorials of Lond. and Lond. Life*, 677.   [5] Rep. 3, f. 270.

[6] Jorn. 4, f. 166 *b*. Inserted under the year 1447.

[7] *Cal. Lr. Bks. G*, 272.

[8] *Mun. Gild.* I. 46. For the date see p. 184 n. 8, above.

[9] *Cal. Lr. Bks. H*, 209–10.

proclaimed that any citizen who was aggrieved by the actions of
the officials of Newgate or other lesser city officers might lay his
grievances at the feet of the mayor and aldermen.[1] This proclamation was reiterated in 1382.[2]

As a yet further means of ensuring good conduct on the part
of its gaolers the City had begun, by the mid-fourteenth century,
actually to draw up regulations for the good government of the
gaols. The regulations of 1356, already referred to, may possibly
be looked upon as the first of these codes. In 1393 a further code
of rules was framed which embodied these and added many more.
It controlled all four prisons.[3] A revised code for Newgate was
issued in 1431,[4] for Ludgate and the Counters in 1463,[5] and for
all four in April 1488.[6] Meanwhile, in 1434, price-fixing rules for
all prisons were put forth[7] and in 1462 for Ludgate and the
Counters.[8] Further price-fixing for all prisons followed the code
of April 1488 five months after its promulgation.[9]

It is to the credit of the city that it did not content itself with
merely framing the regulations but did what it could to see that
they were observed, by sending bodies of visitors to inspect the
prisons. These men were to report back to the court of aldermen
or the common council on the state of the prisons and the way
in which the *ministri* were behaving themselves. The first record
of the appointment of such visitors comes from 1448, when two
aldermen were enjoined by the common council to visit all four
prisons.[10] In October 1463 two incumbents of city parishes and
two commoners were chosen to visit Newgate and Ludgate once a
month and report cases of extortion.[11] By the following December
these arrangements had become statutory. Henceforth the visitors
were to be chosen each year on St Matthew's Day (21 September).

[1] *Cal. Lr. Bks. H*, 112.   [2] Ibid. 199.
[3] *Mun. Gild.*1. 522–4 (*Liber Albus*). There is a brief abstract of the same code in
Cal. Lr. Bks. H, 402, which was the source for the *Liber Albus* version. There is,
however, an addendum to one clause of that version which alters the sense of it.
See p. 191.
[4] *Cal. Lr. Bks. K*, 124 ff.   [5] Ibid. *L*, 40 ff.
[6] Jorn. 9, f. 170b–173, 175b–180.   [7] *Cal. Lr. Bks. K*, 183.
[8] Jorn. 7, f. 17b.   [9] Jorn. 9, f. 209b.
[10] Jorn. 5, f 3b.   [11] Jorn. 7, f. 45.

They were to have access to prisons at any time, and were to report on the observance of the ordinances, the manner of distributing the alms collected, and the causes of each man's imprisonment. They were given power to fine and in the last resort to expel unsatisfactory keepers and also to 'dispose' the waters of the conduits.[1] By 1471 the Counters were apparently being included in the scheme.[2] Certainly they were expressly covered by the revised regulations of 1488.[3]

Such visitors continued to be constantly appointed, although in 1521[4] and 1530[5] the remark is made that visitation had been allowed to lapse and must be revived. More often than not the panel was constituted of two priests[6] and two laymen according to the original design. There were, however, some variations upon that pattern. In 1471 three laymen were chosen.[7] In 1499 there were two panels, one of two priests and two aldermen and the other of four commoners.[8] Perhaps, if the records had been kept more carefully, we might find that both the court of aldermen and the common council regularly aimed at maintaining separate visitatorial boards. By Henry VIII's reign officials began to be associated with the elected representatives and clergy. In 1526 a serjeant was ordered to be in attendance[9] and in 1530 the place of one of the two commoners was taken by the town clerk.[10] In 1532 we notice what appears to be the inception of a new system. Three separate boards, for Ludgate and the two Counters, were then set up, each consisting of a priest, a layman, and an official. The common clerk served the Ludgate boards, other clerks the others. No board for Newgate was at that time formed.[11] The association of officials with aldermen and commoners suggests, though it does not prove, a serious desire to record irregularities that might require correction.

[1] *Cal. Lr. Bks. L*, 42–3.
[2] Jorn. 8, f. 8*b*, which refers in general terms to 'the gaols of the city'.
[3] Jorn. 9, f. 180.   [4] Jorn. 12, f. 147.   [5] Jorn. 13, f. 244.
[6] The master of the college of St Michael Paternoster was chosen in 1511 and 1523 (Rep. 2, f. 120; Jorn. 12, f. 245*b*).
[7] Jorn. 8, f. 8*b*.   [8] Rep. 1, f. 44*b*.   [9] Jorn. 12, f. 363.
[10] Jorn. 13, f. 244.   [11] Rep. 8, f. 265.

Imprisonment in medieval England

Very little has been discovered about the work of the visitors. In 1521, however, they appear to have reported back to the court of aldermen according to their obligations.[1] They had then recently visited Ludgate and the Bread Street Counter and had detected many faults in the keepers of those prisons. This, as has been shown, was after the system had fallen into abeyance for some years.[2] It was they who in 1514 were ordered to regulate the use of certain 'colliers' sacks' which had been put at the disposal of the prisoners in Newgate.[3] It was they, too, to whom some dispute between two unknown persons, perhaps a prisoner and his keeper, was referred in 1523.[4] One thing is clear: the visitors had no responsibility for the repair or condition of buildings. Bodies of men, quite distinct from the visitors, examined the state of the fabric of Newgate in 1450,[5] 1455,[6] 1497,[7] and 1513,[8] and the 'corrupt air' of that prison in 1509.[9] It was also by a distinct body that the activities of the Skinners Company were investigated, when, in 1524 or thereabouts, that company allowed the buildings of St Mary Spital to encroach upon the Poultry Counter and block up the windows.[10]

One of the most prominent subjects in the city codes was the regulation of fees. This has already been examined.[11] Another was the control of those other forms of money-making in which, as we have already seen,[12] the gaolers and their servants indulged.[13]

In 1393 the hire of bedding was prohibited in Newgate and Ludgate. It was permitted in the Counters, but the price (1d. a night) was fixed and prisoners were allowed to bring their own.

[1] Rep. 5, f. 228.
[2] There is no record of the appointment of a board between 5 February 1516 and 28 September 1521: Rep. 3, f. 127; Jorn. 12, f. 147.
[3] See p. 329.   [4] Rep. 6, f. 54b.   [5] Jorn. 5, f. 47b.   [6] Ibid. f. 260b.
[7] Rep. 1, f. 28.   [8] Rep. 2, f. 157.   [9] Ibid. f. 71b.
[10] Rep. 4, f. 181b, Rep. 6, f. 90b (1524); Rep. 7, f. 96b (1526).
[11] See p. 170.   [12] See p. 175.
[13] Except where otherwise stated the substance of the next six paragraphs is drawn from various sets of regulations controlling some or all of the prisons. The sources are: *Mun. Gild.* 1. 522–4 (1393); *Cal. Lr. Bks. K*, 124 ff. (1341), 183 (1434); Jorn. 7, f. 17b (1462); Jorn. 7, f. 45 (October 1463); *Cal. Lr. Bks. L*, 40 ff. (December 1463); Jorn. 9, fos. 170b–173, 175b–178, 179–80 (April 1488); ibid. f. 209b (September 1488).

In 1431 prisoners in Newgate might hire beds with blankets and sheets at 1*d.* a week, and coverlets at the same rate. They were, however, also free to bring in their own. In December 1463 these regulations were extended to Ludgate and the Counters. In April 1488 a bed with blankets, sheets, and coverlet was to cost 1*d.* a week and a 'couch' the same sum, but prisoners might bargain with the keeper for something less. The same sum was authorized for beds in the Counters, but 'couches' are not mentioned.

In 1393 the purchase of lights was forbidden in all four prisons. In 1431 the charge for lights in Newgate was fixed at 4*d.* weekly. In December 1463 this provision was extended to the other prisons. In September 1488 it was decided that the maximum price of candles in all prisons should be fixed by the mayor for the time being.

The sale of food was prohibited in the Counters in 1393, in Newgate in 1431, and in Ludgate in December 1463, prisoners being authorized to buy where they pleased. The regulation was, however, partially rescinded in September 1488 in all four prisons when the price of the loaf, as sold to prisoners, was fixed, although permission for prisoners to be at their own commons was continued. The sale of liquor, always so profitable to gaolers while the opportunity lasted, was another matter. The old Newgate had possessed a 'tap', and it was the clear intention to perpetuate it in the new one. Indeed the retailing of beer is expressly authorized, though gaolers were told that they must not exceed the old prices. These regulations were formally extended to the other prisons in December 1463. There is, however, little doubt that the sale of liquor had been permitted in them long before, for in 1434 the price of a gallon of the best ale was fixed at 2*d.* for all prisons, and in 1462 it was laid down that only the best beer should be sold in Ludgate and the Counters. The regulations of April 1488 add that ale shall only be sold in sealed measures. Those of the following September authorize the sale of 'small' ale or beer, the price of which is then fixed at half that chargeable for the best.

The sale of coal and firewood was forbidden at all four prisons in the same way and at the same periods as the sale of food had been and, as with food, prisoners were to be free to bring in their own. These prohibitions, however, are in apparent conflict with others issued in 1434 fixing the price of coal at 1*d.* a bushel and others issued in September 1488 confirming that decision and limiting the price of firewood to ½*d.* a faggot. The sale of cloth, presumably for clothes, is not mentioned until the regulations of April 1488, when it is prohibited in all prisons.

Finally, there are regulations about chamber hire. In 1393 it was ordained that prisoners who wished to remain in the Counters for their greater comfort might do so, provided that they were not held for treason or felony. They might pay 4*d.*, 6*d.*, 8*d.*, or 12*d.* a week in rent, according to the degree of comfort that they demanded. A new scale, which applied also to Ludgate, was introduced in 1462, when the best rooms were rated at 8*d.* and the others at 6*d.* In October 1463, however, all chamber rent in Ludgate was apparently forbidden. Further regulations on the subject were drawn up in December of that year. They are not very clear but seem to imply that lodging charges cannot be insisted upon. On the other hand a new scale of maximum charges was at the same time laid down, namely, 3*s.* for gentlemen and freemen and 2*s.* for yeomen. The regulations of April 1488 extend these charges to all prisons. Any prohibition against chamber hire that may once have prevailed seems now to have gone.

These regulations leave the impression that originally the city authorities were opposed to this traffic in chambers and commodities. They felt, on the contrary, that prisoners, or at any rate freemen, should enjoy a right of entry into prisons, with the power to introduce their own food, bedding, clothes, and the like. Gradually, however, it became apparent to them that the provision of these amenities by the keepers could not be prevented and was indeed often of advantage to the prisoners. Accordingly, while preserving the prisoner's right to bring in his own property and thus preventing the keeper from establishing a monopoly except in the sale of liquor, they found it prudent to accept the situation. They were, however, prepared to mitigate the consequences by prescribing fair trading rules and by fixing prices. This conclusion seems to be confirmed by the fact that the original version of the code of 1393 read 'qe le porter ne nul autre officer du dit Countour vende a le prisoners pain...nautre vitaille...' but that at a later date the words 'sinoun par mesure et a resonable pris' were added.[1]

One of the practices in which gaolers indulged was to charge prisoners who brought in their own bedding for the right to use it and also to charge them for the use of beds and lights where those amenities had already been provided by charity. John Bottisham, the keeper of Ludgate whom we have already met,[2] was accused of forcing a prisoner fully equipped with bed, bedclothes, and clothing to pay him for the privilege of their use.[3] Charging for charity lights, bedding, and beds was forbidden in Newgate in 1431, and in the other prisons by December 1463.

The evidence for the control of gaolers in provincial towns is much sparser than it is in London. We know, however, that by the fourteenth century Bristol gaolers were required to swear that they would treat their prisoners 'bonement' or to contract to do so on pain of loss of office.[4] In 1481 the corporation of Coventry framed a code of rules which covered the conduct of gaolers, and reissued it in 1515.[5] But long before then they had followed London's lead in fixing the price of beds, chambers, and ale. Prisoners, it was said in 1430, should be entitled to bring their own beds into prison. If, however, they hired them from the gaoler they should only pay 1*d.*, the London figure. Charity beds were not to be charged for.[6] Five years later these charges were reduced to $\frac{1}{2}d.$ for a night or 3*d.* a week. At the same time chamber rent was fixed at 1*d.* a week for those bringing their own beds.[7] In 1432 it was laid down that prisoners should import their own ale and gaolers should not sell it,[8] a rule less favourable to the gaoler than any that London was prepared to promulgate.

---

[1] *Cal. Lr. Bks. K,* 126 n.; *Mun. Gild.* 1. 523.   [2] See p. 181.

[3] *Cal. Plea & Mem. R.* 1381–1412, 158.

[4] *Little Red Book of Bristol,* ed. F. B. Bickley, 1, 55. The oath is? *temp.* Edward II. Much later, in 1592 in fact, the gaoler of Cambridge castle entered into a contract to treat his prisoners well on pain of loss of office: Palmer, *Cambridge castle,* 33.

[5] *Coventry Leet Bk.* 11, 643.   [6] Ibid. 1, 130.   [7] Ibid. 184.

[8] Ibid. 142.

IX

COMMITMENT, BAIL, AND
ENLARGEMENT

No one interested in imprisonment can be indifferent to the ways in which men and women actually got into prison. The subject, however, must be treated most selectively. The ways were numerous and to examine them in detail would lead quickly to a full inquiry into the history of arrest.

From very early times there was a common-law obligation to arrest and imprison not only red-handed thieves but also those to whom felony might be clearly imputed and even those of whom no worse could be said than that their conduct openly verged on the felonious.[1] By the mid-thirteenth century it was also not uncommon to arrest appellees. Indeed in 1300 it became the law that any appellee delated by an approver lying in a deliverable prison should be arrested and taken to that prison so that appellor and appellee might be kept together.[2] Many such arrests were effected either by official persons, that is to say by sheriffs and their officers, by coroners, or by the bailiffs of liberties, including, of course, municipal liberties. It is indeed also true that many suspects were merely attached by pledges after the minimum of custody or none at all, and that many others fled to sanctuary and later abjured. But that there was much arrest even in very early times by the officers of shires, hundreds, and liberties cannot be disputed, and the multiplicity of prisons attests it.

A few thirteenth-century incidents illustrate the way in which uch arrests occurred. In 1206 a king's serjeant in Lincolnshire is

---

[1] Some brief remarks about arrest will be found in Pollock and Maitland, *History of English law*, II, 582–4. Much more is to be incidentally collected from *Crown pleas of the Wilts. Eyre, 1249*, esp. pp. 69–78, 92–8. Sanctuary and abjuration are dealt with in J. A. A. J. Jusserand, *English wayfaring life in the middle ages*, translated by L. T. Smith (4th ed. London, 1950), and R. F. Hunnisett, *The medieval coroner* (Cambridge, 1961).

[2] *Stat. Realm*, I. 141.

found visiting Bardney fair and arresting for burglary some men
whom he found there. The men were claimed by Bardney abbey,
the owner of the fair, and removed into the custody of abbey
officials. They then escaped and were recaptured by the serjeant's
garciones.[1] In or about 1275 a king's bailiff entered a private
liberty to attach a suspect felon. The felon resisted and was
injured and the liberty bailiff imprisoned both the king's bailiff
and the felon.[2] In 1299 a York beadle perambulated the Whitsun
fair in that city seeking cutpurses.[3] Documents of later date contain such stories in greater abundance, as the roll of the Northampton eyre of 1329 will testify. In 1317, for example, a Weldon
man was arrested by a sheriff's bailiff errant, who took him to
Northampton to prison.[4] In 1321 a man of Stamford went to
Oundle and was there arrested for wounding by the abbot of
Peterborough's bailiff.[5] About the same time another man was
arrested for theft at Brigstock by the bailiff of the honor of
Gloucester.[6] Such sorties and perambulations by the officers of
shire and liberty were some compensation for the lack of a ubi-
quitous police force.

Arrest, leading to imprisonment, was also effected by groups
of villagers, often, no doubt, led or accompanied by a hundred
officer, tithingman, or township constable.[7] They had observed
or suspected the occurrence of crimes, arrested the culprit on
the spot, and either placed him in a near-by house[8] or lock-up[9]
or carried him across country to a gaol[10] or castle. These are
thirteenth-century instances. In the fourteenth century, however,
such arrests could still be made, for the eyre of Northampton of
1329 learned of a man arrested by the men of Towcester and
handed on by them to four men and the reeve of that place.[11] In

[1] *Earliest Lincs. Ass. R.* 266–7.　　[2] *Cal. Pat. R.* 1272–81, 88.
[3] *Sel. Cases in K.B.* III, 87–8.
[4] *Assoc. Archit. Soc. Rep. & Pap.* XXXII, 438.
[5] Ibid. 472.　　[6] Ibid. 460.
[7] E.g. *Pleas before king and his justices,* II (Selden Soc. LXVIII), 68; W. M.
Palmer (ed.), *The assizes held at Cambridge in A.D. 1260* (Linton, 1930), 14
(Fulbourn).
[8] Ibid. p. 10 (Cheveley).　　[9] Ibid. p. 5 (Chesterton).
[10] Ibid. p. 9.　　[11] *Assoc. Archit. Soc. Rep. & Pap.* XXXII, 480.

that century, however, arrests in villages were more often made by the tithingmen and constables. Thus in June 1321 a man of Thrapston was arrested by the tithingman and constable of Irthlingborough and put for some days in the stocks. He was then recovered by Thrapston officers and taken off to gaol.[1] At much the same time the corresponding officers in Naseby effected an arrest there and took steps to dispose of their prisoner in the same way.[2]

The system which these incidents illuminate was complemented by the well-known sequence of ordinances enforcing watch by night in the summer.[3] The first of these ordinances comes from 1233,[4] the second from 1252;[5] the third was the Statute of Winchester (1285).[6] The watchmen, varying in number according to the size and ultimately the status of the settlement from which they were drawn, had power to arrest strangers entering the towns and imprison them for the night. The second ordinance and the statute further provided that those who were suspected of ill-doing were to be delivered to the sheriff on the morrow. The Statute of Winchester was reaffirmed in more general terms in 1331.[7]

Where a man was arrested by a sheriff's officer and taken to a gaol, the gaoler presumably knew the escort and was satisfied that he was authorized to receive the man. Where the arrest was made by a coroner, the coroner in earlier times handed the prisoner to the sheriff, and the sheriff passed him on.[8] Here again the case was clear. Where a man was ordered into custody in court the sheriff or gaoler could no doubt often plead the authority of the court roll, as we know was done by a sheriff in 1291–2 when a forest trespasser alleged unlawful imprisonment.[9] Where, however, arrests were made by townships, the gaoler might be involved in considerable risk if he accepted every prisoner whom

[1] *Assoc. Archit. Soc. Rep. & Pap.* xxxii, 199, 872.   [2] Ibid. 479.
[3] Pollock and Maitland, *History of English law*, I, 565.
[4] Stubbs, *Charters*, 8th ed. 362–3.
[5] Ibid. 9th ed. 362–3.   [6] C. 4.   [7] 5 Edw. III, c. 14.
[8] Hunnisett, *The medieval coroner*, 22.
[9] *Sel. Bills in Eyre*, 32.

an escort might bring in. Mistakes, misunderstandings, prejudices could influence the townships, not to mention vindictiveness and revenge. Often the gaoler might not know the escorts by sight and might therefore be unable to verify that they were what they purported to be. To avoid the consequences of a charge of wrongful imprisonment it behoved the gaoler to exhibit a cautious attitude towards the escorts. Accordingly we find gaolers refusing to receive prisoners or only agreeing to do so in return for a fee. Thus, about 1258–9 a woman suspected of murder was taken by the township of Fulbourn to Cambridge castle and there offered to the sheriff in full county court. The sheriff would not receive her and the township would not remove her, so she went free.[1] In or about 1253 a suspected horse-thief could not be lodged in York castle until half a mark had been paid.[2] In 1274 the gaoler of York would not receive a man indicted of a theft. In fact he released the prisoner and held one of the escorts to ransom.[3] About 1260 the gaoler of Cambridge demanded money of the township of Ashley as the price of accepting a thief. The township took away the thief and the thief escaped.[4]

By statute of 1330 punishment was ordained for a gaoler refusing prisoners such as these,[5] but this did not stop the practice. It recurs, for example, about 1368–9.[6] About 1384 a subordinate of the under-constable of Salisbury castle required the reeve and hundredmen, who were escorting a suspect to the castle, to bring their charge within the castle gate, declining to accept him until he had been. The escort would not comply and the man escaped.[7] In 1391 the tithingman of another Wiltshire village brought a man to the same gaol. The gaoler refused to take the man without a fee. This the tithingman refused to pay and left the man, in bonds, outside the gate. Rather naturally, the prisoner escaped.[8] According to the view expressed by Chief Justice Gascoigne in 1409 such an escape would not have exonerated the tithingman, who

---

[1] *Assizes held at Cambridge*, 14.   [2] *Cal. Inq. Misc.* II, p. 524.
[3] *Rot. Hund.* I. 111.   [4] *Assizes held at Cambridge*, 9.
[5] 4 Edw. III, c. 10.
[6] *Yr. Bk. Liber Assisarum* (Vulg.), 42 Ass. 5 (pp. 258).
[7] *V.C.H. Wilts.* v, 22.   [8] Ibid.

should have taken the prisoner back whence he had come and kept him until a delivery occurred.[1] The use of groups of villagers to effect arrest undoubtedly declined as time advanced, in face of other and, in intention, surer and more professional methods. Nevertheless it seems that even as late as 1480 a private individual might not merely arrest an evil-doer but take him in person to the gaol,[2] and a curious statute of 1429 empowers the commoners and foresters of the forest of Dean and the adjacent hundreds to arrest and imprison any of their neighbours who may damage the ships and cargo of the people of Tewkesbury.[3]

Every gaoler stood to gain by receiving a prisoner who possessed any means, since profit could be drawn from the charges which could be levied on the prisoner once he had been admitted. There was, however, small chance of drawing much revenue from the destitute, and it was probably the destitute who were mainly turned away. In addition a prisoner might also be rejected because the gaoler was uncertain whether there were good grounds for the imprisonment and scrupled to run the risk of an action staged against him. The statute of 1330 did not help the gaoler to distinguish between the genuine and the bogus suspect and, where the gaoler extorted a fee, bribe, or 'ransom' from the escort, he may have been insuring himself against future prosecution.

While there were thus many cases where the gaoler, confronted by unknown escorts, was left in perplexity, there were others where he was protected by documentary authority. From the thirteenth century many warrants issued out of Chancery addressed to a sheriff, a gaoler, or some other custodian, directing the addressee to receive, often by indenture,[4] and to harbour arrested suspects, sometimes on transfer from another prison. Thus in 1220 the bailiffs of Chichester were to take into the gaol there some men whom the sheriff of Sussex would deliver to them[5] and in 1222 the warden of the Fleet was to receive four men from the sheriff

[1] *Yr. Bk.* (Vulg.), 10 Hen. IV, p. 7a.
[2] Ibid. 20 Edw. IV, p. 6b.   [3] 8 Hen. VI, c. 27.
[4] For a group of transfers by indenture in 1325 see *Cal. Close R.* 1323–7, 417–19, 422–3.   [5] *Rot. Litt. Claus.* I. 440.

of Kent.[1] In 1248 at least six such writs were issued. Three were addressed to the sheriff of Oxford ordering him to receive and imprison men sent to him by the earl of Cornwall's bailiffs at Wallingford, the bailiff of Richard de Harcourt, and the countess of Warwick.[2] The keeper of Nottingham castle[3] and the sheriffs of Buckinghamshire[4] and Wiltshire[5] received similar orders. But where these writs were issued, there seems usually to have been some special reason, as, for example, that the natural custodian could not provide custody, or that the prisoner was an approver whose security was of peculiar importance. Certainly, as time went on, such writs seem nearly always to deal with special cases and not to issue as a matter of routine.

But while the records of the Chancery are ultimately relieved of these procedural documents, the documents themselves undoubtedly increased. By 1380 coroners were sending prisoners to gaolers with letters telling them to bring the men to trial at the next gaol delivery,[6] and a fifteenth-century register of writs contains precedents for transfer warrants.[7] Justices of the peace also used such a document, the *mittimus*, but it is not certain at what period it originated.

It has been shown that the system of unwarranted arrests could create dangers for the gaoler. Escorts, however, were also imperilled by it and so of course were prisoners themselves. The escorts had often to make long cross-country journeys, presumably on foot, to a proper county gaol, using inadequate improvised accommodation on the way. It was such journeys that led to clamours, such as those voiced in the fourteenth century by the commons of Berkshire[8] and Sussex,[9] for gaols to be seated in accessible places. As to the suspect, he was apt to find himself enclosed in gaol, castle, or lock-up upon the basis of the merest rumour. Those who arrested him, whether they were

---

[1] Ibid. 515. [2] *Close R.* 1247–51, 28, 39, 131.
[3] Ibid. 37. [4] Ibid. 66.
[5] Ibid. 67. [6] *Suss. Arch. Coll.* xcvi, 33–4.
[7] B.M. Add. MS 35205: 'de transferendo A. ab una gaola in aliam'; 'de removendo prisones regis ab una gaola in aliam'.
[8] *Cal. Pat. R.* 1313–17, 328–9. [9] *Suss. Arch. Coll.* xcvii, 78–9.

sheriff's officers or villagers, had no formal warrant for their actions and, even had they had, the suspect was unlikely to be able to understand or even to read it. That such wrongful arrests did indeed occur is frequently asserted, and sometimes the crown had to intervene to protect the suspect. Thus in 1251 a Reading woman was declared by the crown to have been falsely accused (*falso irretita est*) and the bailiffs of that town were ordered to release her.[1] A year later five men arrested by the sheriff of Warwickshire as disturbers of the peace were likewise said to have been wrongfully arrested and were released.[2] But more often than not the case did not promptly reach the ears of Chancery and many claims of unlawful arrest were lodged in eyre or before special commissions. Thus about 1253 several charges were brought against the sheriff of Yorkshire and his servants for imprisoning Stephen de Eyan, his clerks and servants, for short periods, usually without cause assigned.[3] The sheriff of Essex in 1267–8 imprisoned a man in Colchester castle unlawfully, and in the same county the steward of Robert de Brus shut up two men, again unlawfully, for two and six days respectively.[4]

Although the appeal of felony and arrests by townships continued to expose to danger men who were actually of good repute, some protection for such men against the activities of sheriffs and the bailiffs of liberties was afforded by Westminster II (1285). Clause 13 of the statute stipulated that sheriffs and bailiffs were henceforth to imprison only those who had been indicted by a jury. This provision, which extended to trespasses, was designed to put an end to the practice of ordering imprisonment at tourns of men who had neither been indicted nor fallen under strong suspicion. In the fourteenth century a similar prohibition begins to be applied to forest officers in their dealings with venison trespassers. It is first found in the Ordinance of the Forest of 1306,[5] is repeated with reservations in the Ordinances of 1311,[6]

---

[1] *Close R.* 1247–51, 403.   [2] Ibid. 1251–3, 202.
[3] *Cal. Inq. Misc.* II, p. 524.
[4] Helen M. Cam, *Studies in the hundred rolls: some aspects of thirteenth-century administration* (Oxford, 1921), 158.
[5] *Stat. Realm*, I. 148.   [6] 5 Edw. II, c. 19.

re-enacted in much the same form in 1327,[1] and reiterated in 1383.[2]

Sheriffs, however, either acting alone or with others might still be empowered by statute or special commission to arrest offenders and imprison them without indictment. Thus by statutes of 1394[3] and 1411[4] they might so act against rioters, in the second instance in conjunction with the justices of the peace, and one of 1383 authorized them to imprison vagabonds who could not find surety of the peace.[5]

As the keepers and justices of the peace became an ever more conspicuous feature of the scene, powers of arrest and imprisonment accrued to them. The keepers' commission of December 1307 authorized those officers to arrest or attach and thereafter to hold those who might resist the enforcement of the peace and the maintenance of the coinage and the price levels of Edward I's reign. These powers were widened by the commission of April 1314 and they were preserved in later commissions of the same reign. The commission of 1287 had instructed the keepers to inquire into offences by sworn inquest, and they continued in the same reign to conduct such inquiries under commissions that did not actually authorize them to do so. These arrangements were carried further by the commission of June 1314 which enjoined the arrest by the keepers of those indicted at the inquiries.[6]

In the next reign the bestowal of authority to arrest and imprison those indicted continued to characterize the commissions of justices of the peace, and so it was until 1352. After that these powers disappear except for the few years between 1364 and 1368. After 1350 the power to determine felonies, in practice minor ones, was normally enjoyed by the justices, as it had been sporadically from 1327, and the need to hold such offenders until delivered by other justices than those acting under peace commissions was proportionately lessened. The power to arrest suspicious characters, which had been a feature of Edward II's commissions to the

---

[1] 1 Edw. III, St. 1. c. 8.   [2] 7 Ric. II, c. 4.   [3] 17 Ric. II, c. 8.
[4] 13 Hen. IV, c. 7.   [5] 7 Ric. II, c. 5.
[6] *Kent keepers of the peace, 1316–17* (Kent Arch. Soc. Rec. Brch. XIII), pp. xvii–xx.

keepers, was lost in 1327 and only once restored in that reign. In general during Edward III's reign it was replaced by the power to take surety of the peace.[1] Over a very long period the justices, like sheriffs and other officers, enjoyed the power of arresting and imprisoning those to whom specific felonies or other offences were imputed.[2] This was sometimes bestowed by statute.[3]

The exact details of the powers of keepers and justices of the peace, differing, as we have seen, from time to time, are not of great practical importance to the story. Here it is enough to recognize that from the early fourteenth century much imprisonment was effected at the initiative of those keepers and justices through officials acting under their instructions. The intention in using them was undoubtedly to make arrest more regular and less arbitrary, though it does not follow that the intention was always realized.

Apart from the activities of the peace commissioners many persons from the time when those commissioners began to imprison were arrested and imprisoned by special commissioners, expressly appointed for that purpose. The commissions, which certainly go back to 1305, the date of the first trailbaston commission, took many different forms but may be divided into two broad types. One type named the individuals who had fallen under suspicion and directed the commissioners to seek out and imprison them; the other described the offences to which the crown took exception and made the commissioners responsible for imprisoning any who were *prima facie* guilty. In either event, of course, the imprisonment was preliminary to a trial. As examples of the second there may be mentioned commissions to arrest the following classes of persons: vagabonds in Kent and Sussex (*c.* 1305),[4] men who, falsely claiming to be of the royal household, requisitioned victuals from private houses (1316),[5] labourers re-

---

[1] *Proc. before J.P.s*, pp. xxii–xxiv, xxviii–xxx.
[2] Ibid. p. 107.
[3] E.g. 1 Ric. II, c. 6.
[4] *Cal. Pat. R.* 1301–7, 351.
[5] Ibid. 1313–17, 534. For similar commissions of 1317 and 1327 see ibid. 1317–21, 56 and 1327–30, 211. Cf. also p. 121.

sisting the collection of a Fifteenth and Tenth (1350),[1] all persons indicted in Essex for committing murder at Maldon (1358),[2] seditious vagabonds in the city and suburbs of Exeter (1461),[3] and riotous persons in and about the same city (1470).[4] Falling into the other group are a commission of 1332 to imprison at Warwick sixteen persons, fifteen of them named, who had been appealed of felony by an approver in that gaol,[5] and another of 1383 to imprison at Lincoln eight persons from different counties similarly denounced.[6] Four commissions, one of 1334,[7] one of 1345,[8] and two of 1382,[9] are for the imprisonment of outlaws; two commissions, one of 1381[10] and the other of 1455,[11] direct the imprisonment of single persons; one orders the arrest of two clerks convict who had escaped from a 'bishop's' prison, and had become vagrants;[12] while a commission of 1452 is for the imprisonment in Kent or Surrey gaols of seventy-two persons belonging to those counties or to Sussex.[13] In addition to the two main types there were also commissions, issued under the statute concerning malefactors of 1336,[14] for the arrest and imprisonment of anyone notoriously suspected of felony. Many such commissions are to be found in the years 1336–8, each naming the suspects and the prisons to which they were to be sent.[15] Powers to imprison rioters were given by the Statute of Gloucester (1378) to specially appointed county commissioners, and the rioters were to remain in prison without the option of bail until delivered by justices of the peace. The statute, however, was much criticized as a violation of Magna Carta. It was accordingly repealed next year, and those imprisoned under it set at liberty.[16] As has been shown, the sheriffs and justices of the peace took the special commissioners' place.[17] The Peasants' Revolt offered another

---

[1] The commissioners so empowered were actually the taxers and collectors of the tax: *Cal. Pat. R.* 1348–50, 456.   [2] Ibid. 1358–61, 153.
[3] Ibid. 1461–7, 35, 101; cf. ibid. 232 (1463).   [4] Ibid. 1467–77, 250.
[5] Ibid. 1330–4, 353.   [6] Ibid. 1381–5, 285.   [7] Ibid. 1334–8, 65.
[3] Ibid. 1345–8, 32.   [9] Ibid. 1381–5, 134, 250.
[10] Ibid. 22.   [11] Ibid. 1452–61, 305.   [12] Ibid. 1364–7, 135.
[13] Ibid. 1452–61, 58.   [14] 10 Edw. III, St. II, c. 3.
[15] *Cal. Pat. R.* 1334–8, 448–9; 1338–40, 145, 357.
[16] *Rot. Parl.* III. 43, 65.   [17] See pp. 199–200.

opportunity to make use of such commissions,[1] and in 1382 commissioners were appointed to imprison the preachers of heresies and errors.[2]

Strange though it may at first sight seem, many men and women in these times put themselves in prison voluntarily to clear their names or to escape the consequences of outlawry. It seems as though this may sometimes have been the practice when suspects were privily indicted before the thirteenth-century eyres,[3] though others so indicted were certainly arrested on the eve of their trials.[4] These were doubtless surrenders before the processes of outlawry had begun to run their course. Later in the century surrenders to avoid the fulfilment of that process begin to be observed. A man put in exigent for flight or non-appearance could, if he chose, surrender to prison and there abide until he should be pardoned or released by writ. In the same way he could escape the consequences of an outlawry published irregularly or inadvertently. This procedure was well known to Bracton,[5] though actual instances of such surrenders do not appear in the records very early. In 1283, however, the case is recorded of a man who was falsely suspected of rape, left his home district, was put in exigent because he was thought to have fled from justice, surrendered to prison, and was released by writ.[6] In 1290 the case is found of a man who was outlawed while overseas.[7] He was told to surrender to Dover, an obvious place for a returning expatriate;[8] if he appeared to be innocent the crown promised to quash his outlawry. That it was necessary for this man to petition for this cassation in Parliament suggests that the procedure was not very well known at the time. Later on, such surrenders were regulated by the Parliament of York (1322)[9] and by statute of 1331[10] and are recorded with great frequency.[11] By

---

[1] *Rot. Parl.* III. 105. [2] Ibid. 124–5.
[3] *Crown Pleas of the Wilts. Eyre*, p. 97. [4] Ibid. p. 92.
[5] *Bracton*, II, 354, 358, 371. Cf. *Britton*, I, 52–3; *Fleta*, II, 72.
[6] *Cal. Inq. Misc.* I, p. 380. [7] *Rot. Parl.* I. 57. [8] See p. 130.
[9] *Cal. Close R.* 1318–23, 558. [10] 5 Edw. III, cc. 12 and 13.
[11] For some examples of exaction and outlawry in the county court followed by pardon upon surrender see *Beds. Coroners' R.* 123, 125, 127.

the fifteenth century it had become the practice for one of the justices before whom the culprit should have appeared, to certify the surrender in Chancery.[1]

The procedure for handing over persons arrested at the suit of a party is in some cases prescribed early by statute. By the Statute of Merchants the mayor or 'chief warden' of the town in which the debt was acknowledged was to be responsible for arresting and delivering to the keeper of the town prison the body of a defaulting debtor. If the keeper would not receive him he was either to assume responsibility for the debt himself or to be himself imprisoned.[2] In London in 1305 and 1308 imprisonment under the statute was being effected by the sheriffs.[3] The merit of these provisions was that they furnished a single, simple method of committal. Westminster II was only slightly less precise in what it had to say about the committal of defaulting accountants.[4] They were to be sent to the nearest of the king's gaols and were to be received by the sheriff or gaoler. No punishment, however, was stipulated if the sheriff or gaoler demurred to the receipt, although he could be punished for an escape.

The variety of methods by which men might reach a common gaol is vividly portrayed in an indenture exchanged between incoming and outgoing sheriffs of Kent on 20 December 1378. There were then to be found in Canterbury castle two men taken red-handed, eleven indicted before coroners, one indicted at a tourn, one indicted before the bailiff of a liberty, six indicted before justices of the peace, and two taken on statute staple writs.[5] A less specific indenture of 18 November 1533 shows that there were then in Guildford and Lewes castles together twenty persons taken on suspicion of felony and three persons indicted of felony, besides six persons who had been tried and reprieved. Two of these six are said to have been 'attainted' and two indicted.[6] It is perhaps doubtful whether those two prisons

---

[1] E.g. *Cal. Pat. R.* 1416–22, 373, 412; 1422–9, 429.
[2] *Stat. Realm*, I. 99.   [3] *Cal. Lr. Bks. C*, 215, 244.
[4] C. 11.   [5] *Arch. Cant.* LXXI. 210–11.
[6] Guildford Castle Arch. Loseley MSS 692/2.

were really void, as the indenture implies, of non-criminal prisoners.

It has by this time become clear that arrest was frequent and could often be arbitrary. Since this was so, it was fortunate for the suspect that the practice of bail and mainprise was so widespread and that there were many inducements to apply it. Bail is an ancient institution, whose history cannot be recounted here.[1] It must suffice to say that sheriffs possessed by prescription the right to grant it and that in Glanvill's time they exercised the right to do so even in grave cases. The procedure then followed was for the arrested party to sue out a writ *de homine replegiando*. This, in the form in which it became set, was available to many types of suspect. A man charged with homicide, with 'any charge for which according to English custom he is not repleviable', or with an offence against the forest law was, however, excepted, as were those who had been taken at the command of the king or the chief justice. Bracton tried to define the 'other irrepleviable charges'. They mainly concern the activities of appellees and charges imputed to strangers who were unknown to any local community and could not find pledges. It is clear, however, that in his time bail was available to those accused of such serious offences as robbery, rape, and mayhem.[2] By *Britton's* time there was a much longer and more precise list of the types of accusation for which bail was available. Many of these would not, if proved, have amounted to felonies, but were in fact various sorts of trespass.[3]

It will be seen that it was only by stages that it became apparent what offences were bailable. Moreover, it seems that it was a disputable question whether men charged with repleviable offences could claim to be bailed of right. On the first point it must be said that many writs survive from the earlier thirteenth century to show that sheriffs or gaolers had failed to release men on bail, although, on the face of it, the law permitted them to do so. Their

---

[1] The subject is dealt with fully in Elsa de Haas, *Antiquities of Bail* (New York, 1940); see also a convenient summary in *Crown Pleas of the Wilts. Eyre*, p. 46.
[2] De Haas, op. cit. 71.   [3] Ibid.

motives for this failure could have been a genuine doubt whether the accused could find adequate security or whether the crown would consider the charge to be one properly falling within the repleviable category. Sometimes, too, there may have been an ignorance of law or custom and this could have been particularly the case where the custodian was not a sheriff but a constable[1] or a municipal community.[2] Later in the century there are numerous accusations that bail could only be secured by bribing the sheriff or the gaoler (or both) and perhaps a number of other officials as well.[3] That the writ had to be purchased from the Chancery at prices that seem to have varied greatly but were often high seems undisputed.[4] That its purchase should give rise to further local payments was rather naturally resented.

In irrepleviable offences the crown, with growing frequency, made available to suspects another writ, the writ *de ponendo*. This was issued of grace, mainly to suspected homicides and trespassers against the forest law. These writs were in principle, though not always in practice, enrolled in Chancery, and by totting the enrolments up we might judge to some degree how frequently they were issued. In the period 1248–53 the annual average for all prisons was 44, with a maximum of 51 in 1250. For the 20 years from 1248 to 1267 the annual average for Winchester, a fairly large prison, was 1·75, and for Guildford, a smaller one, it was one. Writs *de ponendo* were often issued for groups of offenders, so that the total number of prisoners affected would have been larger than these statistics imply. If such were the figures for major offenders, we may judge that those affected by writs *de homine replegiando* would have been much larger. It is therefore clear that quite considerable numbers of prisoners were released on bail or mainprise and this made an important contribution towards relieving congestion in the gaols besides representing an alleviation of hardship.

It is necessary to recall at this point that the system described

[1] *Close R.* 1227–31, 369–70.
[2] *Rot. Litt. Claus.* I. 470 (bailiffs of Wallingford).
[3] De Haas, op. cit. 87–91.   [4] Ibid. 78–84.

above did not operate in some boroughs, notably in London. In London it was the custom, from at least King John's time, to admit every suspect to bail, provided he could find suitable pledges. The heinousness of his alleged crime did not affect the privilege.[1] In 1238–9 the citizens claimed this as one of their ancient customs.[2]

The uncertainties by which the old common law was beset were much reduced by Westminster 1 (1275).[3] This laid down thirteen categories of irrepleviable offences and six categories of offences which might automatically lead to replevin, if proper security were available. It did not end the life of the writ *de ponendo*, though the numbers issued were cut down and the security required seems usually to have been increased. Thus in the period 1303–6 the annual average of these writs for all prisons was only nineteen. Their presence has become infrequent by 1318 and after the end of Edward II's reign is distinctly rare. Under one of the Ordinances of 1311 forest offences became automatically repleviable,[4] and though the ordinance was revoked in 1322, this particular provision was re-enacted in 1327.[5] Thereafter bail writs for such offenders continue to be enrolled at least until 1381.[6]

After 1275 a genuine attempt seems to have been made to prevent the bailment of irrepleviable offenders. The sheriff of Warwick and Leicester, in 1293, was condemned in parliament to prison for bailing a suspected murderer and another man committed by an order of the crown.[7] It was found in 1304 that a sheriff of Shropshire had released on bail two persons charged with abetting a homicide; the justices of gaol delivery sent the sheriff to prison for allowing bail in such a case, although they acquitted the suspects.[8] After this, although there are many complaints that sheriffs and gaolers allowed prisoners to go at large either through negligence or venality, there is less to suggest the excessive use of bail by local officials for the benefit of serious

---

[1] *E.H.R.* xvii, 721–2. [2] *Mun. Gild.* i. 113.
[3] C. 15. [4] 5 Edw. II, c. 19.
[5] 1 Edw. III, St. 1, c. 8.
[6] E.g. *Cal. Close R.* 1360–4, 74; 1369–74, 159; 1377–81, 435.
[7] *Rot. Parl.* i. 95–6. [8] *Sel. Cases in K.B.* iii, p. cxci.

misdoers. On the contrary the complaint now rather is that persons of good fame are appealed by approvers and kept in prison against all reason. This practice was forbidden in general terms by one of the Ordinances of 1311, and sheriffs and gaolers directed to grant bail to such suspects without taking fees or bribes for doing so.[1] The ordinance, however, was revoked in 1322.

The bailment by local officers was thus temporarily controlled but special measures had to be taken to deal with bail granted by the marshal of the King's Bench. In 1320[2] he was accused of bailing irrepleviable felons, and the justices of that court were ordered to make sure that indicted homicides and other indicted felons were kept shut up. Such complaints were repeated in the next parliament. The petitioners claimed that the released suspects thus freed injured the parties at whose suits they were delivered, those parties being presumably the felons' victims or the friends of those victims. The previous orders were thereupon reiterated and aggrieved parties were given an action against the marshal.[3] The trouble, however, continued. A statute of 1331 shows that marshals were still releasing on bail persons indicted and appealed of 'felonies, robberies, and larcenies'. On the face of it some such persons would have been bailable, but presumably the meaning is that the marshal was not exercising due discretion in applying the outlets of the law. Alternatively, it may mean that suits could not have been removed *coram rege* at all unless the charges were so heinous that bail was inadmissible. The statute laid down that prisoners of this sort should be kept in prison both during and out of term, places of custody being assigned in court to the marshals. If prisoners were found in future to be at large, the marshal should be subject to six months' imprisonment or a fine in lieu. And the justices were to inquire into such incidents.[4] No doubt this singling of the marshal out was partly due

[1] 5 Edw. II, c. 34.

[2] In the parliament of York, which may be either the parliament that was summoned to meet on 6 May 1319 or that summoned for 20 January 1320, but was probably the latter.

[3] *Rot. Parl.* I. 372.   [4] 5 Edw. III, c. 8.

to the lack, at the time, of any permanent place of detention for King's Bench prisoners.

In the mid-fourteenth century complaints about an insufficiency of bail are renewed. In a petition to parliament in 1355 it was alleged, as in 1311, that sheriffs and gaolers were declining to bail persons of good fame taken on the lightest charges until they had been bribed. The petitioners also urged that two categories of suspects not included in the repleviable categories in 1275 should be made repleviable. These were those who were arrested by a *capias* on a writ of account and those appealed by an approver in his lifetime. The crown pronounced the petition to be 'reasonable', declared that the statute of 1275 should be kept, but ignored the Commons' desire to extend the repleviable classes.[1]

It is not very surprising that those arrested by a *capias* should not have been included in the repleviable class. As is shown elsewhere, there was a great deal of feeling, and long had been, that prisoners committed at the suit of a party were insecurely held.[2] To have afforded the accountant the opportunity of being bailed would have seemed to contemporaries nothing but an encouragement to the lax custody of debtors. In 1347–8 a complaint was lodged against the warden of the Fleet, a place very full of debtors, because he admitted a debtor to bail,[3] and in 1377 he was prohibited by statute from doing so on his own authority.[4]

Many of the statutes of the fourteenth and fifteenth centuries which made new offences punishable by imprisonment positively forbade bail. Such prohibitions were particularly characteristic of the Statutes of Labourers and Vagabonds, and are in fact included in the statutes of 1360,[5] 1388,[6] 1406,[7] 1423,[8] 1427,[9] 1495,[10] and 1515.[11] The first of these actually imposed a fine of £10 on the 'keeper' who bailed a defaulting labourer together with damages of half that amount to the labourer's aggrieved lord. The statute of 1423 also imposed a cash penalty on 'keepers'

---

[1] *Rot. Parl.* II. 266.   [2] See p. 242.   [3] *Rot. Parl.* II. 211.
[4] 1 Ric. II, c. 12.   [5] 34 Edw. III, c. 9.   [6] 12 Ric. II, c. 9.
[7] 7 Hen. IV, c. 17. This prohibition applies only to imprisonment in the stocks.
[8] 2 Hen. VI, c. 18.   [9] 6 Hen. VI, c. 3.
[10] 11 Hen. VII, c. 22, s. 6.   [11] 6 Hen. VIII, c. 3, s. 5.

but it was now no more than £1 for mainprise. Wherever such a prohibition is present, the imprisonment is obviously meant to be punitive.

To offset these prohibitions a mid-fifteenth-century statute, framed in the spirit of earlier legislation, regulated bail in the interest of the party arrested. Sheriffs, under-sheriffs, and franchise bailiffs were required to bail automatically all arrested persons of sufficient credit, provided that those arrested had not been committed by what is called 'condemnation', by execution, by certain writs of *capias*, by surety of the peace, or by the special order of a justice, and provided that they were not labourers or vagabonds disobeying the Statutes of Labourers. The cost of the bail bond was at the same time limited.[1]

A leading defect in the system of granting bail in its earlier phases lay in the fact that the person with whom it rested to interpret the law was so often the actual or nominal keeper of the prison in which the prisoner seeking bail was enclosed. Since it was established custom for the keeper to make a profit out of his charges, he was well placed to manipulate bail to his own advantage. In fact the system was apt to be very irresponsibly administered and the consciousness that this could be so is no doubt reflected in an order issued by Abbot Richard of Wallingford of St Albans (1328–36) that his own consent was required before bail could be granted to a prisoner in his gaol.[2] But in general what was required to correct the defect was to entrust the processes of bail to an authority purely judicial. Probably from early times the justices of the king's central courts granted bail on particular occasions. At any rate, in 1292 gaol-delivery justices are ordered to bail a prisoner,[3] and in 1320 the king's justices clearly enjoyed the power of bailment.[4] But such arrangements were not for day-to-day use. In the end a partial solution was

---

[1] 23 Hen. VI, c. 9.   [2] *Gesta Abbatis Sancti Albani* (R.S.), II. 206.
[3] Order addressed to the Worcester gaol-delivery justices: *Cal. Close R.* 1288–96, 233.
[4] *Rot. Parl.* I. 372. Note also that in 1455 servants charged with embezzling their deceased master's goods were to be committed to the King's Bench but might be bailed by the justices: 33 Hen. VI, c. 1.

found by enabling justices of the peace to grant bail, a power which they were in practice exercising by the third decade of the fifteenth century, if not before.[1] After two sterile petitions to that effect had been lodged in parliament in 1455 and 1467–8,[2] the power became statutory in 1484, when individual justices were suffered to grant bail out of sessions.[3] In 1487 the power was limited to two justices sitting together.[4]

Rather naturally, the king remained free to release prisoners, with or without security, if it was advantageous to him to do so. Two such instances are to be found in the mid-fourteenth century. In 1348 or 1349 a man called Paul de Monte Florum was released from the Fleet until Easter 1349 on the understanding that he would not go far from the city and would appear before the council to answer some charge laid against him. He did not observe his day but was forgiven and his temporary enlargement was thrice prolonged until 1350.[5] In this case mainprise is not mentioned. At about the same time William Pouche, who was also in the Fleet awaiting the settlement of a crown debt, was released on bail in order that he might carry out some business for the queen and subsequently that he might act as the king's agent in Flanders. His temporary enlargement was repeatedly extended and possibly he never returned to prison or answered the charge.[6]

It was by such methods that men were taken into custody and temporarily released pending trial. How were they discharged? Suspect felons were of course brought before a court, commonly of gaol delivery,[7] and there either acquitted or sentenced to death. The rolls of the court were no doubt the sheriff's warrant for the action taken, and besides this both he (or the under-sheriff) and the gaoler were normally present in court and heard judgement pronounced. Two pieces of fourteenth-century evidence suggest that hanging was immediate. At the gaol delivery of Maidstone held on 4 and 5 December 1299, twelve men were hanged the

---

[1] *Proc. before J.P.s*, p. cvii; Bertha H. Putnam, *Early Treatises on...J.P.s* (Oxford Studies in Social & Legal History, vii, Oxford, 1924), 86.

[2] *Rot. Parl.* v. 332, 620–1.   [3] 1 Ric. III, c. 3.

[4] 3 Hen. VII, c. 3 (4).   [5] *Cal. Close R.* 1349–54, 85, 190, 210.

[6] Ibid. 93–4, 141, 212, 353, 463.   [7] See chapters xii–xiv.

first day and eight the second.[1] At the gaol delivery of Northampton castle on 19 February 1389 one man was hanged on the
sessions day.[2] The acquitted presumably left the gaol as soon as
they had paid any outstanding charges to their gaolers.[3] In the
sixteenth century we find prisoners who are said to have been
'attainted and reprieved', 'indicted and reprieved', 'condemned
and reprieved', or simply 'reprieved'.[4] These, no doubt, were
hoping for a pardon, perhaps one procurable almost of course,
where a plea of *per infortuniam* or *se defendendo* had succeeded.

We have seen that from the thirteenth century there was much
imprisonment which was liquidated in practice by the payment
of a 'ransom'.[5] The arrangements for extracting this are not described and no doubt varied greatly with circumstances. There
seems, however, to have been at this time a more or less stereo-
typed procedure, exhibited in writs,[6] for dealing with one class
of redeemable offenders, namely, redisseisors imprisoned under
the Statute of Merton. In this case the payment of a fine was an
openly admitted means of terminating the imprisonment.[7] In two
instances, both coming from 1259, the sheriff was required to
assess the fine according to the quality of the trespass and the
capacity of the delinquent to pay. This done and the fine paid,
the sheriff released the man.[8] A writ of 1306 varies the procedure
slightly. This directs the sheriff to bail his prisoners to appear
in the Exchequer and make fine there.[9]

It also seems that in the closing years of the thirteenth century
there was some kind of routine for releasing trespassers in parks
and vivaries, condemned to terms of three years' imprisonment
under chapter 20 of Westminster I.[10] In the period 1290–6 there
will be found instances of the release of men at or shortly after

---

[1] Lambeth Palace MSS, C.R. 658. [2] E 364/25 m. D.
[3] See p. 167.
[4] Guildford Castle Arch. Loseley MSS. 962/1, /2, 969/2 (1532, 1533, 1559).
[5] See pp. 15, 30.
[6] The earliest noticed is 1259, the latest 1296: *Close R.* 1256–9, 372; *Cal. Close R.* 1288–96, 497. For original writs of 1289 and 1290 see E 143/3/1.
[7] See p. 18.   [8] *Close R.* 1256–9, 372, 438.
[9] *Cal. Close R.* 1302–7, 374.   [10] See p. 32.

the completion of that period.[1] In other cases men were released after four years,[2] six years,[3] and eleven years.[4] In yet another case there is no period expressed but it is said that the men had been imprisoned for so long that they had suffered enough.[5] This overrunning of the term may have been due to the crown's hope that a release fine could be collected, as the statute declared should, if possible, be done; or to the failure on the part of the culprits to find at the end of the statutory term the needful security upon which the statute insisted. It has not up to the present been possible to establish for how long this vigilance lasted.

In general, however, we are not well informed about the methods adopted for freeing men sentenced to penal imprisonment. We do not know who saw to it that the prisoner was eventually released if his term was unlimited by statute or regulation or, if it was so limited, that the sentence was fully worked out or, alternatively, not exceeded. The truth may well be that no one did, but that, if the prisoner was sufficiently influential or rich, he could memorialize the crown, who might thereupon issue letters close which had the effect of terminating the imprisonment. At all events this seems to have been done in 1304 for the benefit of two redisseisors,[6] in 1350 for the benefit of a man who claimed improperly that he was the mayor of London's attorney,[7] in 1352 for a trespasser against the Statute of Provisors,[8] in 1421 for a group of rioters who had violated the statutes against forcible entry,[9] and in 1518 for the customer of Poole who had lain in the Fleet for a triennium.[10]

If a prisoner was coercively imprisoned for a statute merchant debt or in an action of debt or account, we may guess that he was free to leave prison once his creditor or prosecutor was satisfied. But did the gaoler demand any written evidence that satisfaction had been made? If not, there must surely have been the risk that the creditor would allege that the debtor had been allowed to go

[1] *Cal. Close R.* 1288–96, 406, 474.   [2] Ibid. 434.
[3] Ibid. 432.   [4] Ibid. 72.   [5] Ibid. 156.
[6] Ibid. 1302–7, 189.   [7] Ibid. 1349–54, 172.   [8] Ibid. 443.
[9] Ibid. 1419–22, 145. For the legislation see p. 33.   [10] *L. & P.* II (2), p. 1227.

at large prematurely and, as we shall see,[1] such an allegation, if sustained, could lead to the prosecution of the gaoler by the creditor. But of such acquittances examples are rare,[2] and statutes lay no procedure down. The best that can at present be said is that by the fourteenth century the prisons of the city of London were keeping some kind of records and that these must surely have contained entries of the kind described. Indeed we know that the keeper of Ludgate maintained a 'calendar of deliveries' in Richard II's time[3] and the 'books' of the Counters, destroyed by the mob in 1381,[4] must surely have included registers of admissions and releases.[5]

The foregoing paragraph presupposes that private debts and similar obligations were eventually discharged. But some debtors were permanently insolvent and might in theory lie in prison their whole lives long. To meet this difficulty testators began from the fifteenth century to leave money for the express purpose of paying such debts,[6] and by 1560 this type of bequest had become very fashionable.[7] Nor were such gifts the only means of cutting out of the prison population the swarming crowd of debtors, for we are told that in 1506–7 Henry VII released from Ludgate and the Counters many debtors owing 40s. apiece, and even, it is added, some owing as much as £10.[8] This cannot have been popular with creditors.

Hitherto we have thought chiefly of the regular methods of discharge. Besides these there were particular occasions when the

[1] See p. 242.
[2] For a release writ (1333) in favour of a statute merchant debtor see *Cal. Close R.* 1333–7, 39. For a similar writ in favour of another type of debtor (1352) see ibid. 1349–54, 419. The second of these looks at first sight like an imprisonment under 25 Edw. III, St. v, c. 17 (see p. 46), but since the statute was passed by a parliament that had adjourned by 11 February 1352 and the prisoner was ordered to be released on 24 March this is perhaps unlikely.
[3] *Cal. Plea & Mem. R.* 1381–1412, 159.
[4] *The Brut*, II (E.E.T.S. cxxxvi), 337. Cf. p. 223.
[5] Admission registers were kept by the gaolers of the Paris Châtelet in the fifteenth century: *Revue Hist.* LXIII, 50.　　　　[6] See p. 174.
[7] W. K. Jordan, *Philanthropy in England 1480–1660: a study of the changing pattern of English social aspirations* (London, 1959), 43, 265.
[8] *Gt. Chron. of Lond.* 334.

crown was moved to terminate an imprisonment either out of compassion or from a desire to secure a ransom. In 1294 two men sentenced to three years' imprisonment for unlawful fishing were released, the one after serving a year,[1] the other after only a few months.[2] In 1305 an impoverished clerk, who had lain in prison for a year in consequence of a redisseisin, was, owing to his poverty, released without the payment of the customary fine.[3] In 1408 a Wiltshireman, who had suffered a 'long' imprisonment for unspecified offences, was similarly treated.[4] Elizabeth of York just before her death (1503) secured through her personal intervention the release of two men from the King's Bench prison who had been implicated in the earl of Suffolk's conspiracy.[5] It would no doubt be easy to multiply examples of such pardons and indulgences.

The release of whole classes of prisoners in time of revolution or to signalize some feast or junketing has not been uncommon in world history and the good fortune of Barabbas has ever kept the possibility before the minds of Christians.[6] Such wholesale enlargements, however, have occurred only rarely in this country. The most notable exception comes from an extremely early time. Immediately after Henry II's death Eleanor of Aquitaine sent commissioners throughout England to liberate prisoners. Some indeed were only released upon conditions and were pledged to appear if charged. Offenders, however, against the forest law and those who were not imprisoned *per commune rectum* nor in consequence of an appeal were pardoned outright.[7] The conclusion has been drawn that this was done because in Henry's later years many had been imprisoned by administrative order and not in accordance with the principles of the assize of Northampton.[8]

[1] *Cal. Close R.* 1288–96, 350. [2] Ibid. 351. [3] Ibid. 1302–7, 301.
[4] Ibid. 1405–9, 332. [5] *Brit. Arch. Jnl*, XVII, 317–18.
[6] For fourteenth-century Italian practice see Anna T. Sheedy, *Bartolus on social conditions in the fourteenth century* (New York, 1942), 88 n.; for fifteenth-century French practice see *Revue Hist.* LXIII, 49.
[7] *Chronicle...known* [as] *Benedict of Peterborough* (R.S.), II. 74–5.
[8] F. M. Powicke, 'Per Judicium Parium vel per Legem Terrae', in *Magna Carta commemoration essays*, ed. H. E. Malden (Aberdeen, 1917), 114–15; cf. A. L. Poole, *From Domesday Book to Magna Carta* (Oxford, 1951), 349.

The growing use of eyres, quasi-eyres, and gaol delivery commissions no doubt supplanted such extraordinary expedients, while the consequences for public order in the sudden release of so many suspected evil-doers may have been too tragic to warrant repetition. Of releases on festive occasions only one example has been traced and it comes from a late date. When Charles V visited London in 1522 he secured the enlargement of some of the prisoners in Newgate.[1]

It would be useful to know how often prisoners were released by the crown in return for service in the wars. There is actual evidence of this from Edward I's reign. In 1294–7 commissioners were appointed to 'draft' into the armies in Wales, Gascony, and Scotland men who had been indicted or appealed of serious crimes.[2] Their service done, the men were to return home to stand their trial. Some of the men were actually in prison or were outlaws; others no doubt were released on bail. During the ensuing years large numbers of pardons were granted in consideration for foreign service. Among the crimes pardoned was prison breach, and it is tempting to believe that in these instances, which are not particularly common, the escapes were engineered in order to increase the supply of soldiers still further. Among the prisons in question were Plumpton,[3] Stafford,[4] and Warwick[5] and the crimes imputed included robbery and homicide.

This chapter has already made it clear enough that in the middle ages imprisonment was often capricious or insufficiently authorized. In theory this was reprobated. The thirty-ninth clause of the Magna Carta appears to have extended in intention even to imprisonment *per mandatum regis* and certainly the Charter could be invoked in the fourteenth century to limit the crown's prerogative of imprisonment.[6] Despite this, however, that prerogative continued to be wide, and redress against the crown direct

---

[1] Rep. 4, f. 164.

[2] *Cal. Pat. R.* 1292–1301, 107, 186, 289. See also the index to that volume and the next s.v. Army.

[3] Northamptonshire: *Cal. Pat. R.* 1301–7, 165.

[4] Ibid. 170; ibid. 1292–1301, 614.   [5] Ibid. 1292–1301, 615.

[6] See Powicke in *Magna Carta commemoration essays*, especially pp. 110–21.

was difficult. At the same time the subject was to some degree protected against arbitrary imprisonment, through the action of false imprisonment, which might lie against the crown's officials as against other sorts of men.

The appeal of unjust imprisonment was known as early as 1198, when an actual case was being tried.[1] It crops up regularly in the thirteenth century,[2] and was quite familiar to Bracton[3] and to the author of the *Mirror*.[4] In 1232 it could constitute the grounds for a plaint in a hundred court.[5] Ten years before that it was already beginning to form the basis of an action for trespass and from then onwards writs are found enrolled similar in type to one of the writs of imprisonment that ultimately established a place for itself in the Register. By Edward I's early years damage is usually alleged as a concomitant and by 1283 *vis et arma*.[6] By 1285 the action had been given a statutory sanction, for Westminster II[7] provided that men who were sent to prison by sheriffs in their tourns or by franchise bailiffs in hundred courts and similar assemblies without indictment should have an action of imprisonment against their captors.

In trying such actions it must often have been difficult to determine how far the person effecting the imprisonment acted maliciously. Some thirteenth-century instances do suggest that the imprisonment complained of had been 'wrongful', but 'wrongful' only owing to misunderstandings or mistakes.[8] At other times there is at least a *prima facie* case for supposing that some minor official was only carrying out his duty by placing under arrest some person who was thought to have committed or condoned a felony. When about 1217 the bailiff of the Norfolk village of Gunton put a man in the stocks and in 'irons' because he thought he had committed arson,[9] he may have been acting in good faith.

[1] *Pleas before the king and his justices*, II. 10.
[2] *Crown Pleas of the Wilts. Eyre*, pp. 74, 83, 197, 201; *Introd. to Cur. Reg. R.* (Selden Society LXII), 309.
[3] *Bracton*, II, 410–12.
[4] *Mirror*, 103.
[5] *Sel. Cases of Procedure without Writ*, 62.
[6] *Law Quarterly Rev.* LXXIV, 209–10.
[7] C. 13.
[8] *Crown Pleas of the Wilts. Eyre*, p. 73.
[9] *Norfolk Ant. Misc.* II, 180.

So at times at least may Richard Stocket, a hundred bailiff, whose doings were so unfavourably represented to the Wiltshire eyre of 1281.[1] So also may the village bailiff whose case was heard in 1294. He exhorted a man who had wounded one of his neighbours to find surety of the peace. The man refused, so the bailiff imprisoned him, and the prisoner thereupon brought a writ of imprisonment.[2] At other times the accused sheltered himself beneath the plea that the prisoner was his villein,[3] and such a plea may not have been unreasonable. Many other arrests and imprisonments, however, can claim no extenuating circumstances, and naturally they are suspect whenever the captor appears to have been holding out for a 'ransom'. An excellent instance of this is to be found in 1325–6,[4] and the practice became common enough to qualify for a special mention in Fitzherbert.[5]

Where the offence was proved against the person effecting the imprisonment, the consequences in *Britton*'s time were the imprisonment of the imprisoner or a 'ransom' proportioned to the offence.[6] A case of 1292 seems to make it plain that this was not only theory but practice.[7]

[1] *Collectanea*, (Wilts. Arch. Soc. Rec. Branch, XII), pp. 94, 60.
[2] *Yr. Bk. 21 & 22 Edw. I* (R.S.), 556–9.
[3] *Introd. to Cur. Reg. R.* 311; and cf. chapter III.
[4] *Sel. Bills in Eyre*, 92.
[5] *New Natura Brevium* (1652 ed.), 192. [6] *Britton*, I, 47–8.
[7] *Sel. Cases in K.B.* II, 116.

X

ESCAPES AND THEIR CONSEQUENCES
FOR THE ESCAPER

IN the middle ages the word 'escape' covered a multitude of different activities. It might be used where a prisoner broke out of prison or where he simply walked out. It might signify that a sheriff, gaoler, or other officer had corruptly allowed a prisoner to purchase his release, or that a prisoner who was being escorted to prison by a tithing, township, or village constable eluded the vigilance of the escort. Eventually it could even be used where a man arrested at the suit of a party was subjected to a form of detention too mild to achieve the coercive aims of his antagonist-at-law. These various forms of 'escaping', if proved against the prisoner or his keeper, usually brought punishment to one or the other or to both. To fix the blame and to settle the punishment occupied much time and thought and resulted in the end in the erection of a gigantic mound of legal learning.[1] Owing, however, to the feebleness of many prisons and the venality of many officials no effective means of prevention was ever contrived. The existence, too, of the right of sanctuary eased the escaper's path.

References to escapes can be traced as far back as the Pipe Roll of 1130 and are to be found in many other Pipe Rolls of the same century.[2] The rolls, however, naturally give no details. The early rolls of the king's courts, whether *coram rege* or in eyre,[3] are much more revealing, but nothing would be gained by cataloguing and analysing the relevant entries. It may, however, be said that the incidents are of a most varied character, and some illustration of that variety may not be out of place. Thus in the late twelfth century and in the thirteenth some escapes were

---

[1] E.g. Sir M. Hale, *Historia Placitorum Coronae* (1800 London ed.), I, cc. 51–4.
[2] See p. 232. [3] For the eyre see p. 224.

directly due to warfare. Shortly before 1194 several men escaped
from Salisbury castle because Count John, the later king, had
broken the castle with his troops.[1] Again, in consequence of the
civil war that ushered in the reign of Henry III, escapes occurred
from the gaols at Kenilworth, Warwick, Worcester, and York
and seem, except in the case of Warwick, to have been quite
unavoidable. In particular Worcester was said to have been captured by the enemy and none but the enemy was blamed for
the consequences.[2]

Neither in these nor in later times was escaping often the result
of events so stirring. Most men escaped singly or in little groups
through their own initiative, as they have been doing ever since.
One early story of an individual escape is worth repeating for its
peculiarity. About 1225 a man who had already escaped from
Oxford prison was rearrested and imprisoned at Northampton.
While at Northampton he had an attack of claustrophobia which
induced the hallucination that the devil had appeared to him in
the form of a monk. To defend himself from the devil, as he said,
he began to pull stones out of the prison wall and this appears to
have led him to break down a substantial piece of the wall itself.
At the eventual inquiry it was reported that he made three breaches
from which he severally extracted a cart-load, a barrow-load, and
a bowlful of stones and through one of these breaches he made
his exit.[3] No accomplices are mentioned and it is extraordinary
that the man could have demolished so much unaided and
undetected.

It is very easy to find examples of collective or multiple escapes.
In the two years 1229–31 no fewer than thirty-one thieves escaped
from Winchester prison.[4] In the next century, about 1356, some
clerks convict imprisoned in the archbishop of Dublin's prison
at Swords dug an underground passage and escaped through it.[5]

[1] *Rolls of the king's court 1194–5* (P.R.S. xiv), 103, 106, 108.
[2] *Rolls of Justices in Eyre for Gloucestershire, Warwickshire and Staffordshire*
(Selden Society, lix), 344, 381; *Rolls of Justices in Eyre for Lincolnshire and
Worcestershire* (Selden Society, liii), 565, 586; *Rolls of Justices in Eyre for
Yorkshire* (Selden Society, lvi), 203.   [3] *Cur. Reg. R.* xii, pp. 215–16.
[4] *Close R.* 1227–31, 516.   [5] *Cal. Pat. R.* 1354–8, 355.

A few years before, in 1347, twelve prisoners in Old Salisbury castle had dug a pit 4 feet deep under the wall of the gaol and would have left the castle by that means had they not been disturbed by the keepers.[1] Ten years later some men got out of one of the gaols in the castle of Newcastle upon Tyne *per sedem latrine*.[2] At a much later date (1455) certain felons released themselves from York city gaol by breaking through the floor above the chamber or vault in which they were confined.[3] Another daring escape was staged in Winchester gaol about 1441. When the gaoler's servant was leaning over the stocks to search several of the prisoners, his keys were seized by those whom he was searching. With them the prisoners undid the fastenings of the stocks and their fetters and chains. They then beat the servant and, opening the prison doors, got easily away.[4]

Newgate, as the chief criminal prison and the place of custody of the worst type of offender, was naturally the scene of many escapes. In 1275 nineteen persons broke out.[5] Ten years later four men and a woman broke from custody, climbed on the roof, and held the prison officers at bay *a mane* until prime.[6] In 1325 three events occurred in Newgate in such rapid succession that they look like parts of a concerted operation. In June the prison gate-keeper was killed by an escaped prisoner in the 'high street' of Farringdon Within, whither he had gone in pursuit of his murderer and three other fugitives.[7] In September six approvers and four others cut a hole in the prison wall and escaped through it,[8] and in November a woman was detected in the act of supplying prisoners with 'iron instruments' and otherwise abetting escapes.[9] A riot occurred during the Cade revolt which resulted in much damage to the fabric and the dismissal of the gaoler.[10] It is not quite certain whether on this occasion escapes actually occurred but, when another riot was staged in 1456, the prisoners

[1] J.I. 3/130 m. 133. [2] *Arch. Ael.* n.s. IV, 127.
[3] *Quendam solum desuper illam gaolam*: *Cal. Pat. R.* 1452–61, 273–4, checked with MS. [4] Ibid. 1436–41, 489.
[5] *Chrons. Edw. I and II*, 1. 85. [6] Ibid. 93.
[7] *Cal. of City Coroners' R.* 121–2. [8] Ibid. 130.
[9] Ibid. 136. [10] *Speculum*, XVIII, 241.

actually broke custody, ascended to the leads, and threw down stones and other missiles. The sheriffs and their officers could not withstand the rioters unsupported and only induced their antagonists to surrender by calling upon the generality of the citizens for aid. This riot seems to have been set off by the escape of Lord Egremont and his brother Sir Richard Percy, but it is not clear how near in time to one another the two incidents were. According to one account the riot followed immediately upon the escape, according to another within the same month.[1] Other London prisons were also troubled by such incidents, for in 1504–5 many or most of the prisoners in the Marshalsea broke out. The disturbance, however, seems to have been successfully quelled.[2]

Among stories of sensational escapes one might, of course, justly number those occasions when men of eminence, confined for political offences or as prisoners of war, broke their captivity. There is space only for a very few examples. Many will recall how in 1233 Hubert de Burgh, then imprisoned in Devizes castle, took sanctuary in a church near by, was reclaimed, and then escaped again.[3] In 1244 Gruffydd ap Llywelyn, the Welsh prince, irked by his very long confinement, made a rope of linen cloths and let himself down from a turret in the Tower of London. He was, however, so fat that the rope would not support him and he fell to his death.[4] Later, in 1323, Roger Mortimer escaped, also from the Tower. He and one of his servants made a *potum ingeniosum*, otherwise described as *pestiferum*, with which they drugged the guards to sleep. While the *potum* was having its effect, Mortimer and his companions smashed a wall which connected their prison with the king's privy kitchen. Thence they managed to enter a ward of the castle (*custodiam castri*) and from it gained access to another ward by means of a rope ladder. Thus

[1] *Gt. Chron. of Lond.* 189; R. Flenley, *Six town chronicles of England* (Oxford, 1911), 144; C. L. Kingsford (ed.), J. Stow, *A Survey of London* (Oxford, 1908), I, 37. [2] *Gt. Chron. of Lond.* 328.
[3] For a recent concise account see F. M. Powicke, *Henry III and the Lord Edward* (Oxford, 1947), I, 138–40.
[4] *Chrons. Edw I and II*, I. 41; see also plate facing p. 97.

they reached the Thames where a boat awaited them.[1] In the same year Maurice of Berkeley tried to escape from Wallingford castle. He invited the constable and many of his attendant watchmen and porters to have supper with him. While the meal was in progress a squire, whom the constable had allowed to enter the castle to pay Berkeley a visit, got up from the table and demanded the castle keys. These were delivered and the squire then went to a private door and admitted ten of his companions. A boy, lodging in the castle gate, thereupon raised the alarm, and first the sheriff and then the earls of Winchester and Kent arrived. Thereupon the conspirators surrendered.[2] The attempt was, therefore, foiled, and Maurice remained in the castle prison until his death.[3] If it was possible for such people, who were often closely watched by individual guards,[4] to get away, how easy must it have been for the common suspect or debtor to do so, whose security was of no particular concern.

Not only did men either individually or in groups break out of prison. Prisons were often broken into from outside by excited mobs or desperadoes and the prisoners released. Such 'releases' were described as rescues. The first case yet noticed comes from 1268 when armed men broke open the bishop of Lincoln's prison at Thame and released a man.[5] In 1298 nine men, eight of them aldermen, broke into the London Tun and effected a rescue.[6] A much more sensational incident occurred in 1312, though it is a curious mixture of breaking out and breaking in. Some prisoners in the Tower rushed out from the fortress, armed, and assaulted the wardsmen of Tower ward. The wardsmen retaliated and pursued the prisoners to an open space outside the Tower, presumably Tower Hill. The prisoners then forcibly closed the outer gates,

---

[1] *Abbrev. Plac.* 343; *Chron. Monast. S. Albani*, III (Trokelowe and Blaneforde), 145–6. The second source gives the fuller account but under the wrong year. The correctness of 1323 seems to be proved by the concordance of *Ann. Paul.* (*Chrons. Edw. I and II*, I. 305–6) with *Abbrev. Plac.* and with *Cal. Pat. R.* 1321–4, 425.   [2] *Chrons. Edw. I and II*, II. 273–5.
[3] Sir J. Maclean (ed.), J. Smyth: *The lives of the Berkeleys, lords of the manor of Berkeley in the county of Gloucester from 1066 to 1618* (Gloucester, 1883), I, 272.
[4] See p. 162.   [5] *V.C.H. Oxon.* VII, 115.
[6] *Gt. Chron. of Lond.* 23, 400.

to prevent the wardsmen from drawing upon assistance from within, and rang the bells of All Hallows, Barking, to summon a crowd. The crowd then effected a breach in the gates and walls and released two London citizens who had been imprisoned there against the liberties of the city. The government tried to fix responsibility upon the city of London, but this was repudiated. In the end, the alderman of the ward empanelled an inquest jury, but the findings are not known.[1]

Later in the century, in 1325, there was a rescue of notables from the Tower after the murder of Walter Stapleton.[2] In 1337 the archbishop's prison in Ripon was broken into from without and criminous clerks removed.[3] In 1381 Wat Tyler and his crew broke the gaols of Canterbury and Rochester and indeed all the gaols of Kent. At Rochester they laid siege to the castle for half a day until the constable surrendered. On reaching Southwark they broke the Marshalsea and King's Bench prisons. Later they broke all the London prisons, so that all the prisoners were enlarged.[4] Other rioters broke into the abbot's gaol at St Albans, held a mock delivery, and released nearly all the prisoners.[5] Soon afterwards, probably in 1382, it was alleged that other insurgents broke into Lewes castle, which had been temporarily appointed in that year as an additional prison for Sussex.[6] It was declared in 1421 that Oxford scholars were in the habit of breaking into 'bishops'' prisons and releasing the prisoners who thereafter sometimes rode about the countryside with their rescuers in semi-military or hunting bands.[7] Jack Cade broke the King's Bench and Marshalsea prisons in 1450 and released the prisoners,[8] not without some

[1] *Chrons. Edw. I and II*, i. 215–18.   [2] *Flor. Hist.* iii. 234.
[3] *Memorials of the church of Ripon*, ii (Surtees Soc. LXXVII), 117–20.
[4] *Cal. Pat. R.* 1381–5, 409; André Réville, *Le Soulèvement des Travailleurs d'Angleterre en 1381* (Paris, 1898), 187, 192; C. Oman, *The great revolt of 1381* (Oxford, 1906), 38, 39, 46; *Anonimalle Chron.* 136, 140–2; *The Brut*, ii (E.E.T.S.), 336–7.
[5] *Gesta Abbatum* (R.S.), iii. 291.
[6] *Cal. Pat. R.* 1381–9, 119, 259; cf. ibid. 119.
[7] 9 Hen. V, St. i, c. 8.
[8] Gregory's Chronicle in *Historical collections of a London citizen* (Camden Soc. n.s. XVII, 193).

assistance from inside,[1] and in the same year a traitor, who may have been one of Cade's supporters, was taken out of Colchester town gaol.[2] In October 1470 a crowd of some 300 people came to the Marshalsea, broke down its grates and walls, and released 99 prisoners.[3] On 'Evil' May Day 1517, the mob of London apprentices released their fellow rioters from the Counters and even took two men away from Newgate.[4] Such events remind us that prison life, which was as dreary in the middle ages as it is today, was occasionally relieved by excitement.

However incapable the authorities may have been of preventing escapes, they never showed any inclination to treat escaping as a matter of no importance. As has been said, escapes at Salisbury are recorded on the earliest eyre roll to survive.[5] Reporting such escapes in eyre continued. At the Lincoln eyre of 1202 two were reported and possibly a third,[6] and two each at the Gloucester and Worcester eyres of 1221.[7] By that time a special chapter (now commonly numbered 32) *de evasione latronum* had come to be included in the articles of the eyre and it remained thereafter a constituent of the corpus.[8] The Chancery, however, does not seem to have felt that it was good enough to place reliance upon this article alone, for it sometimes reinforced the standing orders by the issue of express instructions. An example of such instructions to the eyre is to be found in 1238,[9] and the special commissioners of 1274 were similarly charged.[10] In pursuance of these orders, whether general or special, the justices persisted in their investigations. They are found doing so, for example, in Buckinghamshire in 1227,[11] at Durham in 1242,[12] and at Wilton in 1249.[13]

---

[1] Jorn. 5, fos. 47b, 48. [2] *Cal. Pat. R.* 1446–52, 415, 503.
[3] *Rot. Parl.* VI. 49–50. [4] E. Hall, *Chronicle* (1809 ed.), 588–9.
[5] See p. 219. [6] *Earliest Lincs. Ass. R.* 129, 150, 152.
[7] Maitland, *Glos. Pl.* pp. 69, 75–6; *Rolls of Justices in Eyre for Lincolnshire and Worcestershire*, 542–3, 610.
[8] *Crown Pleas of the Wilts. Eyre*, p. 30; Helen M. Cam, *Studies in the hundred rolls*, 88, 92–3. [9] *Close R.* 1237–42, 56.
[10] Helen M. Cam, *The Hundred and the hundred rolls* (London, 1930), 252.
[11] *Rolls of Justices in Eyre* [for Bucks.], *1227* (Bucks. Rec. Soc. VI), 50.
[12] *Miscellanea*, II (Surtees Soc. CXXVII), 1.
[13] *Crown Pleas of the Wilts. Eyre*, pp. 42–3.

In the last instance no fewer than 16 incidents had to be examined.[1] Wherever possible the justices were expected to determine the veracity of the allegations and this was made mandatory by Westminster I.[2] Unless there had been a judgement in eyre no penalty could be inflicted. After judgement the fine could be estreated by green wax summons.[3] The statute was not allowed to remain a dead letter. In 1295 a sheriff who, acting on the crown's behalf, was claiming fines for escapes before such judgement had been delivered was ordered to desist.[4] Even as late as 1343 men were arguing, though without effect, that escapes could only be adjudged in eyre and that even the King's Bench lacked competence to do so.[5]

The gradual disappearance of the eyre rendered this provision ineffective and other methods of inquiry had to be devised. It is perhaps likely that from the early fourteenth century gaol-delivery justices, who were certainly charged by statute[6] to investigate grave abuses of custody, investigated escapes as well. But other devices were also adopted. Thus, at the time of the amnesty of 1357,[7] the justices of the peace throughout England were enjoined to inquire into and indeed to 'adjudge' escapes, as the justices in eyre had formerly done. Special commissions were also issued. Not relying wholly on the justices of the peace for the county, the crown appointed in 1358 such a commission to inquire into the guilt of the Yorkshire sheriff for conniving at such escapes.[8] In 1400 another such commission was told to inquire into escapes within the bailiwick of the sheriff of Surrey.[9] In 1397 the Colchester gaol-delivery justices had been expressly ordered to report upon recent escapes from Essex gaols.[10] By the early sixteenth century, a set form of words existed requiring such justices to

---

[1] Ibid. subject index, s.v. escapes. [2] C. 3.

[3] *Britton*, I, 88. [4] *Cal. Close R.* 1288–96, 413.

[5] *Sel. Cases in K.B.* VI, p. 45; *Yr. Bk. Liber Assisarum* (Vulg.) 21 Ass. 12 (p. 79).

[6] E.g. 1 Edw. III, St. I, c. 7; *Rot. Parl.* II. 141 (1343).

[7] *Cal. Close R.* 1354–60, 363–4; see p. 247.

[8] *Cal. Pat. R.* 1358–61, 160. [9] Ibid. 1399–1401, 270.

[10] Ibid. 1396–9, 157.

inquire,[1] and this suggests that they were often employed on this work. In the fifteenth century we begin to encounter a regular series of such commissions, issued either partially or wholly for that purpose. Thus the justices of the King's Bench, peace, and assize were authorized by statute in 1414 to inquire into escaping suspect Lollards.[2] The justices of assize, together with the sheriffs and escheators of and in the counties which it was the justices' duty to visit, were told in 1426 to make such inquiries,[3] and in the next year[4] and in 1434[5] other sets of persons were commissioned similarly, with an authority which was practically nation-wide. How effective these measures were has not been ascertained.[6] They seem to show a genuine concern for the state of criminal justice, though the desire to collect fines may have been an additional motive. Later in the century, in 1484, the justices of the peace were permanently charged by statute to inquire into escapes.[7] This followed the precedent of 1357.

The culmination of these measures was the Statute 'of Negligent Escapes' of 1504,[8] which introduced elaborate provisions for fining the keepers of county gaols and some others who had charge of suspect traitors and felons. The statute will be re-examined later.[9] Here it is enough to say that it shows every sign of having been seriously devised to correct a serious abuse.

Such in outline were the general arrangements, but some special ones also existed. By the mid-fourteenth century the coroner of the King's Bench was reporting as a matter of routine upon escapes from the custody of the marshal of that court.[10] This practice was still being followed in 1460 when the coroner visited the prison once or twice a term.[11] Secondly, by the middle of the next century, in fact in 1448, the city of London, never behindhand in the reform of prison administration, had tried to put its own house

[1] 'De inquirendo de escap' felonum commissio': B.M. Add. MS 35205.
[2] 2 Hen. V, St. I, c. 7.   [3] *Cal. Pat. R.* 1244–9, 361.
[4] Ibid. 406.   [5] Ibid. 1429–36, 359.
[6] For a return of 1448 see C 145/313/9.   [7] 1 Ric. III, c. 3.
[8] 19 Hen. VII, c. 10.   [9] See p. 236.
[10] *Sel. Cases in K.B.* VI, pp. xliv–xlv, 77; *Yr. Bk. Liber Assisarum* (Vulg.), 21 *Ass.* 12 (p. 79).   [11] *Yr. Bk. 39 Hen. VI* (Vulg.), p. 33.

in order by appointing two aldermen to examine its own prisons and report upon defects of custody.[1] It was perhaps this body which secured the dismissal of the gaoler of Newgate for negligence in 1450.[2]

The prime object of all these inquiries was to establish the truth or falsehood of the incidents and, where truth was found, to prevent recurrence. For prevention reliance was naturally placed in part on punishment and the inquirers had to assess the punishment appropriate. This involved determining the culpability of the escaper and his keeper.

Punishment for escaping can be traced back to Henry I's reign.[3] Though the references are unilluminating, the punishments then recorded were almost certainly inflicted not upon the prisoner but the keeper. The punishment of the prisoner, however, is also very ancient. It might be achieved either by 'rough justice' or by more formal means. If a prisoner escaped, it was strictly necessary to raise the hue and, this done, the townsmen were to pursue the fugitive. If the pursuers recovered him while in flight and before he had taken sanctuary they might behead him on the spot. Such was the fate of two men who escaped from the Tower in 1283 and were hunted down in St Paul's cathedral and churchyard.[4] Henry de la Mare, imprisoned at Wallingford about 1315, was treated in the same way,[5] and so was a rebel imprisoned at York in 1324 and pursued into Herefordshire.[6] Such executions were perfectly regular. The executioners, however, sometimes deemed it prudent to secure a pardon. Seven men who hanged some fugitives from Northampton about 1227 took this course,[7] as did the man who chased the fugitive from York who has just been mentioned.

Where escaped prisoners were restored to custody it was the original practice to treat them as though they were convicted felons, an attitude which seems to have been exhibited in Roman

---

[1] Jorn. 5, f. 3*b*. [2] Ibid. fos. 48, 51.
[3] See p. 232. [4] *Chrons. Edw. I and II*, i. 91.
[5] *Rot. Parl.* i. 296. [6] *Cal. Pat. R.* 1324–7, 13.
[7] *Close R.* 1227–31, 4.

law.[1] It was not altogether an unreasonable attitude since, in certain circumstances at least, the escaper, by the very act of escaping, admitted his own guilt and, if a suspect felon, might be expected to suffer a felon's fate.[2] Accordingly a man appealed of homicide who was recaptured after escaping from York prison in 1208 was ordered to be put to death.[3] A man 'of evil report' suspected of theft, who likewise was recaptured after escape, was condemned to be hanged.[4] It was decided at the Warwick eyre of 1221 that two fugitives from Warwick gaol who after several years were still at large should be deemed to have been convicted.[5] By Bracton's time it had become a doctrine that escaping suspect felons condemned themselves[6] and *Britton* endorsed Bracton.[7] *Britton* said further that coroners might hold inquests of prison breach and that if the jury found against the prisoner he was *ipso facto* guilty of felony.[8] Thus all the evidence contributes to the view that throughout the greater part of the thirteenth century prison-breaking was a felony in itself, and by Westminster I (1275) it was numbered among irrepleviable offences.[9]

This very rigorous attitude was modified by a statute of 1295, which declared that none should have judgement of life or members merely for the offence of breaking prison, *licet temporibus preteritis aliter fieri consuevit.* Such punishment was only to be inflicted if it was the one appropriate to the offence with which the prisoner had been charged.[10] In days such as these were, before treason had been properly defined, the effect of this ruling was to confine the extreme penalty to escapers who were suspect felons. The statute did not abolish prison-breaking as an offence,

[1] Anna T. Sheedy, *Bartolus on social conditions in the fourteenth century* (New York, 1942), 98.
[2] Cf. *Crown Pleas of the Wilts. Eyre*, p. 65.
[3] *Cur. Reg. R.* v. 268.   [4] Ibid. VIII. 142.
[5] *Rolls of Justices in Eyre in Gloucestershire, Warwickshire and Staffordshire*, 338–9, 381.
[6] *Bracton*, II, 350.   [7] *Britton*, I, 43.
[8] Ibid. 8–9. This was still held to be true in 1313–14 (*Eyre of Kent*, I, 80), but there is no evidence that such inquests, if taken, were ever enrolled (R. F. Hunnisett, *The medieval coroner* (Cambridge, 1961), 110).
[9] C. 15.   [10] 23 Edw. I: *Stat. Realm*, I. 113.

but tempered the punishment which it attracted to the circumstances. As the reporter of the Kentish eyre of 1313–14 somewhat ineptly put it, if one who was a mere trespasser escaped no 'escape' had occurred.[1]

If prison-breach by suspect felons was a felony, prison-breach by suspect traitors was logically a treason. After treason had been statutorily defined, the logic of this was put to the test. Thomas Exeter, indicted of treason in 1421, escaped from prison before he could be tried. He was retaken on a charge of theft, but was indicted not for theft but for prison-breach. He was found guilty of the offence and condemned to suffer the death of a traitor. In the same year Sir John Mortimer was likewise imprisoned for treason and after various escapes and recaptures was in 1424 similarly charged and similarly sentenced.[2] After these two convictions escaping suspect traitors, if convicted of escape, were deemed to be traitors.[3]

How far these doctrines were consistently applied is naturally not easy to determine, since the offences for which escapers were being detained are often quite unknown. It seems to have been held, however, in 1351 that escapers from the custody of the King's Bench marshal, if not able to account satisfactorily for their escape, must suffer death.[4] Some of these at least were felons. The men, however, whose technical escape provoked this expression of opinion, were not convicted of prison-breach.[5] The men who tried to dig themselves out of Salisbury castle in 1346[6] were presumably felons. They were hanged, although their offence seems to have been attempted rather than actual escape. Hanged too, it seems, were all the escapers from the Marshalsea (presumably of the household) in 1504, irrespective of their offences.[7] On the other hand a man who escaped about 1313 from Canterbury castle and was recaptured was merely flogged.[8] Though he died in consequence, he did not suffer a felon's death. He was

---

[1] *Eyre of Kent*, I. 87.
[2] *Yr. Bk. 1 Hen. VII* (S.S.), pp. xxvi–xxvii
[3] 2 Hen. VI, c. 21.
[4] *Sel. Cases in K.B.* v, p. xxvii.
[5] Ibid. VI, p. xlv.
[6] J.I. 3/130 m. 33.
[7] *Gt. Chron. of Lond.* 328.
[8] *Eyre of Kent*, I, p. lvi.

possibly a trespasser or misdemeanant. The men who rioted in Newgate in 1456 were punished only with 'irons', though it must be said that they did not manage to get beyond the leads.[1]

It is not clear how clerks held in 'bishops'' prisons, either pending trial or penally, were punished if recaptured. Plainly they could not be treated in accordance with the statute of 1295, since the death penalty could not be inflicted upon them. Eventually, in 1532, a statute declared that such escapes were to be deemed felonies,[2] so that at last the law of Edward I was made to apply to such people. The preamble asserted that hitherto the punishment for such escapers had been insufficient. The best intervening evidence is furnished by the statute of 1414 against Lollards which provides that the lands and chattels of such people are to be seized by the crown until the escapers surrender again to their keepers. If the escapers had been convicted of Lollardy they would have lost their property anyway, but presumably if they were acquitted the property would have been restored.[3] Perhaps, however, this provision is more in the nature of a coercive power to ensure appearance at a trial than a punishment.

In order to incur the pains of 'escaping' it was necessary, according to the view that eventually prevailed, for the prisoner to have 'broken' prison, an act which is once or twice called 'burglary'.[4] If the door stood open through the negligence of the gaoler or was forced open by the activities of other prisoners or a mob without, the prisoner was himself exonerated. He had 'gone out', not 'broken out', and any culpability was transferred from him to his rescuers or keepers. This seems to have been on the way to settlement in Edward IV's time.[5] At all events a Star Chamber action of 1482 turned on the question whether an escaper had 'broken out of ward' or whether he had 'come out'.[6] With the rescuers themselves the law dealt severely. Coke, quoting Billing and Choke, justices at the time when the foregoing

---

[1] *Gt. Chron. of Lond.* 189.   [2] 23 Hen. VIII, c. 11, s. 1.
[3] 2 Hen. V, St. 1, c. 7.
[4] *Beds. Coroners' R.* 111 (1304); *Sess. of Peace in Lincs.* 11, 16 (1383).
[5] Coke, 2 *Instit.* (1671 ed.), 589.
[6] *Sel. Cases in Star Chamber*, [1], pp. lxxiii–lxxv.

distinction between 'breaking out' and 'going out' was established, declared that rescuing was always felony at common law,
and reported cases confirm that opinion, though not quite un-
equivocally. A *garcio* of the constable of Oxford castle, who
helped a woman to escape in 1306, was hanged,[1] and a man who
helped the traitor Exeter to escape suffered with him a traitor's
death.[2] The man, mentioned above, who broke the door in 1485–6
through which the prisoner walked was deemed to have committed felony. On the other hand an Oxford clerk, who about
1421 rescued a clerk from a 'bishop's' prison, did not suffer the
clerk's punishment for felony, though he was outlawed and expelled from the university.[3]

[1] *Abbrev. Plac.* 253.   [2] *Yr. Bk. 1 Hen. VI* (S. S.), pp. xxvi–xxvii.
[3] *Rot. Parl.* iv. 131.

XI

THE CONSEQUENCES OF ESCAPES
FOR THE GAOLER

THE punishment of a 'keeper', however defined, who suffered his prisoners to escape is much more fully documented than is the punishment of the prisoner himself, his accomplices, or rescuers. It has a long and complex history.

In the earlier twelfth century this punishment took the form of heavy fines,[1] which as the century advanced appear to have grown more moderate.[2] Fines were also common in the thirteenth century and were inflicted on gaolers in fee[3] and townships[4] alike. There were, however, severer punishments as well. In 1230[5] and 1246–7[6] gaolers in fee lost their office for this cause. In 1254 the sheriffs of London when they failed to keep safely John of Frome, a man in whose punishment Henry III was directly interested, were in like manner deprived and were also imprisoned for a month, while the gaoler of Newgate was outlawed for complicity in the same offence.[7]

Such penalties seem to have rested upon custom, for no known ordinance imposes them. It may, however, be mentioned that failure to pursue and arrest felons both within franchises and without became statutorily punishable under Westminster 1,[8] and

---

[1] Aubrey de Vere (Essex) owed £550 and 4 palfreys for a prisoner who escaped from his custody and for penalties incurred in shire courts (*pro forisf' comitatuum*); Osbert the palmer (Lincs.) owed 15 marks for a forger who escaped; *Pipe R.* 1130 (Rec. Com.), 53, 113.

[2] In 1186–7 a servant of the prior of Coventry owed 20s. for the escape of a cobbler from his prison, apparently in Gloucestershire: *Pipe R.* 1187 (P.R.S. xxxviii), 138. In 1192–3 the town of Wallingford owed 1 mark for a thief who escaped: ibid. (P.R.S. n.s. ii), 130.

[3] *Rolls of Justices in Eyre for Lincolnshire and Worcestershire* (Selden Soc. liii), 610.   [4] See p. 250.

[5] *Close R.* 1227–31, 362, 516.   [6] Ibid. 1247–51, 19, 20.

[7] *Chron. Maiorum et Vicecomitum Lond.* (Camden Soc. o.s. xxxiv), 21–2; *Cal. Pat. R.* 1258–66, 8.   [8] C. 9.

since, as we have seen,[1] releasing a man actually in custody and failing to arrest and hold a man who ought to be in custody did not seem to contemporaries to be logically far apart, it may perhaps be said that subsequent practice owes something to that statute. It may at least be worth recalling what the statute provides by way of punishment for such offences. The common man who fails to take part in the hue and cry and to arrest where need be incurs a heavy fine; the lord of a franchise so failing shall lose the franchise; a 'bailiff' so failing shall be imprisoned for a year and shall make fine as well; and a sheriff, coroner, or other 'bailiff', within franchise or without, who corruptly conceals felonies or corruptly fails to arrest felons, shall be treated in the same way. In the last instance, if the defaulter be too poor to pay the fine, his imprisonment is to be prolonged to three or four years.

The earliest express definition of the punishment falling upon those responsible for escapes is to be found in *Britton*.[2] It must be admitted that his statements are disorderly and confusing. They seem, however, to tell us this. If anyone who claims the custody of a prison in fee suffers an escape, he is to lose his franchise; if a sheriff or other royal officer is similarly guilty, he should be fined £5; if a township or the owner of a private prison be guilty, the township or that person should be amerced. The implication is that in none of these instances would the escaper have been an approver. If he was, the 'keeper' was to be imprisoned and 'ransomed' at the king's will. It is also implied that the escapes were due to pure negligence. If corruption entered in, and the 'keeper' was found to have connived at the escape, he was to be indicted of felony and if convicted was to suffer a felon's death. *Fleta* in like manner declares that the death penalty ought to be inflicted on the marshal if convicted of such corrupt connivance.[3] Thus *Britton* and *Fleta* draw a distinction between what were later to be called 'negligent' and 'voluntary' escapes,[4] a 'voluntary' escape being one that had occurred by the 'will' of

---

[1] See p. 218.   [2] *Britton*, I, 43, 87.   [3] *Fleta*, II, p. 115.
[4] Sir M. Hale, *Historia Placitorum Coronae* (London, 1800), I, c. 51. The words are perhaps first juxtaposed in the statute of 1504, see p. 236.

the 'keeper'.[1] *Mutatis mutandis* the clause in Westminster I, already referred to, had drawn a similar distinction.

It is not possible to show that all *Britton*'s doctrines formed a correct statement of the law as it was subsequently applied in practice. This is particularly true of 'voluntary' escapes. Such escapes are indeed constantly imputed to 'keepers'. They are traceable in the records of the Gloucestershire eyre of 1221[2] and the Buckinghamshire eyre of 1227.[3] The visitatorial commissioners of 1274–5 were told to be on the watch for them.[4] Later generations were just as familiar with them[5] and they are comprehensively condemned in the preamble to the Statute of Escapes of 1504, referred to below.[6] It is, however, uncommonly hard to find a 'keeper' suffering the punishment which *Britton* and the other authorities said was his due. Perhaps the explanation is in part that the doctrine was a Roman or quasi-Roman one,[7] never really assimilated into English practice. No doubt, too, the offences alleged were not always very serious, amounting often to no more than unauthorized replevins, and that the evidence available tended to come from suspect sources. Consequently, although the pains of felony may have hung *in terrorem* over the head of every conniving 'keeper', they seldom fell upon it.

That a sheriff or other 'keeper' who allowed an approver to escape was sent to prison cannot be proved from documentary sources. That such a lapse, however, was seriously regarded is shown by the conduct of the prior of Dunstable's gaoler in 1295 who, after an approver had escaped from his hands, took sanctuary for three weeks.[8] In any event such officials were from time to time imprisoned for allowing escapes of other types of prisoner,

[1] 'Wilful' is the word used in 14 and 15 Hen. VIII, c. 17, s. 7 (1523) and is better than 'voluntary'.
[2] Maitland, *Glos. Pl.* pp. 86, 96–7.
[3] *Rolls of Justices in Eyre* [for Buckinghamshire], *1227* (Bucks. Rec. Soc. VI), p. 49.   [4] Helen M. Cam, *Studies in the hundred rolls*, 158–9.
[5] Thus in 1358 the sheriff of Yorkshire was accused of allowing many people to escape from York castle by conspiracy and bribery: *Cal. Pat. R.* 1358–61, 160.
[6] 19 Hen. VII, c. 10; and see p. 236.
[7] Anna T. Sheedy, *Bartolus on social conditions in the fourteenth century*, 99 n.
[8] *Ann. Mon.* (R.S.), III. 395–6.

especially where the crown was directly interested in keeping the prisoner safe, as indeed it was in the case of approvers. This, as we saw, was the fate of the sheriffs of London in 1254,[1] and of the mayor, bailiffs, and certain citizens of Winchester in 1304 for their failure to keep in proper confinement a hostage of Bayonne.[2] When in 1305 the sheriff of Essex let a Scottish prisoner go he was deprived of his property and imprisoned.[3] Another man, similarly negligent while escorting a Scotsman to the same sheriff in the same year, was also imprisoned.[4] Under-marshals of the King's Bench who did not keep their prisoners in ward might be imprisoned for an indefinite period,[5] and such a punishment was statutorily ordained in 1331.[6] Other instances of later date could also be cited where keepers were imprisoned for this cause, as was the keeper of Newgate in 1450 for the collective escape that occurred in that year.[7]

That a gaoler in fee might, as *Britton* says, lose office if he suffered an escape is proved by incidents that occurred before the time at which the tract was written. Other 'keepers' might be similarly punished, as were the sheriffs of London in 1254[8] and the King's Bench marshals in 1323–4.[9] As has been said, they were imprisoned as well. According to *Fleta*, the marshal and his deputies, if they suffered escapes, were to be imprisoned and deprived.[10] Escapes could also lead to a permanent loss of franchise. In 1297 the crown threatened to close the London Tun as a punishment for the rescue already described,[11] and, although the threat was not carried out, the citizens had to purchase a pardon before they were forgiven.[12] The prison at Milton-next-Sittingbourne, probably at that time a franchise prison,[13] was confiscated for a like cause in 1313–14.[14]

---

[1] See p. 232.   [2] *Rot. Parl.* I. 176–7. He was later 'ransomed'.
[3] Ibid. 216; cf. *Cal. Close R.* 1302–7, 419. Later, on the Scotsman's recapture, the property was restored and the sheriff released.
[4] *Mem. de Parl.* 59.   [5] *Rot. Parl.* I. 365.   5 Edw. III, c. 8.
[7] Jorn. 5, f. 48.   [8] See p. 232.   [9] See above.
[10] *Fleta*, II, p. 115.   [11] See p. 222.
[12] *Cal. Lr. Bks. B*, 75; *C*, 37–8. The prison is concealed under the word 'cask'!
[13] See p. 83.   [14] *Eyre of Kent*, I, 82.

But though loss of franchise, loss of office, imprisonment, or even death might be the reward of lax or unfaithful custody it is clear that the common punishment was a fine. This fine was very often £5 for the escape of each ordinary suspect if a layman. It could stand at that figure in both Henry III's earlier[1] and middle[2] years and, as we saw, *Britton* held it to be normal in straightforward circumstances.[3] Certainly in the fourteenth and fifteenth centuries it was very commonly imposed.[4] In the mid-fourteenth century it could also be due from the marshal of the King's Bench *pur cescun comune prison de felonie*[5] although escaping from that prison was subject to special regulations.[6] Finally, it figures in the tariff of fines for escapes from sheriffs' gaols embodied in the Statute of Escapes (1504), where it is declared to be the appropriate penalty for the escape of a suspect felon charged with a crime less serious than murder.[7] Of course the sum forfeited by the gaoler is not always expressed, and if expressed is not always £5. But whatever the rate of the fine, its infliction, both on 'keepers', escorts and townships, is frequent.

The Statute of Escapes, which to an extent tidied up for a while a tangled mass of custom and case law, is worthy of a little more attention than it has yet received. It opens by reciting that in the past escapes had all too often been fraudulent, the fraud consisting on the sheriff's part in suffering the prisoner to go free in return for a bribe while representing the escape as done without his knowledge. Where escapes had been detected and punished, the preamble continues, the punishment had consisted of imposing fines too small to deter. Accordingly it lays down a tariff of fines varying with the degree of guilt attaching to the escaper. By reuniting castles with counties[8] it brought as many common gaols as possible within the tariff. Others apart from sheriffs who had charge of suspect traitors and felons and let them go were to be

---

[1] *Close R.* 1234–7, 254. [2] *Sel. Cases in Exchq. of Pleas*, p. 22.
[3] See p. 233.
[4] E.g. *Cal. Pat. R.* 1361–4, 265; 1381–5, 372; 41399–101, 114–15; 1405–8, 39, 180; *Yr. Bk. 25 Edw. III* (Vulg.), p. 82a.
[5] *Sel. Cases in K.B.* v, pp. xxvii, cxxii. [6] See p. 235.
[7] 19 Hen. VII, c. 10. [8] See p. 151.

fined by 'the justices that shall have authority to assess such fines'. The effect of the statute seems to be to blur the distinction between 'voluntary' and 'negligent' escapes, with both of which, according to its title, it purports to deal, and to treat most escapes as 'negligent'. In the interests of ensuring that escapes if proved do not go unpunished altogether, it relaxes the serious consequences of corrupt participation on the keeper's part.

Escapes of clerks from 'bishops'' prisons were treated differently from escapes of laymen from common gaols. They were punished severely, normally by the imposition of a fine of £100 for each escape;[1] this sum seems to have been customary by 1253[2] and was accepted as a matter of course in the earlier fourteenth century.[3] That such a punishment sometimes proved too heavy is attested by numerous pardons.[4] Abatements of the fines are also found. Thus a fine of £1,200 imposed upon the bishop of London in 1357 was reduced to a twelfth of that sum,[5] the fines for which a later bishop became liable in 1430 were respited for ten years, and[6] in 1414 the bishop of Chichester paid only 100 marks instead of £100.[7] But such indulgence was by no means invariable. As early as 1270 the bishop of Norwich, as late as 1472–3 the bishop of Winchester, secured no remission, and in the latter instance the Receipt Roll of the Exchequer confirms the actual payment of the money.[8] If such profits could be made, small wonder that the crown when, by a process which will later be traced, it granted the proceeds of escapes to the Commons of England in 1357, limited the grant to the escapes of laymen.[9]

The reason for this severe discrimination against the owners

---

[1] Leona C. Gabel, *Benefit of clergy in England in the later middle ages* (Northampton, Mass., 1928–9), 111.

[2] It is the sum which the bishop must forfeit if he fails to produce before itinerant justices for trial a clerk handed over to him by the lay power: *Councils & Synods*, ed. F. M. Powicke and C. R. Cheney, II (1), 471–2. Cf ibid. II (2), 883, 1355.

[3] *Yr. Bk. Liber Assisarum* (Vulg.), 21 Ass. 12 (p. 79); A. Fitzherbert, *La graunde abridgement* (London, 1577), Coron. 370.

[4] See p. 245.
[5] *Cal. Pat. R.* 1354–8, 355.
[6] Ibid. 1429–36, 35.
[7] Ibid. 1413–16, 198.
[8] Gabel, *Benefit of clergy*, 111.
[9] See p. 247.

or keepers of 'bishops'' prisons is at present a little speculative. It appears, however, to have been an ancient doctrine, though how ancient is uncertain, that if a felon was 'attainted' of felony and escaped, the penalty for the escape was £100; if, on the other hand, he was only indicted, i.e. was being held for trial, the penalty was only one-twentieth of that sum.[1] Criminous clerks, if they were convicted of felony in a lay court or if they pleaded guilty there, were, as has been shown,[2] handed over to a diocesan to be lodged in prison. It was held by Edward II's reign[3] that they should not be admitted to purgation. If this was observed and they remained in prison unpurged they were in fact 'attainted' felons. Indeed they must have formed the main element in that category, since 'attainted' lay felons should have been hanged immediately after their conviction, and usually were,[4] unless they were remanded. There were possibly other reasons for these heavy fines. 'Bishops'' prisons seem to have been exceptionally insecure and they held men on life-long imprisonment who but for their clergy would have been put out of the way. The temptation to terminate a theoretically interminable sentence was strong and attempted escapes proportionately more frequent. Secondly, the bishops themselves could neither be imprisoned nor removed if the escapes in which they were implicated were 'negligent' nor prosecuted for felony if those escapes were 'voluntary'. The enormous fine of £200 which the abbot of Westminster, who had the powers of an ordinary,[5] was required to pay in 1292 seems to support such an argument. He had connived at the escape of a man whom he had undertaken to have *coram rege* and there was no other way of punishing him.[6]

One of the liberties that the crown sometimes bestowed on its subjects in early times, or allowed them to exercise, was that of taking the fines arising from escapes. The privilege was sometimes called 'utslat' or 'utsslac', a word that may perhaps be the

---

[1] Sir W. Stanford, *Pleas del Corone* (1607 ed.), 35, referring to Fitzherbert's *La graunde abridgement*, though the reference seems inaccurate.
[2] See p. 48.
[3] Gabel, op. cit. 104–6; cf. *Yr. Bk. Liber Assisarum* (Vulg.), 21 Ass. 12 (p. 79).
[4] See p. 210.   [5] See p. 134.   [6] *Abbrev. Plac.* 286.

equivalent of 'slipping away'. Under that name it appears to have
been granted to Peterborough abbey by its charter of 1198,[1] and
to have been confirmed to it by charters of 1200[2] and 1253.[3]
The privilege was challenged by the crown in 1330 on the ground
that the word was unintelligible,[4] but there is no evidence that it
was abandoned. The abbot of Byland made a similar claim under
his charter of 1271–2[5] and the archbishop of York in 1293–4.[6]
While it is not known for how long these particular claims were
sustained, it is clear that the privilege was one which the crown
was prepared to sanction, and even expressly to grant, well after
the end of the thirteenth century. Thus in 1395 the bishop of
London was granted such fines, except for the escapes of clerks
convict,[7] and his rights were confirmed in 1462.[8] The priory of
Bridlington was similarly indulged in 1446.[9]

Apart from such permanent devolutions of the royal prerogative, individuals were sometimes given the right to collect the fines
due for particular escapes. The earliest instance yet noticed comes
from 1270 when Imbert de Montferrand was authorized to collect
a fine which the bishop of Norwich had incurred for the escape
of a clerk convict.[10] Many later examples could be cited particularly
for Richard II's reign and the years immediately following.[11] Such
grants, of course, served as a means of liquidating claims against
a semi-bankrupt Exchequer.

Apart from a few incidents in London little is known about the
fate of municipal 'keepers' who let their prisoners escape. Sometimes, no doubt, special regulations were made for them. At all
events the governing body of Coventry laid it down in 1515 that

---

[1] *Plac. de Quo Warr.* 70. The MS reading is 'utslat' 'utslath'. The printed
text reads 'utflac'.

[2] *Rot. Cart.* 82, where it is printed 'ullath' (checked with MS).

[3] *Cal. Chart. R.* 1257–1300, 142, where it is printed 'utsslac'. In an abstract
of the same charter in the Chronicle of the Abbey (Soc. Ant. Lond. MS 60, f. 123*b*)
the word is written 'utlath'.

[4] *Plac. de Quo Warr.* 71, where it is printed 'utflach' or 'utfak'.

[5] Ibid. 223. [6] Ibid. 221.

[7] *Cal. Chart. R.* 1341–1417, 351. [8] Ibid. 1427–1516, 162.

[9] Ibid. 67. [10] *Cal. Pat. R.* 1268–72, 435.

[11] E.g. ibid. 1381–5, 220; 1399–1401, 114–15; 1413–16, 198.

if their gaoler released a prisoner before his trial he would be fined 3*s*. 4*d*. and if he repeated the offence the fine should rise in geometrical progression.[1]

Hitherto we have been mainly concerned with attempts to discipline or punish 'keepers' who in the normal course of duty failed to secure the ordinary run of prisoners. It is necessary to add that in the fifteenth century several statutes were passed or promoted to provide special punishments for special types of escape. In 1415 the Commons failed to substitute a fixed fine of £100 for an arbitrary fine for those responsible for the escape of a man held for forgery or the debasement of the currency.[2] By a statute of 1455 the keeper of the King's Bench prison was made liable to a fine of £400 if he released without warrant servants imprisoned for the embezzlement of their deceased masters' goods. This was payable to the dead man's executors.[3] This was a very heavy fine indeed, but in the same century fines of quite fantastic proportions were sometimes imposed with the aim of securing the safe custody of individuals. Thus in 1439 the marshal of the Marshalsea, if he should set at liberty a man charged with levying public war upon another,[4] was to forfeit £1,000. Likewise it was enacted in 1439 that the unlucky gaoler who might allow Thomas Percy, Lord Egremont, and his brother Richard, charged with riot, to escape was to pay £2,000.[5] The gaoler who might release Robert Poynings and his two associates, all adherents of Jack Cade, was to forfeit twice that amount.[6] The sheriffs of London and Middlesex, if they should allow a former sheriff of Cornwall to escape from Newgate, were condemned in 1475 to a fine of 6,000 marks.[7] It seems unlikely that such enormous sums could have been collected, and their insertion in Acts of Parliament looks like 'window-dressing' or the result of panic.

Besides prison-breach and prison-rescue and escapes due to sheer acts of carelessness there are many instances from the later

---

[1] *Coventry Leet Bk.* II, 644.   [2] *Rot. Parl.* IV. 82.
[3] 33 Hen. VI, c. 1.   [4] *Rot. Parl.* V. 17–18.
[5] Ibid. 395; *Peerage*, s.v. Egremont. As mentioned above (p. 221), Egremont did escape from Newgate a little later, but this was a separate imprisonment.
[6] *Rot. Parl.* V. 397.   [7] Ibid. VI. 139.

thirteenth century of men escaping because a prisoner had been allowed by the gaoler to go out of prison without due protection. This form of 'escape', eventually called 'wandering abroad', is so special that it is justifiable to treat it in isolation.

Accusations that gaolers allowed this latitude tend to merge into accusations of the injudicious or unlawful concession of bail, but they may in logic be distinguished from one another by the fact that on the face of it the replevied prisoner was not expected to return to prison before his trial. At Christmas 1291 Matthew of the Exchequer, who was undergoing a sentence of two years' and two days' imprisonment in the Fleet for official misconduct, was allowed by the warden to go out to dinner at a friend's house. He was accompanied by a *garcio* of the warden. A few days later he was taken by the warden's deputy to the Carmelite church in London and even to the king's court at Westminster. These antics resulted in an increased sentence for Matthew and his removal to the Tower, the imprisonment of the deputy in Newgate, and the removal of the Fleet from the custody of the warden.[1] In 1293 a man who had been appealed for abetting a homicide, and who had been outlawed in Kent, was observed hearing mass at Black-friars and in St Paul's and wandering about the streets, squares, and inns of London without 'irons'. He should have been in the custody of the deputy-marshal of the King's Bench. The deputy-marshal said that the prisoner had always been in the company of his *garcio*, who was merely taking him from Kent to London for trial, and that he was without 'irons' only because he could not walk in 'irons'. The punishment was similar to that inflicted in the previous case: the deputy, though subsequently pardoned, was handed over to the sheriff of Kent, the *garcio* was put in custody, and the marshalsea was taken into the king's hand.[2] In 1306 Hengham, then a justice of oyer and terminer in Kent, reported that several men committed to prison by the justices, together with certain outlaws, were wandering about the country. The sheriff of Kent was called upon to account.[3] About 1313–14

---

[1] *Sel. Cases in Exchq. of Pleas*, pp. 141–3; *Sel. Cases in K.B.* II, pp. cliv–clv.
[2] *Sel. Cases in K.B.* II, pp. 149–51.   [3] Ibid. p. clvi.

a man arrested for petty larceny in the Kentish hundred of Milton
was allowed by the keeper of the prison in which he was shut up
to go to a neighbouring town on the understanding that he would
return. He actually went to another town in a different hundred
and was held to be trying to escape.[1] At about the same time a
man detained on remand for killing another man in self-defence
was allowed by the sheriff of Kent to wander without an escort.
Though the prisoner would doubtless have been acquitted in the
end, the sheriff was fined £20 for this indulgence.[2] Similar allegations that prisoners were wandering at will were levelled against
the keeper of Windsor gaol in 1315,[3] the keeper of Stafford gaol
in 1336,[4] and the keeper of Warwick gaol in 1342.[5] In 1342 ninety-
one indicted persons were found to be missing from the custody
of the King's Bench marshal, and in 1350 twenty-two were
missing from the same custody. Some members of the latter
group were recovered and succeeded in excusing themselves on
the plea that they had bound themselves with the deputy-marshal
in a substantial sum to appear in court by a certain day.[6] This
was a kind of unlawful bail.

In the late thirteenth century, as we have seen,[7] imprisonment
for debt begins to be provided for by statute. The Statutes of
Acton Burnell, of Merchants, and of Westminster II are of that
century and are reinforced in the next by the statute of 1352.[8]
These Acts introduced a new feature into prison-keeping, namely,
the obligation upon the gaoler to act in such a way as to protect
the interests of the creditor or other party initiating the imprisonment. The Statute of Merchants says that the keeper of the prison
in which the statute debtor is confined shall answer for the debtor's
body as for the debt, the meaning being that if he allow the
debtor to escape he shall become liable for the debt or else shall be
himself imprisoned.[9] Westminster II stipulates that the defaulting
accountant shall not be replevied or allowed to leave prison by

---

[1] *Eyre of Kent*, I. 80.
[2] Ibid. p. lxxii.
[3] *Cal. Pat. R.* 1313–17, 329.
[4] Ibid. 1334–8, 365.
[5] Ibid. 1341–3, 499.
[6] *Sel. Cases in K.B.* vi, pp. xliv–xlv.
[7] See p. 45.
[8] 25 Edw. III, St. v, c. 17.
[9] *Stat. Realm*, I. 99.

any other means without the assent of his master. If a sheriff or gaoler allows him to do so, he shall be answerable to the master for the damages done by the servant.[1] In other words he is to be placed under the same obligations as the escaper himself. That such releases did occur and the gaoler came to be liable for the escape is attested by suits of 1311,[2] 1318,[3] 1344,[4] and 1363.[5] The first and third of these were prosecuted under the Statute of Merchants, the second under Westminster II. Two of these suits will have to be referred to again later.[6] In addition to these two statutes, in which the responsibility for 'letting out' was clearly defined, other cases can be found where the defendant in a civil suit had been imprisoned and released. Thus two cases could be cited of the release of persons taken in pursuance of an action of conspiracy, in one of which (1314) the sheriffs of London were held to be to blame and were ordered to satisfy the plaintiff.[7] Once, however, it became possible for the creditor in an action of debt to distrain upon a debtor's person,[8] there was much greater scope for allowing prisoners to go at large. Persons imprisoned in such actions were not of course common felons or dangerous to the public. They were often of good standing in society and might sometimes be well-to-do. They were therefore very apt to be in a position to make terms with a gaoler, and gaolers were not slow to take advantage of the situation. The practice was particularly notorious in the Fleet, and in 1377 resulted in the enactment of a corrective statute.[9] Prisoners taken at the suit of a party were said to be frequently allowed by the warden to go at large either under bail or without bail in the custody of a baston. They were then free to conduct their business and could not readily be restored to prison. The result was that the coercive effect of prison was destroyed; debts and other actions might remain unsettled. In future no prisoners were to leave the Fleet until they should

---

[1] C. 11.
[2] *Yr. Bk. 5 Edw. II* (Selden Soc. LXIII), 9–10.
[3] *Yr. Bk. 11 Edw. II* (S.S.), 265–7.
[4] *Yr. Bk. 18 & 19 Edw. III* (R.S.), 64–70. The suit was undetermined.
[5] *Cal. Plea & Mem. R.* 1323–64, 266.
[6] See pp. 253–4.
[7] *Rot. Parl.* I. 320, 463.
[8] 25 Edw. III, St. v, c. 17.
[9] 1 Ric. II, c. 12.

have made 'gree' to the plaintiff, in fact until they had afforded him the satisfaction which he hoped to secure by their imprisonment. It appears from the same statute that debtors imprisoned in other prisons habitually alleged that they were crown debtors and thus were able to claim admittance to the Fleet. There, where 'suet' of prison prevailed by custom,[1] they could enjoy that liberty to go abroad which was a part of that indulgence and which at the time was apparently not available to them in other prisons. This practice was also forbidden. Henceforth no such transfer was to be made unless the prisoner was, of record, a crown debtor. Instead he was to be remanded to his original prison. The penalty resting upon the warden for such practices was loss of office. Moreover, the plaintiff was given an action of debt against him. Thus, as in the case of the Statutes of Merchants and of Westminster II, the defaulting warden was put in the position of the debtor. The result of this was that the wardens began to purchase letters of protection from the crown. This practice was in turn forbidden in 1406,[2] but probably without success.

The statute of 1377 seems to have been provoked by a curious incident that took place in the year before it was passed. A man had been prosecuted in the Common Pleas for rape and had been sentenced to a fine and damages. He refused to pay either. For refusing the fine he was outlawed and steps were also taken to outlaw him for his failure to pay the damages. Before process was complete he borrowed money from one of the auditors of the Exchequer, declined to repay it, and was collusively imprisoned in the Fleet. Here he at once arranged for his temporary release so that he was able to carry on a normal life by day, perhaps returning to the Fleet at night. By entering the prison of his choice on his own terms, with the cooperation of a friendly plaintiff who would not pursue his claim, he was able to protect himself from the consequences of his conviction in the earlier suit. This shows how the Fleet could form a kind of haven of refuge not very different from a sanctuary.[3]

---

[1] See p. 336.   [2] 7 Hen. IV, c. 4.   [3] *Trans. R. Hist. Soc.* 4th ser. v, 42–3.

It seems to have been doubted in 1470 whether a debtor who had been allowed to go at large and was then recaptured was still in execution for the original debt.[1] It was because of the existence of such doubts that when the earl marshal and his officers were indemnified by statute for the rescues effected from the King's Bench prison in that year, the rights of creditors to execution against the debtors were expressly saved.[2] This provision, how-ever, affected only a particular group of debtors. The doubts seem to have been finally removed in 1475 when it was decided in the Exchequer Chamber that a debtor might be recaptured at any time and would remain in execution, but that if a creditor success-fully brought an action for the escape against a gaoler, the debtor would be cleared of his debt.[3] Any risk that the creditor would 'have it both ways' was thus removed. That creditors sometimes tried to do so is a reminder that in disputes with gaolers creditors were not always the innocent party. Thus in 1474–5 a prisoner in Ludgate who owed money to a London draper escaped either by a prison-breach or by evading his baston. The creditor pro-ceeded against the sheriffs, but the sheriffs said that the debtor escaped through the 'covin' of the creditor. The action was com-promised,[4] a result which suggests that at any rate the sheriffs were not exclusively blameworthy.

Such in outline is the story of 'wandering abroad' so long as 'wandering' was in the nature of an abuse or an irregularity. Later it became a recognized custom and merits attention in another place.[5]

Much space has been devoted to the punishment of gaolers, but naturally the facts alleged against them were by no means always substantiated and many pardons are on record. Thus in 1238 the king granted the gaoler of Exeter a pardon conditional upon proof that a homicide had not escaped with his connivance.[6] Pardons were also issued to the keeper of Guildford gaol in 1271[7] and

---

[1] *Yr. Bk. 10 Edw. IV & 49 Hen. VI* (S.S.), 92–5.
[2] *Rot. Parl.* VI. 50. Cf. p. 224.
[3] *Sel. Cases in Exch. Chamber* (Selden Soc. LXIV), II. 34.
[4] *Gt. Chron. of Lond.* 222–3.   [5] See p. 336.
[6] *Close R.* 1237–42, 56.   [7] *Cal. Pat. R.* 1266–72, 505.

the sheriff of Essex in 1307[1] because they had pursued and re-captured prisoners, to the sheriff of Surrey and Sussex in 1391 because his prison was out of repair,[2] to the keeper of Winchester about 1441, when his servant lost his life and his keys in the course of searching prisoners,[3] to the keeper of Nottingham in 1442, when a man escaped through the 'covin' of his servant,[4] and to the keeper of Cambridge in 1452 when a prisoner fled while ostensibly making his dying confession.[5] On the face of it these look like valid excuses. There were also many precautionary pardons, excusing the beneficiary from the pains arising not only from escapes which had actually occurred but from those which might occur in future.[6] Pardons were also frequently granted to diocesans. Thus in 1382 the bishop of Lincoln, fourteen of whose clerks had fled from his prison at Newark, received such a pardon.[7] The bishop of Winchester was similarly pardoned in the same year for the escape of twenty-three who had been enclosed at Wolvesley.[8] Between 1386 and 1413 no fewer than five such pardons were granted to the archbishop of York for the escape from various prisons in York and elsewhere of prisoners both clerical and lay.[9] Other pardons in respect of a more limited number of individuals were received between 1440 and 1479 by the bishops of Chichester[10] and Exeter[11] and by the abbot of West-minster.[12] About 1486 the abbot of St Albans was petitioning with the same object.[13] This ecclesiastical preponderance is naturally due to the severity of the fines imposed upon the clergy.[14]

From the middle of the fourteenth century a succession of statutes was passed releasing in general terms all fines due to the

---

[1] *Cal. Pat. R.* 1301–7, 490.   [2] Ibid. 1388–92, 389, 487.

[3] See p. 183.   [4] *Cal. Pat. R.* 1441–6, 91.

[5] Ibid. 1446–52, 551.

[6] E.g. Walter Mauny, under-marshal of the King's Bench who, with his subordinates, was exonerated in 1342 from all escapes and all other 'excesses' committed in his time: ibid. 1340–3, 561.

[7] *Cal. Pat. R.* 1381–5, 120, 143.   [8] Ibid. 161.

[9] Ibid. 1385–9, 125; 1388–92, 328; 1396–9, 268, 466; 1408–13, 465.

[10] Ibid. 1436–41, 492; 1476–85, 161.   [11] Ibid. 1441–6, 376.

[12] Ibid. 1467–77, 340. For the abbot's status as ordinary see p. 134.

[13] *Chron. Monast. S. Albani*, VI (2) (*Registra...Abbatum*), 279.

[14] See p. 237.

crown for escapes, together with many other outstanding claims against the subject. Some of the foregoing pardons to individuals may have been sued out under them. The first statute,[1] passed, it is said, at the instigation of William Montagu, earl of Salisbury,[2] dates from 1340 and was made to last until the king should go to Brabant. A second was passed in 1357, in return for a vote by the Commons of a Fifteenth.[3] It was more limited in scope than most of the other releases, for it did not extend to the escape of clerks convict nor to escapes unadjudged or occurring in the future, and it incorporated special orders to justices of the peace to inquire into such escapes. Amnesty, therefore, was on this occasion accompanied by administrative reform. The exclusion of the fines for the escape of clerks is intelligible when it is remembered how much larger they normally were than fines for the escapes of laymen,[4] and how much importance was attached to the safeguarding of clerks. A third measure, and a more sweeping one, was enacted in 1362[5] and was extended in 1377[6] to cover escapes occurring up to that year. A fifth,[7] promulgated, once again in return for subsidies, in 1380, empowered the keepers of prisons or their lawful representatives to petition for pardons for the escape of both suspect felons and clerks convict, provided that those escapes had not already been 'adjudged' and were not known to be due to corruption on the keeper's part. It was renewed in more comprehensive terms, and without positively requiring the suing out of pardons, in 1398,[8] repealed in 1399,[9] and brought back into force in 1401.[10] The precedents established in the fourteenth century were still remembered in the sixteenth for, by an Act of 1523, Henry VIII, in return for a subsidy, pardoned all negligent (but apparently not any voluntary) escapes occurring before a day named therein.[11]

It might seem at first sight that measures to facilitate the purchase of pardons must be at variance with the evident desire of the

---

[1] 14 Edw. III, St. I, c. 2. [2] *Peerage*, XI, 387.
[3] 31 Edw. III, St. I, cc. 13 and 14. [4] See p. 237.
[5] 36 Edw. III, St. II. [6] 50 Edw. III, c. 3. [7] 4 Ric. II, c. 2.
[8] 21 Ric. II, c. 15. [9] 1 Hen. IV, c. 3. [10] 2 Hen. IV, c. 13.
[11] 14 & 15 Hen. VIII, c. 17, ss. 3 and 7.

crown to prevent or reduce escaping. This, however, is not necessarily the case. In the middle ages most wise men, even when wholly cleared by judgement of a court of the charges brought against them, took the precaution of securing a pardon if the charges were grave ones. The crown and the Chancery officials on their side were not averse to the habit, since the pardons were issued in return for fees and fees never came amiss. The statutes, therefore, do not so much indicate laxity and indifference as the extreme frequency of the imputation of negligent custody, which the special commissions of inquiry of the time[1] almost certainly brought forth, and the probability that many such charges were, if not baseless, at least incapable of verification.

Before the immensely complicated subject of escaping can be dismissed, there is one special aspect that must be examined, namely, the award of liability. If an escape seemed to have occurred through the fault of a 'keeper' it was necessary to establish who the 'keeper' was. The answer to this question varied from one type of prison to another,[2] and also to some extent from age to age. For escapes in the thirteenth century from county gaols not held in fee the sheriff was normally responsible,[3] though prolonged investigation would no doubt yield a number of exceptions. Thus, when the gaoler of Cambridge castle some time before 1260 suffered a prisoner to escape, it was he and not the sheriff who was held to blame,[4] although, as far as is known, he was a common gaoler appointed directly by the sheriff. It is true that in this instance the escape was a technical one caused by the gaoler's corrupt desire to extort a fee from the prisoner before admission. The gaoler of Cambridge, however, was still held liable, in different circumstances, in 1295.[5]

If a county gaol had been entrusted to a gaoler in fee, it was he and not the sheriff who was responsible. Worcester gaol was

---

[1] See p. 225.
[2] The best existing accounts of the subject will be found in *Crown Pleas of the Wilts. Eyre*, pp. 42–3; *Eyre of Kent*, I, p. lxviii.
[3] *Crown Pleas of the Wilts. Eyre*, p. 42.
[4] W. M. Palmer (ed.), *The assizes held at Cambridge in A.D. 1260* (Linton, 1930), 9.   [5] *Cal. Close R.* 1288–96, 413.

originally in such custody,[1] and consequently it was the fee-holder who in 1221 answered for an escape.[2] The fee-holders of Winchester and Exeter were similarly liable.[3] If the sheriff had lost control of the castle in which his gaol was seated, it was the constable who was called to account and not he. At least this is true from the early fourteenth century onwards. At Colchester the evidence for this is quite specific,[4] and it is easy to add to it. Thus it was Amaury of St Amand, when constable of Oxford in 1305,[5] and Nicholas of Segrave, when constable of Northampton between 1308 and 1315,[6] who were required to answer for escapes from those castles, and not the sheriffs of the counties.

When the crown began the practice of appointing gaolers by patent, the patentees, like gaolers in fee, seem to have been liable. Pardons for escapes and inquiries about the degree of negligence displayed are usually addressed to them.[7] Nevertheless, the incidence of liability could easily be uncertain. In April 1383 Richard Hurel, keeper of Aylesbury gaol, was pardoned for allowing escapes. More than a year later the sheriff of Buckinghamshire was also pardoned for the same offence. He had what was described as the 'chief' custody whereas the keeper had the 'immediate' custody, and he did not recognize that the pardon to the keeper was necessarily tantamount to his own exoneration. Accordingly he was detaining the keeper in prison.[8] The sheriff was no doubt wise, for no patent of appointment for Hurel has been found. A very similar case occurred in Nottinghamshire in 1406 where once again two pardons had to be issued.[9] It was not only sheriffs who indulged in this form of insurance. When a large-scale rescue

---

[1] See p. 146.
[2] *Rolls of Justices in Eyre for Lincolnshire and Worcestershire*, 610.
[3] See pp. 143, 146. [4] See pp. 69–70. [5] *Mem. de Parl.* 280 7.
[6] *Assoc. Archit. Soc. Rep. & Pap.* XXXII, 447. In fact the record states that the liability rests upon Segrave's tenants.
[7] E.g. the gaolers at Warwick: *Cal. Close R.* 1341–2, 499; *Cal. Pat. R.* 1381–5, 183; 1388–92, 431; 1399–1401, 447; 1405–8, 39; 1452–61, 290.
[8] Ibid. 1381–5, 271, 481.
[9] Ibid. 1405–8, 180, 263. There had been patentee gaolers before this time (see p. 150), but no patent appointing the gaoler who was thus pardoned has been found.

took place at the Marshalsea in 1470, the duke of Norfolk, as
earl marshal, thought it prudent to indemnify himself, although
the effective custody of the prison had been devolved upon
an under-marshal.[1] Perhaps, however, the duke's action really
reflects *Fleta*'s doctrine already alluded to, namely, that if a
prisoner escapes from the custody of the marshal of the household both the marshal himself and his subordinates are to be
punished.[2]

Where prisoners escaped from the custody of towns without
a fully developed municipal personality and from villages, liability
was sometimes fixed upon the lord, sometimes upon the community at large. Thus at the Wiltshire eyre of 1249 escapes from
the 'prisons' of the abbot of Glastonbury at Christian Malford,
of the abbess of Shaftesbury at Bradford-on-Avon, and of Parnel
de Tony at Britford were fastened upon the lords and not upon
the townships.[3] On the other hand escapes from the 'prisons' of
Bishopstone (in Ramsbury hundred), Brocklees (in Corsham),
Patney, and Stratton St Margaret were fastened upon the townships and not upon the lords.[4] Again at the Cambridgeshire eyre
of 1260 townships and not lords had to answer for escapes from
the 'court' of Peter of Savoy at Bassingbourn, the 'prison' of the
prior of Barnwell at Chesterton, and the 'house' of the prior of
Ely at Melbourn.[5] For an escape from Alan Basset's prison at
High Wycombe *c.* 1227 the township and not Basset answered,[6]
and so it was in 1259 with the men of 'Graham' who owed a fine
for an escape from the prison there which belonged to the lord
Edward.[7] In the next century, on the other hand, it was held
that the abbot of Peterborough was liable for an escape from the
stocks in his 'court' at Oundle (1321).[8] The lords of Far Cotton

[1] See p. 159.   [2] See p. 235.
[3] *Crown Pleas of the Wilts. Eyre*, pp. 162, 179, 251.
[4] Ibid. pp. 169, 173, 192, 229.
[5] *Assizes held at Cambridge*, 2, 3, 5–6.
[6] *Rolls of Justices in Eyre* [for Bucks.], *1227*, p. 50.
[7] *Sel. Cases in Exchq. of Pleas*, p. 22. The lord Edward's bailiff paid on behalf
of the villagers and recovered the money from them in instalments. The place
is not easily identifiable.
[8] *Assoc. Archit. Soc. Rep. & Pap.* XXXII, 472.

(1353),[1] and Luton (1358)[2] were similarly liable for escapes from those places and not the respective townsmen and villagers. The reason for these divergencies of liability is not immediately apparent. It was declared by the jurors who tried the Far Cotton and Luton cases that the lords were liable because they had the right to keep a prison. The same general right, however, was certainly enjoyed by some of the other lords already mentioned, Peter of Savoy, for example, and the abbot of Glastonbury. The Oundle case may be contrasted with two roughly contemporary ones that occurred in Northamptonshire likewise, in each of which the villagers were liable.[3] On one of these occasions the villagers were escorting a prisoner to a gaol, on the other they appear actually to have reached the gaol precincts. It seems fair that in these instances the escorts should have been accountable and it is possible that in some of the earlier instances, even though the record does not say so, the prisoners were not at rest in a prison or the stocks but on the road.

In municipal communities responsibility rested, as in a village, originally on the community at large, later on the officers chosen by the community. Thus at Gloucester in 1221[4] the town was collectively liable, presumably because at that time the organs of local government were primitive. At York in 1278–9 the bailiffs were liable for escapes occurring in the daytime.[5] At Wallingford in 1294 an under-bailiff assumed responsibility under mainprise.[6] But there is also an early case of liability resting upon a municipal gaoler, a case indeed fit to parallel that of the gaoler of Cambridge castle already mentioned.[7] The gaoler in question was employed at Kingston upon Thames in 1264,[8] and presumably was the

---

[1] *Cal. Inq. Misc.* III, pp. 50, 51.

[2] Ibid. p. 103. It was, however, argued that if the escape had occurred after the enactment of 31 Edw. III, St. 1, c. 13 the men of Luton would have been liable. For this statute see p. 247.

[3] *Assoc. Archit. Soc. Rep. & Pap.* XXXII, 199, 479. Curiously, in the first of these instances the village was Oundle.   [4] Maitland, *Glos. Pl.* p. 107.

[5] J.I. 1/1057 m. 55 *d* [58A*d*]. The butchers of the city were collectively responsible for escapes that took place at night: *V.C.H. Yorks., City of York*, 491.

[6] Berks. Rec. Off. W/JB a 30.   [7] See p. 248.

[8] *Cal. Pat. R.* 1258–66, 475.

nominee of the bailiffs of that town. Perhaps, much later on, such devolution of responsibility became quite common in larger towns. At all events in 1515 the gaoler of Coventry was expected personally to ensure that his prisoners remained in custody until their trial.[1]

In London the responsibility usually rested upon the senior elected municipal officers. It was, however, not always easy to decide which officers were the appropriate ones. This uncertainty is early illustrated by the story of John of Frome, mentioned above.[2] He escaped from Newgate in 1254, and the king summoned the mayor and citizens to account for the escape. The citizens replied that the custody of Newgate did not belong to them but to the sheriffs. The king rejoined that it was they who made the sheriffs. The citizens countered that they merely chose the sheriffs, who could not act until they had been admitted in the Exchequer. In the end the sheriffs were imprisoned for a month and then deposed.[3] Thus the crown admitted the citizens' case. But this was not the limit of liability, for the keeper of Newgate, the sheriffs' nominee, was also inculpated though eventually pardoned.[4] The decision in Frome's case seems to have created a precedent, for when in 1300 the mayor and sheriffs were summoned to produce certain prisoners at a provincial gaol delivery the mayor returned that since he had not the custody of any prison he ought not to answer for any prisoner. The return was accordingly made by the sheriffs alone, who repudiated the demand.[5]

When statute law began to invest judgement creditors with rights against persons whom the statutes themselves called 'keepers' of prisons, it became a matter of importance to decide whether the principal or his agent was truly the 'keeper'. The Statute of Merchants (1285) gave the creditor an action against the 'keeper of the prison' if he released a debtor before that debtor had satisfied his creditor. In 1311 the mayor of Exeter was charged by a creditor with having released a debtor in such

---

[1] *Coventry Leet Bk.* II, 644. 　 [2] See p. 232.
[3] *Chron. Maiorum et Vicecomitum Lond.* 21.
[4] *Cal. Pat. R.* 1258–66, 8. 　 [5] *Cal. Lr. Bks. C,* 68–70; and see p. 290.

circumstances. Was the creditor justified in treating the mayor as 'keeper'? Was it not rather Thomas of Halscombe, who actually bore that title, or the mayor and bailiffs collectively who delivered the debtor into Halscombe's hands and who appointed Halscombe in the first place? It was decided that the mayor alone was liable. The issue may perhaps have been befogged in this instance because the mayor intervened in person and unwarrantably released the prisoner, and it may have been the better view that the mayor and bailiffs were jointly to blame.[1] But at least it was made tolerably clear that the person who lived in a prison and had the immediate custody of its inmates was not necessarily the statutory 'keeper', even though he might bear that title. Westminster II (c. 11) similarly gave the creditor an action against the 'keeper' in the event of an unwarranted release. The statute, however, contained the proviso that, if the 'keeper' was without means, the action would lie against the 'sovereign'. The same ambiguity arose here also over the identity of the 'keeper'. In 1318 a creditor brought an action under the statute against the sheriffs of London, who had released his debtor from Newgate.[2] Counsel debated whether the 'keeper' meant the sheriffs, against whom the writ had been issued, or whether it meant Roger Sporon to whom the sheriffs had deputed the custody. According to one account Sporon was said to possess means, according to another to lack them. In his judgement Chief Justice Bereford declared that in London the mayor and citizens were sovereign and the sheriffs were keepers under them, a judgement that corresponded with what had been settled in Frome's case in the preceding century.[3] In his view the action could only lie against the 'keeper' or against the mayor and citizens. It could not lie against the sheriffs, who were the parties sued in the writ. Where, as in London, a sheriff did not hold in fee but was annually removable, it was into the sheriff's hands that the court would deliver a prisoner. The sheriff was accordingly the 'keeper'. A nominal 'keeper', like Sporon, was under the permanent protection of a superior, in this case the sheriffs. The

---

[1] *Yr. Bk. 5 Edw. II* (Selden Soc. LXIII), 9–11.
[2] *Yr. Bk. 11 Edw. II* (S.S.), 265–7.   [3] See p. 252.

plaintiff appears to have lost his case on the technical ground that the writ he had sued out was void for uncertainty, but at any rate the issue of liability was now settled.

Bereford amplified his judgement by saying that where lords had the franchise of a prison and put others in their place, the keeper must answer, since it was he who must receive a prisoner from the court. One effect of this seems to have been that the keepers of franchise prisons bore a personal responsibility which the keepers of prisons appointed by removable sheriffs avoided. There is evidence to prove that this was at least sometimes so. In 1339 the keeper of Westminster prison, which belonged to the abbot of Westminster, was held accountable for an escape under Westminster II;[1] in 1344 the gaoler of the liberty of Ely was similarly deemed to be liable under the Statute of Merchants.[2] So it also was with the bailiff and under-bailiff of Cotton in the escape of 1353 from which the men of Far Cotton exculpated themselves.[3]

It was of course possible for a principal to escape liability by entering into a contract with his agent to save him harmless if escapes occurred. Thomas de Cantilupe[4] concluded such a contract with his gaoler, the prior and convent of Dunstable with theirs in 1295,[5] the sheriffs of London with the keeper of Ludgate in 1419.[6] When an escape from one of the Counters took place in 1455 the sheriff concerned looked to his secondary to indemnify him,[7] no doubt because there was a contract. Conversely, the view was taken in 1351 that the deputy-marshal in the King's Bench could not be held liable since he had given the marshal no security.[8]

[1] *Yr. Bk. 13 & 14 Edw. III* (R.S.), 38–50.
[2] *Yr. Bk. 18 & 19 Edw. III* (R.S.), 64–70.   [3] See p. 251.
[4] *Roll of household expenses of Richard de Swinfield, Bishop of Hereford, Abstract* (etc.) (Camd. Soc. o.s. LXII), p. cxlvi. The bond is there printed.
[5] *Ann. Mon.*, III. 396.
[6] *Memorials of Lond. and Lond. Life*, 677.   [7] Jorn. 5, f. 244.
[8] *Sel. Cases in K.B.* v, p. xxvii.

XII

THE EARLIER HISTORY OF GAOL DELIVERY

IN so far as gaols were places of detention for suspect felons they needed to be regularly cleared or 'delivered' of their populations. It is possible that before 1170 this was sometimes done by sheriffs or by local justices,[1] although before 1166 sheriffs' gaols, at all events, were probably few. It was also sometimes done in the same century by justices at Westminster. The costs, so often mentioned, of taking prisoners to London, must sometimes at least have been incurred so that those prisoners could reach a place of trial;[2] and the actual records of such trials are to be found upon the rolls of the king's court.[3] Gaols were also delivered in eyre and by the king and his justices when perambulating, and for such deliveries the evidence is similar: records of the trials themselves[4] and expenses claimed for removing prisoners from one provincial town to another.[5]

The eyre grew less frequent after 1194. To fill the intervals between its visitations justices travelling in circuits but acting under more limited commissions were fairly frequently appointed.[6] These also delivered gaols.[7] Such commissions can, indeed,

[1] At least sheriffs seem often to have determined crown pleas before the Inquest of Sheriffs: *Crown Pleas of the Wilts. Eyre*, p. 3.

[2] E.g. prisoners taken from Nottingham to London: *Pipe R.* 1181 (P.R.S. xxx), 121, and 1188 (P.R.S. xxxviii), 201; from Canterbury to London: ibid. 1184 (P.R.S. xxxiii), 144, and 1187 (P.R.S. xxxvii), 47; from Lewes to Lambeth: ibid. 1192 (P.R.S. n.s. ii), 204. It must be remembered that some 'prisoners' are more likely to have been taken in war than arrested on suspicion of felony.

[3] For some probable examples drawn from Hants, see *Cur. Reg. R.* ii. 195.

[4] E.g. Launceston gaol, 1201: *Pleas before the king and his justices*, i (Selden Soc. LXVII), 130, ii, 176–8; York and Worcester gaols 1212: *Cur. Reg. R.* vi. 351, 400–1, and cf. p. vi.

[5] E.g. from York to Carlisle: *Pipe R.* 1166–7, 173; from Aylesbury to Bedford: ibid. 1192, 197.

[6] *Crown Pleas of the Wilts. Eyre*, pp. 4, 5.

[7] E.g. *Rot. Litt. Claus.* i. 83 (commission *inter alia* to deliver Lincoln gaol).

be detected even before Richard I's reign. The last time that they were issued on a nation-wide scale was in 1225 when, by a single instrument, nineteen separate panels were appointed,[1] of each of which a professional justice was a member. In fact in one way or another there was a great deal of delivery by itinerants before Henry III's reign, so much indeed that by John's reign a plot of ground on which trials could take place was beginning to be set aside.[2]

By 1220 these deliveries by itinerants were being supplemented by newer methods. The older ones were not, however, abandoned. Justices of the bench continued to deliver gaols in the London area, especially Newgate, and justices in eyre and the King's Bench in its perambulations continued to try and sentence suspects. But for routine work the crown preferred the appointment, as the need arose, of small bands of justices or of a single justice to deliver a designated gaol. Occasionally the justices might be assigned to deliver all the gaols in a named county or the chief gaols in adjacent counties,[3] but much the commoner practice was 'one gaol, one commission'.

The justices thus appointed acted under commissions enrolled in Chancery and it is from these commissions that our knowledge of the system is derived. Enrolment first begins in 1220 and was indeed somewhat haphazard at first; there are some early commissions that are known to have been acted upon of which the enrolment cannot be found;[4] but there is reason to suppose that by the early forties enrolment had become much more the rule. However this may be, it has been necessary to base the ensuing analysis upon enrolled commissions alone.

The commissions were of two kinds: a general one to deliver

[1] *Rot. Litt. Claus.* II. 76. The Somerset roll is printed in translation in *Somerset Pleas* [1] (Som. Rec. Soc. XI), 1. For a description of the circuits and their records see *Cur. Reg. R.* XII, p. xi, and XIII, p. xii.　　　　[2] See p. 308.

[3] Of the former practice there seem to be but six examples: Hunts. (1232–3), Kent (1233–4), Suffolk (1236–7), Northumberland (1236–7), Somerset and Dorset (1241–2), Cornwall (1247–8). The other practice was somewhat commoner but seems to have died out after 1263–4. It was confined to counties that shared a sheriff, particularly Norfolk and Suffolk, Shropshire and Staffordshire.

[4] E.g. the records of gaol deliveries at Oxford, Hereford, and Worcester in 1223–4: *Cur. Reg. R.* XI, pp. 118, 381–2.

all prisoners within a stated gaol or gaols, and a special one to deliver a gaol of certain named prisoners or a certain category of prisoners. The first type was much the commoner but the second was by no means rare. The commissions were also variously composed. Perhaps the most usual arrangement was to commission four justices, often called 'the four knights', who were drawn from the neighbourhood in which the gaol falling to be delivered lay. These four might include a professional justice, who had local connections. 'The four knights' has become a conventional name for the system, but smaller and larger groups of individual justices were also appointed with the same object.

The same set of gaol-delivery justices (or same justice), usually[1] acting under separate but parallel commissions, was in the earlier years of Henry III's reign sometimes appointed at more or less the same time to try one or more of the possessory assizes. Gaol deliveries and assizes had of course already been linked together through the common responsibility of justices in eyre and other itinerants for both. The system of parallel commissions to 'four knights' may have done something to preserve the link and helped to give our still surviving system of itinerant justice its usual name. By the 1240s assize commissions were more usually being conferred either on a justice of the central courts sitting with local associates, or on two professional justices.[2]

The system of 'four knights' described above was not radically modified until 1292. For the purpose of examining it here it is convenient to divide the long period in which it operated into two parts, which will be called Period A and Period B. The dividing line has been drawn in 1258. The division is largely arbitrary, although the baronial reformers of 1258 did try to influence the composition of these commissions[3] by increasing the local element. In the analysis no distinction is drawn between general and special commissions.

[1] There are a few examples of commissions to deal with both types of business, e.g. C 66/43 mm. 5*d*, 7*d*, 9*d* (1232–3); *Close R.* 1237–42, 442 (1242); *Cal. Pat. R.* 1258–66, 49–50 (1259).

[2] *V.C.H. Wilts.* v, 19.

[3] From information supplied by Mr C. A. F. Meekings.

In Period A we have record of nearly a hundred different gaols that were ordered to be delivered on at least one occasion.[1] Of these hundred, however, a bare forty are mentioned before 1235–6, nearly half of which occur but once. Among these forty the gaols most frequently delivered were those at Gloucester (6 times), Ilchester (5), Lincoln (7), Northampton (5), and York (5), and those in Nottinghamshire and Derbyshire (6), Shropshire and Staffordshire (10), and Warwickshire and Leicestershire (11). Thus it seems that it was for gaols in regions which, while reasonably well populated, were remote from London, and therefore barely accessible to the king's court at Westminster, that commissions were commonest. It was not only the gaols managed by the sheriffs that were delivered. Almost from the beginning private prisons were delivered too. Thus in the earlier thirties the prison of the archbishop of Canterbury at Otford,[2] of the abbot of Reading at Leominster[3] and Reading[4] and of the abbot of St Albans at St Albans[5] were cleared by such commissions. Commissions to deliver town prisons were also already being issued. Southampton (1234–5) is a fairly obvious case,[6] Bristol (1230) a not impossible one,[7] while it is not easy to see why the plural should have been used in issuing commissions for Hereford in 1220 and Gloucester in 1234 unless the justices were meant to concern themselves with the respective municipal as well as with the respective county gaols.[8] The best example of all, however, comes from

---

[1] These statistics of deliveries are drawn from the enrolled commissions and from references of other sorts where the evidence for delivery is clear. Most commissions were enrolled on the dorse of the patent rolls. Those up to 1232 are printed in *Pat. R.* From the later *Calendars* they are omitted, and recourse must be had to the rolls themselves. For 1272–9 they are printed in 42–50 *D.K. Reps.* While all unpublished commissions have been sought for, it is quite possible that a few have been missed, if only because a few membranes are partially blind. A small number of commissions was enrolled on the close rolls. Up to 1272, at any rate, all these have been published. The presumption has been made for the purpose of this chapter that all commissions issued were executed. It is naturally possible that this was not invariably the case.

[2] *Cal. Pat. R.* 1232–47, 79, 124.   [3] *Close R.* 1227–31, 506–7.
[4] *Pat. R.* 1225–32, 365.   [5] C 66/44 m. 16*d.*
[6] C 66/45 m. 9*d.*   [7] *Close R.* 1227–31, 389.
[8] *Rot. Litt. Claus.* I. 437 (Hereford); *Cur. Reg. R.* IX. 198 (Hereford); C 66/45 m. 13*d* (Gloucester).

Orford, where in 1244 the sheriff of Suffolk was told to return to the bailiffs of that town the prisoners whom he had removed from the town prison, so that they might be tried on the spot.[1]

After Henry III's twentieth year the number of commissions issued annually tended to increase. In the ensuing twenty-two years the annual average was about twenty-seven, and in 1257–8 there were actually fifty-four. On the other hand there were two years when the number issued was as low as eight.

The frequency with which in Period A particular prisons were delivered naturally varied a good deal. If we group all the gaols lying within a single county together and treat as a single county those counties that were in charge of the same sheriff, we find the order of frequency to be as follows:

Over 50: Norfolk and Suffolk.

Over 40: Warwickshire and Leicestershire.

Between 30 and 40: Bedfordshire and Buckinghamshire, Essex and Hertfordshire, Gloucestershire, Lincolnshire, Oxfordshire, Shropshire and Staffordshire, and Somerset and Dorset.

Between 20 and 30: Cambridgeshire and Huntingdonshire, Berkshire, Derbyshire and Nottinghamshire, Kent, and Northamptonshire.

Between 10 and 20: Devon, Hampshire, Herefordshire, Northumberland, Surrey, Wiltshire, Worcestershire, and Yorkshire.

Under 10: Cornwall, Cumberland, Lancashire, Rutland, Sussex, and Westmorland.

The Berkshire and Oxfordshire figures have been shown separately, although from 1244 those two counties formed a single bailiwick. If they had been united throughout the period the bailiwick would have fallen into the first class. The Surrey and Sussex totals have also been kept apart, although those counties were linked in 1242. For the gaols in London and Middlesex no commission is to be found. Rather naturally the palatinates of Chester and Durham formed no part of the system. The delivery of their gaols will be considered elsewhere.[2]

It is evident from these figures that the frequency of delivery depended in part upon the populousness of the areas surrounding

---

[1] *Close R.* 1242–7, 346.　　　　[2] See pp. 295–6.

the gaols. It is in no way surprising to find Cornwall, Cumberland, Rutland, and Westmorland in the lowest group, nor East Anglia, the midland shires, and four of the home counties in the second. The infrequency of deliveries in Hampshire, Surrey, and Sussex and, to a lesser extent, in Kent is less easily explained. It is probably due, however, to the easy communications between those counties and London, with the consequence that their suspects were often sent to London prisons and delivered there. The low position occupied by Lancashire and Yorkshire is more remarkable and for it there is no evident explanation. Nor is it clear why Somerset and Dorset stand so high when Wiltshire stands so comparatively low.

It might have been expected that there would have been a close correlation between frequency of delivery and inception of delivery, that is, that those counties or groups of counties whose gaols were most frequently delivered would be the ones in which delivery exhibited itself at the earliest date. This, however, is not so. Of the first ten commissions of which there is record five relate to gaols in sheriffdoms in the fifth of the foregoing classes, three to gaols in the third class, and one to gaols in the second class. Unless the records are gravely deficient, it looks as though these novel methods were tried out upon the less important gaols and, having proved their merits there, were then extended to the greater ones.

If we turn now to Period B, and examine the thirty years from 1258–9 until 1285–6, we find some increase in the number of gaols ordered to be delivered and a marked increase in the frequency with which commissions were issued. The number of separate gaols falling to be delivered now amounts to about 125, but of these a little over thirty were delivered only once, and about a dozen only twice.[1] This is not in very striking contrast

---

[1] In making any calculation of the number of separate prisons actually delivered two difficulties must be remembered: (i) the possibility that a town and a county gaol lying in the same place may have been reckoned only once; (ii) the use by the Chancery of different names for the same prisons. For example, it is probable that the prison usually called Wimbotsham was once delivered under the name of Clackclose.

to what we learnt about Period A. The annual average of commissions issued, however, has now mounted to nearly eighty. It is true that the variation from year to year is still large. In 1262–3 there were as few as eleven and in 1280–1 as many as 172, but there is no doubt that from Henry III's closing years it had become the policy to deliver frequently. This acceleration seems to date from 1270–1, when over seventy commissions can be counted. The frequency with which particular prisons were visited was, naturally enough, uneven. Thus there are only twelve commissions for Appleby, and only once was that prison visited twice in a year. A large prison like Oxford, however, was the object of nearly ninety visitations, and was once visited as often as fifteen times in a single year, or more than once a month.[1]

Owing to the uncertainty of some of the identifications it is not easy to analyse by sheriffs' bailiwicks the 2,100-odd commissions issued in this period. If, however, we make the attempt, we shall find a fairly close correspondence between the number of deliveries and the presumed density of population. Excluding London and Middlesex once again, the situation seems to be somewhat as follows. Berkshire and Oxfordshire, Norfolk and Suffolk, have something like 200 commissions each. Next come Bedfordshire and Buckinghamshire with about 150, and Essex and Hertfordshire with about 130. Cambridgeshire and Huntingdonshire, Kent, and Northamptonshire amount to a little over a hundred. Hampshire, Lincolnshire, Shropshire and Staffordshire, Somerset and Dorset, and Surrey and Sussex have between 100 and 80, Gloucestershire, Nottinghamshire and Derbyshire, Warwickshire and Leicestershire, and Wiltshire between 80 and 60, Devon, Herefordshire, Worcestershire, and Yorkshire between 68 and 40. The rest are below 40 and Westmorland has only 12. Thus the gaols comparatively close to London were delivered most often and those in the north and far west least so.

As was the case in Period A, visitations were not limited to the long-established sheriffs' gaols, but extended to gaols in royal castles not normally used by sheriffs, and to those in liberties and

[1] In 1284–5.

towns. Some of the franchise prisons were at the centres of well-known ecclesiastical liberties like Battle, Bury, or Peterborough. Others, like the prisons at East Dereham[1] or Melton,[2] were at outposts of such liberties, in counties other than those in which the *caput honoris* was seated. Others again, like Arundel, were in the castles of lay lords. There were, however, many important franchises, the prisons belonging to which were never delivered.[3] The reasons for this variation from area to area, from castle to castle, from liberty to liberty, we can only hope to learn when a close study has been made of the history of each locality. We may take it, however, that they are partly to be accounted for by variations in population and by the vigour or supineness of different sheriffs.

Strictly speaking, perhaps, franchise prisons, or at least those in the ownership of lay lords, ought never to have held suspects awaiting delivery. In Edward I's reign the crown, when testing claims to prisons, argued that suspected felons, unless there was a strong presumption of their guilt, should not be kept in private prisons beyond a few days' span but sent instead to the proper county gaol.[4] This rule, however, if rule it were, was probably unenforceable, at any rate at certain times and in certain districts. Congestion in the sheriffs' gaols or the perils and problems of transport could easily have made it so. The crown seems, therefore, to have arranged instead to have the prisons delivered. One thing at least is tolerably clear: franchise and even municipal prisons were not rigidly confined to suspects belonging to those liberties. Indeed the Ramsey annalist makes this plain, for when he notes the delivery of the prison at Wimbotsham in 1258 he mentions that the thieves within it were drawn not only from within the liberty but from outside it.[5]

If we examine the composition of the commissions between 1220 and 1292 we find, as has been said, a good deal of variety at

[1] The prison of the liberty of Ely in Norfolk.
[2] The prison of the same liberty in Suffolk.
[3] E.g. the prison or prisons of the abbot of Glastonbury.
[4] For the Sussex evidence see p. 94.
[5] *Chron. Abbat. Rameseiensis*, 344.

different times. This is particularly true of the period when the system of *ad hoc* commissions was in its infancy. The first 60 commissions, those that were issued between 1220 and 1234–5, do not consistently conform to what became the pattern a little later on, namely four local knights or gentlemen. Only about half were commissions of four, and there were two of five, eleven of three, seven of two, and three of one. Justices of the Bench or of the Jews formed an element in some 20 commissions, and probably it could be shown that several more contained some other royal servant no less trustworthy. In two instances a Bench justice was appointed alone; in three more, two Bench justices were appointed. In three instances the sheriff was appointed with other local commissions and in one of these a Bench justice sat with him.[1] Twice a Bench justice was chosen to sit with coroners.[2]

Two conclusions seem apparent. First, the crown had evidently not yet established enough confidence in local prudence to leave the groups of local worthies altogether on their own. While this conclusion is often a mere matter of deduction it is twice a virtual certainty. In 1228 the delivery of Gloucester gaol was adjourned because Stephen de Segrave, a Bench justice and one of the commissioners, could not attend, and the crown was reluctant to proceed to delivery unless he or some person equally trustworthy was present.[3] Similarly, in 1232 the four local gentlemen appointed to deliver Exeter were to act only upon the advice of William de Raleigh,[4] a Bench justice who had also close connections with Devon and might be expected to be on the spot when the visitation took place. Secondly, the crown was making experiments which do not seem to have been worth repeating. Neither sheriffs nor coroners were again included in commissions as official members,[5] though in Wiltshire at any rate it was possible

[1] York (1227), Gloucester (1229), Reading (1230): *Pat. R.* 1225–32, 159, 365; *Close R.* 1227–31, 228.
[2] Gloucester (1228), Bedford (1230): *Pat. R.* 1225–32, 183; *Close R.* 1227–31, 397.
[3] *Close R.* 1227–31, 104–5. [4] *Pat. R.* 1225–32, 516.
[5] For the use of the sheriff of Durham in delivering gaols in the palatinate see below, p. 295.

in the thirteenth century for a coroner to be appointed a justice of gaol delivery by name.[1] Later on, this was not so, for it was held in 1291 that a coroner could not be a gaol-delivery commissioner as well,[2] or, if he became one, a replacement for him as coroner had to be found.[3] Nor was the choice of local knights ever again left to the sheriff, as had been the case in Lincolnshire in 1230.[4]

In the ensuing eighteen years, that is from 1234 to 1253, the pattern is a good deal more symmetrical. All but 15 per cent are commissions of four. Of that excepted percentage, commissions of two form the most numerous class and after that commissions of one. There are three commissions of five. There are two examples of commissions, one of four and the other of five persons, who are to act in concert with other persons who are specially singled out as though they were men of outstanding reliability.[5] All these exceptional types have been noticed in the preceding period, though they are now proportionately less numerous. There are also five examples of a commission, not previously encountered, which appoints a Bench justice to act with any whom he may wish to associate with him. The first of these *una cum hiis* commissions was issued in 1236–7 to Adam Fitzwilliam for the delivery of Bedford gaol.[6] Once, in 1235, a justice of the king's court (William of York) and his fellows are given the responsibility of choosing four local knights to deliver the gaol at Lincoln.[7]

This period, when commissions of four are so much more the rule than the exception, is followed by another extending over seven years and therefore up to 1260–1 in which the pattern is

[1] Hamon of Beckhampton, who was a justice of gaol delivery in 1236–7, had been a coroner in 1232 (*Close R.* 1231–4, 46) and probably was still so when commissioned. William Druce was a coroner 1268–81 (J.I. 1/1005 m. 113(115)) and a justice of gaol delivery once during that period.
[2] *Sel. Cases in K.B.* II, 56.   [3] *Cal. Close R.* 1313–18, 358.
[4] *Close R.* 1227–31, 386.
[5] York (1238); the nominated person was William Percy, perhaps once a bench justice: C 66/48 m. 9d. Oxford (1250); the nominated person was Laurence del Brok, later a Bench justice: C 66/61 m. 5d.
[6] C 66/47 m. 10d.   [7] *Close R.* 1234–7, 159.

quite different. Of the 225 or so commissions more than a hundred are addressed to one person and rather fewer than a hundred to four. The figures for commissions of intermediate size are in comparison negligible and there is but one *una cum hiis* commission. The commissions of one rise to their peak in 1257–8, when they number 30. The next year they fall sharply and the commissions of four rise to 38. There were 19 of these solitary commissioners and nearly all of them were professional justices or royal servants.[1] Of the professionals those most frequently commissioned were Laurence del Brok, the king's attorney, and William le Breton. The reason for the practice is fairly obvious. To an increasing degree after 1240 possessory assizes were taken in the provinces by professional justices and the like, though often in conjunction with local associates.[2] Such professionals being in any case on the spot, it was natural enough to use them also for the less difficult work of clearing gaols.

When we advance into the period from 1260–1 until 1274–5 there is yet another change of pattern. In these years commissions of four are more than five times more numerous than commissions of three, two, and one put together. After the four-man commissions, which number over 460, the one-man commissions come next, followed by two-man commissions (22) and three-man commissions (16). There is also one commission of five justices (Gloucester, 1260–1) and one of six (Ilchester, 1271–2). Of *una cum hiis* commissions there is now no instance. By this time William le Breton was dead, but Laurence del Brok, who became a justice about 1268, continued until his death in 1274–5 to be a most popular commissioner. Of the 58 one-man commissions issued in this period, no fewer than 23 were addressed to him. He was six times appointed to deliver Newgate and Westminster, and conducted ten visitations of prisons in the home counties. He also visited five prisons in what became the Norfolk

---

[1] The exceptions seem to be Alexander de Montford (Winchester, 1256–7), John de Wuull (Lancaster, 1256–7), R. de Percy (York, 1257–8), William de Swinford (Norwich and Ipswich, 1258–9), and the constable of Dover (Dover, 1258–9).

[2] *V.C.H. Wilts.* v, 19.

circuit and two in Berkshire and Oxfordshire. He never went farther afield.

When we reach 1275–6 we are confronted with yet further changes. Out of some 160 issued in that year about 140 are addressed to two justices. In 1276–7 the total number of commissions is much reduced, but once again commissions of two preponderate. In fact they are more than twice as numerous as all other commissions. In 1277–8 commissions of four have regained first place, though commissions of two are nearly half as numerous. After this commissions of two gradually decline and in 1283–4 are reduced to four. In 1278–9 commissions of one are finally abandoned. Of abnormal commissions there is only one in this period—a panel of five for Lancaster in 1280–1. Contrasting the two major groups, the fours and the twos, we find that there are some 390 of the first to set against some 1,300 of the second.[1]

Is there any way of accounting for the change in 1275–6? If we look at the names of the commissioners one thing becomes clear at once: the use of local knights has not been given up; sometimes they sit in pairs, sometimes they are associated with professional justices or serjeants, but in any case they sit. On the other hand professional justices and serjeants also sit in pairs and may range widely over the kingdom.[2] What we seem to be encountering is an attempt to reduce as many panels as possible, however composed, to two. So far as local knights are concerned, the experiment evidently failed, perhaps because of the difficulty of ensuring adequate attendance. The great increase in four-man commissions that occurs in 1277–8 is probably to be attributed to the resumption of the eyre in that year, a visitation that extended with interruptions until 1289. The professionals were too busy in eyre to occupy themselves with routine deliveries.

Besides the great increase in provincial deliveries that took place in Edward I's early years, steps were also taken to deliver

---

[1] No analysis has been made of the commissions for 15–20 Edw. I. There is little reason to think that the situation in those six years differed very much from that which prevailed in 11–13 Edw. I.

[2] E.g. J. Lovetot and R. Loveday visited together gaols in Cambridgeshire, Essex, Hertfordshire, Norfolk and Suffolk, besides a gaol at Alveley (Salop).

Newgate regularly. The first recorded commission had indeed been issued as long before as 1241–2 and this was followed in 1250–1 by a second commission, though a special one. The justices appointed, two on each occasion, were professionals or royal servants.[1] In 1255–6 Laurence del Brok was appointed alone,[2] and reappointed, though as a special commissioner, in 1260–1.[3] Three other commissions were issued between 1261–2 and 1267–8, and then no more, as far as the enrolments show, until 1272–3. Up to that time Newgate prisoners continued to be tried at places remote from the gaol. Thus in 1258 Hugh Bigod, the chief justice, was appointed to try at a time and place of his own choice two prisoners into whose alleged crime the sheriff and coroners of London had conducted a preliminary inquiry.[4] But as the number of such prisoners increased, the risks of transporting them to Westminster or other places increased as well. It was therefore not an unnatural development to send justices to the prison rather than prisoners to the justices. It also suited the pretensions of the Londoners who claimed quittance of external pleading. During the period between 1272–3 and 1285–6 about sixty Newgate commissions were issued. Of these about three-fifths were composed of two persons.[5]

Hitherto we have been looking at England as a whole and have been trying to describe the system on the basis of figures collected for the country. It may be useful to supplement this by looking closely at the limited area of a single county, choosing Wiltshire for that purpose. Wiltshire was neither a very large nor a very small county, its population was neither dense nor sparse, and it lies neither very close to Westminster nor very far away. It may be looked upon, therefore, as an area in which the system of the 'four knights' could be fairly tested.

The first recorded Wiltshire commission was issued in 1236[6] and therefore some time after the inception of the system.

---

[1] C 66/50 m. 13*d*; *Cal. Pat. R.* 1247–58, 116.   [2] C 66/70 m. 22*d*.
[3] *Cal. Pat. R.* 1258–66, 186.   [4] Ibid. 1247–58, 666.
[5] This number includes a commission of 1275–6 for the delivery of the Tower as well.
[6] C 66/47 m. 8*d*.

Between that year and 1285–6, a span of 50 years, 89 commissions
were issued. Of these 77 were for Old Salisbury castle, five for
Marlborough castle, four for New Salisbury, two for Wilton,[1]
and one for an unnamed gaol.[2] Sixty-nine commissions were
addressed to four, 14 to two, five to one, and one to three justices.
The average frequency of delivery amounts to rather more than
one a year, but the average is deceptive. While there were eleven
regnal years between 1236 and 1256–7 when no commissions were
issued at all, for the remainder of the period there are only four
in which that is true. Moreover, in some of Edward I's earlier
years the number of commissions issued is large: 5 in 1275–6,
8 in 1277–8, 6 in 1278–9, and 10 in 1281–2. Thus deficiencies in
the earlier part of the period are offset by superabundance in the
later.

The commissioners appointed under Henry III were mainly
local men, without known professional connection with the law
or with direct royal service. Out of 31 commissions only about a
third seem to have been composed of or to have included outsiders. Three of these were commissions to a single professional
justice,[3] and two others included such a justice. One of these two,
a commission to four issued in 1266–7, was a body of peculiar
character and exceptional strength.[4] Adam de Grenville[5] and
Henry de Montfort,[6] both professional justices, led it, and its
other members were Richard of Worcester, one of the king's
serjeants, and William de Dun. Montfort, Worcester, and Dun
succeeded one another as sheriffs of the county, the first two
coming to that office from outside, and one at least of them must
have sat as a commissioner while exercising that office. Perhaps
the sequel to the civil war demanded a rigour in the trial of suspect

[1] One of these is C 66/104 m. 8*d* (1284–5). The other, issued in 1253–4, refers
strangely to 'Wilton and Salisbury gaol': *Close R.* 1253–4, 161.
[2] *46 D.K. Rep.*, App. II, 227.
[3] Henry of Bath (1253–4), William le Breton (1256–7), Nicholas of Hadlow
(1259–60). In 1249 the first two had been justices in eyre in the county: E 372/94,
/95.
[4] C 66/85 m. 20*d*.
[5] He often took assizes in the county: *V.C.H. Wilts.* V, 20.
[6] He was a justice in eyre in Wiltshire in 1268: E 372/111,/112.

felons that no purely local bench could hope to exercise. Two other commissioners appointed in this reign were men who, while neither professional justices nor royal servants, are not known to have had anything to do with Wiltshire. One, who sat six times in all, was Alexander Dando, a Somerset landowner.[1] Another unusual commission was that issued in 1267–8 to Peter de Scudamore, who sat again, in association with a professional justice, in 1272–3. He was a member of a local family, but he was evidently something more than one of the ordinary knights of the shire, and a few years later the trust that the crown reposed in him was to earn for him one of the first keeperships of the peace in Wiltshire.[2] Among the purely local justices were others who had held or who were to hold purely local office, two as sheriff,[3] four as county coroner, and seven as escheator or sub-escheator.

Of the local knights only about a fifth were called upon to sit on more than five occasions. Of these Dun was the most notable, for between his first appointment in 1266–7 and his last in 1284–5, he sat no fewer than eighteen times. Others were more regularly resummoned, though less frequently. Between 1236–7 and 1246–7 Hamon of Beckhampton was named in six out of the seven commissions issued, between 1257–8 and 1263–4 Ralph Daungens in six out of nine, and between 1246–7 and 1270–1 William Druce in ten out of eighteen.

The situation is rather different in Edward I's reign. Although many more commissions were issued over a shorter span of years, the number of separate commissioners, forty-one in all, was rather fewer. Whereas in commissions issued under Henry III the local men were more than four times as numerous as the outsiders, under Edward I they outnumbered them less than three times. William de Braboef, a Wiltshireman but also a professional justice,

---

[1] He first sat in 1263–4 (C 66/81 m. 8*d*). For his connection with Somerset see *Feud. Aids*, IV, 290, 291, 297.

[2] *V.C.H. Wilts.* V, 31.

[3] Godfrey de Scudamore (sheriff 1258–9) sat five times between 1240–1 and 1263–4; Ralph Daungens (sheriff 1264–6) sat six times between 1257–8 and 1263–4.

sat nine times,[1] and two other professionals once each.[2] A person
called Hereward del Mareys, who appears to have been a Dorset
knight[3] married to a Hampshire woman,[4] sat eleven times and
his presence upon so many commissions calls for some comment.
We noticed that in Henry III's time there was at least one justice
who, while not a professional in any sense, did not belong to
Wiltshire. In his successor's there were several justices of this
class. While their number has not been precisely ascertained, there
were, besides Mareys from Dorset, three Hampshire men[5] and
one who came from Somerset.[6] On two occasions, moreover, if
on no more, the same men were appointed by separate instruments to deliver both Winchester and Salisbury gaols,[7] so that
Wiltshire knights were trying men of Hampshire while Hampshire knights were trying those of Wiltshire. Fifteen of the Wiltshire knights, who were not connected with other counties, sat
only once or twice. On the other hand John of Grimstead was
appointed to 26 out of 45 commissions issued in a span of ten
years and Richard de Coleshill to 25 out of 33 in a span of eight,
while Dun's 18 sittings, mentioned above, lapped over into
Edward's reign. Only one commissioner served as sheriff,[8] but
two commissioners at some time or another served as coroners
and four as escheators. To be a gaol-delivery justice was part of
the local *cursus honorum*. The figures seem to show that purely
Wiltshire knights were being used rather less freely than before,
while those that were employed carried a rather heavier burden
than their predecessors.

[1] From 1275–6 until 1281–2. He was a justice in eyre in Wiltshire in 1281:
J.I. 1/1005.
[2] Henry of Woolavington, who was a justice in eyre in Wiltshire in 1268
(E 372/112), and Walter de Helion.
[3] *Cal. Close R.* 1272–9, 214; *Cal. Pat. R.* 1272–81, 324.
[4] *Cal. Pat. R.* 1266–72, 349.
[5] John Windsor, who sat twelve times, 1282–5, was lord of Stoke Charity:
V.C.H. Hants, III, 448. Richard Portsea and William Pagham (both sat 1285–6)
seem to have belonged to Hampshire families: *Feud. Aids*, II, 310, 320, 336.
[6] Humphrey de Kael (sat 1282–3) held land in Somerset: *Feud. Aids*, IV, 286.
[7] 1284–5 (C 66/104 mm. 12d, 14d); 1285–6 (C 66/105 mm. 22d, 26d).
[8] Richard de Cumbe (sheriff 1289–93) sat twice in 1285–6.

Earlier history of gaol delivery

Up to the present, whether we have been viewing the system nationally or locally, we have drawn no distinction between general and special commissions. The bulk of commissions were general ones. This is particularly so in earlier times. In Period A, as defined above, only about 3 per cent are special. Of this fraction four are for the delivery of clerks, whose guilt or innocence the justices would have tried to establish although they would have surrendered them to the bishop for judgement.[1] Four are for the trial of persons appealed by approvers. Six are for the trial of single individuals or small groups whose names are usually given and offences usually specified. One, at Reading, declares somewhat verbosely that it is for the trial of all those then recently attached at Woodstock, who belonged to Berkshire, to the liberty of Reading abbey, or to the honor of Wallingford.[2] One commission, for Warwick in 1249–50, excludes from the purview of the justices those suspected of homicide.[3] There are also a few commissions, not included in the excepted fraction, which direct the justices to do certain specified acts as well as, in general terms, to deliver the gaol. Thus in 1248–9 the justices at Gloucester were not only to deliver the gaol but also to do justice on false coiners.[4]

The number of special commissions in the period from 1258–9 to 1271–2 has not been measured. In the first fourteen years of Edward I's reign it stood at between 9 and 10 per cent of the total, a notable increase over the number issued during the period from 1220 to 1257–8. Nineteen of these, all but one of which[5] were issued in the first or third year of the reign, were for the trial of trespassers who did not put themselves within the king's peace after the proclamation of June 1267.[6] Some of these commissions are in one way or another further limited. Thus three of 1272–3, one for Ipswich and two for Norwich, exclude those then recently

---

[1] Earliest: Newcastle upon Tyne, 1232 (*Pat. R.* 1225–32, 512–13). Latest: Nottingham, 1235 (C 66/45 m. 11*d*).
[2] *Cal. Pat. R.* 1232–47, 262.   [3] C 66/61 m. 6*d*.
[4] *Cal. Pat. R.* 1247–58, 53.   [5] Maidstone, 1280–1.
[6] F.M.Powicke, *The Thirteenth Century* (Oxford, 1953), 214.

indicted in East Anglia before Thomas de Clare. One, for Nottingham, also issued in 1272–3, confines itself to prisoners arrested after Henry III's death. Two, for Colchester and Winchester, issued in 1274–5, do not extend to men charged with homicide or released on bail or mainprise.[1] The men who came before these tribunals were rather rebels than felons and their delivery from prison has nothing to do with the administration of criminal justice. To mention the commissions here, however, is not so irrelevant as might at first sight seem, since eleven of them were composed of 'four knights'. We thus see that that system was not meant to be confined to common criminals but rather to all persons whose local delivery was deemed expedient.

About sixty more commissions are for the trial of named prisoners, most of whom were to be tried singly. Homicide is the offence alleged in nearly thirty cases. There are also eight commissions to try those vaguely accused of trespass, and there are charges of clipping coin,[2] arson,[3] and holding treasure trove.[4] Twenty commissions are for the trial of persons whose offences are not declared, and there are three commissions for the trial of unspecified numbers of unnamed persons charged with clipping,[5] homicide,[6] and receiving an outlaw.[7] It looks as though some of the accused were involved in *causes célèbres*. Thus in 1274–5 two commissions, each to a single justice, were issued for the trial, once at Bedford and once in Newgate, of Sewall le Fam. Presumably his case was difficult, and he had to be removed from one place to the other to secure evidence; or his escape was apprehended and he had to go from the provinces to London. Then in 1277–8 there are three commissions for the trial of persons charged with killing a merchant of Almain, of whom one was at Huntingdon, two at Lincoln, and one at Nottingham. In 1292 Rhys ap Meredith, then in York gaol, was tried by a commission of four knights for 'seduction' to the king, demolishing the king's

[1] Undefined reservations are written into a Salisbury commission of 1272–3.
[2] Newgate, 1276–7.　　[3] Windsor castle, 1280–1.
[4] Newgate, 1274–5.　　[5] Tower of London, 1278–9.
[6] Colchester, 1278–9.　　[7] Lincoln, 1278–9.

castles and other offences.[1] But much more commonly there is nothing in the commissions to suggest that a 'story' lies behind them.

Commissions to try criminous clerks have now been reduced to one. On the other hand a new type of commission, of which there are numerous examples, makes its appearance at Ilchester in 1280–1. It is for the trial of persons, usually named individuals, who have been put in exigent and who, hearing rumour of it, have thereupon surrendered themselves to gaol. In and after 1281–2 these commissions often state that the surrender has taken place since the departure of the last eyre for the county in which the prisoner is confined.[2]

Considering all the administrative difficulties of an age of poor communications, it is rather remarkable that we should find so many commissions for the trial of individuals. One might have expected that the crown would have been content to leave them in prison until there was a group of prisoners to be tried. That it did not always do so could be due to the fear of escapes, or to a desire to secure felons' chattels if the suspect was condemned. It can, however, hardly be doubted that more often some attorney of the suspect moved the crown to try his principal quickly and to that end sued out a writ at a price that was attractive. For example, it was reported in 1275–6 that Walter Scalpin had obtained a patent (*impetravit litteras domini regis*) for the trial of his wife, who had been shut up at Oxford, but that the sheriff had declined to take the steps preliminary to the trial until he had been bribed.[3] That such is no isolated incident is perhaps implicit in a passage in the *Mirror*, whose author enumerates among 'abuses' a failure to deliver gaols quickly once a writ has been procured,[4] and from the evidence brought to light in 1291 when the existing system of delivery was on the eve of extinction.[5]

Commissions, whether general or special, sometimes give us

---

[1] *Cal. Close R.* 1288–96, 267.
[2] A commission for Salisbury appears to be earliest in this form: C 66/101 m. 19 *d*.
[3] *Rot. Hund.* I. 19.   [4] *Mirror*, 160.   [5] See p. 279.

details about the time and place of deliveries. About half of the earliest commissions, those issued before 1231, name either the day or place at which the justices are to sit. From 1231 until 1254 the day is usually specified. In the ensuing six years it is named with decreasing frequency until in 1261–3 it is named for the last time. Sometimes the writ expressly states that the day is to be arranged, particularly when the trials were to be held before a single professional justice or serjeant. In the period 1257–9 this formula is very common, but rare thereafter. Once a king's justice, Thurkilby, is ordered to deliver a municipal prison when he is next in the district.[1]

The place is mentioned very much less often. Indeed it is only between 1231 and 1237 and between 1248 and 1251 that its inclusion is at all common. By Edward I's time it had ceased to be the custom to mention either day or place. Naturally it must not be supposed that the omission of either detail from the enrolment necessarily implies that the full commission did not contain both.

When the delivery of more gaols than one is committed to the same group of justices the days on which they are to deliver each are very often named. On two widely spaced occasions it is left to some chosen individual to name the day: in 1231 Ralph Fitz-Nicholas, the king's steward, was to report it to the Nottingham gaol commissioners,[2] and in 1250–1 the sheriffs of London and Middlesex were to name it to the Newgate justices.[3] Twice, in the case of the linked counties of Shropshire and Staffordshire, it was laid down that delivery should take place at the next county court,[4] and once a day is named not on but before which delivery is to have been completed.[5] A few commissions make provision for recurrent deliveries. The first Newgate commission (1241–2) was to be executed 'when it should be necessary'.[6] Into two Northumberland commissions of 1283–5 the same formula was introduced but with the addition of a date after which the authority

[1] The gaol was Orford: *Close R.* 1242–7, 346.
[2] *Pat. R.* 1225–32, 448.
[3] C 66/62, m. 4d.   [4] C 66/49 m. 4d;/50 m. 10d.
[5] C 66/59 m. 7d.   [6] C 66/50 m. 13d.

would become invalid;[1] a third, of 1285–6, was to be valid during the king's pleasure.[2]

The place of delivery, when mentioned, was usually the same as the place at which the gaol to be delivered was seated. Where, however, a single bench of justices was appointed to deliver more gaols than one, it was sometimes, but not always, the practice to deliver one or all at the same place. Thus in 1227 the gaols of Nottingham and Derby were delivered at Nottingham,[3] in 1232 those of Colchester and Hertford at Colchester and those of Cambridge and Huntingdon at Cambridge.[4] The gaols of Shropshire and Staffordshire were usually entrusted to the same commissioners and delivered at Bridgnorth. Kenilworth was thrice delivered at Warwick, Rothley twice at Leicester, Salisbury twice at Wilton, all the 'gaols of Cornwall', as they were on those occasions called, twice at Launceston, and the gaol of Melton once at Ipswich. If the number of prisoners in a gaol was few, as must sometimes have been the case, there can have been no great inconvenience in moving them into a neighbouring town or even county.

The places of trial already mentioned, and many others that could be named, were the customary meeting-places of county courts. Since justices of gaol delivery and assize were often the same people, and since petty assizes were supposed to be tried in county courts,[5] this is natural enough. Deliveries, however, were sometimes carried out neither at the gaols themselves nor at the meeting-places of county courts. Thus, in early times, two special deliveries of private gaols took place at a considerable distance from the gaols themselves: in 1232 the abbot of Reading's gaol was delivered at Whitsbury near Fordingbridge,[6] and in 1234–5 the prison at Otford, which belonged to the archbishop of Canterbury, was delivered at Lewes.[7] The two ecclesiastics held lands in or near these places of delivery and possibly in the first case

---

[1] C 66/103 m. 10*d*;/104 m. 30*d* (Newcastle upon Tyne).
[2] C 66/105 m. 11*d* (Wark on Tyne).   [3] *Pat. R.* 1225–32, 160.
[4] C 66/43 m. 7*d*, 9*d*.   [5] Magna Carta, c. 18.
[6] *Pat. R.* 1225–32, 521.   [7] C 66/45 m. 14*d*.

and certainly in the second had prisons in them.[1] It is therefore likely that the small number of prisoners that each prison would contain was in each case being tried at a single centre. Less easy is it to understand why 'the gaols in Suffolk' should have been delivered at 'Leylond', i.e. Nayland, in 1236–7[2] or the gaol of Rochester at Malling (presumably a Kentish Malling) in 1240–1.[3] In 1285 the four prisons in Bristol were delivered at four separate points, the Monkbridge prisoners in the Guildhall, the prisoners in the market prison in the market, those imprisoned on Sir Thomas Berkeley's fee in Redcliffe Street, and those imprisoned on Sir Richard Arthur's fee in his court belonging to that fee.[4]

From the inception of the system that is being described the crown was strict in its insistence that gaols should not be delivered without warrant. A chapter was inserted into the articles of the eyre in 1227 directing inquiries into unwarranted deliveries and stayed there.[5] The only answer so far traced comes from Buckinghamshire in 1284–6 and was reassuring to the crown,[6] but there is other evidence of both possible transgressions and royal vigilance. Commissioners doubting the extent of their authority might refer their doubts to the king, as was done in 1251–2.[7] In 1252 a Warwickshire man was summoned before the king's court to show why he had intruded himself into a gaol-delivery commission in place of another man lawfully appointed.[8] A Leicestershire man, Peter de Neville, was in like trouble in 1269.[9] In his case the prisoners were held for forest offences and not for felonies, but the principle that delivery required the king's express authority is precisely the same. Much more important is the prohibition of unwarranted delivery in 1280 against the sheriff of

---

[1] The archbishop had a prison at South Malling, Sussex, in 1266–7: *Suss. Arch. Coll.* XCVII, 72.

[2] C 66/47 m. 5 *d*.   [3] C 66/49 m. 11 *d*.

[4] *Great Red Book of Bristol* I (Bristol Rec. Soc. IV), 107.

[5] Helen M. Cam, *Studies in the hundred rolls: some aspects of thirteenth-century administration* (Oxford, 1921), 92–3.   [6] *Feud. Aids*, I, 90.

[7] *Cal. Pat. R.* 1247–58, 156 (a Lincoln case of 1251–2).

[8] *Close R.* 1251–3, 193.   [9] *Sel. Pleas of Forest*, 52.

Westmorland, after Edward I had personally investigated complaints against the sheriff on the spot.[1] Here, it seems, perhaps
because of the remoteness of Westmorland, the sheriff and his
serjeants had been trying suspect felons *virtute officii*, which was
declared to be against Magna Carta. A few years later, in 1291, a
trial held before justices who lacked the king's commission was
looked upon as invalid.[2]

It is probable that from the beginning the justices kept records
of a kind. A roll is mentioned in 1242–3,[3] but the earliest one to
survive does not go back beyond 1250.[4] The first surviving roll
of a delivery by 'four knights' is dated 1271.[5] It seems as though
about 1291 the individual justices, or perhaps groups of justices,
kept separate rolls.[6] Through this lack of records, the work of
the thirteenth-century justices may tend to have been unduly
minimized. It forces us, in any event, to base our conceptions of
the state of early criminal justice in the provinces largely on the
records of the eyres. The eyre appeared in the county but seldom
and, so far as criminal justice went, was mainly concerned with
the failures and abuses of administration. If, as is sometimes
pointed out,[7] few suspects came before it in person, this was not
because suspected felons 'got away with it' but because the
justices of gaol delivery had already done their work.

[1] *Cal. Close R.* 1279–88, 109.   [2] *Sel. Cases in K.B.* II, 56.
[3] *Pipe R. of Cumberland and Westmorland* (Cumb. and Westm. Antiquarian
and Archaeological Society, extra ser. XII), 98.
[4] From information supplied by Mr C. A. F. Meekings.
[5] J.I. 3/14/1, a Devon roll for 1271–8, 1281.
[6] *Sel. Cases in K.B.* II, 54–17.
[7] Maitland, *Glos. Pl.* p. xxxv; *Eyre of Kent*, I, p. xlii. The second of these, of
course, concerns a late eyre, that of 1313–14. In general Maitland seems to
underemphasize the importance of thirteenth-century gaol-delivery justices:
Pollock and Maitland, *History of English Law*, II, 645 and n.

XIII

LATER HISTORY OF GAOL DELIVERY

THE system of gaol delivery which Edward I inherited exhibited two leading characteristics: first, the inception of each delivery depended upon the issue of a distinct commission relating to the gaol to be delivered; secondly, more commonly than not, commissions were composed wholly or partially of non-professional judges. This system, as we have seen, remained unaltered for the first twenty years of the reign. It was then transformed, not suddenly but over a period of forty years. After the close of that period of experiment the system which has in effect lasted until our own time had in all essentials been worked out.

The chief features of the new system were these: gaols were delivered by judges travelling in circuits from county to county and from gaol to gaol; the judges were professionals; and the same judges who tried suspect felons tried civil suits at the same sessions and at the same places. It is the last of these characteristics that requires attention first.

As has already been explained,[1] professional justices, sitting either alone or with local associates, were from the 1240s increasingly used to try possessory assizes in the provinces. After the accession of Edward I these arrangements were made more systematic. In 1273 panels of assize commissioners began to be appointed for groups of counties and these groupings as time went on tended to crystallize. Westminster II (1285) required such sessions to be held at least once yearly, but not often more than thrice yearly.[2] In 1293 four assize circuits were established by statute,[3] each staffed by two paid commissioners who were not

[1] See p. 257.
[2] C. 30. In fact that maximum was occasionally exceeded: *V.C.H. Wilts.* v, 37.
[3] *Stat. Realm*, I. 112.

278

judges.[1] The justification for this was that the justices of the two benches and in eyre were often hindered by other business from hearing pleas at the times and places appointed. The new justices were to make themselves constantly available and were to hold their sessions at places most convenient to suitors and jurors. Middlesex pleas were to be heard at Westminster.[2] The assize commissioners were empowered to hear by writs of *nisi prius* cases started in the central courts. It was of course these writs that gave a name to the civil work of the later judges of assize and to the courtrooms in which they sat, but it was the earlier title, derived from the petty assizes, which the judges themselves assumed.

In the course of 1292 the 'four knights' system as a method of delivering gaols came to an end. An analysis of the commissions issued round about this time shows that between November 1291 and June 1292 90 panels of 4 justices were appointed, 11 of 3, and 8 of 2. In the next six months the figures are as follows: 1 panel of 4, 6 of 3, and 22 of 2. For the next twelve months the figures are: 1 of 4, 2 of 3, and 83 of 2.[3] Contemporaries tried to show that the old system had condemned itself by its abuses. At all events it was alleged, at the time when the system was first abandoned, that the 'four knights' were in the habit of trying prisoners by means of juries of tainted reputation, suborned juries, or juries drawn from areas remote from those in which the prisoners to be tried had been arrested (*per patriam longinquam*). It was said, too, that the 'knights' sometimes did not observe the terms of their commissions: where, for example, four were appointed, only three would sit. The justices of assize going on circuit in that year were told to investigate these charges and to take corrective measures.[4]

These general charges are corroborated by some evidence provided by a case heard in the King's Bench in 1291. A man was suing the sheriff of Nottinghamshire and his clerks for procuring

[1] From information supplied by Mr C. A. F. Meekings.
[2] For the justices' names see *Cal. Close R.* 1288–96, 319–20.
[3] From information supplied by Mr C. A. F. Meekings.
[4] *Rot. Parl.* I. 86.

an approver to appeal him of felony.[1] Four 'knights' had been appointed to try the appeal and with them two others had been later associated. The rolls of the various justices were examined and were found to be in disagreement, and one of the justices turned out to be a coroner. Since, naturally enough, none of the justices had taken the judicial oath recently imposed on justices of assize,[2] but rather, as the record says, were persons chosen by the parties, it was decided to ignore the testimony of their rolls. The outcome of the case does not concern us. We do, however, get by this means some insight into the way the system worked. Evidently the parties could apply for the appointment of named justices,[3] about whom the Chancery might well know little. The trial might then proceed under the superintendence of men of dubious impartiality.

In place of the panels of 'four knights', commissions were issued whose members were partly judges and partly sworn permanent commissioners. The latter category was made up of some of the more important local knights and a few royal servants. The commissioners were grouped into circuits, but these circuits did not coincide with those organized for assizes.[4] They were not, indeed, all of them geographical circuits; some were related to the movements of particular individuals and therefore might be called personal.

The organization of gaol delivery by circuits was not entirely new. In 1242–4, for example, two commissions had been issued, each requiring the justices to visit two gaols in succession.[5] In 1270–1, Geoffrey of Lewknor, a king's serjeant if not indeed then a judge, was sent to deliver five prisons in turn—Warwick, Oxford, Reading, Wallingford, and Leicester;[6] and, as has been said above,[7] panels of two commissions might go from gaol to gaol in Edward I's early years. Moreover, the assize justices who had been appointed in and after 1273 had occasionally tried suspect felons.[8]

---

[1] *Sel. Cases in K.B.* II, 53–7.
[2] See p. 285. [3] Cf. p. 307.
[4] For the circuits of 1294 see *Cal. Close R.* 1288–96, 394.
[5] *Close R.* 1242–7, 109; C 66/55 m. 12*d*. [6] C 66/89 m. 5*d*.
[7] See p. 266. [8] *V.C.H. Wilts.* v, 37.

The circuit system, however, was not seriously applied to gaol delivery until the closing years of the thirteenth century. Thereafter there was a close but not a continuous connection. It was through the justices of assize, whose evolution has just been described, that the connection was established. By the Statute of Fines of 1299 these justices were given the task of delivering gaols.[1] The statute enjoins that the justices, immediately after they have taken the assizes, shall remain together and deliver all the gaols, including the franchise gaols, within the shires.

While the linkage, first given statutory authority in 1299, was eventually perpetuated, so that it has become the system that is known to us today, it was interrupted in 1305–7 by the appointment of justices of trailbaston. These justices, among other duties, delivered gaols, and other machinery for that purpose was consequently superfluous. After the then trailbaston commissions were spent, the original assize circuits were altered and the judges of the central courts introduced into the assize commissions. The gaol delivery circuits and commissions were also altered and still more radically than the assize commissions. Between 1308 and 1328 any coincidence between assize and gaol-delivery circuits and commissioners became largely personal through the activity of particular individuals. Where such individuals were absent, gaol delivery reverted for a while to non-professional 'knights' of the type with which men had been so familiar in the thirteenth century.

By the Statute of Northampton (1328) the whole country was regrouped into six assize circuits, which were to come into being with the spring sessions of 1329.[2] Owing to visitations of the eyre and trailbaston justices these arrangements were not brought fully into effect at once. A further statute of 1330, however, completed the process.[3] By this the linkage of 1299 was re-established. It is from this statute rather than from the Statute of Fines that the historical system of 'assizes' is to be dated.

[1] *Stat. Realm*, i. 129.
[2] From information supplied by Mr C. A. F. Meekings.
[3] 4 Edw. III, c. 2.

By the later 1330s the six assize circuits had come to be constituted as follows:[1]

Home: Essex, Hertfordshire, Kent, Middlesex, Surrey, and Sussex.

Midland: Derbyshire, Leicestershire, Lincolnshire, Nottinghamshire, Northamptonshire, Rutland, and Warwickshire.

Norfolk: Bedfordshire, Buckinghamshire, Cambridgeshire, Huntingdonshire, Norfolk, and Suffolk.

Northern: Cumberland, Lancashire, Northumberland, Westmorland, and Yorkshire.

'Oxford': Gloucestershire, Herefordshire, Shropshire, Staffordshire, and Worcestershire.

Western: Berkshire, Cornwall, Devon, Dorset, Hampshire, Oxfordshire, Somerset, and Wiltshire.

Somewhat later Oxfordshire and Berkshire were added to the 'Oxford' circuit,[2] which thus acquired the name it eventually bore, and Middlesex was withdrawn from the Home circuit.[3] Middlesex prisoners were being tried at Newgate sessions in the fifteenth century and probably long before.[4] Monmouthshire was added to the Oxford circuit in or after 1542. By the seventeenth century the Northern circuit had acquired Durham.[5] Otherwise the circuits were not significantly changed until the nineteenth century.

The qualifications of a gaol-delivery justice, of the ordinary sort, were not narrowly defined. A statute of Edward I had laid it down that justices of assize must be 'lawful' men 'having knowledge of the law', and the Statute of Northampton (1328), when bringing gaol deliveries finally within the purview of those justices, made it clear that gaol-delivery justices should be the same.[6] The statute of 1330 said that the justices must be 'good and discreet' men, who were not 'of the places'.[7] The Statute of

---

[1] For the circuits of 1–10 Edw. III see J. F. Willard, W. A. Morris, and W. H. Dunham (eds.), *The English government at work 1327–36* (Cambridge, Mass. 1940), III, 248–52; for those of the nineteenth century see *Guide to the ... Public Record Office* (London, 1963), I, 127.

[2] From information supplied by Mr C. A. F. Meekings.   [3] Ibid.

[4] Jorn. 5, f. 196.

[5] From information supplied by Mr J. S. Cockburn.

[6] 2 Edw. III, c. 2. The earlier statute has not been identified.

[7] 4 Edw. III, c. 2.

Fines[1] had debarred any commissioner in Holy Orders from trying suspect felons and had required that such a justice should be replaced by a senior knight of the shire. Such a disqualification seems natural enough. It had not, however, always existed, for in the long-distant past, in 1207, the archdeacon of Stafford had joined in a gaol delivery. Nor, it would seem, was the new statute in practice observed.[2] In 1340 it was declared that only a justice of one of the two benches or a king's serjeant could be a justice of assize and therefore, by implication, deliver gaols on circuit.[3] Serjeants had never been expressly mentioned before, but the power to take associates had already been conferred on the justices of assize in 1318.[4]

The exclusion of natives or residents was evidently intended to prevent corrupt alliances between justices and local magnates, as a petition in Parliament of 1382 makes plain.[5] That petition attests the fact that the statute of 1330 was not strictly observed, and it was confirmed by a new statute in 1384.[6] A further petition to the same effect had, however, to be lodged in 1411, when once again it was ordained that the existing law should be enforced.[7] It remained the law until 1739,[8] although at times circumvented: Anthony Wood was shocked to learn that a puisne judge of the King's Bench, though born in Oxford, should have 'got himself' into the Oxford circuit in 1685 and 1686.[9]

One means of circumvention was contrived only a few years after the statute had been passed. As we shall see,[10] legislation of 1394 enabled justices of the peace, if 'men of law', to deliver gaols within their counties. Since the justices of assize and gaol delivery had by that time come to sit on those commissions, they could deliver prisoners in their own counties by means of peace commissions even if they could not properly do so by means of gaol-delivery commissions.

---

[1] See p. 281.
[2] *Rot. Litt. Claus.* I. 83.
[3] 14 Edw. III, St. I, c. 16.
[4] 12 Edw. II, c. 4.
[5] *Rot. Parl.* III. 139.
[6] Ibid. 200; 8 Ric. II, c. 2.
[7] *Rot. Parl.* III. 661; 13 Hen. IV, c. 2.
[8] 12 Geo. III, c. 27.
[9] *Life and Times*, III (Oxf. Hist. Soc. XXVI), 134.
[10] See p. 305.

Other qualifications and disqualifications of gaol-delivery justices deserve to be mentioned. Until 1384 the two chief justices were not authorized to sit. The Chief Justice of the Common Pleas was then allowed to do so. His brother in the King's Bench, however, continued to be excluded. Eventually, in 1411, he was suffered to sit in Lancashire, but in Lancashire alone.[1] The reason for this prohibition was that he might be required to sit in error upon a case which he had already tried at first instance. At the very end of the thirteenth century it was held that justices might only deliver prisoners against whom charges had been laid in that county or in those counties whose gaol or gaols the justices themselves had been appointed to deliver. Thus a justice appointed to deliver Windsor gaol was not qualified to try a man charged in Hertfordshire.[2] This very inconvenient rule was still in force in the fifteenth century in Cambridgeshire and Huntingdonshire.[3] It is not known how strictly it was enforced at other times and in other places. It can hardly have applied to Newgate at any time.

Sheriffs occasionally delivered gaols in Henry III's early years[4] but later were only used in the remotest counties. One of these was the palatinate of Durham, whose arrangements were, in any case, distinct from those of the kingdom. Another was Westmorland. Here, as we have seen, sheriffs and their serjeants were delivering, however illegally, before 1280. Even thereafter they were not forbidden to do so provided that they secured a commission.[5] For most of the thirteenth century, however, they were not used in England at large, and in 1317 the Council expressly debarred them from exercising this or any other judicial office.[6] Coroners were implicitly debarred by 1316[7] if not long before,[8] and were formally debarred next year with the sheriffs.[9] The

---

[1] *Rot. Parl.* III. 200, 661; 8 Ric. II, c. 2; 13 Hen. IV, c. 2.
[2] *Sel. Cases in K.B.* III, p. cxcviii, 205–11. The case was heard in 1298.
[3] Marguerite Gollancz, 'The system of gaol delivery as illustrated in...gaol delivery rolls' (London M.A. dissertation, 1936), p. 24.
[4] See p. 263.
[5] *Cal. Close R.* 1279–88, 109; and see pp. 276–7.
[6] R. F. Hunnisett, *The medieval coroner* (Cambridge, 1961), 170.
[7] *Cal. Close R.* 1313–18, 358.   [8] See p. 263.
[9] Hunnisett, op. cit.

disqualification, however, did not apply to the coroner of the King's Bench, who, contrary to every expectation, delivered the King's Bench marshalsea at sundry times between 1343 and 1362.[1]

From 1290 all justices of assize, not being members of the king's council, were required to take oaths before they could act,[2] and were so doing by 1294.[3] By a statute of 1346 all justices of assize, gaol delivery, *nisi prius*, and oyer and terminer were required to swear similarly before receiving their commissions.[4]

It was said above[5] that it had become possible in 1285 to hold assizes thrice yearly if necessary. That maximum was converted into a minimum frequency in 1330[6] and so into the minimum frequency for gaol delivery. But in this matter, as in many others, there was much experiment in the early years of the new system. At first Newgate was delivered much more often than three times a year; sometimes indeed it was visited once a month.[7] Later, as we shall see, visitations became much less frequent.[8] After 1330 the statutory frequency was at first sometimes observed but even in Edward III's early years two annual visitations seem often to have been common,[9] and by the later sixteenth century had become the rule.[10] Judging from the evidence of the extant rolls alone deliveries took place in fourteenth- and fifteenth-century Wiltshire once or twice a year with almost equal frequency.[11] In 1382 the justices on the Northern circuit were reproved for failing to deliver the gaols of Northumberland, Cumberland, and Westmorland with the same regularity as that with which they delivered those of Yorkshire. It was said that they had overlooked such deliveries for two years.[12] While this may have worked some improvement, the assizes were not held in the three counties more

---

[1] *Sel. Cases in K.B.* I, p. xxix and n.

[2] L. Ehrlich, *Proceedings against the crown (1216–1377)* (Oxford, 1921), 222.

[3] *Sel. Cases in K.B.* I, p. lxiv n. 4.   [4] 20 Edw. III, c. 3.

[5] See p. 278.   [6] 4 Edw. III, c. 2.

[7] P.R.O. List of Gaol Del. R. (typescript).   [8] See p. 278.

[9] Willard and others (eds.), *English government at work*, III, 235–6.

[10] L. Alston (ed.), Sir T. Smith, *De Republica Anglorum* (Cambridge, 1906), 95.

[11] *V.C.H. Wilts.* V, 39.   [12] *Rot. Parl.* III. 139.

often than once a year until the early nineteenth century.[1]
Prisoners in the stannary gaols fared far worse than this for,
according to a petition of 1376, delivery took place only once in
ten years.[2]

Even where visitations were frequent and regular, individual
prisoners were not always delivered very promptly. In the fourteenth century trials of prisoners indicted on coroners' inquisitions
were often adjourned because a coroner had failed to send his
indictment to the justices in time for trial. In an extreme instance
a woman indicted of murder in 1369 remained untried in 1378,
by which time she was dead.[3] Of five persons who were in
Northampton castle by 23 March 1388, one was not tried until
19 February in the next year, and the other four not until 16 July
1389.[4]

Gaols, whether of counties or of liberties, were usually delivered on the spot, that is to say in the towns in which the gaols
stood. Most counties, of course, possessed one obvious administrative centre which housed the gaol and received the justices
on their circuits. Thus the county gaol of Hampshire was delivered at Winchester, where it stood, the county gaol of Warwickshire at Warwick. There were, however, some counties in
which there were more places of delivery than one, and these were
visited either successively in the same circuit or alternately in
succeeding circuits.[5] When delivery did not take place in the gaol
town the reason perhaps often was that some other town seemed
a more suitable place for hearing the civil pleas. Such arrangements, however, were unpopular. Moving prisoners away from
the gaol to take them to assizes was probably a nuisance and a
danger. At all events, in 1376 the Commons petitioned in Parliament that justices of assize should hold their sessions in gaol
towns. The request was tactfully evaded.[6] In 1382 the Commons

[1] John, Lord Campbell, *The lives of the chief justices of England* (1874
London ed.), IV, 160.
[2] *Rot. Parl.* II. 344.
[3] Hunnisett, *The medieval coroner*, 130–1.   [4] E 364/25 m. D.
[5] From information supplied by Mr C. A. F. Meekings.
[6] *Rot. Parl.* II. 334.

again raised the matter, complaining that the justices were apt to
hold their sessions in 'the remotest places'.[1] The crown's answer
to this was that the sessions ought to be held in the 'principal
and chief towns' in each county, where the shire courts were
held, and so it was enacted.[2] This was a somewhat foolish answer.
It was too vague. For example, the Wiltshire county court sat at
Wilton[3] but by no stretch of imagination could it be called the
'chief town' of Wiltshire. But even if we except such anomalies,
the statute really gave no guidance, but rather provided scope for
disagreement. Accordingly, in 1387 another petition was lodged
in which it was shown that the statute was objectionable to the
people of some counties. The suggestion, on the face of it a
sensible one, was made that assize towns should be fixed by the
Chancellor and assize judges in conjunction at places convenient
to the local population. This became the law.[4]

It may be worth illustrating how this discretion was exercised
in a few counties. Wiltshire deliveries, which up to 1335 had
invariably taken place at Old Salisbury, were now held there
most infrequently and not at all after 1414. New Salisbury was
used instead.[5] Between 1410 and 1530 Surrey and Sussex assizes
and gaol deliveries were held in a variety of towns, no doubt in
part because the counties lacked obvious centres.[6] Excluding those
sessions which are simply called 'assizes', we find that gaol deliveries occurred at Lewes (1463–6), Horsham (1483–4, 1525–6,
1530, 1532, 1533),[7] East Grinstead (1515,[8] 1518–20, 1523–4, and
1524–6), and Southwark (1518–21,[9] 1523–7, and 1530).[10] 'Assizes',
not expressly called gaol deliveries, were held repeatedly at East
Grinstead between 1410 and 1464, and also at Lewes (five times
between 1412 and 1465), Hailsham (1412–13), Crawley (1458 9,

---

[1] Ibid. III. 139.   [2] 6 Ric. II, St. 1, c. 5.
[3] *V.C.H. Wilts.* v, 9.   [4] 11 Ric. II, c. 11.
[5] *V.C.H. Wilts.* v, 40.
[6] Unless otherwise stated these details are collected from Huntington Library,
San Marino, California, Battle Abbey Muniments, Beadles' R.
[7] *Suss. Arch. Coll.* CII, 47, 48, 50.   [8] Ibid. 45.
[9] Treating as Southwark one delivery said to have occurred in 'London'.
[10] Guildford Castle Arch. Loseley MSS 961.

1462–3), and Horsham (1458–9, 1461–2). In 1484 a special commission delivered some Sussex prisoners lying in Guildford gaol at Crawley,[1] while in 1530 the same gaol was being delivered at Southwark.[2] Shortly before 1535 Dorset gaol deliveries had been moved from Dorchester to Shaftesbury,[3] no doubt a more convenient place for the justices on their way from Salisbury to Exeter. In 1535 Dorchester was restored as the assize town by patent, but in Edward VI's reign the justices again took to sitting at Shaftesbury, and Dorchester was not restored until 1559.[4] By 1435 the Cumberland assizes were being held outside Carlisle, but the practice was forbidden by a special statute.[5]

A franchise gaol was nearly always delivered in the gaol town of the franchise, since one of the objects in maintaining the gaol was to secure that prisoners, jurors, and officials should not have to leave the confines of the franchise. There were, however, exceptions. Thus in 1331–2 prisoners in the archbishop's gaol at Maidstone were tried at Rochester and perhaps also at Canterbury,[6] although in 1317–18 the trials seem to have taken place in Maidstone itself.[7]

Most liberties in this period were of course municipal ones, the cities and boroughs of England. Many of these enjoyed by charter exemption from external pleading. It has yet to be ascertained whether it could have been legitimately argued that such exemption automatically entitled the towns possessing it to separate gaol deliveries. It is not unlikely that it could have been, though there were certainly some exempt towns whose gaols were never delivered or only very rarely. The issue is obscured by the fact that many such towns were also the seats of county gaols which were delivered on the spot. The justices would therefore be

---

[1] *Cal. Pat. R.* 1476–85, 519.

[2] Guildford Castle Arch. Loseley MSS 961.

[3] C. H. Mayo (ed.), *Dorchester municipal records* (Exeter, privately printed 1908), 32–4.   [4] *Ibid.* 35.   [5] *Rot. Parl.* IV. 490.

[6] Lambeth Palace MSS, C.R. 664: costs of moving prisoners to Rochester and Canterbury, hiring a house for them at the first, and accommodating them at the second. Prisoners, however, were also taken from Rochester to Maidstone.

[7] Lambeth Palace MSS, C.R. 664: making a bar at Maidstone against the justices' coming.

visiting the towns in any case, so that the townsmen, whether theoretically entitled to a separate delivery or not, need never go outside their walls.

In the earlier fourteenth century four municipal gaols were actually granted deliveries by patent. They were Norwich (1315),[1] Grimsby (1318),[2] Derby (1327),[3] and Coventry (1345).[4] Derby and Coventry are not known to have had deliveries or even prisons before the grants were issued. Thereafter they enjoyed both. Coventry was a growing town and certainly the most important one in Warwickshire at the time. Derby had for long ceased to see the justices, since the county gaol there had evidently been abandoned some forty years before.[5] Though Grimsby had once been delivered in the long-distant past (1276–7),[6] there is no evidence that it exercised its privileges after the patent was issued. Delivery in this case, therefore, is perhaps to be looked upon as a 'status symbol'. The reason for the grant to Norwich is not altogether clear, since the town gaol had been delivered from the earliest years of the century.[7] It seems possible, however, that the grant was made because King's Lynn, Thetford, and Great Yarmouth were occasionally chosen for Norfolk deliveries[8] and, when this occurred, the city would, but for the charter, have been omitted. Perhaps it was intended to treat Seamer (1346)[9] in the same way as the other four towns but the promise to send justices thither is not so specific as in the other cases. In any case the justices never went. It stands to reason that once a town became a county in itself its gaol became deliverable *ipso facto*. Apart, however, from Hull, all towns upon which such privileges were bestowed within our period were receiving gaol-delivery visitations before they became counties.

That some towns and liberties did not think it worth while to clamour for or preserve their rights of visitation may possibly be

---

[1] *Cal. Chart. R.* 1300–26, 284.
[2] Ibid. 411.
[3] Ibid. 1327–41, 51.
[4] Ibid. 1341–1417, 39–40.
[5] See p. 65.
[6] See p. 101.
[7] J.I. 3/47/3 (1299–1302).
[8] From information supplied by Mr C. A. F. Meekings.
[9] *Cal. Chart. R.* 1341–1417, 53.

attributed to motives of economy. The costs of visitation were not inconsiderable and would have had to be borne by the town or liberty visited. Of such costs there is no little evidence. Thus at Maidstone in 1299–1300 the archbishop had to pay the expenses of the justices,[1] as he did again in 1316–17.[2] The corporation of Nottingham was making a small payment to the justices in 1463–4.[3] We shall later have need to notice that the cost of purchasing the Newgate commission was a charge upon the sheriffs and mayor of London in the fifteenth century.[4] In addition in that century either the mayor or the sheriffs had to entertain to dinner the justices, four aldermen, the recorder and common serjeant, the clerks of the court, and the grand jury.[5]

Naturally London was never daunted by such expenses. On the contrary, it upheld its right to internal delivery, and on sundry occasions refused to allow its prisoners to be tried elsewhere: in the eyre of Kent in 1288–9,[6] at a Gloucester gaol delivery in 1300,[7] in the King's Bench or elsewhere at Westminster in 1332,[8] 1371,[9] 1383,[10] and 1386.[11] Instead the men were to be delivered at Newgate or in the second instance at the Tower, part of whose precinct lay within the city boundary.[12] Nor did the matter end there. Londoners detained in prisons outside London were removed to Newgate to stand their trial at the delivery of that prison.[13]

It has been shown that by the later thirteenth century Newgate had become in effect a national gaol for felons.[14] Accordingly it is not surprising that it should have been subjected to a system of delivery all its own.[15] So far as is known, it had never been delivered by 'four knights' during the period when that system prevailed. In fact from 1241–2, when we first read of its delivery, a senior justice of one of the central courts was normally ap-

---

[1] Lambeth Palace MSS, C.R. 658.   [2] Ibid. C.R. 659.
[3] *Recs. of Nottingham*, II, 377.   [4] See pp. 292–3.
[5] *Cal. Lr. Bks. L*, 137.   [6] *Mun. Gild.* I. 297–8.
[7] *Cal. Lr. Bks. C*, 68–71.   [8] Ibid. *E*, 281.   [9] Ibid. *G*, 277.
[10] Ibid. *H*, 224–5.   [11] Ibid. 285.   [12] Ibid. *I*, 3 and n.
[13] Ibid. *C*, 163–6.   [14] See p. 105.
[15] This and the next paragraph owe much to Mr C. A. F. Meekings.

pointed, or else the king's attorney.[1] When the assize circuits were first tentatively created in 1273 and their commissioners nominated, two justices were appointed at the same moment for the delivery of Newgate.[2] The commissioners always consisted of or included senior judges of the king's courts, each of whom tended to remain upon the commission for a number of years. Mayors, ex-mayors, and ex-sheriffs were often included in the commissions from 1273 until 1286, but were not appointed in the period 1286–98 when the city was in the hand of the crown. During that period Ralph of Sandwich, the keeper of London, was always a commissioner. After the king's hand had been removed, mayors began again to be commissioned, occasionally from 1302, fairly regularly from 1307. During the period 1305–7 the prison was delivered by the trailbaston home circuit.[3]

In 1327, on petition of the city in parliament,[4] it was settled that the mayor should for the future sit on the commission *ex officio*, and this decision was embodied in the city's charter of 6 March 1327.[5] As has been said, the charter merely 'confirmed a practice that had long been growing'.[6] Henceforth the mayor is always included in commissions and plea roll headings up to 1334. The city Letter Books, in which from 1332 until 1431 a selection of commissions, possibly arbitrary, is entered, tell the same story. This being so, there is no immediately obvious reason why it should have been necessary to issue a writ to the Exchequer in 1358 to ensure the inclusion of the mayor in such commissions.[7]

The entries of commissions in the city records[8] show that from 1345 to April 1377 the commissioners numbered either four or

---

[1] See p. 267.

[2] *Cal. Close R.* 1272–9, 52. The practice of occasionally using the early circuit assize justices to deliver gaols is mentioned above (p. 280).

[3] From information supplied by Mr C. A. F. Meekings.

[4] *Rot. Parl. hactenus inediti* (Camden Soc. 3rd ser. LI), 127.

[5] W. de Gray Birch (ed.), *Historical charters and constitutional documents of the City of London* (London, 1884), 53.

[6] *Speculum*, XVIII, 243 n., and see above.

[7] *Mun. Gild.* I. 414.

[8] These figures exclude special commissions.

five, though in 1370 there were six. In Richard II's reign there were two commissions of four, eleven of five, two of six, seven of seven, five of eight persons.[1] In the period 1403–31 the size increased still further. The figures then were: one commission of six, four commissions of seven, one commission of eight, three commissions of nine, four of ten, five of eleven, three of twelve. Of the eleven-man commission of December 1431[2] all were judges except the mayor and the recorder. In the period 1492–1513 there were five commissions of nine, eight of ten, one of fifteen, and two of eighteen. The last three, however, which contained several noblemen and knights with no professional qualifications, look, on the face of it, like something quite exceptional. Excluding these three all the commissions are constituted like the commission of December 1431.[3]

In the early fourteenth century deliveries, as has been said, were very frequent.[4] Later they became less so. In February 1341 a special delivery by the mayor and two justices was ordered, notwithstanding the impending eyre at the Tower, because the prison was over full.[5] This implies an undue interruption of a normal or at least an optimum sequence. If we were to judge merely from the actual entries of commissions in the city's books the average interval between one delivery and the next was, in the period 1345–April 1377, a little under eighteen months. There is reason to think, however, that in the 1370s trials of doubtful legality were conducted by the city officials,[6] a practice that could easily have been induced by the comparative infrequency of deliveries. In Richard II's reign the frequency with which commissions were issued increased to about once in eleven months.[7] We must not, however, attach too much importance to the dates of the commissions. It was naturally possible for several successive deliveries to be conducted under the same commission.

In 1471 it was ordained that the sheriffs should procure an

[1] *Cal. Lr. Bks.*   [2] Ibid. *K*, 140.
[3] *Cal. Pat. R.* 1485–94, 1494–1509; *L. & P.* I and II (Newgate gaol delivery commissions).   [4] See p. 285.
[5] *Cal. Close R.* 1341–3, 106.   [6] See p. 301.
[7] Figures based on *Cal. Lr. Bks.* and commissions enrolled in Chancery.

annual commission at their own charge.[1] In view of what is said below, the meaning of this ordinance is far from clear. Perhaps, however, it might be assumed that it was directed at ensuring a minimum frequency and at settling a minimum financial liability. This order was followed in December 1475 by another which stipulated that thereafter the 'sessions at Newgate' should be held at least five times a year. The sheriffs were to 'hold' the first four of them, and the mayor the fifth or, if necessary, a sixth.[2] The author of the *Great Chronicle of London*,[3] commenting upon this ordinance, says that at one time there had been two yearly sessions, one 'kept' by the sheriffs and the other by the mayor; that subsequently there had been three sessions, two of which had been 'kept' by the sheriffs and one by the mayor; that the mayor's turn had often been omitted on grounds of expense and that the sheriffs were consequently obliged to bear the whole burden of five or six sessions. The best sense that can at present be made of all this is that by the beginning of the fifteenth century at the latest sessions were occurring twice a year and that gradually the frequency increased to five or six times a year. A foreign observer confirms that in 1500 deliveries took place more often than twice a year.[4] It may be that these variations in frequency were in part due to the cost of holding the sessions and that the long intervals that occurred in an earlier time between one delivery and the next may in part have been attributable to a general disinclination on the part of both mayor and sheriffs[5] to bear the cost of purchasing commissions and furnishing hospitality,[6] or to a dispute between the mayor and the sheriffs over their respective liabilities.

As has been shown, the normal system of delivery was by means of circuit justices, and with the circuit system the delivery of

---

[1] *Cal. Lr. Bks. L*, 101. [2] Ibid. 137.

[3] *Gt. Chron. of Lond.* 224.

[4] *A relation of England* (Camden Soc. o.s. xxxvii), 36.

[5] The common council required the sheriffs in 1450 to bear the costs of commissions and writs for the delivery of Newgate, according to ancient custom: Jorn. 5, f. 51.

[6] For the costs of hospitality see pp. 289–90.

Newgate must be associated. But the circuit justices enjoyed no monopoly. So long as it lasted the eyre continued to deliver gaols, and the trailbaston justices and the King's Bench in its perambulations were used for the same purpose. Special commissioners, not fitting properly into any of these categories, were also appointed. It would be tedious to collect particulars about many of them. A few, however, of fourteenth-century date are worthy of particular mention. In 1312 the steward and marshal of the household, together with another man, were appointed to deliver from the marshalsea prison a man charged with counterfeiting the privy seal and another man charged with receiving it from him.[1] Two commissions dealt with men arrested during the civil war with Thomas of Lancaster. The first, issued in 1321, affected men in Warwick gaol who had captured Warwick castle and held it against the king;[2] the second, issued in the following year, affected men 'in the marshalsea' and in York castle.[3] A commission of 1324 delivered the Marshalsea prison of six men who, under the pretence of being members of the household, had committed larceny.[4] In 1326 the admiral of the fleet towards the north and another justice were appointed to deliver Colchester of seven pirates.[5] Much later in the century a commission of eight delivered the Tower of John Northampton, the mayor of London, and his associates.[6]

With one isolated exception, in 1301, the King's Bench when on circuit did not deliver gaols before Edward II's reign. In 1318, however, when it was transferred to York, it delivered the prisoners in the castle there and after this time made a regular practice of delivering gaols in whatsoever county it might visit.[7] The evidence for delivery has been carefully collected for the period up to 1336[8] and there is nothing to suggest that the practice was abandoned until the migrations of the court ceased in 1421.[9]

[1] *Cal. Pat. R.* 1307–13, 538.
[2] Ibid. 1321–4, 59.
[3] *Cal. Fine R.* 1319–27, 152.
[4] *Cal. Pat. R.* 1324–7, 69.
[5] Ibid. 294.
[6] *Cal. Lr. Bks. H*, 264.
[7] *Sel. Cases in K.B.* iv, pp. liii, lviii, lix.
[8] Ibid. p. lviii, n. 8.
[9] Ibid. p. lxv; *Proc. before J.P.s*, pp. lviii, lxxi, lxxii, 33.

XIV

EXCEPTIONAL TYPES OF
GAOL DELIVERY AND THE CONDUCT
OF TRIALS

IT is fully apparent that the crown acknowledged the right of franchise-owners to keep their prisons. Towards claims by franchise-owners, however, to deliver those prisons it took a much less indulgent view. It is time to consider how far such claims were conceded not only in the period after 1292 but from the earliest times.

Inevitably the palatinates were suffered to make their own arrangements. Except during vacancies of the see, as in 1237,[1] the crown never sought to deliver the gaols of Durham. In the thirteenth century the sheriff of Durham, who was the bishop's nominee, is supposed to have effected delivery. Most probably he did so, for deliveries by sheriffs seem at the time to have been characteristic of the remoter regions of the country.[2] He was certainly delivering the gaol of Durham itself in 1317 without the aid of associates.[3] On the other hand, by this time the practice of appointing panels of justices also prevailed, for about 1314–15 three men were delivering Durham gaol[4] and two Sadberge.[5] It is impossible to say which system was chiefly favoured in the next half-century. In 1340 there were certainly panels of two or three commissioners for Durham,[6] so the impression is conveyed that the thirteenth-century system was obsolete. On the other hand Bishop Bury in 1344, as though instituting a new system, associated a commissioner with the sheriff for the trial of prisoners, though the power of delivering homicides was withheld.[7] In the

---

[1] *Close R.* 1234–7, 543.   [2] See p. 277.
[3] *Hist. Dunelmensis Scriptores Tres* (Surtees Soc. IX), pp. cxiv–cxv.
[4] *Reg. Palatinum Dunelmense* (R.S.) II. 1258.   [5] Ibid. 716–17.
[6] Ibid. III. 238, 240, 341.
[7] G. T. Lapsley, *The county palatine of Durham* (Cambridge, Mass., 1900), 83–4.

late fifteenth century and in the sixteenth the practice was to appoint panels for both prisons varying in number from twelve to three. At times these certainly contained professional judges and serjeants-at-law.[1] In 1519–20 a separate commission of eyre and assize was being appointed.[2] It consisted of six persons, five of whom were also members of the concurrent gaol-delivery commission. An 'assize' for Norhamshire existed in 1345–6,[3] but whether there was then also a gaol delivery is unknown. In the first few years of the sixteenth century there were also commissions of nine or ten justices for Islandshire and Norhamshire.[4]

Of the system of delivery prevailing in the palatinate of Chester very little has at present been collected. That it was different from that in force in the kingdom admits of no doubt. The best that can yet be said is that the justice of Chester appears to have gone on circuit throughout the shire with or without the sheriff.[5]

The grant to Henry of Lancaster in 1351 of palatine powers included the power to appoint justices for the quasi-palatinate who were to hold both crown and civil pleas.[6] Four justices were at once appointed.[7] When the quasi-palatinate was revived for John of Gaunt's benefit the number of justices was reduced to three and later in the fourteenth century to two.[8] The justices were, among other things, justices of gaol delivery,[9] but at best they enjoyed only a concurrent jurisdiction, for Lancashire never ceased to be treated as part of the northern circuit.

The palatine privileges of the duchy were supposed to be modelled on those of the earldom of Chester. In this respect, however, they more closely resembled those of the bishopric of Ely. In the thirteenth century the *curia Eliensis* possessed within

---

[1] *36 D.K. Rep.*, App. I, pp. 36, 58, 60, 66, 98. The years are 1492–3, 1495–6, 1501–2, 1502–3, 1519–20.

[2] Ibid. 98.   [3] *31 D.K. Rep.*, App. I, p. 133.

[4] *36 D.K. Rep.*, App. I, pp. 60, 61, 81, 99. The years are 1501–2, 1502–3, 1507–8, and 1512–13.

[5] From information supplied by Mrs Margaret Sharp.

[6] R. Somerville, *History of the duchy of Lancaster* (London, 1953), I, 42.

[7] Ibid. 467.

[8] *Transactions of the Historic Society of Lancashire & Cheshire*, CIII, 64.

[9] Ibid. 65.

the liberty the powers of a royal eyre, which of course included the delivery of gaols. When the eyre began to fade away, the bishop seems to have taken to appointing his own justices of gaol delivery. At all events there is a reference to them in 1286. In the same year, however, Edward I claimed to appoint such justices as well.[1] There was nothing revolutionary in this, for the crown had long been delivering the liberty gaols, even though there was no vacancy in the see: Dereham from 1252–3,[2] Melton from 1259–60,[3] and Ely itself from 1273–4.[4] In the earlier fourteenth century the bishop alone seems to have delivered his liberty gaols.[5] In the later part of the century, however, the crown did so,[6] though whether exclusively or concurrently it would be hard to say. In the later fifteenth century the crown seems to have nominated the justices, who were thereupon reappointed by the bishop. The bishop, however, appointed his own justices of assize, and it is quite possible that he also continued to appoint justices of gaol delivery.[7] At all events the Chief Justice of Ely, to use his later title, exercised a criminal jurisdiction within the Isle until 1836.[8] Three conclusions are therefore possible. One is that throughout the middle ages, with the possible exception of the earlier fourteenth century, crown and bishop tried suspect criminals concurrently; a second, that the crown appointed the commissioners and the bishop reappointed them; and a third, that the crown tried the major felonies and the bishop the minor ones. The second conclusion is the most convincing, though there is a strong probability that the crown never felt itself debarred from exercising a concurrent jurisdiction if need arose.

Several other ecclesiastics asserted rights of delivery with varying success. In 1293 the archbishop of York claimed a gaol delivery for Ripon and Beverley[9] and also for Hexhamshire.[10] The

---

[1] *V.C.H. Cambs.* IV, 13.   [2] C 66/55 m. 7*d.*

[3] C 66/74 m. 14*d.* For an unexplained reason the mandate in pursuance is addressed to the sheriff of Essex.

[4] *43 D.K. Rep.*, App. I, 437.

[5] *V.C.H. Cambs.* IV, 13; P.R.O. List of Gaol Del. R. (typescript).

[6] P.R.O. List of Gaol Del. R.   [7] *V.C.H. Cambs.* IV, 17.

[8] Ibid. 20.   [9] *Plac. de Quo Warr.* 221–2.   [10] Ibid. 591.

crown made the not unexpected rejoinder that such deliveries must depend on express grant, and to such a grant the archbishop could not point. The case was thereupon adjourned without judgement. A gaol in Beverley was certainly delivered by the king's justices in the late thirteenth century and at various times in the fourteenth.[1] Only once,[2] however, is it called the archbishop's gaol, and the other references (apart from one which names the provost's gaol)[3] may be to the town gaol. The archbishop's gaol in Ripon was also once delivered by the king's justices.[4] There are no other references to deliveries, and possibly in Ripon's case the archbishop was long successful.[5] The abbot of Battle claimed to deliver his prisons at Bromham (Wilts.) at some time in Edward III's reign[6] and Wye (Kent) in 1328.[7] He seems to have succeeded in his claim over Wye for the time being, though there are many fourteenth-century deliveries by the crown.[8] In the other case it was decided to meet the claim, if the evidence supported its justice. Numerous commissions to deliver the gaol at Battle itself were issued by the abbot in the fourteenth century.[9] The crown, however, delivered concurrently.[10] There is some reason to think that the abbot of Ramsey was delivering the prison at that place in 1312.[11] It has been asserted that the abbot of Bury habitually delivered the gaol of the banlieu of Bury.[12] However this may be, the crown repeatedly delivered 'the gaol of Bury' from 1243–4.[13] St Albans was constantly delivered by the crown from 1233–4.[14] At some uncertain date a grant of delivery was made to the abbot but in 1406–7 he was adjudged

[1] P.R.O. List of Gaol Del. R.   [2] In 1403: J.I. 3/82/3.
[3] In 1343: J.I. 1/1141 m. 7.   [4] In 1402: J.I. 3/82/2.
[5] Cf. C. Hallett, *The cathedral church of Ripon* (London, 1909), 21, 31.
[6] *Rot. Parl.* II. 15.   [7] Ibid. 393.
[8] P.R.O. List of Gaol Del. R.
[9] Huntington Library, Battle Abbey Muniments, Gaol Delivery Rolls, 1–7. The years range from 1327 to 1358.
[10] P.R.O. List of Gaol Del. R.
[11] W. O. Ault, *Private jurisdiction in England* (New Haven, Conn. 1923), 118. The abbot took the amercements.
[12] *Proc. Suffolk Inst. Arch.* XXI, 206.
[13] C 66/44 m. 16*d* records the first delivery commission. See also P.R.O. List of Gaol Del. R.   [14] C 66/44 m. 16*d*.

to have lost the privilege through failure to exercise it.[1] Later he evidently recovered it for, after the Dissolution, his successors in title possessed the right of delivery.[2] The abbot's gaol at Westminster, which the crown frequently delivered from 1259,[3] seems in 1266 to have been deliverable by the abbot's justices also.[4]

While these abbots, eminent though they might be, were unable to assert their rights or claims consistently, two other heads of houses were more successful. Of these the abbot of Glastonbury was the more notable. When in 1287 the crown sent justices to try a prisoner in his gaol, the abbot refused to admit the emissaries. Instead he reappointed two of them, with two of his own nominees, to hold the trial.[5] The crown was so far successful in resisting the abbot's claim on this occasion as to be able to have the prisoner removed to the Tower. Whatever may have been the outcome of this particular case, Glastonbury presumably maintained the right to deliver prisoners taken in the Twelve Hides until the Dissolution.[6] The second was the abbot of Fécamp. From 1248 until the disappearance of the eyre he had been exempted from the national eyre system,[7] and in 1333 was maintaining his privilege of delivery in his Gloucestershire hundreds of Slaughter[8] and Cheltenham.[9] To these rights the abbess of Syon succeeded and still claimed to exercise them in both hundreds in the earlier sixteenth century,[10] though under peace commissions.[11]

Besides such extensive rights as these, whether exercised or not, some ecclesiastical franchise-owners laid claim to a right that was more restricted. This was to deliver prisoners charged only with larceny or at least prisoners not charged with homicide. The known claimants were the abbots of Cirencester and Tewkesbury and the chapters of Beverley and Ripon. The Cirencester

[1] Coke, 2 *Instit.* (1671 ed.), 43. For the date of the forfeiture see p. 96 n. 7.
[2] *Archives*, [I], no. 4, p. 17.   [3] C 66/74 m. 14*d.*
[4] *Cal. Pat. R.* 1258–66, 681.   [5] *Sel. Cases in K.B.* I, 166.
[6] C. A. Ralegh Radford, *The Tribunal, Glastonbury* (Min. Public Bdg. and Works, Guide, 1961).
[7] *V.C.H. Glos.* VI, 6.   [8] Ibid.   [9] S.C. 2/175/25.
[10] S.C. 2/175/27; *V.C.H. Glos.* VI, 6.   [11] S.C. 6/Hen. VIII/1179.

claim, which is not positively known to have extended beyond Rapsgate hundred in Gloucestershire, but probably did, was asserted in 1230–9.[1] The Tewkesbury claim, which was limited to the inhabitants of Tewkesbury borough, was advanced in 1273.[2] The Ripon claim, advanced at an uncertain date, affected part of the city and some of the surrounding districts. It seems to have extended to all crimes except homicide, in which excepted case a royal justice was bound to sit beside the justices appointed by the chapter.[3] Beverley's privilege, as accepted by the crown in 1403, amounted simply to the delivery of larceners. The charter, however, which conceded this privilege, purported to be a form of confirmation of a much more comprehensive grant by Henry III. That grant comprised the determination by the canons' justices, though in the presence of the king's justices, of all pleas of eyre, including pleas of the crown.[4] The charter of 1403 seems, therefore, to have truncated an originally more extensive privilege. It should be added that in 1317 the prior of Durham had the right to deliver prisoners taken on his fee except for homicide.[5] This declaration represents a very similar limitation although, of course, it was to the bishop of Durham's justices and not to the king's that the power of trying homicides was reserved.

In the present state of knowledge it is impossible to say whether the alleged privileges of Tewkesbury, Ripon, and Beverley were exercised. There is no evidence that royal justices ever visited Tewkesbury, but this may show either that the abbot delivered the gaol himself or that it was not delivered at all. Prisons at Ripon and Beverley were indeed often delivered by the king's justices, but it is only rarely that we learn which prisons in those towns they were. They could have been archiepiscopal, capitular, or even municipal. There is one recorded delivery of the provost

[1] C. D. Ross (ed.), *The cartulary of Cirencester Abbey, Gloucestershire* (London, 1964), I, pp. 215, 218. Cf. ibid. p. 222.
[2] William Dugdale, *Monasticon Anglicanum* (2nd ed. London, 1817–30), II, 83.
[3] Hallett, *The cathedral church of Ripon*, 21.
[4] *Cal. Chart. R.* 1341–1417, 457.
[5] *Hist. Dunelmensis Scriptores Tres*, p. cxv.

of Beverley's gaol[1] but even here the precise nature of the gaol is uncertain.

It has just been shown that the canons of Beverley claimed to have received a charter from Henry III which authorized them to try pleas of the crown in eyre, including by implication those of gaol delivery, in courts presided over by mixed benches composed of their own and the king's justices. A charter to Battle abbey of 1271 contains the very same provision, the abbot's nominee in this case being his steward *ex officio*.[2] The abbot of Glastonbury partially conformed to the same principle in 1287 when he reappointed the king's justices of gaol delivery to sit with his own.[3] Probably other instances of these mixed benches could be discovered in non-municipal liberties, whether in the days of the eyre or in later ones. The creation of such benches represents a compromise between the absolutely unrestricted choice of justices by either party, the crown on the one hand and the franchise-owner on the other.

The impression we are bound to form is that in general the crown viewed with extreme distaste the claims of lords of liberties, apart from the great ones, to deliver their own gaols, and that where it admitted the claim at all it limited it in some fashion. The three systems of limitation seem to have been the creation of mixed benches, the alternate delivery by royal and franchise justices, and the reservation to royal judges of the graver pleas. At least until the fifteenth century even municipal communities, indulged though they were, could not hope to escape some such limitation, or unrestrictedly to usurp the crown's prerogative to deliver. London herself was granted that freedom only once and that was in a moment of crisis in 1363, when 'the citizens', whatever that phrase may have meant, were suffered to deliver gaols and try offenders without waiting for the king's justices.[4] In the next decade, though apparently without authority, they appear to have continued the practice,[5] perhaps because the properly

---

[1] See p. 298.   [2] *Cal. Pat. R.* 1266–72, 601–2.   [3] See p. 299.
[4] J. Tait (ed.), *Chronica Johannis de Reading et Anonymi Cantuariensis, 1346–67* (Manchester, 1914), 158.   [5] *Cal. Close R.* 1374–7, 174.

constituted benches sat too rarely.[1] In 1327 London did of course
secure that her mayor should be a justice *ex officio*,[2] but the crown
appointed him together with the other commissioners. From 1363
the recorder also said that he was expressly commissioned likewise.[3] In 1373 Bristol expressed the wish that her gaols should be
delivered by the mayor, bailiffs, and coroner,[4] but the crown was
only prepared to grant her the privileges of London.[5] From the
early fifteenth century there was a separate commission of gaol
delivery for Norwich composed of the mayor and other local
worthies. The crown, however, appointed the commissioners.[6]

To the generalization that towns could not control their own
gaol deliveries the Cinque Ports form at least a partial exception.
Dover castle seems in early times to have been used as the main
prison of the liberty. Though in the later thirteenth century this
was on five recorded occasions delivered by commissioners appointed by the crown, on two of them the constable was appointed as sole judge.[7] By the early fourteenth century the
constable had become, and perhaps even in the preceding half-
century already was, the supreme president of the Cinque Ports
franchise, appointed by the crown but pledged to support the
liberties of the Ports.[8] Delivery by him, therefore, might have
been, or perhaps was, the equivalent of delivery by the portsmen
themselves. Moreover, on one of these five occasions the justices
were instructed to deliver according to the law and custom of the

[1] See p. 292.   [2] See p. 291.

[3] Men who are known to have been recorders are invariably named in the
commissions enrolled in the Letter Books from this year, usually at the tail end
of the commissions: cf. *Speculum*, XVIII, 243, where it is stated on the authority
of C. Pendrill, *London life in the fourteenth century* (London, 1925) that the
recorder was first summoned to sit in 1368.

[4] *Little Red Book of Bristol*, ed. F. B. Bickley (Bristol, 1908), I. 123.

[5] *Bristol Chart.* (Bristol Rec. Soc. I), 125–7.

[6] *Recs. of Norwich*, I, pp. cxxxi, 299–300.

[7] 1251–2, 1258–9, 1273–4, 1281–2 (twice). In 1258–9 the constable was
appointed under the name of his office; in 1273–4 Stephen of Pencestre, who was
both warden of the Cinque Ports and constable of Dover, was appointed by
name.

[8] Katherine M. E. Murray, *The constitutional history of the Cinque Ports* (Manchester, 1935), 77.

Ports.[1] Deliveries by the crown of Dover or any other Cinque Port prison are not encountered in later times, except in 1487 when Winchelsea gaol was delivered by the mayor and six others because the wardenship was vacant.[2] This implies that delivery by the warden was the normal practice.

Towards the end of the fifteenth century the old strictness was in one or two instances unexpectedly relaxed. First the crown granted by charter the right of delivery to the small and remote Shropshire boroughs of Ludlow (1462)[3] and Wenlock (1468).[4] The prisoners in the borough gaols were to be tried by the borough bailiff or bailiffs and either the recorder or the steward. Since these officers were chosen by the boroughs themselves, the crown lost all effective control over the choice of justices. Almost at the same time two ecclesiastics, one of them significantly enough a Shropshire one, were similarly privileged: the abbot and convent of Shrewsbury in 1466[5] and the bishop of Salisbury in 1479.[6] The first was to use as justices his steward and one or two persons learned in the law. The choice of the bishop was in no way limited. The bishop's area of jurisdiction was presumably meant to coincide with the boundaries of the city of Salisbury. At all events in the year of the grant he appointed his steward, the mayor of the city, and four other men.[7]

The Act of 1536 for Recontinuing Liberties in the Crown prohibited for the future all appointments of gaol-delivery justices by the owners of franchises, whether the franchises were ecclesiastical or municipal. Instead all such appointments were to be made by the crown.[8] How quickly and how completely the statute was observed has not yet been measured. Durham was merged in the national system of deliveries, but precisely when and in what circumstances is not easy to establish.[9] Hexhamshire also ceased to have a separate bench appointed by the archbishop, but

---

[1] C 66/73 m. 14*d*.   [2] *Cal. Pat. R.* 1485–94, 214.
[3] *Cal. Chart. R.* 1427–1516, 159.
[4] Ibid. 232.   [5] Ibid. 213.
[6] *Cal. Pat. R.* 1476–85, 152.
[7] Registrum Beauchamp episcopi Sar. II, f. 25 *b*.
[8] 27 Hen. VIII, c. 24, s. 2.   [9] See p. 282.

this would have occurred in any case when the crown acquired the shire in 1545.[1]

Although the Act of 1536 put an end to autonomous appointments, it protected those boroughs and towns that already possessed a gaol-delivery commission in the enjoyment of that privilege. Accordingly the Salisbury justices are found delivering their own gaol in 1540, though the commission appointing them is in the king's name.[2] Such town commissions were not a recent growth and their history must not be overlooked. They represent one form of 'local' commission, by which is meant a body of justices not formed exclusively or mainly of professional circuit judges or serjeants. It has already been mentioned[3] that after 1299 there was a partial resumption of the system of using local knights, usually three to each panel, for gaol delivery, though in conjunction with circuit judges and not in substitution for them. The same knights were often peace commissioners. Thus throughout Edward II's reign criminal justice of both the lower and the higher order was at times concentrated in local hands. After the circuit system was reorganized in the early years of Edward III on lines now familiar, commissions addressed to local knights became relatively fewer.[4] Nevertheless such knights and gentlemen, and indeed townsmen,[5] continued to be frequently commissioned in association with circuit justices. This practice lasted until 1530 at any rate,[6] and very likely much later.

Besides these *ad hoc* commissions addressed to local knights and gentry the county peace commission itself sometimes served as the authority for delivery. This practice seems to have originated in a clause which is first found in the commission of 1329 which empowered keepers of the peace to determine felonies imputed to men and women indicted before them. This clause was unusual until 1350 but is found thereafter except in the periods

---

[1] *History of Northumberland* [Northumberland County History Committee], III, *Hexhamshire*, pt. 1, 53.

[2] Roll *penes* city of Salisbury.   [3] See p. 281.

[4] From information supplied by Mr C. A. F. Meekings.

[5] *Recs. of Norwich*, I, p. cxxxi.

[6] *L. & P.* IV (3), pp. 2918–19.

1364–8 and 1382–9.[1] It received statutory confirmation in 1344,[2] 1361,[3] and 1394,[4] but all those statutes provide that the power can only be exercised when 'men of law' sit with or as members of the commission. The commission itself and the statutes of 1344 and 1361 do not mention gaol delivery and are permissive. The statute of 1394 positively enjoins delivery upon the justices if in their opinion too long an interval was elapsing between one delivery and another, with the consequent danger of escapes. It does not seem to limit the justices' power to the delivery of prisoners indicted before themselves.

It is not clear how these arrangements worked out in practice. It is known, and has already been stated,[5] that justices of the central courts sometimes delivered under peace commissions, perhaps because by this means they could avoid the prohibition against delivery by 'natives' embodied in the Acts of 1330 and 1384.[6] It is also known that, to take one example, Salisbury castle gaol was being delivered in 1373 and 1376 by benches presided over or consisting of men who were indeed justices of the peace but were neither judges of the central courts nor serjeants.[7] On the other hand a parliamentary petition of 1421 complains that the power of delivery by justices of the peace had been 'restrained'[8] and a further petition of 1455 implies that those justices could not deliver prisoners arrested on suspicion by the king's ministers.[9] Neither petition was granted. It is perhaps the case that in the fifteenth and sixteenth centuries the crown when it wished to use local justices for gaol delivery preferred to commission them expressly for the purpose. At the same time it was held in the seventeenth century that the then commission and the Acts of 1344, 1361, and 1394 gave justices of the peace all the authority to deliver that they needed.[10]

---

[1] *Proc. before J.P.s*, pp. xxviii–xxix.
[2] 18 Edw. III, St. ii, c. 2.
[3] 34 Edw. III, c. 1.
[4] 17 Ric. II, c. 10.
[5] See p. 283.
[6] See p. 283.
[7] *V.C.H. Wilts.* v, 39.
[8] *Rot. Parl.* iv. 146.
[9] Ibid. v, 332.
[10] M. Dalton, *The country justice, containing the practise of the justices of the peace out of their sessions* (London, 1635 ed.), 50.

The petition of 1455 had asked that the power of delivery might be enjoyed not only by county benches but by cities and boroughs with their own commissions of the peace. Although the petition was not granted, some towns' benches at least enjoyed such a power in the fifteenth century. In Norwich, which had had a gaol-delivery commission from at least 1423,[1] the custom had grown up by 1492 of holding gaol-delivery and peace sessions together[2] or at least (1509) on the same day.[3] In Slaughter Hundred, in Gloucestershire, in 1510–11, the two types of session were also being held together,[4] as they were in Salisbury in 1540.[5] The municipal gaol of Colchester seems to have been delivered by notables of the town in 1423.[6]

The various types of commission already described were issued for the delivery of all the prisoners in a particular gaol or gaols. Special commissions, however, for the delivery of named persons or limited groups of persons, which had been so very common in Edward I's early years,[7] continued to be issued in later times. Until the end of the thirteenth century they are frequently encountered, particularly at gaols that were not regularly delivered.[8] Various causes operated to promote their decline in the century that followed. The disappearance of the eyre eliminated the mopping-up commissions for the delivery of those who had surrendered to prison after outlawry in eyre.[9] The greater frequency and regularity of deliveries by justices on circuit and the use of justices of the peace for delivering gaols[10] may be assumed to have much reduced the need for such special measures. Nevertheless, in the short period from 1318 to 1323 three such commissions were issued to deal with prisoners in Exeter gaol alone. One of

[1] *Recs. of Norwich*, I, 299–300.
[2] Ibid. 305.
[3] Ibid. 307.
[4] S.C. 6/Hen. VIII/1179.
[5] Roll of peace and gaol-delivery session *penes* city of Salisbury.
[6] *Red paper book of Colchester*, ed. W. G. Benham (Colchester, 1902), 48.
[7] See p. 271.
[8] R. F. Hunnisett, *The medieval coroner* (Cambridge, 1961), 98.
[9] The last such commission to be noticed of *c.* 1303 was for a man in Ely gaol: *Cal. Close R.* 1302–7, 194. It appears to have been re-enrolled on the patent roll, but the entry is not calendared.
[10] See p. 305.

these prisoners was a forger[1] and another a man who was charged with appropriating treasure trove.[2] The third, however, was, as so often before, a suspected homicide,[3] and special commissions for other homicides were also issued at the same time.[4] In the same period individuals might still successfully petition the crown in parliament for writs of gaol delivery, for three such petitions from prisoners survive from the period 1318–19.[5] In the later fourteenth century such special commissions are infrequent though not unknown.[6] In the fifteenth century they are rather more numerous. Taking only four gaols and looking no further than the face of the patent roll, we find six such commissions for the delivery of prisoners in Exeter and Nottingham, five for those in Guildford, and three for those in Colchester.[7] Of these twenty, twelve affect a single prisoner. Of the remainder three affect large groups, one of nine,[8] one of fourteen,[9] and one of sixteen persons.[10]

The practice, noticed in the earlier period, of issuing commissions for the delivery of all prisoners in a particular gaol except certain defined categories continued for a little while into this one. Thus such commissions were issued for Eye in 1295[11] and York in 1303.[12] There was also a sequence of commissions at about the same time, for the trial of all prisoners held in Surrey and Sussex prisons except those accused of trespassing in the warrens and chaces of John de Warenne, earl of Surrey, and of murdering his parker. Chichester (1294),[13] Arundel (1295),[14]

---

[1] *Cal. Pat. R.* 1321–4, 381.   [2] *Ibid.* 55.
[3] *Ibid.* 1317–21, 185.   [4] *Ibid.* 477, 537.
[5] H. Cole (ed.), *Documents…from the records of…the Queen's Remembrancer of the Exchequer* (Rec. Com.), 35–7. Cf. *Mem. de Parl.*, 10–11.
[6] E.g. *Cal. Lr. Bks. G*, 2 (Newgate, 1352), *H*, 322 (Newgate, 1388); *Cal. Pat. R.* 1364–7, 281 (Battle, 1366); *ibid.* 1381–5, 428 (Old Salisbury, 1384); *ibid.* 1385–9, 383 (Exeter, 1387).
[7] The patent roll calendars have been searched for these four places with some care.
[8] *Cal. Pat. R.* 1446–52, 433. At this page there are two separate commissions, addressed to different groups of persons, for the delivery of the same group. They have been counted as one commission.
[9] *Ibid.* 1429–36, 350.   [10] *Ibid.* 1452–61, 308.
[11] *Ibid.* 1292–1301, 162.   [12] *Ibid.* 1301–7, 192.
[13] *Ibid.* 1292–1301, 72.   [14] *Ibid.* 166.

Chertsey (1297),[1] and Guildford (1299–1301)[2] were all treated in this way. At Chertsey and often at Guildford other classes of prisoner were also excepted. Some of the trespassers against Warrenne were tried by a special gaol-delivery commission sitting at Chichester (1294).[3] It is not known what happened to the others.

It is possible to construct a somewhat imperfect picture of the actual conduct of a normal gaol delivery. We know that the county court was often the place of trial.[4] In some counties that court sat in the castle and in these we find the county and the circuit courts sharing the same home. This seems to have been the case at Cambridge.[5] In the thirteenth century there was a county hall (*aula comitatus*) in the outer bailey of Hereford castle,[6] and in 1335 the county court of Lincolnshire was sitting in the great hall of Lincoln castle.[7] At York the county court was sitting in the castle as early as 1212. Many generations later, in 1360, the little hall of the castle was furnishing a joint home for both county courts and assizes. By 1446 all the courts seem to have moved to the 'Motehall', which was either another name for the great hall of the castle or a building on the site put up to meet the special needs of justice.[8] At Northampton we know that the great hall of the castle was being used for circuits in 1329,[9] but we are uncertain about the whereabouts of the county court.

In other towns where the gaol was not in the castle special buildings were provided for the gaol deliveries. The earliest example comes from Warwick, where in 1202–3 a piece of ground was bought contiguous to the gaol 'to hold the pleas of the gaol'.[10] Thereafter gaol and gaol hall seem to have stood side by side in Gaolhall Lane, now Gerrard Street,[11] and indeed by the

---

[1] *Cal. Pat. R.* 1292–1301, 320.

[2] Ibid. 161–2 (1295), 254, 260, 286, 319, 375 (1297), 355, 378, 382, 459 (1298), 423, 461–2 (1299), 547 (1300), 627 (1301). One of the 1299 commissions also excepts other categories.   [3] Ibid. 116.   [4] See p. 275.

[5] *V.C.H. Cambs.* III, 118.   [6] *King's Works*, II, 675.

[7] Ibid. 705.   [8] *V.C.H. Yorks., City of York*, 522–3.

[9] *King's Works*, II, 753.   [10] *Pipe R.* 1203 (P.R.S. n.s. XVI), 28.

[11] *Rot. Hund.* II. 228; *Cal. Inq. Misc.* I, p. 302; *P.N. Warws.* (Eng. Place-Name Soc.), 261; Hollar's plan of 1654 in W. Dugdale, *Warwickshire* (2nd ed., London, 1730, I, 424).

mid-fifteenth century seem to have formed a single structure.[1] Edward II ordered the construction of a gaol hall at Leicester to stand beside the gaol. After long delays it had been completed by 1344.[2] The 'shire houses' at both Ipswich and Norwich were rebuilt in the last years of the fourteenth century. The 'house' at Ipswich had completely disappeared by 1397,[3] that at Norwich was ruinous in 1389.[4] At Stafford there was a shire hall by 1398.[5] The 'great halls' at Nottingham and Hertford, both contiguous to the gaols of those places and neither at the time within its castle, are mentioned in the fifteenth and sixteenth centuries, the former first in 1444,[6] the latter in 1506.[7]

Town halls or guild halls were also no doubt sometimes used for the delivery of county gaols. Sir Thomas Smith specifies the 'town house' as a possible location.[8] It is probable that Salisbury forms an actual example, for there the council house seems always to have accommodated the assizes. But Smith implies that even as late as his own day trials were sometimes held in the open.[9] If this is a correct conclusion, some temporary booth was no doubt put up within the open space.

The gaols of towns and liberties may often have been delivered within the gaol itself. In the fourteenth century the gaol for St Mary's liberty, York, was delivered within the abbey gatehouse, which was itself the prison.[10] In earlier times the same practice prevailed at Newgate, for in 1241–2 the justices were ordered to

[1] E.g. guttering between the 'long hall' of the gaol and the prisoners' house (1444): E 101/621/21; wall between the hall and the 'chamber' within the prison (1448–9): E 101/590/29; stone staircase built to connect the 'chamber' of the gaol with the hall: E 101/621/19 (1462).

[2] *V.C.H. Leics.* II, 92. Allusions up to 1462–3: E 101/591/1. And cf. *V.C.H. Leics.* IV, 338.

[3] E 101/575/28. Later allusion 1409: E 364/43 m. B.

[4] E 101/575/27. Allusions up to 1466: E 101/575/38.

[5] W.S.L., H.M. Chetwynd, 7. Later allusion 1433–4: W.S.L., D 1850/2/6.

[6] E 101/581/3. Allusions up to 1458: E 364/93 m. J.

[7] E 101/557/21. There are subsequent sixteenth-century allusions, of which the last is 1526–7: E 101/557/25.

[8] L. Alston (ed.), Sir T. Smith, *De Republica Anglorum* (Cambridge, 1906), 96.

[9] Ibid.   [10] From information supplied by Mr C. A. F. Meekings.

meet at the prison[1] and in 1281–2 a room in the prison 'in which the justice sits' is named.[2] In 1329 or thereabouts the justices seem to have sat at the Guildhall,[3] but in 1334 steps were taken to provide a purpose-built sessions house. A plot of ground measuring some 180 feet by 40 feet, and stretching northwards from a point just outside Newgate towards Smithfield, was in that year leased by the city to one William of Langford, who was to build thereon a hall and three 'chambers' in which to hold the Newgate sessions. The buildings were to lie at the south end of the plot, the northern extremities of which were presumably meant for a garden.[4] No doubt Langford thought he could make some profit out of renting the premises to the city. The building was presumably erected and commonly used, though the delivery commission of February 1365 appears to have required the justices to sit at the Guildhall. This was evidently disliked, for in the next year it was declared that this arrangement was not to be taken as a precedent or construed as prejudicial to the city's liberties.[5] During the rebuilding of Newgate, delivery took place at the Counters,[6] whither the prisoners had been removed.[7] Probably the sessions house was rebuilt on its old position at the same time. At all events it occupied a very similar site by 1456.[8] But we know that at that very time the prison itself was overcrowded and perhaps the sessions house had to be turned into an extension to the prison soon after. Be this as it may, it seems to have been abandoned by 1539, when a new sessions house, the first in then living memory, was built in the Old Bailey.[9]

York had its own 'hall of pleas' by the fourteenth century and here trials took place.[10] Some other towns and liberties would have been likewise equipped; the 'Tribunal' at Glastonbury which under the name of 'county hall' may be traced to the

---

[1] C 66/50 m. 13d.
[2] E 101/467/11.
[3] *Chrons. Edw. I and II*, 1. 346.
[4] *Cal. Pat. R.* 1334–8, 158.
[5] *Cal. Lr. Bks. G*, 213.
[6] Ibid. *K*, 39, 49.
[7] See p. 110.
[8] Jorn. 6, f. 87b.
[9] R. R. Sharpe, *Memorials of Newgate Gaol and the Sessions House* (London, privately printed 1908), 9–10.
[10] From information supplied by Mr C. A. F. Meekings.

thirteenth century, was used for the gaol delivery of the Twelve Hides.[1] The court house at Battle, repaired or equipped between 1367–8 and 1519–20, was doubtless put to the same use.[2]

The justices sat upon the bench,[3] which at first was doubtless literally no more. The prisoners stood at the bar, which at Maidstone in 1317–18 was specially constructed in preparation for the justices' visit.[4] Large numbers of officials attended: the sheriff, the under-sheriff, their clerks, hundred bailiffs, stewards and bailiffs of liberties, and coroners.[5] From an uncertain date the justices of the peace were also there; juries of presentment must needs attend of course; so must the knights and freemen of the county to act as trial juries. Both in the thirteenth[6] and the early fourteenth centuries[7] such juries seem to have been compounded of a mixture of presenting juries and other men of the vicinity.

The trial jury which was used in eyre by at least the mid-thirteenth century was also a conspicuous feature of gaol delivery,[8] and care was taken to secure attendance. In 1253 the sheriff of Kent was ordered to make sure that the hundreds adjacent to Maidstone gaol made full appearance at a forthcoming delivery.[9] In 1273–4 tenants of the abbot of Waltham were expected to be present when the abbot's prison was delivered.[10] By the same time the bailiffs of Wiltshire hundreds were sending in lists of knights and freeholders within their areas of jurisdiction if men from those areas were waiting to be delivered either in prison or on bail. The men listed were then summoned by the sheriff who picked the jurors.[11] Attendance was not always easy to secure. In 1249

---

[1] Radford, Min. Public Bdg. and Works, Guide.

[2] Huntington Library, Battle Abbey Muniments, Beadles' R. 8, 10, 42, 76, 78, 84, 94, 95, 280.

[3] Smith, *De Republica Anglorum*, 96.   [4] Lambeth Palace MSS, C.R. 660.

[5] For coroners see Hunnisett, *The medieval coroner*, 98, 112; for the practice in Cambridgeshire in the early fifteenth century see Marguerite Gollancz, 'The system of gaol delivery as illustrated in...gaol delivery rolls' (London M.A. dissertation, 1936), p. 28.   [6] *Crown Pleas of the Wilts. Eyre*, p. 52.

[7] *Kent keepers of the peace 1316–17* (Kent Arch. Soc. Rec. Brch. XIII), pp. xxxvi, 81.

[8] *Crown Pleas of the Wilts. Eyre*, p. 52.

[9] *Close R.* 1251–3, 476.   [10] *Rot. Hund.* I. 150.

[11] *Crown Pleas of the Wilts. Eyre*, pp. 52–3.

the liberties of Malmesbury abbey were temporarily confiscated because the abbot's men had not attended the delivery of Salisbury gaol.[1] Two centuries later, in 1454, the mayor of London was rewarded for enforcing the attendance of the men of Middlesex at Newgate gaol delivery, a practice that had long been in abeyance.[2] In 1518 Londoners were being imprisoned and fined for similar lapses.[3]

Attendances of jurors or potential jurors must often have been large. Seventy men or more had acted as jurors at a Nottingham delivery in or shortly before 1291[4] and at about the same time at least a dozen knights had been present at a recent delivery in the same county, quite apart from men of lesser station.[5] It was partly because the concourse was so large that the public objected to gaols being kept, and therefore to trials being held, in puny places. In 1315 Windsor, where the Berkshire gaol then was, was thought to be too poor a place to be the seat of sessions.[6] It was no doubt for a like cause that Sawley was condemned by the commons of Derbyshire in 1380.[7]

The records of gaol delivery in the Public Record Office have recently been so fully and carefully listed[8] that further description is well-nigh superfluous. They begin, as has already been said,[9] in 1271, and for the fourteenth century and first half of the fifteenth are numerous. Much has been lost but no doubt some of the losses could be made up from ancient transcripts.[10] The records end for no known reason in 1476 with a roll for the city of Bristol,[11] and the series is not resumed until the records of the south-eastern circuit, in different form, begin in 1559.[12] There is no reason, however, to assume that there was any discontinuity.

[1] *Close R.* 1247–51, 529.
[2] Jorn. 5, f. 196.
[3] Rep. 3, fos. 248 *b*–249 *b*, 252 *b*, 253.
[4] *Sel. Cases in K.B.* II, 57.
[5] Ibid. 83.
[6] *Cal. Pat. R.* 1313–17, 328–9.
[7] *Rot. Parl.* III. 95. The assizes at Sawley were presumably held for civil pleas alone, since there was no county gaol in Derbyshire and therefore no need for a gaol delivery. See p. 65.
[8] P.R.O. List of Gaol Del. R. (typescript).
[9] See p. 277.
[10] E.g. C 47/81/5/168.
[11] J.I. 3/20/10.
[12] *Guide to the...Public Record Office* (London, 1963), I, 129.

Indeed, to look no further, an extract exists from a roll of 1479[1] and a roll for the justices delivering Guildford castle in 1530 has been preserved outside public custody.[2]

The surviving records consist of both rolls and files, the files being made up of commissions, writs, indictments, and jury panels. They present a magnificent picture of the state of society over two centuries, though inevitably their credibility is questionable. Not only are they statements of charges and judgements, rather than of fact, but at times they were falsely engrossed. In 1304 the king's attorney noted that certain rolls so contradicted the indictments upon which they were based *quod prefata recorda potius debent dici discordia quam recorda.*[3]

By at least 1289–90 such records were beginning to be laid up for security in the Exchequer.[4] In 1293 Hamon Hauteyn's son was ordered to surrender the records, which he had retained, of his late father's deliveries of Newgate.[5] In 1320 the executors of twelve judges were told to send in the rolls of the judges whose estates they were administering.[6] Five years later the sheriffs throughout England were told to proclaim that such rolls must be surrendered,[7] and in 1335 the requirement was made statutory.[8] In the fifteenth century this statute does not seem to have been observed; often the records of a circuit delivery were handed from one presiding justice of the circuit to his successor.[9]

No doubt the respective justices or their families kept the records in their own hands for some time in case they should be called for either by the King's Bench or, while it lasted, by the eyre. A case of 1291 has already been cited where all the rolls of a delivery were brought into the King's Bench.[10] At the London eyre of 1320–1 the gaol-delivery justices and other functionaries came with their rolls done up in bags. These bags with their

---

[1] C 47/81/6/202. Cf. *Cal. Pat. R.* 1476–85, 166.

[2] Guildford Castle Arch. Loseley MSS 961.

[3] *Sel. Cases in K.B.* II, p. xxxvii.   [4] Ibid. I, p. clxi.

[5] *Cal. Close R.* 1288–96, 335.   [6] Ibid. 1318–23, 240.

[7] Ibid. 1323–7, 341.   [8] 9 Edw. III, St. I, c. 5.

[9] Gollancz, 'The system of gaol delivery as illustrated in...gaol delivery rolls', pp. 37, 45.   [10] See p. 280.

contents described on the outside were sealed by the chief justice in eyre and handed over to the coroners to keep.[1]

The rolls of franchise justices, judging from the few specimens that survive,[2] were in much the same form as those of the crown circuits and were in principle preserved. In the earlier fourteenth century the bailiff of the liberty of St Albans was ordered by the abbot to deliver such rolls to the abbey treasurer every year.[3]

[1] *Mun. Gild.* II. 295–6.
[2] Six rolls, one of which is the duplicate of another, for Battle abbey liberty (1327–58), exist in the Huntington Library. A roll for Salisbury city (1540) is in the Salisbury council house.
[3] *Chron. Monast. S. Albani,* IV (2) (Walsingham), 206.

XV

THE WELFARE OF PRISONERS

How were prisoners kept alive? There is no single answer. In fact the answer varies with the different types of prisoner, and from one period to another.

Prisoners of war and hostages[1] were normally maintained out of the Exchequer and so, at times at least, were state prisoners. Certainly some state prisoners were so maintained both in the eleventh[2] and in the thirteenth centuries;[3] and in 1425 the Commons of England believed that traitors and Lollards held in the Tower and other castles and 'holds' were being treated likewise.[4] They argued that such people ought to be quickly tried, for otherwise the crown would be overburdened with their keep. Since, however, the petitioners included felons, as well as traitors and Lollards, in their demand, it is permissible to ask whether they knew what they were talking about.

Approvers were always maintained by the state or, where appropriate, by the lord of a franchise prison. Liveries to them, which possibly included the men's clothing, go back to early times. Thus no fewer than 9 approvers received liveries in 1170-1[5] and 4 in 1182-3.[6] In the second of these years the rate of pay was 1d. a day. It stood at the same figure in 1196-7,[7] though in 1212 it

---

[1] E.g. 'hostages', 1162-4, *Pipe R.* 1163 (P.R.S. VI), 4; 1164 (P.R.S. VII), 25; 'hostages' and Roderic FitzGriffin, 1242-5 (*Cheshire in Pipe R.*, Lancs. and Ches. Rec. Soc. XCII), 77; bishop of St Andrews, 1306 (*Cal. Close R.* 1302-7, 456-7); Earl of Moray, 1339-40 (C. P. Cooper, *History of the castle of York* (London, 1911), 109); Breton prisoners, 1513-14 (*L. & P.* I (2), pp. 1078, 1223, 1423).

[2] Rannulf Flambard in 1100 for his food: A. le Prévost (ed.), *Orderici Vitali...shistoriae ecclesiasticae* (Paris, 1838-55), IV, 108.

[3] Geoffrey Marsh (1244) and John le Poor (1254) seem to fall into this class: *Cal. Lib. R.* 1240-5, 214; 1251-60, 161. The subject, however, merits further investigation.   [4] *Rot. Parl.* IV. 292.

[5] *Pipe R.* 1171 (P.R.S. XVI), 19, 41, 55, 61, 148.

[6] Ibid. 1183 (P.R.S. XXXII), 83, 138, i.e. 11s. for 2 men for 69 days.

[7] I.e. 18s. 6d. for 222 days: *Pipe R.* 1197 (P.R.S. n.s. VIII), 144.

was a little less.¹ The penny rate is found again in 1243.² In 1250, however, it was 1½*d.*,³ and so it was in 1316–17.⁴

In the Laws of Alfred provision was made in emergencies for the king's reeve to feed perjurers correctively imprisoned.⁵ Some vestiges of these humane principles may have survived into the twelfth century for the benefit of suspect felons and similar offenders. Certainly, as has been said, sheriffs claimed allowances in Henry II's reign for supporting thieves.⁶ Did they continue to do so for a while after his reign had ended? If not, who was Richard the prisoner, *qui fuit cum utlagatis*, for whom the sheriff of Northamptonshire claimed 11*s.* 4*d.* in 1190–1?⁷ Who were the prisoners Mark and Garsus, for whom another sheriff made a claim in 1206–7?⁸ Were they common suspects, testifying to the vestigial survival of an earlier system, or were they approvers or prisoners of war?

Such questions are unlikely to be answered. Whatever the situation may have been in the twelfth century, it becomes clear in the early years of the next that suspect felons and the like normally received no royal bounty. While awaiting trial they had to find their keep out of their lands and chattels. If they were eventually cleared of their imputed guilt or died before conviction,⁹ their property was restored to them, less the costs of their support in prison. Such, as the records show, was the system in the earlier thirteenth century. In 1218–19 the chattels of a Yorkshireman, who had escaped from prison, were valued at nothing because, in a quaint phrase, he had eaten them in prison.¹⁰ In 1228 the chattels of a man hanged for murder were appraised at 13*s.*, out of which the sheriff was allowed 4*s. pro victu dum fuit in gaola.*¹¹ In 1230 the bailiffs of Yarmouth were ordered to sustain

¹ I.e. £4 6*s.* 8*d.* for 3 men for 360 days: ibid. 1212 (P.R.S. n.s. xxx), 27.
² *Cal. Lib. R.* 1240–5, 186.   ³ Ibid. 1245–51, 302.
⁴ Lambeth Palace MSS, C.R. 659.
⁵ Alf. 1, s. 3: *The Laws of the earliest English kings* (Cambridge, 1922), ed. F. L. Attenborough.   ⁶ See p. 4.
⁷ *Pipe R.* 1191 and 1192 (P.R.S. n.s. II), 153.
⁸ Ibid. 1207 (P.R.S. n.s. xxII), 31.   ⁹ *Close R.* 1237–42, 447.
¹⁰ *Rolls of Justices in Eyre for Yorks.* (Selden Soc. LVI), 203.
¹¹ *Cur. Reg. R.* xIII, p. 169.

a suspect murderer out of his chattels,[1] and a similar order was directed twenty years later to the bailiffs of Winchelsea who had charge of the chattels of two suspect pirates.[2] In 1252 a man suspected of rape was, with his wife and family, to be maintained out of his property.[3]

There is thus much evidence of what the practice was. It was also declared by Bracton to be the law,[4] and after Bracton's day such special directions as have been cited above probably became unnecessary. Bracton, however, merely says that prisoners are not to be disseised of their lands or despoiled of their goods before conviction but that the lands and goods are to be kept for their support. Later authorities are more specific. The author of the *Mirror*[5] says that the lands and goods of those indicted before the coroner, whether principals or accessories, after the former have been put in custody and the latter replevied, are to be taken into the king's hand, extended or appraised, and then entrusted to 'the townships', who are to use a part for maintenance and are to answer for the remainder to the king. *Fleta*[6] tells the same story except that, according to him, it was the bailiffs of the accused man himself to whom the assets were to be entrusted, and nothing is said about accessories. In such a state the law remained. Perhaps, however, it did not remain the practice, for in 1484 it was necessary expressly to forbid sheriffs, escheators, and other officials to confiscate the property of unconvicted felons.[7]

Presumably it was normal thirteenth-century practice to require trespassers also to support themselves. A trespasser shut up in the Fleet in 1259 was certainly maintained out of his own lands.[8] On the other hand in 1244 two men charged with forest offences appear to have received 1*d.* a day out of the issues of Windsor.[9] In 1225 Richard FitzNiel was clothed at the crown's expense,[10]

[1] *Close R.* 1227–31, 365.   [2] Ibid. 1247–51, 476.
[3] Ibid. 1251–3, 75.   [4] *Bracton*, II, 346.
[5] *Mirror*, 33.   [6] *Fleta*, II, p. 67.
[7] 1 Ric. III, c. 3.   [8] *Close R.* 1259–61, 17, 98.
[9] *Cal. Lib. R.* 1240–5, 266.
[10] *Rot. Litt. Claus.* II. 84; for the arrangements for FitzNiel's custody see p. 162.

and John le Poor, who was in various prisons during the middle years of the century, was both fed and clothed.[1] The first of these, who, as we have seen, was placed under a special guard, may have been some kind of 'state' prisoner, the second simply the object of Henry III's compassion.

Defaulting accountants who were committed to gaol by auditors under the Statute of Westminster were expressly required to support themselves while there.[2] It follows that when in 1352 the benefit of the statute was extended from the writ of account[3] to writs of debt and detinue, and imprisonment for debt by mesne process began, the creditor was likewise free of any liability to maintain the debtor. The Statute of Acton Burnell (1283) required creditors to furnish their debtors if in prison and destitute with bread and water,[4] and in certain circumstances the Statute of Merchants (1285) imposed the same requirement.[5] It seems clear, however, that by these statutes the creditors merely acted as paymasters and recovered the cost of maintenance out of their debtors' estates.

Even in an age of administrative sophistication it would be hard to ensure that the goods of a suspect felon were so managed by his neighbours that he and his family, while he himself was in prison, should draw upon them for their livelihood. Moreover, such a rule could not be applied to the destitute nor to husbandmen. Equally hard would it have been to ensure the delivery of bread by statute merchant creditors. And there were certain classes, such as outlaws surrendering to a prison in anticipation of a pardon, for which the law made no provision. In fact, in order to support life, very many prisoners must have looked rather to their friends' than to their own purses. That even the Chancery expected the suspect's friends to play their part is testified to by the terms of a writ of 1277 which authorized the release of a venison trespasser on bail because he was himself poor and was lacking friends who might support him while in prison.[6]

[1] *Cal. Lib. R.* 1245–51, 196–7; 1251–60, 48, 108, 161.
[2] Westm. II, c. 11.   [3] 25 Edw. III, St. v, c. 17.
[4] *Stat. Realm*, I. 54.   [5] Ibid. 99.   [6] *Cal. Close R.* 1272–9, 391.

Not all suspects had friends prosperous enough to lend them aid, or even friends at all. Moreover, they might be imprisoned in towns distant from their homes, which their friends could hardly hope to reach. To meet such a situation the law provided no remedy and many must have starved to death. To this reminder of the grimness of prison life many a coroner's inquest bears witness. Thus in 1323 hunger was a contributory cause of the death of seven people shut up in Northampton castle.[1] In the early years of Richard II it was stated that a prisoner who died in Reading gaol starved to death. The coroner's jury, perhaps wisely, added that it did not know who ought to have fed him.[2] Long before this, in 1295, a horrible incident had occurred at York. The eyre had just been sitting and had put in exigent a considerable number of people who had been indicted before it. Many, hearing of their exaction, had surrendered to the gaol and would no doubt have been tried in eyre. The session, however, was suspended because of the Welsh war and the poor prisoners were left behind untried. A 'great multitude' is said to have died of hunger and a special commission of gaol delivery had to meet to try the remainder, who were in danger of death.[3]

Though many died, many survived. Where Exchequer grants, the prisoners' own resources, the gifts of friends and kinsmen, and the bread of creditors were all alike lacking, how was this achieved? It was achieved above all by private charity. Such charity was already being bestowed in 1248 when Henry III ordered alms to be distributed to all prisoners in Newgate on the first Monday in Lent.[4] This perhaps was a once-for-all gift, meant to supplement the proper system of support which the law enjoined. By the early fourteenth century, however, it seems to have been generally assumed that prisoners could not exist without alms, for one of the arguments used in 1315 against retaining the gaol of Berkshire in Windsor was that the local community was too small to contribute much and that many prisoners might

[1] *Sel. Cases from Coroners' R.* (Selden Soc. IX), 79–81.
[2] R. F. Hunnisett, *The medieval coroner* (Cambridge, 1961), 36.
[3] *Cal. Pat. R.* 1292–1301, 161.   [4] *Cal. Lib. R.* 1245–51, 168.

therefore starve before they could be tried.[1] That it had become
a fully established feature of the prison system by the middle of
the next century is proved by the terms of the oath administered
in the fifteenth century to the keeper of Newgate.[2]

It might perhaps be expected that the nourishment of prisoners
would have been a task assumed by the brethren of hospitals. So
far, however, there is only one piece of evidence to connect a
hospital with such acts of mercy. The hospital in question was
St Leonard's, York, which by 1289 was regularly delivering half
a rye loaf a week to each prisoner in York castle.[3] This practice
still prevailed in 1295[4] and apparently in some form in 1364.[5]
Although St Leonard was the patron saint of prisoners, and there
were over fifty hospitals in the country dedicated in his honour,[6]
no other hospital than that at York, so far as is yet known, interested itself in the prisoners' fate. Perhaps the truth is that hospitals by custom housed rather than furnished outdoor relief to
unfortunates, and prisoners naturally could not be housed.

Some ecclesiastical persons and corporations had a direct responsibility for large numbers of prisoners. Such were the heads
of those greater religious houses that possessed franchise gaols.
Such also were all diocesans, each of whom after a certain date
was bound to maintain a prison for clerks convict and very often,
as we saw,[7] kept custody of laymen also. There seems no doubt
that they normally supported their prisoners, or at least their
clerical prisoners. This benevolence perhaps originates in a requirement which is as old as Justinian and is reiterated by
ecclesiastical councils. It is that bishops should visit their prisoners
weekly, inquire into the grounds of their detention, and exhort
the magistrates to treat them well.[8]

The earliest evidence of episcopal alms comes from the prison of

[1] *Cal. Pat. R.* 1313–17, 329.　　[2] See p. 185.
[3] D. and C. Lichfield, MS Qq. 7.　　[4] Ibid. Qq. 2.
[5] *Cal. Inq. Misc.* iii, p. 203.
[6] Rotha M. Clay, *The medieval hospitals of England* (London, 1909), 261.
[7] See p. 134.
[8] C. Calisse, *A history of Italian criminal law* (Continental Legal History
Series, viii) (London, 1928), p. 418.

the archbishops of Canterbury at Maidstone. This was a prison for both clerks and laymen, and over a long period, namely from 1279 to 1491–2, the archbishop appears to have supported both classes. Each man normally received ½d. a day, though in 1279–80 some laymen, though not all, received ¼d. In 1316–18 a much-favoured prisoner, Gilbert Lavonder, whose reason for being in prison is unknown, was benefited on a graduated scale descending from 1½d. a day at the outset to ¼d. at the end. In 1316–17 a rather different system of almsgiving prevailed. A lump sum was paid to all the prisoners (except Lavonder) and this presumably they were left to share out among themselves. It was 6¼d. a day from 29 September to 19 February, 12d. a day from then until 2 August, when the gaol was delivered, and 6d. for the rest of the financial year.[1] Presumably the fund varied with the number of prisoners in custody. The early fourteenth-century register of Bishop Sandale shows that clerks convict imprisoned at Winchester also received allowances. The rate was apparently never more than ¼d. a day,[2] which was also the rate paid by the bishop of Coventry and Lichfield to his prisoners, both clerical and lay, at Eccleshall in the fifteenth and mid-sixteenth centuries,[3] and by the bishop of Lincoln to his clerks convict at Banbury in 1510.[4] It could, of course, be the case that these 'alms' were not paid by all diocesans and that the evidence of payment merely reflects the humanity of individuals. That this, however, is most unlikely is shown by the conduct of Archbishop Islip in 1352. Responding to the royal initiative, the archbishop declared that clerical imprisonment was too mild and should consequently be made more rigorous, and

[1] Lambeth Palace MSS, C.R. 656 (1279–80), 658 (1299–1300), 659 (1316–17), 660 (1317–18), 664 (1331–2), 95 (1418–19), 96 (1427–8), 98 (1489–90), 99 (1491–2).
[2] Leona C. Gabel, *Benefit of clergy in England in the later middle ages* (Northampton, Mass., 1928–9), 112, quoting *Registers of Sandale and de Asserio* (Hants Rec. Soc. VIII), pp. xiv–xv.
[3] Lichfield Joint Records Office, B/A/21/123315 (1449–50); W.S.L., D 1734 J/1948, m. [8] (1463–4) and 1949, m. [20d–21] (1541–2); S.MS. 335 (1), m. 19d (1472–3).
[4] W. Potts, *The history of Banbury; the story of the development of a country town* (Banbury, 1958), 49, 50.

in pursuance of this policy he limited the victualling allowance for notoriously infamous clerks in prison to bread and water thrice weekly, bread and small ale on three other days, and bread, ale, and pulse on Sundays. The clerks were to receive no gifts from their friends by way of supplement.[1] While this was indeed the bread of affliction it was in fact a fixed allowance and it is mentioned in such a way as to make it clear that such allowances were the regular thing. An ironical remark in Foxe's *Acts and Monuments* confirms the view that 'the bishop's alms' was a well-recognized institution. The story, coming from the years 1500–6, is there told of a man of Amersham imprisoned in the bishop of Lincoln's house at Woburn. Here the bishop's alms were brought to him, but these alms, the martyrologist adds, were nothing better than taunts and threats.[2]

But whatever such episcopal gifts may have amounted to, they were not enough to furnish even in episcopal prisons a sufficient maintenance. Had it been otherwise we should not find the practice growing up, as it did from the mid-fourteenth century, of leaving sums of money for the benefit of prisoners by will and of making similar gifts *inter vivos*. Among bequests the earliest so far noticed is one made under a will dated 1346, when a citizen of Salisbury left 6*d.* to the prisoners in Salisbury castle and in the bishop's prison at the guildhall in that city.[3] By a will made only a few months later a London pepperer bequeathed 1*d.* to every prisoner in Newgate,[4] while in 1351 a Yorkshire parson left 2½ marks for distribution among the inmates of three of the gaols in York.[5] Thus we see that the practice was widely extended throughout England at this time. Whether its origin was much earlier cannot safely be said. It is curious, however, that though wills proved in the husting of London are registered from 1258, the earliest instance of a bequest to prisoners is the one cited above.

[1] D. Wilkins (ed.), *Concilia Magnae Britanniae et Hiberniae*, III. 13–14.
[2] S. R. Cattley (ed.), John Foxe, *acts and monuments* (London, 1837–41), IV, 124–5.
[3] Salisbury Corporation Muniments, Deed Chest, Drawer C.
[4] *Hust. Wills*, I, 515.   [5] *Test. Ebor.* I. 63.

Welfare of prisoners

Such bequests now became very common. Confining ourselves to the legacies to prisoners in Newgate recorded in the husting of London, we find that in the later fourteenth century such legacies numbered 70 and thus were at the rate of more than one a year.[1] Among fourteenth-century benefactors one must not fail to mention Sir William Walworth (d. 1385) who left £3 to Newgate and the Marshalsea jointly,[2] and a gaoler of Newgate (will proved 1349) who left the residue of his estate to his former charges, perhaps out of contrition for having maltreated them.[3] After the fourteenth century the husting bequests become much less numerous; in fact they number only eight in the next decade. Testators whose wills were proved elsewhere continue, however, to remember Newgate, and it has been reckoned that in the period 1480–1660 the citizens of London devoted as much as 1·84 per cent of their charitable wealth to the relief of prisoners.[4]

Posthumous benevolence towards prisoners was indulged in by many men of no great substance,[5] but there were also some very large bequests. John of Gaunt (1398) left 100 marks to two prisons;[6] Whittington, as we shall see, £500; Cardinal Beaufort (1447) £400 to 8 London prisons.[7] Other men left sums of similar magnitude, though mainly for the different purpose of purchasing releases.[8] Rather naturally there was a good deal of local patriotism mixed up in these bequests. Londoners mostly remembered London prisons—Newgate above all; the citizens of York and Bristol the prisons of those cities.[9] But this was by no means invariable. A London clerk who made his will in 1371

[1] The figures are derived from *Hust. Wills*, I and II. The period chosen for analysis is 1348–97 and the dates those of signature, not of probate.
[2] S. Bentley (ed.), *Excerpta historica* (London, 1833), p. 139.
[3] *Speculum*, XVIII, 237; *Hust. Wills*, I, 552.
[4] W. K. Jordan, *The charities of London, 1480–1600; the aspirations and the achievements of the urban society* (London, 1960), 180.
[5] Ibid. 181.
[6] *Testam. Vetusta*, I. 140; S. Armitage-Smith, *John of Gaunt* (London, 1904), 425, which corrects the date.
[7] *Testam. Vetusta*, I. 250. [8] See p. 173.
[9] See e.g. the York civic wills printed in *Assoc. Archit. Soc. Rep. & Pap.* XXVIII, XXXI–XXXIII. For Bristol see *Trans. Amer. Philos. Soc.* n.s. L, pt. 8, pp. 11, 31–2.

extended his bounty to three prisons in London, five in the home counties, at least four in the west of England, and seven 'bishops'' prisons in different regions.[1] A serjeant-at-law, whose will was proved in 1502, benefited four London prisons and the prisoners in the gaols of Hull and York,[2] and a Kentish knight, whose will was proved in 1525, chose the gaols of Lincoln and Nottingham.[3] Perhaps there is no better place than this to record that the foundation indentures of Henry VII's chapel at Westminster provided that on the birthday of that king and of Lady Margaret Beaufort alms should be distributed to the poor prisoners in London and Westminster prisons. None, however, was to receive more than 2*d*.[4]

At first such legacies were simple doles, not limited to any class or any defined form of benefit. Such doles continued to be bequeathed, but gradually we notice certain refinements. Thus by 1389 the women in Ludgate and Newgate are specially remembered.[5] Sometimes the testator will particularize the neediest prisoners,[6] and once, in 1532, the 'quiet' ones.[7] To guard against the wanton waste of doles, testators begin to provide for spreading the payments over a term of years. Thus it is stipulated in 1392 that each prisoner in Newgate shall receive a 'serteyn' each week throughout one year.[8] In a noble bequest Sir Richard Whittington left £500 to be distributed at the rate of £2 weekly between four London prisons until it was exhausted.[9] If this distribution had been faithfully made, and we know that it was not, the inmates of those prisons would have continued to benefit almost until the Habeas Corpus Amendment Act was passed.

From such arrangements it was but a short step to the creation of charitable trusts. Most notable of these was the trust under the will of John Pulteney (proved 1349) who charged the land that

---

[1] *Hust. Wills*, II, 151. [2] *Test. Ebor.* IV. 196–7.
[3] *North Country Wills*, [I] (Surtees Soc. CXVI), 120.
[4] *Cal. Close R.* 1500–9, p. 143; cf. ibid. p. 291.
[5] *Hust. Wills*, II, 283.
[6] E.g. *Reg. of Hen. Chichele* (Cant. & York Soc. XLII), II. 255 (1423).
[7] Presumably the well-conducted: A. H. Powell, *Ancient borough of Bridgwater* (Bridgwater, 1907), 73 (prisoners at Wells).
[8] *Fifty earliest English wills* (E.E.T.S. LXXVIII), 3.
[9] *Reg. of Hen. Chichele*, II. 242.

he devised to Corpus Christi College, Cannon Street, with quarterly payments to Newgate.[1] The revenues of the chantry of St Katharine in Ilminster church were found at the Dissolution to be incumbered with a small yearly payment to the prisoners at Ilchester.[2] A similar charge was laid upon the estate of a woman of Bury St Edmunds (will proved 1504) for the benefit of the liberty gaol,[3] and in 1514 the London Fishmongers were made trustees under Thomas Kneseworth's will of a perpetual annual payment to Newgate and Ludgate.[4] These are but early examples of many other charitable trusts for prisoners which continued to be a feature of England's eleemosynary provision.[5]

Before the establishment of the Charity Commission it did not follow that charges laid upon estates for the benefit of charities would necessarily be honoured. What was due from the Kneseworth bequest was indeed still being paid in the later nineteenth century,[6] but Pulteney's bequest had a different history. The founder had provided that, if the rent were withheld, a cash penalty should fall upon the College, half of which was to go to the fabric of St Paul's and half to the chamber of the city. The rent was in fact regularly paid up to the time when Newgate was rebuilding. It then lapsed, but in 1431 the city was empowered by Act of Parliament to distrain for it.[7] Neither distraint nor penalty protected the charity. On the contrary, throughout the first three decades of the sixteenth century the city was constantly preoccupied with ways and means of forcing the master of Corpus Christi to honour his obligations. The first evidence of this

[1] *Hust. Wills*, I, 609. Stow says he also endowed a charity for prisoners in the Fleet.

[2] *Somerset chantry certificates* (Som. Rec. Soc. II), 2.

[3] *Bury Wills* (Camd. Soc. o. s. XLIX), 96.

[4] *Hust. Wills*, II, 620.

[5] W. K. Jordan, *Philanthropy in England 1480–1660: a study of the changing pattern of English social aspirations* (London, 1959), 43, 265; idem, *Charities of London*, 180–3. Cf. *Journal of Eccles. Hist.* XVI, 185.

[6] *Hust. Wills*, II, 619n.

[7] *Rot. Parl.* IV. 370–1; *Cal. Pat. R.* 1429–36, 110. The patent is also entered in *Cal. Lr. Bks. K*, 119. Authority to distrain was granted in response to a petition from John Carpenter, Whittington's executor, in which the terms of the bequest appear to differ somewhat from those in the will.

concern dates from 1504,[1] but in 1537, at a later stage in the long-drawn-out proceedings,[2] it was stated that the rent had not been paid for the past eighty years.[3] If this is true, the delinquencies of the master date from 1457 or thereabouts. In the end threats of distraint seem to have induced the master to parley with the city[4] and in the same year the city and St Paul's agreed to excuse nearly all the arrears,[5] no doubt with the idea of securing punctual payments for the future. An 'award' between the two prospective beneficiaries from the potential penalties was then sealed,[6] but, in spite of this, the master was said to be still in default in 1544.[7] What happened after the Dissolution has not been ascertained.

These sums of money, whether large or small, were perhaps destined mainly to be spent on food. Starvation was no doubt the prisoner's greatest peril and many testators expressly made their gifts in meat and drink accordingly. This habit first comes to notice about 1394 when a weekly bread dole is provided for the prisoners in Lincoln castle.[8] Under a will of 1430 bread, ale, beef, and mutton were to be found for the prisoners in three York prisons and for the city poor.[9] Robert Chichele, a London grocer, left enough money to provide each prisoner in four London prisons with a $\frac{1}{2}d.$ loaf each week in the two years following his death.[10] In or about 1502 a beneficiary under a will was bound to provide a 'cade' of red herrings for the neediest prisoners in four London prisons for the ensuing seventeen years.[11] In the 1520s a testator instructed his executors to distribute during the decade following his death a barrel of white herrings every Lent to the prisoners in Ludgate.[12] A dozen other instances could easily be cited, though the provision is often less precise.

[1] Rep. 1, f. 150.
[2] References to this matter will be found in Rep. 2, f. 27 (1507), f. 171*b* (1514), Rep. 9, fos. 127, 128*b*, 193, 194, 212, 225, 227, 242, 243*b*, 244 (1535–7).
[3] Rep. 9, f. 270.   [4] Rep. 9, f. 249.   [5] Rep. 10, f. 10*b*.
[6] Rep. 10, fos. 12*b*, 18.   [7] Rep. 11, f. 33.
[8] A. Gibbons (ed.), *Early Lincoln wills, an abstract of all the wills and administrations recorded in the episcopal registers of the old diocese of Lincoln, 1280 - 1547* (Lincoln, 1888), 74.
[9] *Test. Ebor.* II. 8.   [10] *Reg. of Hen. Chichele*, II. 565.
[11] *Cal. Close R.* 1500–9, p. 260.   [12] *Jnl Eccles. Hist.* XVI, 185.

Money, where it was to be had, naturally could buy not only
victuals but clothing and fuel. Presumably most prisoners entered
in their own clothes and kept them until they were released or
hanged, unless the gaoler robbed them of them. Long imprisonment, however, must sometimes have reduced clothing to rags,
and once, in 1415, a testator specially provides for clothing when
leaving money for the benefit of prisoners in the Gatehouse at
Westminster.[1] Cold is sometimes mentioned as a cause of death
in coroners' inquisitions and was an obvious peril, though doubtless much lower temperatures were tolerated in the middle ages
than in the present century. A Bury St Edmunds woman provided
under her will (1492) for seven faggots to be supplied each week
to Bury gaol from All Saints to Easter.[2] Lights, beds, and bedding
were apparently also provided by charity, in Newgate by 1431[3]
and in the other London prisons by 1463.[4] There were charity
beds at Coventry by 1430.[5] Whether these amenities arose from
bequests or from gifts *pendente vita* cannot be said.

So far we have considered what arrangements were made under
the law for the support of prisoners and how far those arrangements were reinforced by spontaneous acts of piety. These forms
of sustenance were further supplemented by self-help. Begging
by prisoners in the streets or from an aperture in the building was
common in the seventeenth and eighteenth centuries, but the practice is much earlier than that. Some time in the later fourteenth
century, and probably not long before 1373–4, two aldermen of
Colchester, taking pity upon the prisoners constricted in the
stocks within the town gaol, set up two posts outside the entrance
to the gaol to which the prisoners might be chained. So chained,
the prisoners might stand, sit, or lie and beg their sustenance from
passers-by.[6] The account of what these worthy men achieved is

[1] *Reg. of Hen. Chichele*, II. 52. [2] *Bury Wills*, 77.
[3] When the keeper was forbidden to charge for them: *Cal. Lr. Bks. K*, 126.
[4] *Cal. Lr. Bks. L*, 40–2. [5] *Coventry Leet Bk.* I, 130.
[6] *Red paper book of Colchester*, ed. W. G. Benham (Colchester, 1902), 10–11.
The passage is imperfectly transcribed but has been corrected with the MS *penes*
the town clerk. The precise nature of the posts, which were equipped with
iron spikes, is somewhat uncertain.

so particular as to make the reader feel that they were in the nature of pioneers. At almost exactly the same time, in 1375, a man who called himself the attorney of the King's Bench prisoners, but who was not one of them, received royal protection for a year while collecting alms for his principals.[1] A few years later, in 1388, the prisoners in Ludgate were begging in the streets.[2] Such begging was also practised by the prisoners in Newgate. Originally, it seems, they used agents, like the King's Bench prisoners in the preceding century. These agents, however, seem to have secured an excessive 'rake-off'. Accordingly in 1431, when the regulations for the new Newgate were drawn up, begging was confined to the prisoners themselves, and it was stipulated that there should be only two couples of them. One couple was to beg by the riverside, the other inland, and both were to have a box and saucer so marked that their association with Newgate would be easily recognizable.[3] In Nottingham in 1443 it was the custom for alms to be collected thrice weekly. Owing, however, to the excessive concourse of destitute prisoners in the county gaol at the time, these collections were not enough, and the keeper was accordingly authorized to send men, presumably prisoners, on begging expeditions to any part of Nottinghamshire and Derbyshire.[4] At Banbury in 1510 the prisoners begged in the streets on Maundy Thursday, while the prison was being cleaned, and were provided with 'wallets', at the bishop of Lincoln's expense, to hold the cash.[5]

Towards the end of our period we find some authorities taking steps to solve the problem of destitution among prisoners, whether the place of custody was a municipal prison or a county gaol. Thus it was decreed in 1421 that the heads of beasts confiscated in Norwich market should be appropriated to the prisoners in the city prison.[6] In 1438 forestalled salt[7] and in 1464 some fraudulently packed herrings were forfeited by the corporation of

---

[1] *Cal. Pat. R.* 1374–7, 95.
[2] *Cal. Plea & Mem. R.* 1381–1412, 159.
[3] *Cal. Lr. Bks. K*, 125.   [4] *Cal. Pat. R.* 1441–6, 192–3.
[5] Potts, *The history of Banbury*, 47, 50.
[6] *Recs. of Norwich*, II, 86.   [7] Jorn. 3, f. 163 (173).

London's order and assigned to the use of prisoners in Newgate and Ludgate.[1] In 1482–3 the mayor of Southampton caused the loaves baked by defaulting bakers to be sent to Bargate.[2] At about the same time apparently, the burgesses of Launceston declared that it was their custom to apply some of the issues of their lands to supporting prisoners in the county gaol of Cornwall.[3] In 1514 the court of aldermen of London ordered that certain coal sacks, which would otherwise have been burnt, should be put at the disposal of the prisoners in Newgate.[4] Presumably they were meant either for clothing or for bedding. In 1528 a Colchester man, convicted of heresy, was sentenced among other punishments to pay 20d. a week to prisoners in the castle and elsewhere.[5] By 1534 the citizens of Norwich claimed that for some time they had been maintaining, or at least partially maintaining, their prisoners, and took it ill that the gaoler should hold such prisoners in custody after they were due for discharge and thus unnecessarily increase the costs of maintenance.[6] In 1535 the burgesses of Dorchester claimed that they had been accustomed to sustain the prisoners in the county gaol and in 1559 they repeated that claim. On each occasion the town was petitioning that gaol deliveries should once again take place within its boundaries and cited its charitable custom as an argument in favour of that restoration.[7] It can hardly be imagined, however, that the townsmen assumed the responsibility merely in the belief that it would help to induce the justices to deliver the county gaol of Dorset on the spot.

No one who is familiar with the state of the national finances in the later middle ages will expect to find charitable donations for distressed prisoners issuing out of the Exchequer. In 1357 the

[1] *Cal. Lr. Bks. L*, 49. There may be other London instances of similar arrangements: *Speculum*, XVIII, 245.

[2] *Assize of Bread* (Southampton Rec. Soc. XIII), 3, 5, 8, 9.

[3] R. & O. B. Peter, *Histories of Launceston and Dunheved* (Plymouth, 1885), 159. The source there quoted is conjecturally dated 1478.

[4] Rep. 2, f. 194b.

[5] [J. H. Round], *History and antiquities of Colchester castle* (Colchester, 1882), 52n.　　　　[6] *Recs. of Norwich*, II, 165–6.

[7] C. H. Mayo (ed.), *Dorchester municipal records* (Exeter, privately printed 1908), 32–5.

crown did indeed grant to civil prisoners in the Fleet, of proved indigence, a cess called 'Godspence' paid by merchants to the London collectors of the great custom. How continuously the prisoners enjoyed this benefit has not been ascertained. The most that can at present be said is that a payment out of the customs was being made to their successors in the early seventeenth century. The Exchequer lost little, if anything, by this indulgence, since the cess was a deodand, assignable in earlier times to the poor in general, and prisoners were only one class of 'poor'.[1] It was not until the sixteenth century was well advanced that any positive provision for the benefit of prisoners in general was made out of the king's revenues. Henry VIII charged the royal alms with payments to prisoners released from London prisons.[2] A more important step, even if a half-hearted one, was taken under the Gaols Act of 1532. This set forth in its preamble that gaols ought to be sited in populous places so that the largest possible sums could be contributed by the pious as prisoners' alms. This was a mere exhortation to the county justices, but the body of the Act laid down that if the rates set upon the inhabitants of counties to meet the cost of rebuilding gaols should yield more money than was needed for that purpose the excess should be distributed in alms to prisoners. Thus was the first step taken towards providing 'the county allowance' for poor prisoners, which by the Poor Law Act of 1572 was to become a feature of the prison system.[3]

It must be acknowledged that in theory some prisoners could have supported themselves while in prison by the labour of their hands, and we know that this sometimes happened in the eighteenth century.[4] Of any such arrangement in the middle ages, however, we have little evidence and it arises late. In 1515 the corporation of Coventry decreed that suitably qualified craftsmen might work in prison in daylight hours and sell their products,

---

[1] *Toronto Law Jnl*, v, 399–400.   [2] *L. & P.* 1 (1), p. 12.
[3] 14 Eliz. I, c. 5; Sidney and Beatrice Webb, *English prisons* (London, 1922), 10–11.
[4] *V.C.H. Yorks., City of York*, 526.

the gaoler taking 1*d.* in the shilling out of the proceeds.[1] In the late fifteenth century Newgate prisoners made small bone objects and sold them to a haberdasher near by.[2]

This account would not be complete without a word or two about the physical and spiritual health of prisoners. That prisoners often died of diseases, apart from such as might have arisen from starvation and ill treatment, there can be little doubt. It was piously hoped that care would be taken to avoid such fatalities, and the author of the *Mirror* declared that it was against the law to put a prisoner among vermin or putrefaction.[3] But, even given good will, which was often lacking, such an environment cannot have been uncommon, and its consequences are evident in many laconic reports of prison deaths.

Naturally enough, the effects of any nation-wide epidemic are as easily discerned in prisons as in the world outside. The famine and plague of 1315–17 took its toll of prisoners. In 1315–16 just over 60 people died in Newgate.[4] Between 28 June and 4 September 1316 28 men died in Wallingford gaol, four of them on the same day.[5] In the same year, 1316–17, 71 prisoners died at Maidstone[6] and in the next 16 more.[7] A man is said to have died of the 'pestilence' at York castle in 1391[8] and there was a serious epidemic there in 1528.[9] In 1425 nine deaths in the Tower were attributed to 'the plague'.[10] In 1414 the keepers of Newgate and Ludgate and 64 Newgate prisoners died, presumably of some disease.[11]

The impurity of the drinking water was no doubt a leading cause of disease and, if the Tower of London well could be described in 1295 as a place 'where the rats drown themselves',[12]

---

[1] *Coventry Leet Bk.* II, 644. [2] *Speculum,* XVIII, 245 and n.
[3] *Mirror,* 52.
[4] Guildhall Library, London, MS 126, fos. 45–111 (transcript of London coroner's roll).
[5] Berks. Rec. Off. W/JC m. 1.
[6] Lambeth Palace MSS, C.R. 659. [7] Ibid. C.R. 660.
[8] *Sel. Cases from Coroners' R.* 125. [9] *L. & P.* IV (2), pp. 1795–6.
[10] Hunnisett, *The medieval coroner,* 36.
[11] *Survey of London,* I, 36–7.
[12] *Sel. Cases before King's Council,* 15–16.

how unhealthy other prisons must then have been which had not even wells! One of the most important concomitants of the rebuilding of Newgate was the provision in or about 1435 of a supply of fresh water.[1] Besides the lack of pure water there was at times a great lack of cleanliness. The notorious stench of Newgate, before it was rebuilt,[2] can be paralleled by stenches elsewhere, and the name 'Bocardo' may recall them.[3] On the other hand it would be wrong to suppose that prisons were un-drained. By 1535 the new Newgate had been equipped with a windmill to improve the ventilation.[4] Even in 1281 Newgate had quite an elaborate drainage system and privies abounded.[5] Besides all this prisons were from time to time cleaned out. We know that this was done at Bedford about 1239,[6] Maidstone in 1316–18,[7] the women's prison at Oxford at the same time,[8] Newcastle upon Tyne in 1358,[9] Warwick in 1421–2,[10] Banbury in 1510,[11] Battle in 1520–1,[12] and Conway castle in 1534.[13] To help him to keep New-gate decent the keeper of that prison was granted a 'car' in 1526.[14] This was presumably to enable the muck to be removed from the premises.

If disease prevailed, it was not always because the prison was insalubrious within but because of nuisances near by. The health of the prisoners in the Fleet was endangered in 1354 because some butchers deposited the entrails of slaughtered cattle upon an ad-jacent wharf,[15] and in 1356 because some Londoners, without authority, had established tanneries and latrines upon the banks of the surrounding ditch.[16] Likewise, in 1441 the prisoners in Lud-

---

[1] See p. 362. [2] *Speculum*, XVIII, 244–5.
[3] See p. 360. [4] Rep. 9, f. 94.
[5] See p. 363. [6] *Cal. Lib. R.* 1226–40, 420.
[7] It was the privy that was cleaned. At least that is what *in fimis in puteo spargendis* appears to mean: Lambeth Palace MSS, C.R. 659, 660.
[8] *Mun. Civitatis Oxonie* (Oxf. Hist. Soc. LXXI), 259.
[9] *Arch. Ael.* n.s. IV, 127. [10] E 101/590/26.
[11] Potts, *The history of Banbury*, 47.
[12] Huntington Library, Battle Abbey Muniments, Beadles' R. 93.
[13] A. J. Taylor, *Conway castle and town walls* (Min. Public Bdg. and Works, Guide, 1961), 20.
[14] Rep. 7, f. 114. [15] *Cal. Lr. Bks. G*, 31.
[16] Ibid. 49.

gate were exposed to risk because a joiner tried to stop the efflux of Ludgate gaol into the city ditch on the north side of the prison.[1]

It is not impossible that somewhat greater care was shown for the spiritual than for the physical health of prisoners. That there were chapels in some prisons there is no doubt. One was designed for York as early as 1237;[2] there was one in the rebuilt Newgate by 1431,[3] and one at Bury in 1492.[4] Even where there was nothing that might properly be called a prison chapel there must often have been a substitute. First, where gaols lay inside a castle, some consecrated building, part of the castle itself, stood handy to the purpose. During the middle ages the hill now called Old Sarum seems never to have been without some chapel to which the prisoners might reasonably have had access.[5] Secondly, where, as in the Fleet, a system of exeats prevailed, there might be opportunities for hearing Mass in neighbouring churches or, failing that, in an oratory close to the prison.[6] Thirdly, priests might be imported. About 1452 a Cambridge gaoler, believing one of his charges to be mortally sick, procured him a confessor,[7] and a Bury woman by her will of 1492 provided for the hiring of a chantry priest to say Mass before the prisoners every Sunday and at the leading feasts.[8] Less specifically, we find that a portas, which had been bequeathed for the use of clerks imprisoned in Newgate, was duly handed over to the keeper of that gaol in 1382.[9] In 1388 a prisoner in Ludgate charged the keeper with denying him the rites of Holy Church,[10] notably at Easter, a charge which implies that, but for the keeper's opposition, he would naturally have enjoyed them.

Where confinement was honourable or the prisoner of noble rank, access to a chapel was presumably unquestioned. Indeed it could even be enjoined. When the Scottish earl of Strathearn, captured in war, was sent to Rochester castle in 1306, the constable was told that he was to have freedom to hear Mass in the

[1] Ibid. *L*, 254.
[2] *V.C.H. Yorks., City of York*, 523.
[3] *Cal. Lr. Bks. K*, 127.
[4] *Bury Wills*, 77.
[5] *V.C.H. Wilts*, VI, 59–60.
[6] *Toronto Law Jnl*, V, 400.
[7] *Cal. Pat. R. 1446–52*, 551.
[8] *Bury Wills*, 77, 80.
[9] *Cal. Lr. Bks. H*, 185.
[10] *Cal. Plea & Mem. R. 1381–1412*, 158.

chapel.¹ If, as we know to be the case, the friends of Maurice of Berkeley who were abetting his escape in 1323 could readily enter the chapel, it stands to reason that Maurice could have done so too.²

How much did prisoners mix with one another and with the outside world? As will be shown,³ it was over a long period generally held that suspect felons should be kept apart from 'debtors' and those detained for light offences. The motive was humane: to spare honourable men contamination with a criminal class. However such segregation may have worked out in practice, it is reasonably certain that the constituent members of these two broad classes freely associated, 'felons' with 'felons' and 'debtors' with 'debtors'. Many of the escapes by groups of suspect felons could only have been effected if intercourse was quite easy. Among the 'debtors' in the fifteenth-century Fleet friendships could be made or cemented.⁴ Occasionally, however, prisoners, especially state prisoners whose security was important to the crown, were kept in solitude, and such confinement is observable in all periods. The story of two such prisoners confined in 1236 is told below. In 1418 a man who seems to have been guilty of nothing worse than contemptuous conduct was confined in solitude in a Counter and allowed to speak only with those who came from outside to reprobate his past and correct his future behaviour.⁵

Visiting prisoners was, of course, one of the seven corporal Works of Mercy but, though its importance was emphasized by the Church,⁶ it is surprisingly hard to establish how far its performance was sanctioned by lay authority or, indeed, how far it was performed at all. Certainly visits were sometimes forbidden. In 1236 two men, upon whom the king appears to have had his

¹ *Close R.* 1302–7, 422.
² *Chrons. Edw. I and II* (R.S.), II. 275.   ³ See p. 351.
⁴ *Toronto Law Jnl,* v, 399.   ⁵ Jorn. I, f. 47.
⁶ In *Suffolk and Norfolk* (London, 1930) M. R. James assembled evidence which shows that in the churches of those counties alone many representations of the Works (not excluding the Sixth) are or have been visible in paintings, woodwork, and glass: see esp. pp. 8, 81–2, 105, 110, 142–3, 160, 205.

eye, were handed over by the Bench justices to the constable of the Tower, who was told that he must not allow them to communicate with one another or receive visits from any friar or monk or from anyone at all except the justices of the Bench and the keepers of the prison.[1] While the lot of one of the prisoners was later alleviated,[2] there is no evidence that he was allowed visitors. A writ addressed in 1254 to the porter of Wallingford castle authorizing him *hac vice* to let a woman speak to her two sons who were shut up in one of its towers suggests that visiting was at that time a privilege rather than a custom.[3] It must, however, be assumed that informal visiting was not uncommon even in the thirteenth century. In 1280 a woman came to the prison door of Salisbury castle and 'quarrelled with' the prisoners within. The gaoler said that he removed her, the woman that he imprisoned and robbed her.[4] Whatever the truth may be, the prisoners at least seem to have carried on a conversation with the woman. About 1319 a man appears to have been bigamously married in prison, though it is possible that the woman was herself a prisoner.[5] Certainly at times state prisoners openly received visitors, as the story of Maurice of Berkeley, already quoted, testifies.[6] As more and more use was made of prisons for holding men and women who were free from criminal taint the practice of visiting almost certainly grew. By *c.*1389 the brethren of St Leonard's guild, King's Lynn, were being positively enjoined to visit those of their fraternity who found themselves in prison.[7] It was an injunction particularly appropriate to those who were bound together by a common veneration for that saint.

The hardships of confinement must have been to some extent relieved by the system of granting exeats. A curious example of the practice comes from a very early time. Jordon de Bianney, a much-privileged knightly prisoner, was allowed by King John to leave prison twice daily in order to engage in swordplay. In his

---

[1] *Close R.* 1234–7, 363.
[2] Ibid. 291, 324.
[3] Ibid. 1253–4, 126.
[4] *Sel. Cases in K.B.* I. 64.
[5] *Yr. Bk. 12 Edw. II* (S.S.), 122.
[6] See p. 222.
[7] *English Gilds* (E.E.T.S. XL), 50.

absence another man was to be held as a hostage. As soon as the sport was over the prisoner returned and the hostage was released, to return in time for the next bout.[1] Such an arrangement forms a kind of precedent for those instances of 'wandering abroad' which are part of the story of escapes.[2] Such 'wandering' was indulged in by both suspect felons and 'debtors' and up to the end of the fourteenth century seems to have been treated as an abuse. Like so much else in prison life, however, it was converted from an abuse into a custom, regulated by codes of rules. By 1561 it was claimed as an immemorial custom in the Fleet,[3] which had always been its stronghold, and by that time any idea that its practice was illegal had almost certainly been quietly forgotten. At Ludgate such exeats had originally been forbidden[4] but in 1527 the prisoners there were given permission by the Common Council of London to go at large in a baston's charge, for two days a week in four ensuing weeks, in the hope of reaching agreement with their creditors. After the lapse of that period such indulgence was cut off.[5] Next year these prisoners sought to extend this licence. They were so far successful that they were granted leave, on petition to the mayor, to go about within the city during the four Ember weeks under similar guard.[6] Such arrangements seem at first sight extraordinary. Further reflection, however, suggests that they were useful in promoting the settlement of claims and so relieving the city prisons of a dank mass of hopeless debtors.

But it was not only debtors who enjoyed such liberty. As soon as it became the habit for prisoners to beg in the streets or at gratings,[7] those whose turn or lot it was to do the begging must have seen a little of the life of the town. And at times common prisoners might be let out in other circumstances. To our surprise we read that on 1 February 1520 the court of aldermen decreed that all prisoners in Newgate should be allowed out on Candlemas

---

[1] *Rot. Litt. Claus.* I. 88.   [2] See p. 241.
[3] *Toronto Law Jnl*, v, 397.
[4] At least in the case of executions upon statutes: Rep. 7, fos. 255 *b*, 256.
[5] Jorn. 13, f. 21 *b*.   [6] Jorn. 13, f. 62.   [7] See p. 327.

Day provided that they returned again.[1] One wonders how many of them did.

No doubt the greatest affliction that befell the prisoner was boredom, and this neither visiting nor 'wandering', on the scale described, can possibly have alleviated. Presumably prisoners devised some pastimes of their own which afforded some relief, but of their number and nature were are imperfectly informed. The only evidence of those pastimes that conspicuously survives is furnished by the graffiti that adorn the walls of prisons. The best-known of these sculptures are those in the Tower of London, but they seem mostly to have been executed outside our time.[2] Those in Carlisle castle (see frontispiece) are less familiar but no less remarkable.[3] Many of them show the sculptors to have been possessed of an unexpected creativeness and taste.

[1] Rep. 5, f. 177.
[2] *Royal Commission on Historical Monuments (England), Inventory of...Monuments in London*, v (East London) (London, 1930), 77, 79, 80–3, 84–6.
[3] *Carlisle Castle* (Min. Public Bdg. and Works, Guide, 1966), 19, and see frontispiece.

XVI

THE MAINTENANCE OF
PRISON BUILDINGS

UNDER the instructions of 1166 the cost of building and repairing county gaols was to be met by the crown.[1] Thereafter sheriffs habitually paid the bills out of the issues of their counties and recovered their expenses at the Exchequer, as indeed they had already done before the instructions were drawn up. In the thirteenth century Newgate was normally maintained in the same way, the issues of London and Middlesex being drawn upon for the purpose,[2] and in the same century the same issues were applied to the Fleet,[3] although payments were also made out of the Exchequer immediately[4] or from funds available to the clerks of the works.[5] Franchise-owners and municipal communities may be presumed, as a rule, to have provided and mended their own prisons. Little evidence of this has, however, survived.

In various ways the crown sometimes managed to avoid its liability. First, local revenues might be drawn upon. Thus in 1239 the crown ordered the city of London to bear about a third of the cost of some works then recently done at Newgate, because those works were said to be for 'the protection and improvement' of the city.[6] In 1315 it authorized the city to continue to collect murage upon merchandise sold in London on the understanding that the receipts would be applied to repairs to the gate and gaol.[7]

[1] Stubbs, *Charters*, 171.
[2] For early instances see p. 103, where the building history of Newgate is told. Later instances are *Cal. Lib. R.* 1251–60, 87; 1260–7, 159; E 101/467/11 (1281–2).
[3] There are many early instances on the Pipe Rolls; see also *Cal. Lib. R.* 1267–72, p. 163.
[4] *Rot. Litt. Claus.* I. 504, 513; II. 84; *Cal. Lib. R.* 1226–40, 139.
[5] *Cal. Lib. R.* 1267–72, pp. 251, 253.
[6] *Trans. R. Hist. Soc.* 5th ser. v, 12, as corrected by *Cal. Lib. R.* 1226–40, 396.
[7] *Cal. Pat. R.* 1313–17, 270, 295; *Cal. Close R.* 1313–18, 278. Cf. *Cal. Pat. R.* 1307–13, 61, 273, 495–6.

This was, in effect, to apply a local rate to the relief of the Exchequer, although the rate would not have been lawful without the crown's authority. The extensions to Newgate made *c.* 1406 were also apparently at the city's expense.[1] In Edward I's time three county gaols, those at Dorchester,[2] Hertford,[3] and Leicester,[4] appear to have been built by local public subscription or by some kind of levy upon the local inhabitants. The second of these had fallen out of repair by 1342, and the crown threatened that, unless the commons of Hertfordshire or some individuals in that county would put it to rights, Hertfordshire prisoners would have to be taken to Colchester.[5] It is not known whether the threat had effect, but certainly by 1438 the prison was being repaired at the expense of the crown.[6] More or less the same thing happened at Leicester, where the crown's responsibility had been resumed by 1411.[7]

Secondly, the costs of prison construction were sometimes met or partly met by private charity. Dick Whittington's noble bequest for the rebuilding of Newgate is the most eminent example[8] and at widely spaced intervals some other instances are to be found. About 1237 a parson of Middleham (Yorks.) built a prison for women within the confines of York castle.[9] Nothing is heard of it again; if maintained at all, the costs of so doing were presumably included in the other gaol expenses of the sheriff. In the fifteenth century Agnes Forster enlarged Ludgate.[10] In 1505 a man left a small sum of money towards building a new prison at Scarborough, provided that it was completed within two years from the time of the bequest.[11]

Thirdly, in the fourteenth and fifteenth centuries attempts were made, with varying success, to transfer the burden of maintenance to the keeper. We have seen that in the later fourteenth century the keepers in fee were supposed to repair Winchester gaol.[12] The same story, with modifications, may be told of the Fleet. About

---

[1] See p. 104.   [2] See p. 66.   [3] *Cal. Pat. R.* 1281–92, 473.
[4] See p. 71.   [5] *Cal. Close R.* 1341–3, 483.
[6] E 101/557/20 and later accounts up to 1527 (E 101/557/25).
[7] E 101/590/25 and later accounts up to 1459 (E 364/94 m.B).
[8] See p. 104.   [9] *V.C.H. Yorks., City of York*, 523.
[10] See p. 109.   [11] *Test. Ebor.* IV. 236.   [12] See p. 144.

1335 the then hereditary warden rebuilt it at his own charges,[1] and in 1355 the liability for repair was cast upon the guardian of his successor, who was a minor.[2] Gaolers who were crown nominees might also in the fifteenth century be charged with maintenance. So at least it was with the county gaolers at York in 1439,[3] at Ilchester in 1449,[4] and, to move on into the next century, at Lewes in 1579.[5] The same situation also prevailed in the fifteenth century at Ludgate and Newgate. When in 1414 a London grocer was confirmed in his post as keeper of the gate and prison of Ludgate, it was stated that he had for some time maintained not only the gate itself but its superincumbent 'houses',[6] and his successors in 1419 and 1441 seem likewise to have been expected to keep up the buildings.[7] The regulations for governing Newgate, issued in 1431, similarly declare that repairs to the gate belong to the keeper for the time being and that certain prisoners seeking privileges must in return for those privileges agree with the keeper to contribute toward the repairs.[8] When the prison was damaged in the Cade rebellion,[9] the city bound the keeper to perform his duty, implying that he was responsible for the consequent escapes because the fabric was insecure.[10] The motive for such arrangements is obvious. The prospective gaoler thought he could make a reasonable living out of his prisoners and, in order to persuade the gaol-owners to grant him the custody, offered to relieve them of the costs of repair. Such methods, however, were not lastingly sufficient. Despite the decision of 1355 the clerk of the king's works was accounting at the Exchequer for repairs to the Fleet,[11] and by the mid-fifteenth century the keepers of Winchester were effectively relieved of their responsibility.[12] In 1462 a public subscription for the repair of Newgate

---

[1] *Toronto Law Jnl*, v, 389.   [2] Ibid. 390.
[3] *Cal. Pat. R.* 1436–41, 256. His appointment, originally during pleasure (ibid. 1429–36, 112–13), was extended for life in 1439.
[4] *Cal. Pat. R.* 1446–52, 268.   [5] See p. 345.
[6] *Cal. Lr. Bks. I*, 123.
[7] Ibid. *K*, 254–5; *Memorials of Lond. and Lond. Life*, 677.
[8] *Cal. Lr. Bks. K*, 127.   [9] See p. 220.   [10] Jorn. 5, f. 51*b*.
[11] E 101/471/20; E 101/472/24.   [12] See p. 145.

had to be organized,[1] and in 1468 a plea was uttered for an Exchequer grant.[2] The keeper's responsibility was certainly reiterated in April 1488,[3] but perhaps rather in pious hope than in confident prediction.

Where there was no resort to such devices the thirteenth-century practice was to authorize expenditure on prison fabrics by writs of *allocate* enrolled in Chancery.[4] This expenditure was fairly liberal and it is clear that in consequence a good deal of building and repair took place. Moreover, there were frequent grants of timber, either out of a royal forest or from the spoils of a demolished building, and the crown sometimes saw to it that the work was properly executed, by making its own officers available as inspectors.[5] By the seventies this care seems to have grown less sedulous. Chichester was abandoned in 1269 and not replaced;[6] Derby,[7] Ilchester,[8] and Leicester[9] seem to have fallen out of use in the eighties. In the second decade of the next century Ipswich was allowed to decay,[10] and in 1316 the crown was evidently hoping that it might not be required to repair Huntingdon.[11] It is true that Leicester was rebuilt and that a county gaol for Dorset was set up at Dorchester but, as has been said, this was not in either case at the cost of the crown. The only gaol in this period that is known to have been brought back into service at royal expense was Stafford.[12]

If we may trust a petition lodged in parliament by the sheriff of Warwickshire in 1320,[13] the reason for this neglect was that the sheriffs had no certain means of recovering any expenditure they might incur upon repairs. Either there was at this time an absolute ban upon such expenditure, the existence of which was known to sheriffs, or else preceding sheriffs had spent, tried to recover, been refused, and fought shy for the future. In 1397 similar

---

[1] Jorn. 6, fo 62*b*. The entry is, however, blind.   [2] Jorn. 7, f. 180*b*.
[3] Jorn. 9, f. 172.
[4] E.g. *Rot. Litt. Claus.* I. 502 (Worcester, 1222).
[5] E.g. *Trans. R. Hist. Soc.* 5th ser. v, 13.   [6] See p. 76.
[7] See p. 65.   [8] See p. 66.   [9] See p. 71.
[10] See p. 78.   [11] *Cal. Inq. Misc.* II, p. 63.
[12] See p. 74.   [13] *Rot. Parl.* I. 374.

reasons were advanced for the failure of the sheriff of Suffolk to keep up the shire house in Ipswich.[1]

The condition of Warwick gaol was slowly improved, evidently in consequence of the sheriff's plea, and by the sixties a procedure seems to have developed for claiming the needful allowances by writ.[2] Of these writs, which issued out of the Exchequer, many examples survive.[3] Where decay was not reported to be serious, the Exchequer usually placed a limit of £5 upon the expenditure in any one year. If this sum did not meet the need, a further writ, with a like limit, was issued in the next year or the next year but one, and so on until all was ended. Where an alteration or enlargement of the buildings was required,[4] much larger sums were naturally incurred. While through this procedure sheriffs could to some extent keep pace with deterioration, the general impression left is that, nevertheless, there continued to be a good deal of neglect.

By *Britton*'s time it had become the law that the state of gaols and the responsibility for their repair should be inquired into in eyre.[5] These duties devolved upon the justices of assize and gaol delivery. It appears to have been in consequence of reports by the king's justices, presumably sitting on delivery commissions, that repairs to Newgate were ordered in 1316,[6] 1329,[7] and 1330,[8] and it was the assize justices who ordered repairs to Nottingham gaol in 1455.[9] There is evidence, too, from a later time that circuit judges concerned themselves not a little with the sufficiency of prison accommodation.[10] It may be doubted, however, whether such inquiries as those to which *Britton* refers were ever syste-

---

[1] E 101/575/28.

[2] There are allusions to such writs from at least 1365: E 101/553/1.

[3] E.g. E 101/565/12 (Hereford, 1464).

[4] E.g. Stafford, 1391–4 (E 101/587/8 and /9), Northampton, 1527–9 (E 101/578/6 and /7).

[5] *Britton*, I, 87.   [6] *Cal. Close R.* 1313–18, 278.

[7] Ibid. 1327–30, 483.   [8] Ibid. 1330–3, I, 47.

[9] E 101/581/6. It is possible that the commissioners who superintended the repairs to Northampton gaol in 1527–8 (E 101/578/6) were circuit justices.

[10] E.g. *Warwick County Recs.* VII (Warwick, 1946), p. cxi; [Somerset] *Quarter Sessions Records* (Som. Rec. Soc. XXVIII), 44.

matic or, even where they occurred, that the results were particularly beneficial. For no matter how good the system of inspection might be there was the overriding obstacle that cash was short. This shortage was caused as much as anything by the persistence of the primitive method of raising revenue for local needs and of the nominal reliance upon an annually changing officer for the execution of many measures of local government. Under the crown the gaols belonged to the sheriffs. The sheriffs were tenacious of this form of property, and at times, as the Acts of 1340 and 1504 make plain, the crown was prepared to buttress their prerogatives.[1] On the other hand, the crown would not entrust the sheriffs with that degree of local authority which would have enabled them adequately to finance new projects, nor could officers who changed each year have been expected to devise and execute them.

So far as the provision of gaols was concerned, no national remedy was attempted until 1532 and then it was not very satisfactory. The Gaols Act passed in that year[2] typifies the reluctance to grasp the nettle firmly which has disfigured so much administrative change in England. The Act cast upon the justices of the peace in all but fourteen counties the duty of surveying their counties within a year from the prorogation of Parliament and of deciding in what places it would be right to build a new gaol. In each county this survey was to be undertaken for the justices by two feed surveyors of their own choice. It appears from the preamble to the statute that the crown thought that gaols ought to be sited in towns which were readily accessible to the whole shire, which were the customary meeting-places of 'assizes and sessions', and where the population was relatively dense. Density of population would, it was thought, render escapes more difficult and would help to ensure the health of prisoners by the distribution of alms. Having chosen the sites of their new gaols the justices were, with the advice of constables, tithingmen, and borsholders, to frame estimates of the cost of building and then set a rate, to be collected by feed collectors, upon those people of

[1] 14 Edw. III, St. 1, c. 10; 19 Hen. VII, c. 10.   [2] 23 Hen. VIII, c. 2, s. 1.

the shire who had estates for life and years of 40 shillings annually. The justices were not to meddle with those corporate towns that possessed felons' gaols deliverable by their own justices of the peace nor with the owners of hereditary gaols.

The statute cast no abiding obligation upon the justices; the initial survey once completed, the new buildings, where there was need of them, once constructed, the justices were to drop out of the picture. Day-to-day maintenance, as before, was to rest with the sheriffs, who were authorized to crave allowance out of the Exchequer for the costs of effecting it. The sheriffs were to have the custody of the new gaols as of the old ones and were further protected in their rights by the requirement that 'murderers and felons' were to be sent only to 'the said common gaols'.

The statute was the first to place any responsibility for gaols upon the justices of the peace and as such was the foundation upon which gaol management was in the future to rest until in 1877 the central government replaced the justices. It also expressly laid down for the first time that sheriffs were entitled to recover their expenses, an arrangement which, as has been shown, had previously rested upon the suing out of a writ. It also aimed at rationalizing the distribution of gaols. In other respects it was an imperfect measure. First, it was temporary in its nature, for it set an excessively short term for the completion of a none too easy operation. Secondly, it did not cover all the counties. It is not unnatural that it should have excluded London and Middlesex, and the palatine counties of Chester, Durham, and Lancashire. Cambridgeshire was possibly omitted because of the semi-palatine condition of the liberty of Ely. Devon and Hampshire may have been omitted because in those counties there were or had been gaolers in fee. But there is no immediately obvious reason for the exclusion of Cumberland, Hertfordshire, Northumberland, Somerset, Worcestershire, and Yorkshire. It may be mentioned in passing that Cambridgeshire was eventually brought in by an amending statute of 1570, as the five Welsh counties of Cardigan, Glamorgan, Montgomery, Pembroke, and Radnor already had been by a similar statute in 1563. The third defect of the statute was that it divided control between the justices and the sheriffs. If there was a case for rebuilding, the justices were to rebuild, but the sheriff was thereafter to maintain. If there seemed to be no case for rebuilding, the justices were not authorized to act.

The disadvantages of the temporary nature of the enactment were indeed partially mitigated by expiring-laws-continuance legislation. This prolonged the statute's life until the end of Henry VIII's reign. The Act was then revived by an Act of 1 Mary (1553)[1] and again revived in her successor's reign by an Act of 1563—this time for ten years.[2] A further extension of ten years was granted by an Act of 1570, to run from the expiration of the term limited in the Act of 1563.[3] Thus the legislation did not lapse finally until 1582–3. Apart from the extension of the legislation to new counties, as already mentioned, the amending legislation added nothing to the substantive Act, beyond the re-iteration, in the Act of 1563, that the inhabitants of counties were not to be charged with the 'repair or building' of gaols where other persons or corporations ought by law or custom to bear that burden.

Coke said that the legislation was of little use anyway, since the justices made sparing use of it 'within the time to them pre-scribed by that Act'.[4] How far this is fair to the justices could only be determined by a careful inquiry into their activities which has not yet been undertaken and which is beyond the scope of this book. Certain it is, however, that in some counties acts were performed that conformed in some measure with the spirit of the legislation. By 1541 the gaol in east Sussex appears to have been moved from Lewes, where it had been established as recently as 1487, to Horsham.[5] Strangely enough, the Sussex justices desired the sheriff to move it back again in 1579, because Lewes was the more convenient centre and the county gaoler, who lived in Lewes, was prepared to provide a better building there.[6] In

[1] 1 Mary, St. II, c. 14. [2] 5 Eliz. I, c. 24.
[3] 13 Eliz. I, c. 25, s. 3.
[4] Coke, 2 *Instit.* (1671 ed.), 705.
[5] *Suss. Arch. Coll.* XCVII, 79–80.
[6] Guildford Castle Arch. Loseley MSS 976.

Bedfordshire the crown allowed the sheriff in 1552 400 loads of stone from Warden abbey to rebuild his gaol.[1] The Staffordshire justices grew concerned at the lack of any gaol in Stafford and, somewhat slowly it is true, began to build a new one.[2] The Wiltshire justices, dissatisfied with their accommodation, which apparently was rented, found a new site and built upon it between 1568 and 1578.[3] All these things were done within the sixteenth century, and by the next it is apparent that the justices felt that they and not the sheriff must assume responsibility even though that responsibility was no longer statutory. At the same time the lapse of the legislation may be taken to have been a misfortune for the future of prison government and for the welfare of prisoners. Hitherto a specific obligation to provide county gaols had rested upon the sheriff and a customary procedure for discharging that obligation had been carried out. That obligation had been overridden by the transcendent authority of parliament and a new set of obligations had been created. Now that the legislation had lapsed the legal position was uncertain. Did the sheriff return to the *status quo ante* 1532 or did he not? Certainly there is little evidence that any sheriff felt that the obligation had been restored[4] and the dwindling value of the county farm gave him every excuse for not trying to restore it. Indeed the very fact that he had been given in 1532 a statutory right to recover his expenses and that that right had lapsed could have been enough to excuse the Exchequer from ever allowing a sheriff to make a successful claim again. The decaying state and crowded conditions of some prison buildings in the seventeenth century, of which there was much complaint,[5] may have been due at least as much to the vague state of the law as to lack of humanity or to the pressure of increasing population.

[1] *Acts P.C.* 1552–4, 71.
[2] See above. It was rebuilt in or about 1617: W.S.L., D 1721/1/4, f. 131.
[3] A gaol in Fisherton was repaired by the sheriff in 1531–2 (E 101/595/16), but seems by 1540 to have fallen into private hands. By 1560 it was being leased to the sheriff by a man and his wife: *V.C.H. Wilts.* VI, 182.
[4] There is only one Exchequer account for the repair of a gaol later in date than 1582–3. It is for Lincoln gaol (1601–2): E 101/569/43.
[5] E.g. *V.C.H. Yorks., City of York*, 525; *Warwick County Recs.* VII, pp. cv–cvi.

XVII

THE STRUCTURE AND CONTENTS
OF PRISON BUILDINGS

Whave seen that even in very early times many county
gaols stood within the protective wall of a castle,[1] and
the same was true of many franchise prisons. Where
this was so, the ordinary run of prisoners were most commonly
confined in huts standing in the castle yard.[2] These huts were
small buildings—'cages', in fact, as the word *gaola*[3] seems originally to mean.[4] Apart from the yard there was, indeed, hardly
any other place in which to put the prisoners since, before the
reign of Edward I, many castles were still potentially defensive,
and their gatehouses and turrets could not have been permanently
spared to confine substantial numbers of men; nor would crowds
of suspect felons have been welcome to the garrisons in the
castles' fortified parts. This does not mean, however, that the
more eminent or more dangerous political or quasi-political
prisoners who were sent to castles were not so accommodated;
on the contrary, they were probably kept in turrets or even in
special prison cells embedded in the castle fabric. What has been
thought to be such a cell seems discernible in Skenfrith castle[5]
and two others may still be viewed in the gatehouse at Pevensey.[6]

---

[1] See p. 59.
[2] Occasionally the gaol might be fitted into a tower or turret, as at Hereford
in 1241: *Cal. Lib. R.* 1240–5, 38. This, however, is rather to leave the primitive
history of gaols.
[3] The word first occurs (in the form *gaiola*) in 1155–6: *Pipe R.* 1156–8 (Rec.
Com.), 4.
[4] St Peter's prison in the eleventh–twelfth-century Winchester troper perhaps
approaches a faithful representation of an early cage: B.M. Cotton, Calig. A xiv,
f. 22.
[5] S. Toy, *Castles of Great Britain* (London, 1953), 254.
[6] Charles Peers, *Pevensey Castle* (Min. Public Bdg. and Works, Guide, 1960),
11.

All these castles date from the early thirteenth century.[1] At Windsor in 1295–6 there was a tower *ubi prisones ponuntur* and it seems not unlikely that it was already put to that use in 1233–4.[2]

As time advanced, and particularly after the civil war, many castles in unexposed regions lost their military importance. They were, however, still valued for many other purposes, not least the custody of prisoners. Indeed some of them survived as gaols and gaols alone. The withdrawal of the garrisons now made it practicable to construct larger prison buildings and make them more permanent. This was done partly by converting the old defensive parts of the castles to prison use, partly by replacing the little huts by bigger 'houses'. The former method was adopted at Bridgnorth where, as we have seen, the prison was in the barbican before 1281 and in the keep afterwards.[3] By the mid-fourteenth century two towers flanking the second gate of the castle of Newcastle upon Tyne seem to have been used to enclose the lower gaols of that castle,[4] and at Lancaster castle in 1346 one of the rooms above the gate was a prison.[5] A building account that has survived shows how the 'Jewyn' tower at Oxford, once presumably defensive, was converted in 1420 to prison use.[6] In 1476 towers in Lancaster and Liverpool castles contained 'prison houses'.[7] At Cambridge castle both methods are exemplified. If the evidence has been correctly interpreted, the prison was in a tower or turret in the late thirteenth century. By 1327, however, it had apparently been removed to a free-standing prison 'house' which by 1368 was surmounted by the 'constables' chamber'.[8]

---

[1] For the dates assigned to these castles see ibid. and also the Min. Public Bdg. and Works Guides to Skenfrith by C. Ralegh Radford (1949) and to Launceston by T. L. Jones (1959).

[2] W. H. St John Hope, *Windsor Castle, an architectural history* (London, 1913), 59, 89. Since the prison in the castle was covered with lead in the earlier year it seems unlikely that it would have been a wooden hut.

[3] See p. 74.

[4] *Arch. Ael.* n.s. IV, plan at p. 138. Cf. ibid. 132.

[5] *Lancashire inquests* (Lancs. and Ches. Rec. Soc. LXX), III. 128–9.

[6] E 364/54 m. A.

[7] *Transactions of the Historic Society of Lancashire and Cheshire*, CXV, 15, 21.

[8] The thirteenth-century prison seems to have been the 'heldeprisoun', of unknown location, which was roofless by 1327: *King's Works*, II, 586. W. M.

Structure of prison buildings

The closing years of the thirteenth century did not, however, see the end of all castles as fortresses. In vulnerable areas they continued to be built or altered and, when they were, they were sometimes provided with prison cells. Thus the basement storey of the still extant prison tower at Conway castle (*c.* 1285) appears to have been designed as a dungeon,[1] and when the gatehouse of Chester castle was built or rebuilt *c.* 1292–3 provision was made in it for a prison.[2] The basement of Caesar's tower in Warwick castle is a 'purpose-built' prison of the fourteenth century. In 1378 a contract was entered into to build a new towered gatehouse at Carlisle, and into one of the towers a prison was to be fitted.[3]

Even in very early days some prisons were completely 'purpose-built'. Such was the Fleet and such was Warwick,[4] and in later times there were several others. Town prisons, of course, seldom if ever stood in castles, but were most frequently in gatehouses. Where this was so the economy of the gate had to fit itself into that of the prison and when the gate was altered or repaired it is not always clear how far the prison was affected. But even in quite small towns there might be 'purpose-built' prisons. In 1476 the council of the duchy of Lancaster ordained that a new 'motehall' should be built in Congleton, of which the first floor should form a courtroom, the ground floor shops, and the basement a prison.[5]

It had been decreed in 1166 that sheriffs' gaols should be made out of the king's wood. If such timber was not accessible a common person's timber might be taken.[6] It was, therefore, at first expected that gaols would be wooden, and until the time of Edward I the records show that much wood in fact went into them. Thus in 1221 the lesser timber from the demolished castle

Palmer's surmise that the prison was in the postern tower seems incapable of verification. For his views about the position of the prison in 1368 see *Cambridge Antiquarian Society Communications*, XXVI, 81 and cf. his *Cambridge castle*, 13.

[1] A. J. Taylor, *Conway castle and town walls* (Min. Public Bdg. and Works, Guide, 1961), 19–20.

[2] *King's Works*, II, 611.

[3] L. F. Salzman, *Building in England down to 1540* (Oxford, 1952), 456.

[4] See p. 72.   [5] *Trans. Hist. Soc. Lancs. & Ches.* CXV, 8.

[6] Stubbs, *Charters*, 171.

at Nafferton was ordered to be taken to Newcastle upon Tyne so that a gaol might be made out of it. In 1258 it was the king's carpenter who assessed the works at Oxford. From the early twenties much growing timber was requisitioned for gaol building; Bernwood and Shotover forests, for example, served as the source of supply for the gaols at Aylesbury, Oxford, and Wallingford. The only building in these early times in which the use of stone is expressly mentioned is the Fleet where, in or about 1222, payments were made to a mason. But this relatively important building must surely always have been of stone. Even at Newgate there is no mention of stone at first, although the gatehouse itself must always have been of that material.[1] The ubiquity of wood is not on reflection surprising. If a prison were set down in a castle yard, it might, in a period when a castle was defensive, need to be quickly uprooted so that the castle might be more effectively used as a fortress. If such displacements had to be reckoned with, it would have been both inconvenient and extravagant to build in stone.

When, in the late thirteenth century, and still more in the centuries that succeed, we begin to get fairly full information about prison buildings, the picture of the materials used is altered. Ilchester gaol, before its demolition *c.* 1283,[2] had been partly of stone.[3] Whatever may have happened at Newgate in earlier generations, stone was certainly used freely for the repairs that took place in 1281–2.[4] For other prisons it was now purchased extensively, even for those of much less account than Newgate. Thus, when the prison of the prior of Dunstable was rebuilt in 1295 after escapes from it had occurred, the new building was made of stone and mortar, as the annalist proudly pointed out.[5] Nevertheless, even in much later times, its use was not invariable. At all events there is no evidence that it formed any part of the county gaols at Ipswich, at Stafford, after that prison was rebuilt

---

[1] R. B. Pugh, 'King's prisons before 1250', *Trans. R. Hist. Soc.* 5th ser. v, 13–14.
[2] See p. 67.
[3] C 143/6/16.
[4] E 101/467/11.
[5] *Ann. Mon.* III. 396.

about 1390, at Worcester, or at York,[1] nor, except for the hall of pleas,[2] at Leicester. In the sixteenth century brick supplemented stone at Hertford[3] and Nottingham.[4] By the fifteenth century most prisons were 'tiled', the 'tiling' at Leicester being formed in 1411[5] and 1434–5[6] of Swithland slates. In 1444[7] and 1455[8] Nottingham prison was covered with straw, though before and after with 'tiles'. In 1529 Northampton was likewise thatched.[9] From this bare outline of the general character of prison buildings and the materials out of which they were made, we may turn to examine the parts of the buildings.

Although, as we have already seen, a few prisons were, in principle at least, primarily intended for special classes of prisoner, either those with a particular station in society or those whose offences were of a particular kind or a particular gravity, in general prisons were meant for all. This did not mean, however, that once inside a prison all prisoners mingled indiscriminately together. On the contrary a form of segregation, by no means peculiar to England,[10] was intended to be practised and this in turn had an influence on the form of prison buildings.

Even in a text so early as the *Dialogus* a distinction between honourable and dishonourable custody is drawn. Crown debtors are not to be thrust *in ima* but kept 'apart' (*seorsum*) or 'over' (*supra*) the prison.[11] In 1236 orders were issued to transfer a prisoner in the Tower *a carcere* and place him in *libera prisona*.[12] Two years later a group of Oxford clerks, arrested for demonstrating against the papal legate, were to be put in the depths of Wallingford gaol (*in fundo gaiole*) without distinction of class (*sive nobiles, sive alii, nulli deferentes*).[13] In 1283 a party of men

---

[1] These four seem to have been 'purpose-built', though at Worcester and York they stood within castle precincts.

[2] Wages of mason: E 364/96 m. D (1462–3).   [3] E 101/557/23 (1510).

[4] E 101/581/11 (1532–3).   [5] E 101/590/25.   [6] E 101/590/28.

[7] E 101/581/3.   [8] E 101/581/6.   [9] E 101/578/7.

[10] For segregation practised at the Paris Châtelet in the fifteenth century see *Revue Hist.* LXIII, 47–9.

[11] C. Johnson (ed.), *Dialogus de Scaccario* (London, 1950), 21; and cf. pp. 5–6.

[12] *Close R.* 1234–7, 324.

[13] Ibid. 1237–42, 47; F. M. Powicke, *Henry III and the Lord Edward* (Oxford, 1947), I, 352.

involved in a brawl was arrested and taken to the franchise prison of the countess of Aumale in Carisbrooke castle. The party was made up of monks, lay brethren, and laymen. On arrival at the prison they were segregated. The monks were placed in the lighter prison (*in leviori prisona*), the laymen in 'the gaol', and within 'the gaol' they were disposed according to their social status.[1] This sorting out seems to have been taken as a matter of course. In 1314 a man who considered his offences to be light protested that he had been placed in the depths of Newgate among felons and thieves.[2]

The attitude towards segregation is exhibited with peculiar vividness at Oxford. In 1293 the Chancellor of the University asked that the borough prison, which was a place of custody for academical clerks among others,[3] might be enlarged so that serious offenders and petty trespassers might be kept on separate floors.[4] Some kind of segregation seems thereupon to have taken place, at least to the extent of providing separate accommodation for clerks. The clerks' prison, however, had been removed by 1311 and the crown complained to the borough about its demolition.[5] Nothing was done and the complaint was renewed in 1313.[6] Whether this had any effect in Oxford cannot be said, but certainly in other prisons such segregation was deliberately planned. In 1344 a special room for trespassers was constructed at Warwick,[7] and the 'stres hous' at Nottingham town gaol which in 1505 is distinguished from 'the prison' was probably meant for the same purpose.[8] At York castle in 1360 it was taken for granted that felons would be kept underground, apart from other prisoners, and complaint was made that at the time, owing to defects in the building, this could not be achieved.[9] At Newgate in 1368 the felons, misdemeanants, and women seem to have been

---

[1] *Sel. Cases in K.B.* I, 125. The printed text reads '*leniori*'.
[2] *Cal. Pat. R.* 1313–17, 237.   [3] See 138.
[4] *Sel. Cases in K.B.* II, 153.
[5] *Mun. Civitatis Oxonie* (Oxf. Hist. Soc. LXXI), 20–1. The borough did, however, provide a women's prison about this time: see p. 357.
[6] Ibid. 25.   [7] *Cal. Inq. Misc.* II, p. 483.
[8] I.e. ?distress house: *Recs. of Nottingham*, III. 98.
[9] *Cal. Inq. Misc.* III, p. 131.

housed in separate rooms.[1] After Newgate had been rebuilt the accommodation there was divided into three classes: the best was for freemen of the city and 'honest', i.e. honourable, persons; the second best was for strangers (*foreins*) and people of inferior rank; while the felons and others suspected of great crimes were to be put into basement cells and 'strongholds'.[2] More expressly, in 1488, the two lower 'solars' were allotted to the felons.[3]

The arrangements in London emphasize the distinction not only between felons on the one hand and trespassers and debtors on the other but between citizens and 'foreigners'. Not only were the citizens and the 'foreigners' segregated in Newgate, but Ludgate was created and maintained for the benefit of non-felonious Londoners. Such distinctions had existed in other towns and continued to do so. At Worcester (1467) citizens, unless charged with felony or heinous trespasses, were not to go to the 'common prison' but to one of the chambers of the hall, and at Lincoln (1480–1) the 'franchist mans chamber' was set aside for citizens, clerks, and gentlemen. At the Welsh boroughs of Kenfig (1330) and Neath (1542) free prison in the guildhall was restricted to burgesses, and strangers at the former place were to be housed in the 'lower' prison.[4]

It is thus to be imagined that in many prisons there was a basement storey, which was a place of dishonour. Several examples have been cited already, but others can be added. Thus men are to be found in the depths of the gaol (*in profundo carcere*) at Canterbury castle in 1220,[5] at Norwich castle in 1288,[6] and at Exeter castle in or about the same year.[7] It is clear that there was also such a subterranean place at Leicester castle in 1305.[8]

Although, as is well known, the word had primitively no custodial connotation, such places were in the fourteenth century

[1] *Hust. Wills*, II. 114.
[2] *Cal. Lr. Bks. K*, 124 (regulations of 1431).
[3] Jorn. 9. fos. 170*b*, 171. [4] *Borough Cust.* I, 66.
[5] *Cur. Reg. R.* VIII. 397.
[6] *Leet Jurisdiction of Norwich* (Selden Soc. v), 11.
[7] *State trials of Edw. I* (Camden Soc. 3rd ser. [IX]), 51.
[8] *Leicester Borough Rec.* I, 368.

beginning to be called 'dungeons'.[1] Such was the name applied to the Lying House at Durham in 1385,[2] and it was employed at Stafford in 1391,[3] at Hereford in 1462,[4] and at Hertford in 1508–9.[5] It was also being used in the later sixteenth century at Warwick.[6] More usually, however, these places are called in Latin *puteus* and in English 'pit'. The basement storey of a turret in the castle of Newcastle upon Tyne had been used as a 'pit' before 1334. It was called the Heron Pit and took its name from a thirteenth-century sheriff.[7] By 1357–8 there was also 'the great pit' in the same castle.[8] There was a 'pit' in York castle in 1360[9] and in the borough gaol at Colchester in 1373–4.[10] There was a 'pit' at Warwick by 1344[11] and a 'deep' one at Leicester by 1411.[12] Less certainly there was one at Nottingham in 1532–3.[13]

It is to be supposed that these dungeons or 'pits' were sometimes the lower stages of a tower and were sometimes an excavation. Sometimes, again, they were no more than the ground floor or bottom storey of a building the foundations of which were at ground level. We saw that this was the plan for the borough gaol at Oxford,[14] and the 'lower' gaols at Maidstone in 1316–17[15] and at Hereford in 1467[16] were probably similar. A dungeon of the first type was being used at Salisbury castle in 1330.[17] Like those of the second type they were often ceiled at the top by a trap-door, bolted on the upper side. Beneath the trap-door there was perhaps

[1] *O.E.D.* cites an example of *c.* 1325.
[2] *Durham Acct. R.* 1 (Surtees Soc. XCIX), 265. For this prison see p. 378.
[3] E 101/587/8.　　[4] E 101/565/11.　　[5] E 101/557/22.
[6] E 101/591/14 (1570–1). *Puteus* also means 'well' and 'cess-pit' but in only a few of the instances here cited is this rendering possible.
[7] He was sheriff 1246–8: P.R.O. *List of sheriffs*.
[8] *Arch. Ael.* n.s. IV, 126–7.　　[9] *Cal. Inq. Misc.* III, p. 131.
[10] The word is *vorago*: *Red paper book of Colchester*, ed. W. G. Benham (Colchester, 1902), 10–11.
[11] *Cal. Inq. Misc.* II, p. 483, where it is rendered 'well'.
[12] E 101/590/25. In 1455–6 it is called a 'very deep' pit: E 101/590/32.
[13] An account of that year records one rate of payment for carrying plaster to the gaol and double that rate for carrying it down into the gaol: E 101/581/11. For the idea that the depths of Nottingham gaol were the gaol *par excellence* see p. 355 n. 15.
[14] See p. 352.　　[15] Lambeth Palace MSS, C.R. 659.
[16] E 101/565/14.　　[17] *V.C.H. Wilts.* VI, 59.

a flight of steps or a ladder. Trap-doors of this sort are found at Windsor castle in 1295–6,[1] at Leicester castle in 1305,[2] at the 'great' pit at Newcastle in 1357–8,[3] at Ipswich in 1409,[4] at the Lying House in Durham in 1423–4,[5] at Hereford in 1467,[6] and at Warwick in 1544–5.[7] At Pevensey castle one is still visible. Sometimes it seems as though the pit was grated over at the top, in which case access must have been gained from the side. It is probable that this was the arrangement at Warwick, for at least a part of the gaol was at ground level, abutting the gaol hall. Above it stood the gaol 'chamber', to which it was necessary to ascend.[8] There was apparently a hole in the 'chamber' floor, and through the hole there was a view into the 'pit' which in 1551–2 was covered over with beams.[9] When Warwick gaol was moved to a new site in the late sixteenth or early seventeenth century the form of this building was partially reproduced and the resultant excavation may still be seen.[10] Like the old 'pit' it has a grating at the top and an entrance at the side, though the entrance was cut below and not at ground level. There seems to have been the same grated covering at Hertford in 1526–7.[11] What were called in 1420 the 'gridiron gaol' at Worcester[12] and the 'grate' at Oxford[13] may likewise have been excavations similar to the Warwick 'pit'.

Just as the central object of a gaol was to keep suspect felons safe, so the gaol 'pit' in which they lay may be said to have been the heart of the gaol. Documents of very varying dates seem to imply that the 'pit' alone is the 'gaol' or to contrast the 'gaol' with the 'house' of the gaol or 'prison house'. Such usages prevail in the twelfth,[14] thirteenth, and fourteenth centuries[15] alike.

---

[1] St John Hope, *Windsor Castle*, I, 89.

[2] *Leicester Borough Rec.* I, 368.   [3] *Arch. Ael.* n.s. IV, 126.

[4] E 364/43 m. B.   [5] *Durham Acct. R.* I. 271. For this prison see p. 378.

[6] E 101/565/14.   [7] E 101/591/6.   [8] See p. 356.

[9] E 101/591/9.

[10] It incurred the indignation of Howard: *The state of the prisons in England and Wales* (Warrington, 1780), 265.

[11] E 101/557/25.   [12] E 364/54 m. C.   [13] E 364/54 m. A.

[14] *Domus super gaiolam* at Ipswich: *Pipe R.* 1166 (P.R.S. IX), 17.

[15] At Nottingham in 1391–2 repairs to the gaol and the gaol house were undertaken (E 364/26 m. D). Cf. also the distinction drawn in 1283 between *levis prisona* and *gaola*: see p. 352.

Alternatively, a sixteenth-century document may contrast the 'prison' with the 'dungeon'.[1] It would no doubt be unwise to attribute too much precision to the terminology of such documents. Nevertheless it must be conceded as extremely probable that every prison of any size was equipped not only with a 'dungeon' or 'pit' but also with a 'chamber' or 'chambers' for the use of those to whom close confinement was not applied. These 'chambers' or 'houses' often stood above (*super*) the 'gaol' or 'pit'. Such was the position of the 'house' at Ipswich in 1165–6[2] and at Aylesbury by 1238.[3] In the mid-fourteenth century 'pits' at Newcastle upon Tyne had 'houses' above them, in at least one of which there was a prison,[4] and the chamber above the gaol is mentioned at Stafford in 1391–2,[5] Hereford in 1483,[6] and Warwick from 1325[7] to 1551–2.[8] A similar arrangement apparently existed at Banbury in 1510.[9] But nothing more perfectly illustrates the relationship between 'chamber' and 'pit' than the lower storeys of the prison tower at Conway castle. Here, to this day, visitors may inspect the dungeon, lying below a 'chamber'. Documents of 1532–4 make absolutely plain what may be inferred from an intelligent reading of earlier documents, namely, that the felons lay in the pit and the 'debtors' lodged themselves in the room immediately above it.[10]

Bigger prisons certainly had a number of 'chambers'. This was true of Cambridge in 1363[11] and of Leicester in 1411.[12] At Stafford in 1391–2 there were said to be five doors 'around' the gaol admitting to various 'chambers'.[13] At Oxford in 1420 nineteen doors were mended,[14] which suggests a whole group of rooms. At Winchester in 1462 there was a 'great' prison and two chambers leading out of it.[15] In 1421 the rebuilt Newgate was somewhat spaciously equipped with a hall and chapel and what look like

[1] Hertford, 1509: E 101/557/22. [2] *Pipe R.* 1166, 17.
[3] *Cal. Lib. R.* 1226–40, 313. [4] *Arch. Ael.* n.s. IV. 127–8.
[5] E 101/587/8. [6] E 101/565/16. [7] E 143/8/3/11/2.
[8] E 101/591/9.
[9] W. Potts, *The history of Banbury* (Banbury, 1958), 47, 50.
[10] Taylor, *Conway castle and town walls*, 19–20.
[11] E 101/552/51/1. [12] E 101/590/25. [13] E 101/587/8.
[14] E 364/54 m. A. [15] E 101/563/1.

three day-rooms, two beside the chapel and a third, a large one intended for the women, near the hall. The actual lodging 'chambers' seem to have been fairly numerous in Newgate and some of the more affluent might live in towers or 'chambers' in towers.[1]

Special rooms with special objects are also to be found. Rooms, for instance, were set aside or adapted for Scottish and Welsh prisoners of war. 'Houses' for Scotsmen were made anew at Carlisle in 1299–1300.[2] There was a *camera* for Scottish prisoners at Chester in 1301, which had its own trap-door,[3] and another at Nottingham in 1331.[4] A contract for rebuilding the latter was entered into in 1348. It was to be placed under the 'high tower' and to be furnished with double doors.[5] In 1305–7 a wooden cage bound with iron was built for David ap Gruffydd's son, Owain, inside Bristol castle.[6] In 1316–17 a special 'chamber' was made at Maidstone expressly for Gilbert Lavonder who, as mentioned above, was a person specially indulged.[7]

Quarters must also have been commonly set aside for the gaoler. In 1391 the gaoler at Stafford perhaps lived in a room above the 'pit'.[8] In York in 1377 he lived, more unexpectedly, below the great house of the gaol.[9]

In some prisons women were separately accommodated. We saw that about 1237 the rector of Middleham sought to provide a gaol for women within the walls of York castle.[10] If this scheme was realized it was a pioneer effort. In 1279–80 there was a women's chamber at Maidstone.[11] About 1310, after an agitation instigated by the Chancellor of the University that had lasted over fifteen years, a special room or prison for women was constructed in Oxford borough gaol by the king's command. This was intended primarily for prostitutes and by 1393 was being

[1] *Cal. Lr. Bks. K*, 124.
[2] *Liber Quotidianus Contrarotulatoris Garderobae* (Soc. Ant. London, 1787), 76.
[3] *Cheshire in Pipe R.* (Lancs. & Ches. Rec. Soc. xcii), 211.
[4] *King's Works*, ii, 762.
[5] Salzman, *Building in England down to 1540*, 300.
[6] *King's Works*, ii, 580.   [7] See p. 321.   [8] E 101/587/8.
[9] Salzman, op. cit. 453.   [10] See p. 339.
[11] Lambeth Palace MSS, C.R. 656.

called 'the maidens' chamber'.[1] The initiative in all these cases
came from ecclesiastics, though the Chancellor of Oxford was
probably concerned to protect the morals rather of the men than
of the women. By the fifteenth century the same segregation was
being practised in London, for by 1368 the women in Newgate
were housed in a room of their own.[2] In 1406 this room was said
to be uncomfortably crowded and the women asked that, in view
of their cramped conditions, they might have some land adjacent
on which a separate prison for them might be built.[3] Although the
request was granted, it is not known whether their wishes were
otherwise met. In any case the whole prison was rebuilt shortly
after and when it was completed the women were assigned quarters
of their own in it on the ground floor.[4] By 1455 there was a
separate municipal prison for women in York,[5] and about 1454
one Ralph Segrym gave money for a female prison in Norwich
city.[6] A 'woman's chamber' is found at Nottingham town gaol
in 1505.[7] Otherwise the only evidence for a women's prison or
lodgings that has yet been gleaned comes from Hertford, where
in 1509–10 bricks were bought for the women's prison.[8] The
segregation of women was probably a good deal commoner than
these instances imply, although the lack of it in some prisons
could still be pointed to by Howard.[9]

Before passing to some other features of prison design it may
be useful to spare some words, which must be in the nature of a
digression, for prison nomenclature. Prisons themselves were often
given, not only in England,[10] outlandish nicknames truly or iron-
ically describing their purpose. The nicknames tended to stick
and to become the official titles. Where a prison was divided

---

[1] *Sel. Cases in K.B.* II, 153; *Mun. Civitatis Oxonie,* 5, 257 and n.; *Collectanea*
(Oxf. Hist. Soc. XXXII), III. 101.
[2] *Hust. Wills,* II, 114.   [3] *Cal. Lr. Bks. I,* 49.
[4] Ibid. *K,* 127.
[5] *V.C.H. Yorks., City of York,* 492 and n.
[6] *Norwich Recs.* II, 91 and n. It was possibly a bequest.
[7] *Recs. of Nottingham,* III. 100.   [8] E 101/557/23.
[9] *State of the prisons* (1780 ed.), 28.
[10] E.g. the 'Stinche', in Florence, so named because many did not come out of
it alive.

into rooms these rooms might also be similarly designated.[1] Best remembered, perhaps, of these nicknames is the 'Kidcote(s)', used by the fourteenth century for the municipal prisons of York.[2] The prison in Bridlington bore the same name by 1540–1,[3] and other northern prisons in later times.[4] The Cowhouse, the bishop's prison in Wells (1439),[5] and the Bullpit (1445–6), the prison of Clarendon palace,[6] are comparable names. They suggest the herding together of animals in a foetid atmosphere. An inn in Thame, called the 'Bird Cage', is believed to have been a prison of the bishop of Lincoln.[7] If so, the name originates similarly and shows that 'gaolbirds' are medieval beings.[8] A twelfth-century prison at Berwick was called 'Cole' from its darkness.[9]

Rooms called 'Polard' and 'Jordan' existed in the Tower of London about 1295,[10] and in 1370 there was a 'dreadful' room in Newgate called 'Julianesboure'.[11] No explanation of these names immediately suggests itself. On the other hand, 'Little Ease', a name given to a room in the White Tower, is obvious enough. It was so constructed that a prisoner could neither stand nor sit but only crouch.[12] The name is also found at Woburn, a prison of the bishop of Lincoln, in 1500–6[13] and at Battle in 1520–1,[14] although in Battle's case the cell seems to have been within the walls of the monastery and therefore, strictly speaking, monastic.[15]

---

[1] For the names at the Châtelet in the fifteenth century see *Revue Hist.* LXIII, 47–9.

[2] *V.C.H. Yorks., City of York*, 491–2.

[3] *Archaeologia*, XIX, 271.

[4] E.g. Gainsborough, Lancaster, Wakefield: *O.E.D.*; Wright, *English dialect dictionary*.

[5] *Register of John Stafford* (Som. Rec. Soc. XXXII), II. 233.

[6] *King's Works*, II, 918.   [7] *V.C.H. Oxon.* VII, 115. Cf. ibid. p. 165.

[8] The earliest examples of the usage given in the *Oxford English Dictionary* are, however, of the seventeenth century.

[9] *Reginaldi Monachi Dunelm. Libellus* (Surtees Soc. I), 42.

[10] *Sel. Cases before King's Council*, 15.

[11] *Cal. Plea & Mem. R.* 1364–81, 119.

[12] R. Davey, *Tower of London* (London, 1910), 18. This is supposed to have been the prison of Guy Fawkes.

[13] S. R. Cattley (ed.), John Foxe, *acts and monuments* (London, 1837–41), IV 124.

[14] Huntington Library, Battle Abbey Muniments, Beadles' R. 93.

[15] See chapter XVIII.

At an unknown date the Flint Tower in the Tower of London acquired the name 'Little Hell'.[1] Of course many castle towers in other fortresses had names[2] derived usually from the persons who built them or used them as residences. If such towers were converted to prison use the names were often retained, but they are of no significance in the present context.

One of the more curious of prison names is 'Bocardo', borne by the borough prison in Oxford from at least 1318[3] until the building was destroyed in 1770.[4] By 1368 the same name was applied to a room in Newgate,[5] apparently meant for misdemeanants, and was still in use in 1406.[6] It has been customary to explain the name as a mnemonic representing a logical formula and to declare that it may have been bestowed upon the Oxford prison by academical clerks imprisoned there. The significance is supposed to be that it was as hard to escape from the confines of the prison as from the inexorability of the logic.[7] This explanation seems somewhat far-fetched. More likely is it that the name originates in 'boccard', 'boggard', or 'bog'.[8] In 1495 Peterhouse (Cambridge) made a payment '*pro mundacione bocardi*' and in 1504 '*pro remocione fimi in bocardo*',[9] and this seems to show that by the later middle ages there was a declinable Latin word meaning not a prison but a privy. It is known that in 1406 'Bocardo' in Newgate was on the route from the women's quarters to the privy[10] and it is likely that the smell of the privy permeated 'Bocardo'. Probably

---

[1] Davey, *Tower of London*, 40.

[2] See, e.g. *King's Works*, II, 622n., 623; *Cheshire in Pipe R.* 210; R. H. Morris, *Chester in the Plantagenet and Tudor reigns* (Eccleston, 1895), 96.

[3] *Chrons. Edw. I and II* (R.S.), I. 282.

[4] H. E. Salter, *Records of medieval Oxford* (Oxford Chronicle, 1912), 79.

[5] *Hust. Wills*, II, 114. For its use in 1382 see *Cal. Plea & Mem. R. 1381–1412*, 28, and *Cal. Lr. Bks. H*, 204.

[6] *Cal. Lr. Bks. I*, 49.   [7] *O.E.D.*

[8] For *boggard* and *bog* see *O.E.D.* Cf. *Cambridge borough documents* (Cambridge, 1931), ed. W. M. Palmer, 51: for cleansing a bocard within the tenement of William Currow (1514–15). But what was the burgage in Carlisle called 'bocard' which was held by William Denton in 1461 (E 364/98 m. G)? Surely this was not a privy!

[9] Salzman, *Building in England down to 1540*, 282.

[10] *Cal. Lr. Bks. I*, 49.

the whole of the Oxford prison was as noisome as a 'bocard'. Surely it was this feature rather than a syllogism which struck the minds (as well as the nostrils) of the Oxford clerks?

Sometimes a 'hall of pleas' for gaol deliveries so closely abutted the gaol as to form an inseparable or almost inseparable part of it. This seems to have been the case at Warwick from the early thirteenth century, at Leicester and Nottingham from the mid-fourteenth, and at Hertford from the early sixteenth.[1] At Newgate in the thirteenth century deliveries took place within the gaol but this does not seem to have continued.[2] The hall at Newgate, mentioned in 1431,[3] probably served rather as a kind of common- or even as a dining-room than as a sessions house. That there were sometimes chapels in or near to prison buildings, apart from that in Newgate, we have already seen.[4] There were no doubt also sometimes open spaces in which the prisoners could sit or walk. But only once do we find positive evidence that such a yard existed. This was at Ludgate, where the annexe built in 1463 contained a 'large walking-place' measuring $38\frac{1}{2}$ by $29\frac{1}{2}$ feet. This area seems to have been covered in, with lodgings above; above the lodgings were the leads on which the prisoners might also walk and take the air.[5] At Newgate, too, in 1421 prisoners on making payment to the keeper might walk in the passages of the prison and on the leads.[6]

The coldness of prisons has already been commented upon,[7] but it would certainly be wrong to assume that none of them was ever warmed. Even in 1200–1 two 'louvers' were being provided for Warwick,[8] though these might have been meant to admit light and air rather than to release smoke. In 1377 there were two fireplaces in the gaol at York, one in the great 'house' of the prison and the other in the gaoler's chamber.[9] The first of these

[1] See pp. 308–9. [2] See pp. 309–10. [3] See p. 356. [4] See pp. 333–4.
[5] C. L. Kingsford (ed.), J. Stow, *A Survey of London* (Oxford, 1908), I, 39–40. Although the gate itself had been rebuilt the 'quadrant' of Agnes Forster seems to have survived from its founder's day. The passage, however, is not easy to interpret.
[6] *Cal. Lr. Bks. K*, 127. [7] See p. 327.
[8] *Pipe R.* 1201 (P.R.S. n.s. XIV), 232.
[9] Salzman, *Building in England down to 1540*, 453.

recurs in 1404–7.[1] In 1532–3 a brick chimney was being built at Nottingham.[2] The best 'chambers' at Newgate had fireplaces in 1431[3] and the fourteenth- and fifteenth-century regulations, which affected all London city prisons, about the price of charcoal, faggots, and coal must convince us that the supply was common. The charitable gift of fuel, which, as we saw,[4] was made for the benefit of men in Bury prison, shows that a fireplace of a kind must have existed there.

No doubt a castle could not exist without a well. Accordingly where prisons were sited behind castle walls the castle well provided the prisoners with water. Sometimes, perhaps, there was a stream or river in the neighbourhood. The Fleet may have owed its location to the contiguity of the Fleet river. Of artificial arrangements to provide prisoners with water evidence comes only from Newgate and Ludgate. In the rebuilt Newgate there was a 'fountain' on the north side of the prison.[5] It is not known whence this was fed but by 1435 a pipe was being laid from St Bartholomew's Hospital to Newgate,[6] and formal agreement to provide the water for both Newgate and Ludgate seems to have been reached in the following year.[7] This beneficent arrangement, presumably an augmentation of the earlier supply, was due to Thomas Knolles, a grocer, who had been mayor in 1400.[8] At first the source of supply is merely called the superfluous water belonging to the priory.[9] By 1442, however, it was said more expressly to come from a tank near the 'fountain' and the church of St Nicholas Shambles.[10] In 1459 a board of three common councillors was set up to survey the system of water carriage,[11] though at that moment Newgate alone seems to have benefited. By 1468 the sheriffs were repairing the watercourse, though it was hoped that they would recover the cost from the Exchequer.[12] This hope proved vain, for by 1475 the cost of keeping the pipes

---

[1] E 101/502/26.   [2] E 101/581/11.
[3] *Cal. Lr. Bks. K*, 125.   [4] See p. 327.
[5] *Cal. Lr. Bks. K*, 125.   [6] Ibid. 189.
[7] Ibid. *L*, 4.   [8] Ibid.; Stow, *Survey of London*, I, 37, 108.
[9] I.e. St. Bartholomew's Priory: *Cal. Lr. Bks. L*, 4.
[10] Ibid.   [11] Jorn. 6, f. 153*b*.   [12] Jorn. 7, f. 180*b*.

then serving both prisons in proper order was falling upon the chamber of London.[1]

Every prison must have had its privy. That at Newgate, cleaned and mended at the crown's expense in 1281–2, was a substantial room with two doors.[2] After the rebuilding the number of privies evidently multiplied.[3] There were two at Maidstone by Edward II's time[4] and in 1335–6.[5] Others are found at the castle of Newcastle upon Tyne in 1357–8,[6] at Ludgate in 1441,[7] and at Nottingham castle in 1530 and 1538–9.[8] Some effort was made to carry the sewage away. There was a sewer at Newgate in 1316[9] and perhaps the *fosse* there, which were scoured and covered over with gratings at the cleansing of 1281–2, were in fact sewers. In 1441 the sewage from Ludgate was discharged into the city ditch. At Nottingham, however, at the period in question, it seems to have flowed into the streets.

The documents from which the story of medieval prison buildings has to be painfully pieced together are not of a kind which makes it possible for a comprehensive survey of the layout of any prison to be made. They are mainly surveyors' reports on the need for repairs or accounts of the repairs to particular parts of prison buildings actually undertaken. Naturally we lack plans and elevations, nor have we any descriptions in the least like those furnished in the eighteenth and nineteenth centuries by Howard, Neild, or the Inspectors of Prisons. There are also hardly any pictures of any worth. The well-known one of Charles of Orléans in the Tower of London[10] is perhaps faithful but is certainly not informative. A mid-fifteenth-century drawing inserted in one of the City of London's Journals[11] purports to show the exterior of Newgate, but though it may well be representational it does not help us to understand the internal plan. The sketch of the Bristol

---

[1] *Cal. Plea & Mem. R.* 1458–82, 92.
[2] E 101/467/11. It is called *cloaca*.   [3] *Cal. Lr. Bks. K*, 124.
[4] Lambeth Palace MSS, C.R. 662. Called *garderob'*.
[5] Ibid. C.R. 665.   [6] *Arch. Ael.* n.s. IV. 127.
[7] *Cal. Lr. Bks. K*, 254.
[8] *Recs. of Nottingham*, III. 364, 377.   [9] *Cal. Close R.* 1313–18, 278.
[10] B.M. Royal, 16. F ii, f. 73.   [11] Jorn. 4, f. 79.

Tun, already mentioned,[1] is perhaps the truest to nature of any drawing of its sort, but the prison it depicts is of little importance. Nor do existing buildings help to supply these deficiencies to any degree. We can, of course, examine in surviving castles some towers and turrets which were turned into prisons or built as such. Some of these, especially the Bell, Bloody, Martin, and Salt Towers in the Tower of London do evoke the middle ages, and most of all the Bloody Tower with its crude and massive party-walls of timber.[2] All these have been at some time used as prisons, but they were prisons of a special sort. So it is with the small cells in certain other castles which, even though 'purpose-built',[3] are nothing like one of the larger common gaols.

Leaving aside these cells and turrets and a few vestiges of monastic prisons,[4] we are left, so far as identification has yet gone, with only three examples, none of them certain, of medieval prison buildings. These are what is now called the 'Manor Office' at Hexham,[5] Lydford castle,[6] and the former gaol of the liberty of Ely at Ely.[7] The first of these, which is of fourteenth- and fifteenth-century construction, is a stone building about 80 feet long and 33 feet broad. It is at present about 50 feet high but the parapet and original roof are missing, so it must once have been higher. The walls are about 9 feet thick at the base and about 6 feet thick at the top. The original windows are sparse and on the upper floors confined to the east and west walls. On the ground floor there appear to have been no windows on the long sides except slits to light the stair. That this building was designed exclusively as a prison can by no means be proved, but it was certainly so used in later times and the fewness of its windows and the thickness of its walls suggest that part of it at any rate may

[1] See p. 113.   [2] The timbers are presumably not medieval.
[3] E.g. Pevensey, see p. 347.   [4] See pp. 377–9.
[5] Pevsner, *Northumberland*, 181 and pl. 44 (*a*); *History of Northumberland* [Northumberland county history committee] III, *Hexhamshire*, pt. I, 225–36 and picture on p. 227; and see plate facing p. 112.
[6] For the building history see *Lydford Castle* (Min. Public Bdg. and Works, Guide, 1964), now complemented by the researches of Mr A. B. Saunders.
[7] *V.C.H. Cambs.* IV, 31.

have served such a purpose from the outset.[1] Lydford castle, first built in the late twelfth century, was allowed to fall into decay not long after, but in the mid-thirteenth century was repaired and carried two storeys upwards. The ground floor perhaps represents the 'strong house' for stannary or forest prisoners already described.[2]

Some medieval walling and the central staircase appear to attest the early origin of the Ely building, which may indeed still follow a medieval plan. Much of the present fabric, however, and the internal fittings are of the eighteenth and nineteenth centuries. With the Ely prison may be compared the former municipal prison in Bath.[3] This is a late eighteenth-century building, 'purpose-built', and contains no medieval feature. Yet this, like the Ely prison, is modelled upon one type of medieval prison, namely, the gaoler's house in which, surrounded at close quarters by his charges and sharing with them a common yard, the gaoler lived himself.

So much has here been written about castle gaols and 'purpose-built' gaols that there is the risk that a wrong impression may prevail. There must have been a large number of medieval prisons that were minute and in no way subdivided. The house[4] or inn (*hospicium*)[5] of the under-bailiff or bailiff's serjeant in which, in the thirteenth century, Wallingford prisoners were apt to be confined, must surely have been typical of many town prisons—a single room in the appointed keeper's dwelling. Such places lasted right into the sixteenth century and almost certainly much later. One of the town gaols in Southampton in the early fifteenth century seems to have been a small room surmounted by a one-roomed private apartment[6] and in this century and later many town halls or guildhalls, like the guildhall at Norwich,[7]

---

[1] Thanks are due to Mrs Margaret Tomlinson for kindly examining the building in 1964.　　　　　　　　　　　　　　　[2] See pp. 132–3.

[3] In Grove Street: Pevsner, *North Somerset*, 136.

[4] Berks. Rec. Off. W/JB a.3 (*c.* 1230).　　　　　　[5] Ibid. a.9 (1237).

[6] *Stewards' Acct. Bks. of Southampton* (Southampton Rec. Soc. [XVIII]), I. 2 (1428–9); ibid. II. 55 (1434–5).

[7] The prison was called 'penteney' (1433–47), presumably a form of penitentiary: *Recs. of Norwich*, I, 335.

stood above cells or cellars into which prisoners might be summarily thrust. If we strayed further into the sixteenth century, we should find many single-apartment prisons in the multitude of small boroughs and market towns that covered the face of Tudor England. Surely this must have been the situation over many earlier generations.

The visualization of a medieval prison would be much eased if we knew more than we do about the size of prison populations. Naturally, we should not expect all prisons, even the leading county gaols, to have been equally capacious, nor that any given prison would always contain the same number of prisoners. Prisons have at all times differed much in size and, whatever their size, their populations rise and fall. Even making these allowances, however, the information as we have it is very puzzling. It forms itself into no satisfactory pattern and there is little to be done with it but to set it down.

The earliest available figure is for York castle, where the number of prisoners is said to have fluctuated around 80 in 1289 and around 310 in 1293.[1] So large a total as the second of these is hard to credit. For Maidstone prison in the thirteenth and fourteenth centuries there are three sets of very valuable statistics which can be compiled from the payments of daily alms[2] by the archbishop to his captives. These payments show that between 12 April and 29 September 1280 there were 23 men and women in that prison, of whom 19 were laymen. The number seems to have been unchanged throughout that period.[3] Between 29 September and 4 December 1299 there were 34 prisoners there, and on various days during the same autumn 6 more were added to the number. On 4 and 5 December 20 were hanged. This left 20 on 6 December and these remained in custody until 29 September following. At sundry times during the same period 14 prisoners were added but 6 of these left before Michaelmas, so that at the end of the

[1] D. & C. Lichfield, MSS Qq 2 and Qq 7. The figures are for the weekly provision of half loaves. Cf. p. 320.
[2] For 'the bishop's alms' see p. 320.
[3] Lambeth Palace MSS, C.R. 656.

account there remained 31 prisoners.[1] There are also figures for
1331–2. From 29 September to 15 November there were 32
prisoners; from 15 November to 13 December, 30; from 13 December to 2 February, 35; and for the rest of the year, 38.[2] The
impression we have, then, is that in these periods there were
normally between thirty and forty inmates in this prison at one
time. Evidence of precisely the same kind is also available for
the bishop of Lincoln's prison in Banbury castle. It comes, however, for a much later time and relates to clerks convict alone.
Here, in 1510, 19 nominal 'clerks' were imprisoned. Ten were there
for the whole year, and during the year four were discharged,
four admitted, and one died.[3]

We have for Newgate, Maidstone, and Wallingford figures,
which have already been set out,[4] of deaths occurring in the famine
and plague years of 1315–17, and for Newgate also in 1414. If, as
we are told, as many as 71 people died at Maidstone in 1316–17,
we may suppose that the total population was above that figure
and therefore greater than it was at the periods analysed above.

Another method of computing populations is by means of the
indentures by which outgoing and incoming keepers of prisons
transferred their prisoners to one another. Such documents were
in use by the constable of the Tower by 1323.[5] Medieval examples
of these indentures are scarce, though they grow common later
on. The earliest one known is for Canterbury castle and shows
that that prison contained 23 persons on 20 December 1378.[6] A
similar document records that five felons were in Northampton
castle on 23 March 1388.[7] A much-mutilated indenture for Nottingham county gaol of 4 December 1450 appears to contain six
names.[8] Thirteen prisoners were in Guildford and Lewes castles
together on 25 November 1532,[9] and 29 on 18 November in the

---

[1] Ibid. C.R. 658. The roll states, apparently incorrectly, that 33 prisoners
remained at the end of the year of account.
[2] Ibid. C.R. 664.　　　[3] Potts, *The history of Banbury*, 49, 50.
[4] See p. 331.　　[5] *Abbrev. Plac.* 343.　　[6] *Arch. Cant.* LXXI. 209–12.
[7] E 364/25 m. D.
[8] Nottingham University Library, MS Mi. O. 2.
[9] Guildford Castle Arch. Loseley MSS 962/1.

next year.[1] Fifteen men and women were in Nottingham gaol on 23 November 1537,[2] and 27 in Fisherton Anger on 17 December 1547.[3] Apart from the Kent indenture none of these documents records the presence of any 'debtors', which casts a certain discredit upon the figures. For 'felons', however, they may well be accurate. Only two early indentures for a municipal prison have up to the present come to light. Both are for Nottingham. They are dated 2 October 1499 and 30 September 1505 and show the presence in that gaol of but two debtors in the earlier year and but one in the later.[4] Another figure, apparently exact though not derived from an indenture, shows that on 2 May 1533 22 men and women were in the county gaol at Ilchester.[5]

For the great 'national' prisons there are a few figures from the fourteenth century. It is known that there were 21 prisoners in the custody of the under-marshal of the King's Bench on 12 October 1316 and 17 in the same custody in 1324.[6] Ten prisoners were handed over in 1350 and 14 in 1361.[7] For the Fleet there exist for a short period some computations of the number of prisoners paying admission fees. Little though they tell us, they deserve quotation. From 29 November 1337 until 29 September 1338, 31 men paid such fees; in the next year (a complete one), 50.[8] Between 29 September 1339 and 3 March 1340,[9] 32 paid; and between 7 October and 8 November 1350, ten.[10] If the intake for the whole of 1337–8, 1339–40, and 1350–1 had been at the same rate as for those parts of the years for which figures exist, the annual totals would have been *c.* 34, *c.* 75, and 120. There are similar figures for Guildford gaol for 1294–5, when 101 men paid

---

[1] Guildford Castle Arch. Loseley MSS 962/2.
[2] C 146/7243. The indenture speaks of the 'gaols' of Nottingham and Derby but it is doubtful whether there was a gaol in Derby at this time, and there are other reasons for thinking that only one gaol is meant. Cf. p. 65.
[3] B.M. Add. Chart. 18291.
[4] *Recs. of Nottingham*, III. 98–100, 300.
[5] *L. & P.* VI, pp. 391–3.
[6] *Sel. Cases in K.B.* V, pp. xxi, xxvi n. 3. The second date is that of the roll mentioned at the latter page.
[7] Ibid. VI, p. xliv.   [8] E 372/184 m. 49.
[9] Ibid.   [10] E 372/194 m. 45 (46).

admission fees.[1] Naturally it would be particularly valuable to know the size of Newgate's population. All, however, that we can at present say is that in 1414 64 prisoners died,[2] which gives us a minimum figure for that year.

All prisons contained much prison gear, which formed part of the permanent equipment of the prison and, like the prisoners themselves, was handed on from one keeper to the next.[3] Perhaps the stocks (*cippi*), not uncommonly called 'a pair of stocks', were the most important article. Stocks might be found both within a prison building and outside. The death of prisoners from exposure in the stocks on a December day in 1383—a charge laid against the gaoler of Salisbury castle[4]—suggests an out-of-doors location. In 1418 a new pair was made in and therefore perhaps for the yard of Cambridge castle.[5] The distinction drawn at Nottingham in 1537 between 'the stocks' and 'the stocks in the chamber' suggests that the former were in the open.[6] In 1488 the lower rooms in Newgate, to which the felons were relegated, were furnished with stocks.[7] A woodcut in Foxe's *Acts and Monuments* shows how a pair of stocks would look when fitted into a prison room.[8]

It is probable that any prison of substantial size had several pairs of stocks. At Chester in 1301 four pairs were made, one for each of the four gaols that lay within the castle.[9] Three pairs were made for Huntingdon in 1365–6.[10] There were two pairs at Northampton in 1388[11] and one pair there in 1391.[12] There were five pairs at Stafford in the last decade of the fourteenth century[13] and

---

[1] *Surrey Pipe R. for 1295* (Surrey Rec. Soc. VII), 28. Three men paid admission fees to Guildford between 10 and 13 March 1346: E 372/191 m. 40.

[2] See p. 331.

[3] For an early instance (1337) of an order to surrender gear by indenture see *Mems. of Ripon*, II (Surtees Soc. LXXVIII), 121.

[4] *V.C.H. Wilts.* V, 22.

[5] W. M. Palmer, *Cambridge castle* (Cambridge, 1928), 20.

[6] C 146/7243.   [7] Jorn. 9, f. 171.

[8] E.g. ed. of 1684, II, 9. The pair there shown has hand- as well as foot-holes.

[9] *Cheshire in Pipe R.* 210.   [10] E 101/553/1. They are here called *trunci*.

[11] E 364/24 m. E.   [12] E 364/25 m. D.

[13] E 101/587/8 (1391–2); E 101/485/8 (1400–1).

two new pairs were made for that prison in 1449–50.[1] In 1537 there were three pairs at Nottingham.[2]

The medieval stocks, to judge from illustrations,[3] were very like those which are still so often to be seen on village greens. Some needed locks[4] or 'clasps' to fasten them,[5] others were secured by thongs[6] or pegs.[7] One pair of Stafford stocks of 1391 is said to have been 32 feet long, a gigantic and unwieldy instrument.[8] The other four more modestly measured 7 feet. As these dimensions show, the number of people whom the stocks were expected to secure varied. Early fourteenth-century pictures show pairs for one man, and for two, three, four, and six men.[9]

Additionally, every prison possessed instruments which when spoken of in general terms are called 'irons' (*ferramenta*), payments for the purchase of which occur in the Pipe Rolls from 1194.[10] These irons were of various descriptions. The words most commonly met with to describe them are chains, rings, collars, fetters, bolts, shackles, boys, and manacles. The English word 'guyvies' can be found in an official document by 1505.[11] The use to which chains and collars were put is obvious enough. Fetters were meant for the legs and manacles for the hands. Etymology proves this and in a mid-fourteenth-century document the uses are expressly stated.[12] Bolts were also supposed to be intended for the leg but the document last mentioned shows that they could sometimes be fastened to the hands. Shackles comprised bonds for both

[1] E 101/587/10.   [2] C 146/7243.
[3] E.g. B.M. Royal, 10. E iv, f. 187.   [4] E.g. E 101/587/8 (1391).
[5] Morris, *Chester in the Plantagenet and Tudor reigns*, 97 n.
[6] B.M. Royal, 10. E iv, f. 222 b.   [7] Ibid. f. 187 b; see plate facing p. 97.
[8] E 101/587/8. But when handed on in 1400–1 (E 101/585/8) the length is said to be 22 ft., which is the length expressed in the enrolment of the first inventory (E 364/26 m. A).
[9] B.M. Royal, 10. E iv, fos. 187, 222 b, 223, 223 b, 225 b.
[10] *Trans. R. Hist. Soc.* 5th ser. v, 15.
[11] *Recs. of Nottingham*, III. 100. The word is of course much older: *O.E.D.*
[12] Morris op. cit. 97; Huntington Library, Battle Abbey Muniments, Beadles' R. 84. For clear illustrations of manacles of the mid-fourteenth century see *Illustrations to the book of Genesis* (Roxburghe Club, Oxford, 1921), ed. M. R. James, fig. 140; for those of the mid-fifteenth century see B.M. Royal, E vi, f. 208. The latter is a French MS. Cf. B.M. Egerton 1147, f. 225 b.

ankles and wrists.[1] 'Boys', like 'gyves', appears to have been a word of general meaning.

It would, however, be a mistake to try to attach explanations that are too precise to these various words, at least until a careful examination of any surviving examples of the implements has taken place. Some of the Latin words used, of which *compedes* is a good example, can bear more than one meaning, in that instance both 'fetters' and 'stocks'. Some of the words seem sometimes to have been used loosely and sometimes precisely. Indeed over three and a half centuries such variation in meaning is to be expected. Thus in 1398 at Chester a distinction is drawn between 'bolts' and 'fetters' (*comped'*) and each set of instruments is said to be provided with 'shackles', as though the shackles were a mere appendage to the bolts and fetters.[2] On the other hand, at Hertford in 1509–11 'fetters' are distinguished from 'shackles', the latter being the heavier,[3] and at Nottingham town gaol in 1505 fetters and 'bolts' were the same thing.[4] The mention of 'manacles' in the same list suggests that neither of the other two was intended for the wrists. It is against such a background of cautions that any detailed information about 'irons' must be assessed.

Several pairs of 'fetters' existed in most prisons. As many as 33 were bought for Guildford in 1295,[5] 12 for Huntingdon in 1365–6,[6] and 4 each for Stafford in 1449–50,[7] Leicester in 1455–6,[8] and Hertford in 1509–11.[9] These constant purchases bespeak the need to refresh the supply, which was perhaps being constantly reduced by breakages and escapes. Indeed fetters may not always have been very strong; in 1220 a man broke three pairs which were binding him.[10] More illuminating, however, are the figures for the number of fetters held in particular prisons at particular times. The under-marshal of the King's Bench held 21 pairs in 1350 and nine in 1352.[11] There were nine in Northampton castle in 1388

[1] *O.E.D.* [2] Morris, op. cit. 97. [3] E 101/557/23.
[4] *Recs. of Nottingham*, III. 100. [5] *Surrey Pipe R. for 1295*, 28.
[6] E 101/553/1. [7] E 101/587/10. [8] E 101/590/32.
[9] E 101/557/23. [10] *Cur. Reg. R.* VIII. 397.
[11] *Sel. Cases in K.B.* VI, p. xliv.

and 1391,[1] and seven in Chester castle in 1398 together with nine fetter-locks.[2]

There were five collars at Northampton in 1388 and 1391, three of them with chains,[3] and two at Chester in 1398.[4] Eight were bought for Hertford in 1509–11, each furnished with a chain 4 feet long,[5] and two for the same prison in 1522–3.[6] The under-marshal of the King's Bench had four chains in his possession in 1350 and two in 1352 and 1361.[7] There were four in Northampton castle in 1391,[8] and rather more, it seems, in 1388.[9] There were three at Nottingham in 1537.[10] Chains were often reckoned in 'pairs'. As many as 23 pairs were bought for Maidstone in 1331–2[11] and there were 14 at Stafford in 1391–2.[12] The precise meaning of 'a pair of chains' is not immediately clear. It was said, however, in 1391[13] that they were for binding hands and feet, so that the meaning *pro ista vice* may be that they were attached to different limbs. Chains were sometimes used to secure particular individuals. A chain with a lock was supplied in 1225 for the exclusive use of one man.[14] By the sixteenth century, however, and perhaps long before, chains were being used to bind together gangs of prisoners. At Ilchester in 1533 there were seven people on one chain and five on another.[15] 'Rings' seem to have been less painful than chains. In 1236 a prisoner whose lot was lightened exchanged his chains (*vincula*) for rings.[16] They are not much heard of in later times, although they recur in 1347 as part of the equipment of the marshalsea of the King's Bench, where custodial conditions were comparatively mild.[17] Perhaps they were simply a

---

[1] E 364/24 m. E and /25 m. E.

[2] Morris, *Chester in the Plantagenet and Tudor reigns*, 97n.

[3] E 364/24 m. E; /25m. D. The chains are only mentioned in 1389–90.

[4] *36 D.K. Rep.*, App. II, 90.   [5] E 101/557/23.

[6] E 101/557/24.   [7] *Sel. Cases in K.B.* VI, p. xliv.

[8] E 364/25 m. D.   [9] E 364/24 m. E.

[10] They are called 'teams': C 146/7243.

[11] Lambeth Palace MSS C.R. 664.   [12] E 101/587/8.   [13] Ibid.

[14] *Rot. Litt. Claus.* II. 84.   [15] *L. & P.* VI, pp. 391–3.

[16] *Trans. R. Hist. Soc.* 5th ser. V, 15. In the mid-twelfth century, however, a ring could also mean a link joining two fetters for the feet: *Liber Eliensis* (Camden Soc. 3rd ser. XCII), 268.

[17] *Sel. Cases in K.B.* II, p. cxv n.

light chain, designed to secure the prisoner but not to impede his movements, and may be the same as the 'lenks' found in Nottingham town gaol in 1505.[1] It would be possible to quote further evidence about stocks of manacles, shackles, and bolts. To do so, however, would add nothing to the argument. It is enough to say that the strong presumption is that the means existed in all prisons to bind with iron the necks, hands, and feet of prisoners, as also a prisoner's whole person.

A few minor objects deserve a passing mention. There were two iron columns at Northampton in 1391,[2] possibly for tying up prisoners with begging bowls,[3] and three great iron shoes and three pairs of thumb irons at Hertford in 1509–11.[4] The shoes and thumb irons look suspiciously like instruments of torture. Mallets, hammers, and punches are mentioned in 1350–61 (King's Bench),[5] 1388 (Northampton),[6] 1398 (Chester),[7] 1505 (Nottingham town),[8] and 1537 (Nottingham county);[9] at all these places except Northampton there were also anvils, and at all except Nottingham town, mallets. These implements were needed for fixing and removing 'irons'[10] and were sometimes used by smiths who, as at Durham in the thirteenth century[11] or at Eccleshall in the sixteenth, entered the prison for that purpose.[12] In the fifteenth and sixteenth centuries halters were used on journeys when prisoners were taken away from prisons to be tried. Such at least was the practice at Battle in 1461–2[13] and 1519–20.[14] There is only one mention of the purchase of domestic utensils. It is at Battle, where in 1520–1 an earthen pot and a pair of wooden bowls were bought for the prison.[15]

[1] *Recs. of Nottingham*, III. 98.   [2] E 364/25 m. D.   [3] See p. 328.
[4] E 101/557/23. The 'shoes' were presumably the same as the boots: *O.E.D.*
[5] *Sel. Cases in K.B.* VI, p. xliv.   [6] E 364/24 m. E.
[7] Morris, *Chester in the Plantagenet and Tudor reigns*, 97 n.
[8] *Recs. of Nottingham*, III. 100.   [9] C 146/7243.
[10] At Maidstone in 1317–18 this is expressly said to be the purpose of the punch: Lambeth Palace MSS, C.R. 660.
[11] E 372/94 m. 18.   [12] W.S.L., D 1734 J/1949 mm. 20d–21.
[13] Huntington Library, Battle Abbey Muniments, Beadles' R. 86.
[14] Ibid. 84.   [15] Ibid. 93.

XVIII

MONASTIC IMPRISONMENT

Y leaving the world monks, friars, and nuns cut themselves
out of the judicial system that controlled the destinies of
those who remained within it.[1] Accordingly their correction, when that was needed, owed nothing to any secular or
national code of laws, but to an ecumenical system of discipline
which depended upon legislation originating overseas. For these
reasons monastic imprisonment was something quite distinct
from imprisonment applied to Englishmen living in the world,
even when they were in Holy Orders, and must be described
apart.

Six chapters of the Rule of St Benedict are devoted to monks in
need of correction or punishment, but in none of them is provision made for imprisonment.[2] Excommunication, corporal punishment, seclusion from their fellows, exclusion from the *opus
Dei*, and various forms of humiliation are the punishments enjoined. Bearing in mind the circumstances in which the Rule was
framed and the ardour which pervaded all primitive forms of
monachism, it is not surprising that a punishment so tainted with
sordidness as imprisonment should not have occurred to St
Benedict, and that the earliest communities at Subiaco and Monte
Cassino should not have equipped themselves with prison buildings. Nor, of course, did penal imprisonment form any part of
current Roman law. At what precise stage monastic prisons grew
up it is not profitable to try to determine here, but in 816, in the
statutes framed at the synod of Murbach, they are spoken of as
though they were a commonplace.[3]

---

[1] This chapter owes much to the kindness of Mrs Beatrice Howgrave-
Graham, who allowed the author to use the notes on monastic prisons accumu-
lated by her deceased husband, Peter Howgrave-Graham.

[2] 23–8: J. McCann (ed.), *Rule of St Benedict* (London, 1952), 73–9.

[3] P. B. Albers (ed.), *Constitutiones Monasticae* (Stuttgart, 1900–12), III. 88.

Whether there were such prisons in pre-Conquest England is hardly ascertainable, but they certainly existed soon after the Conquest. The Constitutions of Lanfranc, besides enjoining other punishments, make unmistakable provision for imprisonment,[1] which varied in its nature with the gravity of the fault. Whereas in St Benedict's time there were perhaps but two degrees of iniquity, it seems possible, in the Constitutions, to distinguish three: light offences, grave offences, and arrogance. Light offences did not earn any form of confinement. Graver faults, called *culpe graves*, if proved to be such, brought upon the culprit penance and scourging, followed by a period of unbroken silence spent in a place set apart for that purpose (*locum huic negocio ordinatum*). While the offender was in this place an elder brother was assigned to him as a guardian; the guardian, and others specially chosen by the abbot, alone might talk to him; and the abbot must choose his food. This was obviously a special kind of regulated corrective detention, to which there is no known parallel outside the cloister.

If a brother, when charged with his fault, showed no sign of penitence but rebelliously denied his wrong-doing, his brethren were to rise, lay hold of him, and thrust him into a prison suited to such rebels (*in carcerem hujusmodi arrogantibus deputatum*). In this form of detention there seems to be no directly corrective element. It is a hard and cruel punishment for a fault aggravated by that most unmonastic of offences, disobedience.[2]

In Lanfranc's Constitutions we have the distillation of the best Continental practice of the time designed for imitation by the English Benedictine houses. But before the purely English side of the story is traced further it will be well to study some Continental parallels and also to see how the practice of imprisonment was taken up by the Orders. In the customs of Cluny, as codified by

[1] D. Knowles (ed.), *The Monastic Constitutions of Lanfranc* (Edinburgh, 1951), 102, 103. The provisions are substantially the same in the Westminster Customary of c. 1266 and the customary of St Augustine's, Canterbury, of c. 1330: *Customary of St Augustine's, Canterbury and St Peter, Westminster* (Henry Bradshaw Soc. XXIII, XXVIII), I, 243–6, 250; II, 204–5.

[2] The prison in which a monk of St Mary's Abbey, York, was enclosed in 1312 is called '*locus inobediencium*': *Chron. of St Mary's Abbey, York* (Surtees Soc. CXLVIII), 53.

Ulrich, which are almost contemporary with Lanfranc's work, we find Lanfranc's two forms of imprisonment roughly paralleled.[1] For the second class of offence (*gravior culpa*) a very similar procedure is laid down. After various humiliations and flogging the culprit, on hearing the word *abite* from the abbot, is to depart to a place appointed for the purpose (*ad designatum talibus locum tendit*) and there abide, and to sleep and eat when and what the abbot may ordain. After being led to the church to attend divine office he is to be restored to this place—this *familiaris mansiuncula*.

As in Lanfranc's Constitutions there is also provision for the rebellious. Such monks are to be spontaneously seized by their brethren and consigned either to prison (*carcer*) or to fetters (*boge*). Both these forms of detention are defined. *Carcer* is a place without door or window and accessible only by a ladder (*scala*). *Boge* may be either *leviores* or *graviores*. The latter prevent the monk from walking upstairs to the dorter, so that he must sleep in some kind of a prison (*in custodia*). It seems clear from this that the reforms of Cluny did not contemplate the possibility of dispensing with a hard prison, but on the contrary presumed that every monastery would possess one.

The first statutes of the Cistercian Order (1099 × 1109), on the other hand, do not presume anything of the kind.[2] Like the Rule they draw a distinction between graver and lighter offences, but about rebellion and hard prison they say nothing. In fact the 'lighter' offences of the Cistercians appear to correspond with those offences which St Benedict's Rule, Ulrich, and the Constitutions of Lanfranc call *graves* or *graviores*. The form of punishment is somewhat similar and includes the banishment of the offender from the refectory so that he may eat *in loco quo abbati visum fuerit*. This looks rather like Ulrich's *mansiuncula*. However this may be, the Cistercians did not have to wait long for their prisons. An ordinance of 1187 lays down that an adult member of the Order, sound in body, who kills another member, is to be

[1] Migne, *Patrologia Latina*, CXLIX. 734–6.
[2] J. M. Canivez (ed.), *Statuta Capitulorum Generalium Ordinis Cisterciensis* (Louvain, 1933–41), I. 27, 28.

kept in close confinement and fed on bread and water for the rest of his days.[1] Such a discipline could hardly have been enforced in any place but a *carcer*. In 1206 a general licence was issued to construct prisons for the enclosure of fugitives and evil-doers.[2] A more comprehensive regulation of 1229 converted this permission into a mandate binding upon every abbey where the arrangements could possibly be made. All such were to provide themselves with *fortes et firmi carceres* to which at the discretion of abbots were to be sent sodomites, thieves, incendiaries, forgers, and homicides.[3] That these general provisions did not remain a dead letter is attested by the survival of many instructions for dealing with particular offences by way of imprisonment. These instructions also show that light imprisonment existed, abbots guilty of receiving delinquents or prematurely releasing them being condemned to *levis culpa* for six days and to be fed on bread and water.[4] Whether all other Orders made similar provision has not yet been determined, but it is known that in 1238 the general chapter of the Order of Preachers ordained that there should be a prison in every Dominican convent[5] and in 1261 the general chapter of the Carthusians legislated similarly for the Charterhouses.[6]

The conclusion must be that a prison of a kind for monks, and sometimes more than one, should have been a constituent of all the greater monasteries in England. The tenor of general monastic legislation, which applied to England no less than to other Christian countries, is a sufficient foundation for that conclusion. In addition, by the mid-fourteenth century the provincial chapter of the Benedictines had legislated on the point expressly; their statutes of 1343 decreed the establishment of a *carcer* in every monastery for the punishment of the *enormiter delinquentes*.[7] The references, however, to English prisons in documents and the surviving traces of them do not match their presumed ubiquity.

[1] Ibid. I. 1187, para. 2.
[2] Ibid. 1206, para. 4.
[3] Ibid. II. 1229, para. 6.
[4] Ibid. 1225, para. 36; 1226, para. 22.
[5] *Monumenta Ordinis Predicatorum*, III (Rome, 1898), 10.
[6] E. Margaret Thompson, *Carthusian Order in England* (London, 1930), 127.
[7] *Chapters of the English Black Monks* (Camden Soc. 3rd ser. XLVII), II. 42.

Taking the Benedictine houses first, the best evidence comes from Durham.[1] Here there are good documentary indications of two prisons. The first is the 'Lying House', i.e. prison house, a 'strong' prison or *carcer* forming part of the infirmary and under the superintendence of the infirmarian. First mentioned in 1423–4,[2] it was sufficiently detached from the cloister to serve also as a prison for laymen. Its site is uncertain.[3] The other consisted of two small rooms leading out of the south side of the chapter house.[4] This was for light offences.

Westminster, which in certain respects followed Durham closely, seems also to have been equipped with a strong prison. Long ago J. T. Micklethwaite (1876)[5] identified it with the undercroft of the reredorter, which abutted the infirmarian's house, and subsequent research suggests that his speculations were not inaccurate. The undercroft, however, has been so much altered in quite recent times that certainty is unattainable. It was suggested by the later Peter Howgrave-Graham that the prison for 'light' offences at Westminster was the so-called 'skin-room' on the south side of the entrance to the chapter house, now containing stores and switchgear.[6] Howgrave-Graham rested his argument partly on the similarity of the position of this chamber to that of the 'light' prison at Durham, partly upon certain structural details. It must be said, however, that there is little convincing visible evidence of the use of the chamber as a prison.[7] It has been thought

----

[1] *V.C.H. Durham*, III, 131; *Rites of Durham* (Surtees Soc. CVII), 56, 271.

[2] *Durham Acct. Rs.* (Surtees Soc. XCIX), I. 271.

[3] It has hitherto been assumed (*Rites of Durham*, 271; *V.C.H. Durham*, III, 131) that the Lying House was a large subterranean room situated below what was once the canons' stables on the south of the reredorter of the monastery. The architectural history of this room is very puzzling and its identification with the Lying House entirely speculative. Mrs H. E. W. Turner, of The College, Durham, plausibly suggests as a more likely site for the prison a much smaller room further to the north. Access to this room can now only be gained from the covered way (marked 'Underground Passage' on the plan facing p. 136 in *V.C.H. Durham*, III) constructed in the thickness of the curtain wall of the close.

[4] See plate facing p. 112.

[5] 'Notes on the Abbey Buildings of Westminster': *Arch. Jnl*, XXXIII, 27, 28.

[6] In his notes *penes me*.

[7] Mr A. J. Taylor doubts whether it was a prison.

that a light prison can also be traced at Rochester, where it is supposed to have been formed of two rooms in the choir triforium, called the Indulgence Chambers.[1] Besides Durham, Westminster, and Rochester, there is documentary evidence of prisons, of which no traces have been identified, at Coventry in 1296,[2] Worcester in 1301,[3] and *c.* 1535,[4] York in 1312,[5] and Malmesbury in 1527.[6]

For the prisons in Cistercian houses the evidence is even scantier. It is nowhere better than at Fountains, where there yet survive the foundations of three connecting penal cells adjacent to the abbot's chambers.[7] A small room at Waverley between the parlour and the dorter seems ultimately to have served as a prison for that monastery,[8] probably a 'light' one also, and a cell beside the dorter at Flaxley (Glos.), called 'the Penitentiary', is believed to have fulfilled a similar purpose.[9] At Kirkstall the south-west bay of the infirmary hall was latterly walled off and the floor lowered to form a partially subterranean prison.[10]

Now that the existence of monastic prisons is so well established it may be expected that a few more will be identified *in situ*. Search, however, may not be fruitful. Mean buildings such as prisons are not easy to distinguish from undercrofts and small rooms used for stores. But the remains of a privy are a fairly reliable sign of the presence of prison, whether 'light' or hard, as are rings in the wall for the reception of chains, and a narrow lighting-slit high up in the wall. The first and second Synods

[1] From information supplied by the Very Rev. J. Crick to P. Howgrave-Graham.

[2] *Registrum Roberti Winchelsey, Cantuariensis Archiepiscopi* (Cant. and York Soc. LI), I. 71.

[3] *Chapters of the Black Monks* (Camden Soc. 3rd ser. XLV), I. 152–3; cf. J. Noake, *Monastery and Cathedral of Worcester* (London, 1866), 272–3.

[4] D. Knowles, *Religious Orders in England* (Cambridge, 1948–59), III, 342.

[5] *Chron. of St Mary's Abbey, York*, 53.

[6] *Chapters of the Black Monks* (Camden Soc. 3rd ser. LIV), III. 126.

[7] *Yorks. Arch. Jnl*, XV, 337 and plan facing p. 402.

[8] H. Brakespear, *Waverley Abbey* (Surrey Arch. Soc., extra vol.), 42.

[9] Rose Graham to P. Howgrave-Graham, 2 January 1958 (*penes me*).

[10] W. H. St John Hope and J. Bilson, *Architectural Description of Kirkstall Abbey* (Thoresby Soc. XVI), 43.

of Aachen (816, 817) had decreed that prisons should have fireplaces,[1] but whether these were provided in the relatively milder climate of these islands cannot be certain.

The system of imprisonment within the walls of the criminous monk's own monastery was, from the later thirteenth century, increasingly supplemented by the practice of transferring him to another.[2] There he might perhaps be subjected to outright imprisonment but more often was 'gated' within the precinct. He might also be 'gated' in his own monastery.[3] The habit of making transfers to other houses, which was not peculiar to England,[4] was given formal expression in the statutes of the black monks issued in 1343. It was then laid down that flagrant disobedience was to be visited first with excommunication and imprisonment, but that, if such disobedience were contumaciously persisted in, the offender was to be sent for correction to another monastery, or expelled from the Order for good.[5]

So far as England was concerned, the host monastery might be one of equal status to the one to which the offender belonged or might be a cell or even a grange of the parent. Thus small cells, far distant from the mother house and lying in secluded places, became in certain instances and at certain times little better than prisons. Such was indeed specifically alleged in 1303 of the priory of Earl's Colne (Essex), which the abbot of Abingdon had converted from an infirmary to a penitentiary.[6] To send away an ill-disciplined monk and so remove a source of corruption or unrest was easy for the mother house and often in its immediate interest. The recipients, however, if fated to be often so afflicted,

---

[1] K. Hallinger and others (eds.), *Corpus Constitutionum Monasticorum* (Siegburg, 1963), I. 468, 524.   [2] D. Knowles, op. cit. I, 93–4, III, 47–8.

[3] For a case of 1307 where it was suggested that a monk of Selby, if he had grown sufficiently penitent, might exchange imprisonment for 'gating', see *Reg. of William Greenfield, Archbishop of York* (Surtees Soc. CXLIX), II. 19–20.

[4] See *Statuta...Ordinis Cisterciensis*, III. 1266, para. 6, for a case of 1266 where a wandering French monk on his capture was to be sent to a house other than his own.   [5] *Chapters of the Black Monks*, II. 37–8.

[6] G. G. Coulton, *Five centuries of Religion* (Cambridge, 1923–50), II, 328, quoting *Reg. Radulphi Baldock...episcoporum Lond.* (Cant. and York Soc. VII), 77.

were unlikely to profit. But at its best the system embodied the beneficent feature of giving the errant monk or nun a chance to reform his life in a new environment, and there is evidence that certain bishops, in adopting it, were aware of that advantage.

It is hardly surprising that there should be much less evidence of the imprisonment of nuns, and in nunneries no prison buildings have yet been detected. Imprisonment, however, was not unknown, and sentences of a month, a year, and two years have been at different times recorded. The last was imposed in 1535 upon a nun of Esholt (Yorks.), who bore a child. The system of transfers from one house to another which, as we saw, prevailed with men, prevailed also with women, particularly among the Yorkshire nunneries.[1]

We rarely know what were the actual offences for which English regulars were imprisoned. We may note that a canon of Lanthony Secunda bit his prior's finger in 1283;[2] that a monk of York stole money in 1310, escaped with it, was captured and imprisoned, and escaped again;[3] that some monks of Fountains were in prison for theft in 1423;[4] and that a Carthusian of Hinton was imprisoned as a forger in 1443.[5] In the later fifteenth century the Benedictines found it necessary to impose the penalty of imprisonment upon those convicted of simony, and in certain circumstances upon those who meddled in secular business or promoted the interests of laymen.[6] In general, however, there is not much English evidence. We may suppose that the more sinful English monks were little different from their Cistercian neighbours abroad who in the thirteenth century were being imprisoned for stealing their convent's goods[7] or forging documents and seals.[8] Worse offenders still were charged with sodomy,[9]

[1] Eileen Power, *Medieval English Nunneries* (Cambridge, 1922), 466–7.
[2] *Episcopal Registers, Diocese of Worcester* (Worcs. Hist. Soc. xv), II. 182.
[3] *Chron. of St Mary's Abbey, York*, 47, 53.
[4] *Memorials of St Mary's Abbey, Fountains* (Surtees Soc. XLII), I. 420.
[5] E. Margaret Thompson, *Carthusian Order in England*, 284.
[6] *Chapters of the Black Monks*, II. 221–2, 224.
[7] Canivez (ed.), *Statuta...Ordinis Cisterciensis*, II, 1225, para. 36.
[8] Ibid. 1190, para. 60; II. 1247, para. 15.
[9] Ibid. III. 1266, para. 6; 1277, para. 20.

threatening to kill their abbots,[1] wounding them,[2] or even committing outright murder.[3] These terrible outrages brought upon the perpetrators lifelong imprisonment or at least imprisonment that could only be terminated at the will of the general chapter.

We must regard the imprisonment of religious partly as a means of restraining or punishing those persons who, if they had remained in the world, would have suffered death or degradation for their crimes, partly as a means of correcting purely spiritual misconduct of which no layman could have been guilty. Whether the offender was, in common parlance, criminal or sinful, he had gravely departed from those standards of conduct which he had undertaken to observe. Consequently his soul was sick. For the sick in body the cloister made provision, and it was not unreasonable to make parallel provision for the sick in soul. The geographical and administrative association in some monasteries of the prison and infirmary is an outward demonstration of this attitude.

Those who were physically sick might recover and so could the spiritually sick. In its better and milder manifestations monastic imprisonment was a medicine which, administered as it was in conjunction with monitions and exhortations, was designed to induce contrition and so bring the culprit back to a better way of life. Archbishop Wickwane appears to be expressing this aim in a letter of 1283 to the presidents of the canons regular in the province of York, in which he enjoins them to find a truly safe and strong place, outside Marton priory, in which to confine a canon of Marton, so that the canon, *victui necessariis contentus, commissa lugeat et penitenciam subeat salutarem.*[4] Bishop Giffard of Worcester in the same year directed the prior of Lanthony Secunda to keep a rebellious canon on hard commons and in

[1] Canivez (ed.), *Statuta...Ordinis Cisterciensis*, II. 1226, paras. 25, 26.
[2] Ibid. II. 1241, para. 19; 1246, para. 31 (lay brothers).
[3] Ibid. 1230, para. 20.
[4] *Reg. of William Wickwane, Archbishop of York*, ed. W. Brown (Surtees Soc. CXIV), 153. There is the alternative possibility that the canon was mad.

chains until he should repent.[1] Nor, in later times, was his spiritual recovery left to the uncertain process of self-examination, for a Benedictine statute of 1444 decreed that imprisoned monks should be furnished with service books.[2] When we read of such measures we are reminded of the theories of Victorian penologists.

[1] *Episc. Regs., Dioc. of Worc.* II. 182.
[2] *Chapters of the Black Monks,* II. 208.

XIX

CONCLUSION

No previous attempt has been made to write about the early history of imprisonment in this country.[1] This is no doubt partly because there is no well-organized body of documents on which such a study may be founded. Accordingly the present story has had to be painfully pieced together from sources which are widely scattered and are only partially relevant. Nor could the sources, imperfectly edited and indexed as some of them are,[2] have been examined systematically without greatly prolonging the time taken in compilation. Susbstantial sampling has had to be resorted to. For all these reasons the book is a pioneer. Like all pioneers it is 'rugged'. Like all pioneers it may expect to be followed by a more polished and more sophisticated successor.

The theme of the book is to a certain degree artificial. Imprisonment is a feature partly of judicial process, partly of judicial punishment. It fits into the story of each and cannot be completely understood unless each story is told. Moreover, they are quite

[1] The most serious contributions that have yet appeared are Margery Bassett, 'The Fleet prison in the middle ages' in *Univ. of Toronto Law Journal*, v (1944), 383 and 'Newgate prison in the middle ages' in *Speculum*, XVIII (1943), 233; see also R. B. Pugh, 'The king's prisons before 1250' in *Trans. R. Hist. Soc.* 5th ser. v, 1. Mrs Bassett's hope, expressed in the first of these articles, to complete a series of studies on medieval imprisonment has not as yet been fufilled. Mention must also be made of G. C. Ives, *A history of penal methods* (London, 1914) and of two unpublished dissertations, one by Miss Marguerite Gollancz, 'The system of gaol delivery as illustrated in the extant gaol delivery rolls of the 15th century' (London M.A. dissertation, 1936), and the other by Clifford Dobb, 'Life and conditions in London prisons, 1553–1643, with special reference to contemporary literature' (Oxford B.Litt. dissertation, 1953). Some portions of the second of these are exposed to view in 'London's Prisons' in *Shakespeare in his own age* (*Shakespeare Survey* XVII, Cambridge, 1964), ed. by Allardyce Nicoll.

[2] There are few subject index entries under 'gaol', 'imprisonment', or 'prison' in publications of the Public Record Office. While this omission from older publications cannot be criticized, it is to be hoped that it will not impair future ones.

Conclusion

different stories. They are, however, brought into close association by the fact that in the main the men and women affected by imprisonment were kept in the same buildings, were guarded by the same keepers, and were in like degree objects of compassion to the compassionate.

There are also disadvantages in isolating England from the rest of Europe, of Christendom, and indeed of the world *veteribus notus*. Prisons abounded throughout Europe, and their classification, distribution, management, and layout were no doubt much the same everywhere. In general, prison life was probably milder here and prison buildings less awful than in other countries. It is also most probable that penal imprisonment came to be widely practised in England at a much earlier date than on the Continent, for such imprisonment is foreign to Roman law but was not uncongenial to our own.[1] But these admissions made, the resemblances were perhaps more numerous than the differences, though we shall not know for certain until comparative studies have been undertaken.

Finally, there is some inconvenience, inevitable though it be, in separating what happened before the mid-sixteenth century from what happened afterwards. Much that is first articulated in the seventeenth and eighteenth centuries is of medieval origin and its closer study would illuminate many earlier customs. Conversely, of course, it would be instructive to examine by means of later evidence the longevity of medieval practices. These qualifications made, what are the things, or some of the things, that the preceding pages have to tell?

First of all, it is clear that prisons were perfectly well known before the Conquest and were already being used as places not merely of custody but of punishment. As organized institutions, however, they were probably few in number and unevenly distributed. From Henry II's time conditions began to alter. The

[1] For the late development of penal imprisonment on the Continent see e.g. C. Calisse, *A history of Italian criminal law* (Continental Legal History Ser. VIII, London, 1928), esp. pp. 416–17; C. L. Von Bar and others, *History of continental criminal law* (Continental Legal History Ser. VI, London, 1916), esp. pp. 237, 277, 309–10. For the Roman doctrine see p. 17.

prisons maintained by the king's own officers multiplied, while the crown did nothing to restrict the continuance of prisons in the greater liberties. Although these liberty prisons, so far as they were kept by lay barons, seem to wither away towards the end of the thirteenth century, their loss was more than compensated for by the establishment of municipal and 'bishops'' prisons in ever greater numbers. Naturally the prisons varied greatly from one another in both size and character, but, even if a rather narrow view of what amounted to a 'prison' is taken, there must have been not merely relatively but absolutely far more buildings used as prisons in the fourteenth and fifteenth centuries than there are today. Nor were these prisons or their inhabitants withdrawn from public view. To see prisoners trudging to gaol behind their escorts, begging from gratings or in the streets, and being led to execution were the commonest of experiences. From these spectacles the eyes of Englishmen have long been shielded.

Not only were prisons more familiar from the outside than they are today; they were also more familiar from the inside. There were many more opportunities for being consigned to them. First, there was immensely more coercive imprisonment than is now practised, particularly from the later thirteenth century when commerce increased without any parallel development in the provision of credit. There was also a great deal of penal imprisonment for every type of fraud, contempt, disobedience to authority, failure in public duty, and petty crime, although, except in the case of 'clerks', not for felony. Since, however, the definition of the word 'clerk' was stretched ever more widely there was in fact a great deal more imprisonment for felony than at first sight appears.

The sanction for imprisonment primitively was based on common law principles or what is loosely called 'prerogative'. At an early stage, however, imprisonment in connection with forest offences was authorized more formally, and from Edward I's opening years imprisonment of whatever type came increasingly to rest upon statute law or municipal regulation. So far as it was penal, it could be coupled with a requirement to pay a fine and damages, or one or other of them, or it might stand alone.

Much coercive and some custodial imprisonment could be of long duration. So in practice could penal imprisonment, but where terms for such imprisonment were set at all, they were usually short ones. There was much scope for reducing the length of sentences or terminating them, openly by the payment of compositions or 'ransoms' and covertly by bribes. Moreover, despite strenuous efforts to prevent it, escaping was comparatively easy and must often have been lastingly successful.

In some places in the thirteenth century sheriffs hired working gaolers and threw the costs upon the Exchequer, and in the same period the crown sometimes relieved itself of such expenses, together with the costs of maintenance, by requiring a subject to keep a gaol in return for land, or by selling the right to do so for cash. To a growing extent, however, as that century drew to a close, the crown, by-passing the sheriffs, bestowed gaolerships on minor royal servants as a substitute for pensioning them in any other way. This gave an impetus to the already existing system of allowing prison-keepers of all degrees and types, their deputies and servants, to make a living out of their prisoners by means of fees, lodging charges, and the sale of drink and victuals. That such a system was liable to much abuse crown, parliament, and municipal authorities knew well, but circumstances compelled its toleration and even those who saw its defects most keenly seldom did more than try to impose rules to keep the various charges within bounds.

The law, the church, and what passed for public opinion were opposed to the exploitation of prisoners and the practice of cruelty towards them. From the later fourteenth century London and a few other great cities tried to ensure good standards of conduct in gaolers by inspection and other means. Since, however, prisons were often out of repair and prison staffs probably insufficient in size, some fettering was sanctioned and indeed some brutality condoned. Without them imprisonment could hardly have continued. What, however, made life in prison chiefly painful for the prisoner was the absence, except in 'bishops'' prisons, of any system of maintenance. The helpless notion, prevailing in the beginning, that 'felons' could somehow support themselves out of their own property and 'debtors' be supported by their creditors, seems hardly to have outlasted the thirteenth century. It was succeeded by a system of private almsgiving and licensed begging occasionally supplemented by some contribution from such sources as surplus stores of towns. Despite such efforts, however, prison life bore very heavily upon the poor, though, it must be added, perhaps not very much more heavily than life outside. The well-to-do were in a different condition, for they might sometimes, at least in London, choose their prison. That is to say, their wealth might gain them admission to the Fleet or the King's Bench, both of which were more comfortable than Newgate.[1] At any rate they might choose within an assigned prison the best accommodation that was going. From quite early times accommodation was graded according to the prisoner's rank or reputed wrong-doing.

Though it may be asserted with fair confidence that prison was not intended to be barbarous, it was nevertheless intended to be nasty. Though there are faint signs that the church saw in it an opportunity for amendment of life, it was in general regarded much more as a means whereby society could take revenge upon the culprit or could ensure that, if he was indeed as culpable as he seemed, revenge should be taken in another form. Sometimes indeed we detect the feeling that the 'rumour of the countryside' was at least as sure a test of guilt as any judgement of a court could be and that, if a man got so far as to be committed custodially to gaol, he must be a 'criminal type'. Bracton, for instance, declares that a man who confesses to serious wickedness ought not to be bailed *sed carceris poenam et inclusionem sustineat*, thus implying, for aught that may be said elsewhere to the contrary, that the wicked ought to be punished with imprisonment even before their trial.[2] The author of the *Mirror* tells us that 'mortal

---

[1] *Speculum*, XVIII. 245.   [2] *Bracton*, II, 349–50.

sinners' are to be put in gaol to await their judgement, in order to keep them out of contact with the innocent.[1]

The 'subject', if so he may be called, was not effectively protected from capricious arrest or unjustified detention. In particular the power of the crown to hold the king's personal or political enemies in prison for long periods was very widely used. No attempt has been made here to examine this very complicated subject but there is scope for such an examination in the future. But though the prerogative was extensive and its exercise to some extent acknowledged as proper or at least inevitable, the conviction already prevailed strongly that in many sets of circumstances capriciousness was wrong. From the thirteenth century arrest was supposed to be for proper causes, as the thirty-ninth clause of Magna Carta in effect declared, and as time went on the law was strengthened. But the authorized agents of arrest were so numerous and so little subject to uniform rules that good intentions were apt to be frustrated. Moreover, arrest once effected, the financial advantages of detaining prisoners 'unjustly' were powerful, while the fee system made it difficult to ensure that prisoners were released from prison the moment their presence there was no longer warranted.

Against these evils the writ of false imprisonment afforded a partial protection. So far as felony was concerned, there was the more potent safeguard of gaol delivery. The crown from very early times does seem to have aimed consistently at fairly frequent trials or 'deliveries' by reasonably well-qualified judges. If the word 'efficient' may ever be applied in a medieval context it is perhaps appropriate here. Those who offended against the crown without allegedly committing felony no doubt fared less well. Here again, however, inquiries might be instituted, either at the plea of the prisoner or otherwise, into over-long imprisonments. Thus in 1351 the chief justice of the King's Bench was ordered to find out the causes for the detention in the Tower of four men, one of whom had been there for seven and a half years and another for four.[2] The eventual outcome in this instance is not

---

[1] *Mirror*, 52.   [2] *Sel. Cases in K.B.* VI, pp. 72-4.

at present known but certainly at times the crown instructed keepers to release individuals who, in its estimation, had been detained sufficiently, and cases of this can be collected over a long period.

Every student of medieval administrative or legal history is forcibly impressed by the divergence between theory and practice. This is as true of imprisonment as of other phenomena. Strict injunctions are issued—to control arrest or release, to secure humane conditions, to enforce imprisonment where crimes and misdemeanours occur or are suspected. These injunctions are flouted or only very imperfectly observed. They are thus ignored or by-passed partly because their devisers have never given thought or enough thought to their enforceability. The devisers did not mind this nearly so much as their successors would have done in the later nineteenth and earlier twentieth centuries. 'Men in the Middle Ages', said Creighton,[1] 'loved law, and could not have too much of it—on paper. Our ideas have changed...and we dislike to live under regulations that are not observed by the community.' Perhaps in 1968 this is less true than it was in 1895. If that is so, it is partly for the reason that now, as in the middle ages, there is a desire for good government but a shortage of sufficiently rewarded manpower to achieve it. There is no better note on which to end.

[1] Louise Creighton (ed.), *The church and the nation* (London, 1901), 197. The charge there reprinted was delivered in 1895.

INDEX

Aachen, Germany, synods of, 379
abduction. *See* 'ravishing'
Abingdon, Berks., abbot, 380
abjuration, 21, 30 n.
account, action of, 45, 212
accountants, defaulting or fraudulent,
    7, 45, 106, 116, 118, 124, 178, 182,
    203, 208, 318
admiral of the fleet towards the north,
    294
adultery. *See* sexual offences
Agincourt, battle, 122, 128
Akerman, Richard (d. 1792), keeper of
    Newgate, 183
Alan *Alemannus*, 106
ale, beer, 185
    for prisoners, 176, 189, 191, 322, 326
Alfred, king of England, 1
    laws of, 1, 316
Allertonshire, Yorks., 96
Allexton, Leics., prison, 131–2, 180
Almain, merchant of, 272
alms, for prisoners, 173–4, 187, 213,
    319–27, 343
    withheld, 177, 185
alnagers, 34
Alnod the engineer, 114 n.
Alton, Hants, 81
Alveley, Salop, prison, 266 n.
Amersham, Bucks., 322
appeals, failure in, 10, 15
    failure to prosecute, 9 and n.
    false, 32–3, 42
    withdrawal of, 15
    See also approvers
Appleby, Westmorland, gaol or prison,
    85, 261
approvers, 62, 64, 162 n., 197
    appeals by, 22, 105, 192, 201, 207, 271
    corrupted by sheriffs or gaolers, 22,
        181 and n., 184, 280
    escaping, 220, 233–5
    in the Fleet, 115–16

in Newgate, 105, 220
in the Tower of London, 123
maintenance of, 4, 61, 315–16
Arblaster, Richard, 146
    family, 146–7, 157 n.
arms-bearing, unlawful, 42
arrest, 192–203, 232–3
arrows, 38
arson, 2, 216, 272, 377
Arthur, Richard, knight, 101
artificers, 38–40. *See also* craftsmen
Artois, Janice d', 127
Arundel, Sussex, castle, prison, 77,
    152, 262, 307
Arundel, earl of. *See* FitzAlan, R.
Ashley, Cambs., 195
assault, 11, 27
assize, grand, 10
    justices of, 39, 226, 278–84, 342
        and n.
assizes, possessory, petty, 257, 265, 275
    mort d'ancestor, 11, 141
    novel disseisin, 10, 19, 20, 32
Athelney, Somerset, abbot, 19
Athelstan, king of England, laws, 2
attorney, king's, 291, 313. *And see*
    Brok, L. del
auditors, assignment of, 45
Augustine, of Hippo, St., *Soliloquies*, 1
Aumale, countess of, 12, 167, 352
Aylesbury, Bucks., 77, 255 n.
    gaol or prison, 59, 77 and n., 148,
        165, 350, 356
    keeper, *see* Hurel, R.

Babington, William, and family, 157
bail, mainprise, 3, 5, 31, 34, 169, 177,
    204–10, 241
bakers, 170, 329
Bakewell, Derbys., prison, 99
Baldock, Robert, chancellor, 102, 106,
    181
Balliol, John. *See* John

Cheltenham, Glos., hundred, prison, 299

Chertsey, Surrey, prison, 308

Chester, Ches., borough prison, 99, 169
castle, gaol, 85, 126, 165, 349, 357, 369, 371–3
justice of, 296

Chester, county,
Cheshire, 44, 59, 172, 259, 344
gaols or prisons in, 85, 296. *And see* Chester; Congleton; Darnhall; Over; Weaverham

Chesterfield, Derbys., prison, 65

Chesterton, Cambs., prison, 193 n., 250

Cheveley, Cambs., 193 n.

Chichele, Robert, grocer of London, 326

Chichester, Sussex, 76, 153, 196, 308
bishop of, 135, 237, 246
prisons of, 137, 153
castle. *See* county gaol
city prison, 76 and n., 100, ?307
county gaol, in castle, 75
not in castle, 75–6, 165 and n., 196, 341

Choke, Richard, justice of the Common Pleas, 230

Christian Malford, Wilts., prison, 250

Cinque Ports, courts, 130
prisons, 302–3
warden, 130 and n., 303. *And see* Pencestre, S. of

circuit system, 278–82

circumcision, 55

Cirencester, Glos., abbot, 89
prisons of, 79, 96, 299
seven hundreds belonging to, 96

Cistercian order, statutes of, 376–7

Clackclose, Norfolk, hundred, 89, 91
prison, 91. *And see* Wimbotsham

Clarendon, Wilts., assize of, 4 and n.
palace, prison, 132, 359

Clare, Roger de, 105 n.
Thomas de, 272

class distinctions among prisoners. *See* segregation

claustrophobia, 219

cleaning of prisons, 328, 332

clergy, benefit of, 41, 49–51, 386. *And see* clerks

clerks, escapes from prison, 230, 237–9, 247
imprisonment of, 17, 23–4, 41, 48–51, 112, 271, 333, 367
incontinence of, 51
support of, in prison, 320–2
See also chantry priests; chaplains

clerks, academical, imprisonment of, 51, 137–9, 352, 360–1

Clifford, family, 85

Clifton, family, 160

Clifton-on-Yore, Clifton, Yorks., manor and prison, 92 n.

'Cloere Brien', prison name, 57

close, breach of, 27

cloth, 34, 42, 190

clothing for prisoners, 327, 329

Cluny, dep. Saône-et-Loire, France, abbey, 375–6

Cnut, king of England, laws of, 1 n.

coat, 27

Cobham, Eleanor, 127

Cockermouth, Cumberland, 89, 92

Cok, James, keeper of Oxford castle, 60 n.

Coke, Edward (d. 1634), knight, chief justice, 230, 345

Colchester, Essex, 225, 275, 327, 329
archdeacon of, 135
borough prison, 100, 224, 306, 327
castle, constables or keepers of, 68 and n., 69, 70, 131, 249. *And see* Holebrook, R. of; Muntfichet R. de
gaol, 67–70, 129, 135, 149, 198, 329, 339, 356
delivery, 272 and n., 275, 294, 307

Coldingham, Reynold of, 180

Coleshill, Richard de, 270

Colne, Earl's, Essex, priory, 380

combat. *See* battle

Common Pleas or Bench, court, 116–17, 244
justices, 174 n., 263, 284. *And see* Brok, L. del; Percy, W.; Raleigh, W. de; Segrave, S. de
marshalsea, 119

Durham (*cont.*)
    gaols or prisons in, 85, 295–6, 303.
    And see Barnard Castle; Durham;
    Sadberge
    sheriff, 284, 295
'Dutch' prisoners, 107

earl marshal. *See* marshal
Eastwood, Essex, prison, 70
Eccleshall, Staffs., castle, prison, 136–7,
    152–3, 321, 373
    manor, 152
economic regulations, violation of, 106.
    See also industry; labour legisla-
    tion; trade
Edmund of Almain, earl of Cornwall
    (d. 1300), 133
Edmund of Woodstock (d. 1330), earl
    of Kent, 222
Edward the elder, king of England,
    laws of, 2
Edward I, king of England, 126
    as the lord Edward, 56, 127n.,
    130, 250 and n.
Edward II, king of England, 106, 122,
    128
Edward, the Black Prince, 133
eggs. *See* poaching
Egremont, Vivian of, 128n.
    lord. *See* Percy, T.
Eleanor of Aquitaine, queen of England,
    214
    of Brittany, 79
Eliensis, curia. See Ely
Elizabeth of York, queen of England,
    214
Elmham, North, Norfolk, prison, 135
Ely, Cambs., bishop of, 90, 297
    liberty, 344, 364
    court, *curia Eliensis*, 296
    gaols or prisons, in Ely, 90n.,
    254, 297, 306, 364–5; elsewhere,
    90n., 262n., 297
    justices, 297
    prior, 54, 250
entry, forcible. *See* riot
escapes, 69, 178–9, 182–3, 195, 316, 343
    by clerks convict, 50, 201, 231

by monks, 381
collective, 219–20, 334
consequences for escapers, 227–30
consequences for keepers, 22, 142n.,
    143 and n., 233–40
from franchise prisons, 93, 233
liability for, 144, 146, 153, 248–54
negligent, statute of, 226, 234, 236–7
    distinguished from voluntary,
    233–4
of crown accountants, 7
pardons for, 215, 245–8
under pre-Conquest law, 2, 166
escheators, 124, 226, 317
escorts for prisoners, 4, 105 and n.,
    162–3, 168, 177, 194–7, 235, 251,
    255 and n.
Esholt, in Bradford, Yorks., priory, 381
Essex, county, 60, 69–70, 117n., 131,
    201, 232n., 282
    commons of, 69
    gaols or prisons in, 58n., 67–72, 90
    and n., 99, 225, 259, 261, 266n.
    And see Chelmsford; Colchester;
    Eastwood; Finchingfield; New-
    port; Rayleigh; Writtle
    [and Hertfordshire], sheriff, 67–9,
    106, 135, 149, 198, 235 and n.,
    246, 297n.
essoining, irregularities, 12
Eudes the sewer, 68
Ewerye, Edmund del, 156
Exchequer, court, 5, 116–17, 211, 291,
    313
    auditor, 244
    Barons, 6–7, 45–6, 173
    clerks, 34
    issues from, for prison maintenance,
    338, 340–1, 344
    'Godspence', 330
    marshal and under-marshal, 118–19,
    175
    messenger, 13
    Statutes of, 23
Exchequer Chamber, court, 245
Exchequer, Matthew of the, 241
excommunication, 8 and n., 380
exeats. *See* wandering

Index

hunting lodges, 132
Huntingdon, Hunts., 58, 272
  castle, 78
  county gaol, 77–8, 81 n., 341, 369, 371
Huntingdon, county, 59, 282, 284
  gaols or prisons in, 58 n., 77, 256 n., 259, 261, 275. *And see* Huntingdon; Ramsey; Spaldwick
  sheriff. *See* Cambridge, county
Hurel, Richard, keeper of Aylesbury gaol, 249
hurers, 40

Ilchester, Somerset, 67, 180
  gaol or prison, 65–7, 258, 265, 273, 325, 341, 350, 372
    keepers or gaolers, 150–1, 180, 340
Ilminster, Somerset, 325
imprisonment, coercive, 1, 5, 8–9, 35 n., 44–7
  custodial, 1 n., 3, 5, 51 n.
  duration of, 23, 28–30
  false, unjust, action of, 52, 216–17, 389
  honourable, 5–7, 125, 128, 351–2
  irredeemable, 31
  of poor, unable to pay fines, 31
  punitive, or penal, 1 n., 2, 9, 28, 51 n., 129, 170, 316
  for Jews, 56
  release from, 212
  solitary, 334
  statutory, 27–47
indictments, corrupt, 33, 182
'Indulgence Chambers', prison name, 379
industry, offences connected with, 38
infangthief and *outfangthief*, 1, 91, 92, 101
infant, falsely claimed as progeny, 11
infirmaries, monastic, 382
Ipswich, Suffolk, 275
  borough prison, 100
  county gaol, 78, 265 n., 271, 341, 350, 355–6
  shire house, 309, 342

Ireland, 175
  Exchequer and King's Bench in, marshals, 175
  marshalsea of, 167
  prisons in. *See* Dublin; Swords
'irons', 4, 6, 25 n., 53 and n., 146, 152, 178 n., 216, 230, 241
  use and abuse of, 17, 168, 170, 177–80
  varieties of, 370–3
Irthlingborough, Northants., 194
Islandshire, Northumberland, formerly Co. Durham, prison, 86, 296
Isleworth, Middx., 162
  prison, 90 n.
Islip, Simon, archbishop of Canterbury, 49, 321
Italy, mass release of prisoners in, 214 n.

Jaille. *See* Jayle
Jailler, surname, 148 and n.
James I, king of Scotland, 122 and n., 128
Jayle, Jaille, Eudes de la, 148
  Philip de la, 148 n.
Jews, 22
  imprisonment of, 55–6, 124, 168
  justices of, 13, 263
  tallage of, 55, 124
John II, king of France, 122, 126, 128
John (Balliol), king of Scotland, 122
John of Gaunt (d. 1399), duke of Lancaster, 102 and n., 296, 323
John the porter, and William, his brother, 145 and n.
Johnson, Samuel (d. 1784), lexicographer, 183
joiner, 333
'Jordan', prison name, 359
judgements, upsetting, 11–13, 18–19. *See also* justice
judges delegate, 50 n.
'Julianesboure', prison name, 359
juries, jurors, 10, 16, 23–5, 33, 279, 311–12
justice, defeating or impeding the ends of, 9, 16, 116. *See also* judgements

Index

405

London (*cont.*)
  churches and religious houses, All
    Hallows, Barking, 223
    Blackfriars, 241
    Carmelites, 241
    Corpus Christi college, 325–6
    Holy Trinity, Aldgate, priory, 105
    St Bartholomew's hospital, 362
    St Bartholomew's priory, 362
    St Mary Mounthaw parish, 102
    St Mary Spital, hospital, 188
    St Michael Bassishaw parish, 102
    St Michael Paternoster, college,
      187n.
    St Nicholas Shambles, 362
  citizens of, monopoly of im-
    prisonment within city, 102
    power to deliver gaols, 301
    responsibility for repair of New-
    gate, 338–9
  common council of, 154, 186–7,
    293n., 337
  common serjeant of, 290
  Companies, Fishmongers, 325;
    Skinners, 188
  coroners of, 43, 267, 314
  corporation of, 329
  courts, judgements of, 27, 40, 43–4
  Counters, Compters, history and
    location, 109–11
    porters or gate-keepers, and sub-
    ordinates, 43, 153, 155, 161, 170,
    185
    records of, 213
    regulations, 170, 179, 185–91
    otherwise mentioned,107,112,125,
    181, 188, 213, 224, 254, 310, 334
  diocese, chancellor, 152
  ditch of, 333
  eyre in, 313
  Fleet, prison. *See* Fleet
    river, 114–15, 362
  freemen, imprisonment of, 107, 109,
    353
  gaols or prisons in or near, 58, 75,
    77, 226–7, 256, 324, 326–7, 330,
    362. *And see* Counters, Ludgate,
    Tun *under* London; *and* Fleet;

King's Bench; Marshalsea; New-
    gate; Tower; Westminster
    charities, 323–7
  Guildhall, 109, 310
  Holborn Bridge, 119
  [and Middlesex], issues of, 158, 338
  Jews of, 55
  keeper of. *See* Sandwich, R. of
  lock-ups, 113. *See also under* Tun
  Ludgate, gate and prison, history,
    107–9
    alms and begging, 324–6, 329
    keeper and subordinates, 153–5,
    162, 174, 178n., 185 and n., 254,
    331,333,340. *See also* Bottisham, J.
    records of, 213
    recreation in, 361
    regulations, 179, 184–91
    sanitation, 333, 363
    'wandering', 336
    water-supply, 362
    otherwise mentioned, 104, 110,
    170, 245, 329, 339
  mayor, 212, 252–3, 290–3, 302, 312,
    336. *And see* Bowes, M.; North-
    ampton, J.; Waleys, H. le;
    Walworth, W.; Whittington, R.
  merchants, 128, 175
  Lord Percy's house in, 102
  recorder of, 290, 292, 302 and n.
  St Paul's cathedral, 227, 325–6
    prison in, 102, 136
  [and Middlesex], sheriffs of, 4, 75,
    109–10, 153–4, 189, 203, 221,
    235, 240, 243, 252–4, 267, 274,
    290, 292–3, 362
  Smithfield, West, 119, 310
  soke prisons, 101–2
  streets,
    Bread Street, 110
    Cheapside, 110
    Cornhill, 112
    Farringdon Street, 114
    Farringdon Within, 'high street'
    of, 220
    Fenchurch Street, 113, 125
    Fleet Street, 158
    Giltspur Street, 110

Index

Nottingham (*cont.*)
borough gaol, 156 and n., 168, 179, 352, 358, 368, 371, 373
castle, 65
constable, keeper, or lieutenant of, 64, 197
prison, 64, 126–7, 129, 357
county gaol, 64–5, 309, 324, 328, 342, 351, 355 n., 356, 362–3, 367–8, 370, 372
delivery, 271 n., 272, 274, 312
gaoler, keeper, 150, 161, 246
gaol hall or house, 309, 355 n., 361
Nottingham, county, 59, 64, 151 n., 249, 282, 328
gaols or prisons in, 58 n., 65–6, 258–9, 261, 275, 368 n. See also Newark; Nottingham
sheriff. See Derby, county
nuisances, 332–3
nuns. See monks

Oakham, Rutland, castle, gaol, 85, 131, 151, 166
Oakhanger, in Selborne, Hants, 141
oaths, of gaolers, 191. *And see* Newgate
of jurors, 15
of justices, 285
Odiham, Hants, prison, 163
opprobrious words. See slander
ordeal, 24
Ordinances of 1311, 32, 34 n.
Orléans, Charles, duke of (d. 1465), 122, 126, 363
Orleton, Adam, bishop of Hereford, 102, 106
Orford, Suffolk, 259
prison, 98, 259, 274 n.
Osbert the palmer, 232 n.
ostler, 125
Otford, Kent, prison, 258, 275
Oundle, Northants., 193, 250–1
outfangthief. See *infangthief*
outlawry, 2
pardons of. See pardons
surrender in anticipation of, 117, 121, 202–3, 273, 318

outlaws, 241, 272
imprisonment of, 23, 36, 117, 130, 201, 306
Over, Ches., prison, 89
overcrowding in prisons, 104, 108–9
Owain Gwynnedd, 4 n.
Owain, son of David ap Gruffydd, 357
Oxford, Oxon., 18, 22, 137–8, 283
borough prison, 98, 137, 181, 332, 352, 356–7, 360
bridge. See Stamford
castle, 60 n., 167, 348
constable or keeper, 137, 167, 231.
And see Cok, J.; St Amand, A. de
gaol, 19, 60–2, 64, 106, 138, 149, 219, 273, 350, 355–6; delivery, 256 n., 261, 264 n., 280; gaolers or keepers, 148, 161, 167
Oxford, county, 60, 64, 96 n., 106, 282
gaols or prisons in, 58 n., 60–4, 259, 261, 266. *And see* Banbury; Oxford; Thame
[and Berkshire], sheriff, 61–2, 105 n., 138, 149, 197, 273
Oxford circuit, 282–3
Oxford, university, 51, 137–8, 223, 231, 352, 357–8, 360

Pagham, Sussex, prison, 90 n.
Pagham, William, 270 n.
Paneter, Warin le. See Warin
pardons, 41, 211
for escapes. See escapes
of outlawry, 117 and n.
Paris, France, Châtelet prison, 213 n., 351 n., 359 n.
university, 138
park-keeper, 153
parks, trespassers and poachers in, 21, 32, 115, 124, 132, 178, 211–12.
And see hawks; swans' eggs
parliament, return of members to, 34, 117
Patney, Wilts., prison, 250
peace, breach of, 42, 106
peace, justices and keepers of, 31 n., 33–4, 39–40, 203, 210, 311, 320
arrest by, 199–201

Index

Index

'utslat', 'utslath', 'utsslac', 238–9
Uxbridge, Middx., 105

vagabonds, vagrants, 39–40, 42, 199–200, 208–9
Vale Royal, in Whitegate, Ches., abbot, 89, 92
venison trespassers, trespasses. *See* forest, trespassers, trespasses
Venour, Elizabeth, formerly Elizabeth Sapperton, married successively William Venour and Robert Worth, 157
William, sheriff of London, 154, 157
ventilation of prisons, 332
Vere, Aubrey de, 232 n.
vert, trespasses of. *See* forest, trespassers
Vicar of Wakefield, cited, 183
victuallers, 40
villeins. *See* serfs
vis et arma, allegation of, 26 and n.
visiting prisoners, 118, 186–8, 334–5
vivaries, fishponds, trespassers in, 21, 32, 71, 178, 211–12

Wakefield, Yorks., prison, 359 n.
Wales, armies in, 214
prisons in. *See* Conway; Kenfig; Neath
South, great sessions of, 172–3
Waleys, Henry le, mayor of London, 112
Walkefare, Robert de, knight, 183
Wallingford, Berks., 61, 197, 232 n.
borough officers, 155–6, 205 n., 251
borough prison, 98, 365
castle, 66 n.
cell called 'Cloere Brien', 57
constable. *See* Richard, earl of Cornwall
gaol, 61–4, 87, 126, 127 n., 222, 227, 280, 331, 350, 367; porter, as gaoler, 335
honor of, 271
Wallingford, Richard of, abbot of St Albans, 209

Wallop, Matthew of, 141–2
Walter, son of Aubrey, 140
Walker, John Rolle, 146
Waltham Holy Cross, Essex, abbot, 106, 311
prison, 90, 311
Walworth, William, knight, mayor of London, 323
'wandering', exeats, 118, 178 n., 241–5, 333, 336–7
wapentakes. *See* hundreds
Warbeck, Perkin, 107, 124
Warden, in Old Warden, Beds., abbey, 346
Wareham, Dorset, 163
Warin the porter, 140
son of Geoffrey, 'le Paneter', 142 and n., 144
Wark, Wark on Tyne, Northumberland, prison, 275 n.
Warrenne, John de (d. 1304), earl of Surrey, 89, 94, 307–8
family, 91, 95, 100, 152
Warwick, Warws., 275, 286
castle, 72, 294
prisons, 72 and n., 129, 349
county gaol, 50 and n., 59, 71–2, 81 n., 201, 215, 219, 228, 294, 308, 332, 342, 349, 352, 355–6
delivery, 271, 280
keeper or gaoler, 149–50, 165, 242
gaol hall, 308 and n., 355, 361
Warwick, county, 60, 106, 276, 282
eyre in, 228
gaols or prisons in, 58 n., 70–2, 99, 258–9, 261. *And see* Coventry; Kenilworth; Kineton; Warwick
sheriff. *See* Leicester, county
Warwick, countess of. *See* Philippa
earls of. *See* Beauchamp, G. de and T.
watch by night, ordinances for, 194
water-supply, in prisons, 187, 331, 362
Waterford, Co. Waterford, Ireland, 42
Waverley, in Farnham, Surrey, abbey, monastic prison, 379
weaver, 148 n.
Weaverham, Ches., prison, 89

417

York (*cont.*)
King's Bench, court and marshalsea at, 119, 294
lock-ups, 113
mayor, 103
'Peter prison', 102
prisons, in general, 246, 322–4
St Leonard's hospital, 320
St Mary's abbey, 375 n.
    lay prison, 96, 309
    monastic prison, 379
sheriff, 103
York, county, 282, 308, 316, 322, 344, 381

eyre in, 92, 319
gaols or prisons in, 58 n., 84, 147, 259–61, 285. *And see* Beverley; Bridlington; Clifton-on-Yore; Fountains; Galtres; Kingston upon Hull; Kirkstall; Pontefract; Ravenser Odd; Ripon; Sandal; Scarborough; Seamer; Skipton; Sutton under Whitstone Cliff; Wakefield; York
sheriff, 22, 84, 198, 225, 234 n.
York, province, Augustinian canons in, 382
York, William of, justice, 264